Mobilizing the Metropolis

Mobilizing the Metropolis

How the Port Authority Built New York

Philip Mark Plotch and Jen Nelles

University of Michigan Press
Ann Arbor

Copyright © 2023 by Philip Mark Plotch and Jen Nelles
Some rights reserved

This work is licensed under a Creative Commons Attribution-NonCommercial-NoDerivatives 4.0 International License. *Note to users:* A Creative Commons license is only valid when it is applied by the person or entity that holds rights to the licensed work. Works may contain components (e.g., photographs, illustrations, or quotations) to which the rightsholder in the work cannot apply the license. It is ultimately your responsibility to independently evaluate the copyright status of any work or component part of a work you use, in light of your intended use. To view a copy of this license, visit http://creativecommons.org/licenses/by-nc-nd/4.0/

For questions or permissions, please contact um.press.perms@umich.edu

Published in the United States of America by the
University of Michigan Press
Manufactured in the United States of America
Printed on acid-free paper
First published May 2023

A CIP catalog record for this book is available from the British Library.

Library of Congress Cataloging-in-Publication data has been applied for.

ISBN 978-0-472-07613-0 (hardcover : alk. paper)
ISBN 978-0-472-05613-2 (paper : alk. paper)
ISBN 978-0-472-90348-1 (open access ebook)

DOI: https://doi.org/10.3998/mpub.12009801

The University of Michigan Press's open access publishing program is made possible thanks to additional funding from the University of Michigan Office of the Provost and the generous support of contributing libraries.

Cover illustration: PATH station at the World Trade Center. Photograph by Anthony Quintano, August 18, 2016. Courtesy Wikimedia Commons, CC BY 2.0.

CONTENTS

List of Illustrations   vii
Acknowledgments   ix

1   Introduction   1

2   Creation and First Triumphs   27

3   Grappling with Capacity Problems at the Airports   49

4   Ports Competing on a Global Scale   81

5   Fostering Regional Mobility through Enduring Partnerships   114

6   Turning Point: A Strike at Autonomy and a Blow to the Culture   143

7   Moving Three Bridges from the Periphery to Center Stage   173

8   Building and Rebuilding the World Trade Center   213

9   The Rhetoric and Reality of Political Independence   260

10   Conclusion   280

Notes   309
Index   361

Digital materials related to this title can be found on the Fulcrum platform via the following citable URL: https://doi.org/10.3998/mpub.12009801

ILLUSTRATIONS

Maps

1.1	Major Port Authority Facilities	25
3.1	The Region's Airports	62
7.1	Staten Island	175
7.2	Roadway Network around Midtown and Lower Manhattan	184
8.1	World Trade Center in Lower Manhattan	221

Figures

1.1	Port Authority Commerce Building	2
1.2	Traffic along the Hudson River	6
1.3	Recent Port Authority Organization Chart	26
2.1	New York Harbor in 1893	32
2.2	Aerial View of Manhattan	33
2.3	Hudson River Piers in Manhattan	34
2.4	Railroad Yards along Jersey City Waterfront	35
2.5	Timeline of Major Port Authority Projects	38
2.6	Shaking Hands in the Holland Tunnel	40
2.7	George Washington Bridge	45
2.8	Lincoln Tunnel Ceremony	47
3.1	LaGuardia Field	52
3.2	Great Swamp National Wildlife Refuge	65
3.3	Planes Queued Up at Kennedy Airport	71
4.1	Trucks Lined Up for the Ferry in Hoboken	87
4.2	Unloading Freight on a Manhattan Pier	92
4.3	Manhattan's Banana Docks	93
4.4	Containers on 1956 Maiden Voyage of *Ideal X*	94

4.5	Little Island on the Hudson River	96
4.6	Trade Routes between Asia and New York	99
4.7	Shipping Containers in Elizabeth	106
4.8	Container Ships at Marine Terminal in Elizabeth	107
5.1	Transcom Operations Center	127
5.2	TransitCenter's TransitCheks	134
5.3	Manhattan Traveler Commuter Rail Map	136
7.1	Construction of Outerbridge Crossing	178
7.2	Goethals Bridge Construction	179
7.3	Crossing the Goethals Bridge	181
7.4	George Washington Bridge's Upper and Lower Levels	186
7.5	Narrow Lanes on the Goethals Bridge	197
7.6	The New Goethals Bridge	201
7.7	Governor Chris Christie in Bayonne	209
7.8	Raising the Roadway on the Bayonne Bridge	210
7.9	Container Ship under the Bayonne Bridge	211
8.1	PATH Sign Goes Up	223
8.2	Radio Row in Lower Manhattan	225
8.3	Original World Trade Center Complex	232
8.4	Remains of World Trade Center after September 11	237
8.5	Austin J. Tobin Plaza	241
8.6	Original Site Plan for World Trade Center	244
8.7	New Site Plan for One World Trade Center	245
8.8	Construction of One World Trade Center	248
8.9	National September 11 Memorial under Construction	249
8.10	One World Trade Center	256
8.11	Former Presidents at National September 11 Memorial	257
8.12	Calatrava's PATH Station	258
10.1	Port Authority's Helicopter	283
10.2	Exclusive Bus Lane	287
10.3	Port Authority Officer in Lincoln Tunnel's Catwalk Car	301
10.4	Ramps Connecting Lincoln Tunnel and Bus Terminal	302

ACKNOWLEDGMENTS

Diligence and resourcefulness can only take you so far. Everyone relies on help from family members, friends, colleagues, and even kind strangers. We owe a special thanks to the late Jameson Doig who started us on our journey, inspired us to ask the right questions, and applauded us along the way. Jim was both a revered scholar and an academic who informed ongoing public policy issues.

We were extraordinarily fortunate that so many people connected to the Port Authority of New York and New Jersey shared their stories and invaluable insights. The two of us are especially grateful to Alfred Doblin, Alice Herman, Amit Bhomick, Ann Freedman, Anne Strauss-Wieder, Bethan Rooney, Bill Armbruster, Bill Baroni, Bob Gordon, Bob Kelly, Cherrie Nanninga, Christian Bollwage, Christine Todd Whitman, Chris Rohner, Chris Ward, Dave Judd, David Plavin, Deborah Finn, Edmond Harrison, Enoch Lipson, Floyd Lapp, Frank Lombardi, Frank Caggiano, Frank McDonough, Gary Hack, George Cancro, George Marlin, Gerald Stoughton, Gil Medina, Greg Storey, Herb Ouida, Janet Cox, Jeff Zupan, Jeffrey Green, Jim Devine, Jimmy Diaz, Joan Verplanck, Joann Papageorgis, Joe Doria, Joel Ettinger, John Fruin, John Haley, Jon Peters, Ken Philmus, Laine D'Augustine, Larry Filler, Larry Lennon, Lee Sander, Leon Goodman, Lillian Borrone, Linda Spock, Loretta Weinberg, Lynne Sagalyn, Mark Muriello, Martin Robins, Marygrace Parker, Matt Edelman, Mike Miller, Pat Foye, Patty Clark, Paul Bea, Peter Goldmark, Peter King, Peter Rinaldi, Quentin Brathwaite, Rebecca Marcillo-Gomez, Richard Kelly, Richard Lobron, Richard Mroz, Richard Oram, Richard Roper, Rick Larabee, Robert Boyle, Robert VanDeventer, Ronald Shiftan, Rosemary Scanlon, Sandra Van de Walle, Stan Brezenoff, Stephen Berger, Steve Levine, Steve Rothman, Thom Carafella, Tim Gilchrist, Tom Wakeman, Tony Coscia, Tony Shorris, Victoria Kelly, and Wilfredo Guzmán.

We want to give a very special thanks to Dave Gallagher, Lou Venech and the Port Authority Retirees Association for helping us with every aspect of the book. We do hope that our readers appreciate all the great maps that Md. Shahin Rahman made for us, because we certainly do. We are grateful to Elizabeth Demers and Haley Winkle at the University of Michigan Press who early on recognized the importance of our work. Their team (including editors and designers) is remarkably sharp and diligent. Thanks also to all the archivists who helped us uncover documents and old photographs that have been stored across the United States.

We would also like to thank the friends and colleagues who read drafts of the book and offered their comments and suggestions. Adam Brown, Jen's frequent collaborator and a fellow infrastructure dork, suffered through countless early drafts. Jen's father, H.V. Nelles, read the manuscript with the eyes of a historian and gave us valuable feedback that helped bring our story to life. Her mom, Diane Nelles, was also super valuable, offering encouragement and mostly restraining herself from commenting on Jen's creative use of punctuation, while delivering all-important virtual hugs. Tim Vorley ensured that Jen had time and space for this project and a job to fall back on in the off chance that it's not a runaway bestseller. He doesn't care about ports or authority, but this book is for him. Jen would also like to thank her husband Robby Gutmann, who gamely tolerates her infrastructure obsession and without whom life would be way less fun. Her kids, Ozzy and Archie, are the best snugglers around and every author knows that's key for good writing.

Phil's wonderful wife, Amy, has been a real trooper on this book adventure—tagging along on romantic outings to container terminals, cargo facilities, suspension bridge towers, trash incinerators, and the swamps of Jersey. Phil is thankful for his sister, Laura Gagnon, who splendidly took on a lion's share of family responsibilities so he could go to Seoul for a year as part of the U.S. Fulbright Scholars program. That adventure provided him with tremendous insight into the problems and potential of American cities. Phil also wishes to thank his teachers (from P.S. 128 in Brooklyn to his professors at Hunter College and the New School) along with his remarkable colleagues at the Eno Center for Transportation who provide him the support to continue his important research efforts. And, a special shoutout to Cynthia and Andrew who always give Phil such "naches."

CHAPTER 1

Introduction

A remarkable structure sits on the west side of Manhattan. Although 111 Eighth Avenue is only eighteen floors high, it consumes an entire massive New York City block and was built with big things in mind. The building (see fig. 1.1), which contains 50 percent more square feet than the Empire State Building, was designed with elevators so large they could accommodate trucks weighing twenty tons. It is perhaps appropriate that today it houses Google's New York City headquarters, a firm often described using similar superlatives. However, from when construction was completed in 1933 until 1973, the building had very different uses. It served as an enormous transfer facility for railroads and truckers (President Franklin D. Roosevelt once described it as the first great post office for freight) as well as the city's largest exhibition hall. The owner of the building, the Port of New York Authority, had its headquarters on the upper floors, where ambitious public officials mobilized the metropolis to build even more impressive structures, securing New York's role as one of the greatest cities in the world.[1]

The Authority (since 1972 known as the "Port Authority of New York and New Jersey" or simply the "Port Authority") is a bistate partnership between New York and New Jersey that builds, operates, and maintains critical transportation and real estate assets. It was established in 1921 in an effort to find solutions to infrastructure development and freight mobility conflicts inherent in the economically integrated but geographically and politically fragmented New York metropolitan region. Although the Authority's name suggests that its responsibilities are limited to managing the region's shipping ports, in fact its influence extends to developing, planning, and regulating a wide range of transportation infrastructure on water, roads, rails, and in the air. Almost all its assets are located within a twenty-five-mile radius of the Statue of Liberty, with a portfolio that includes five airports, four marine terminals, three bus stations, four bridges, and two tunnels, as well as numerous real estate sites including the World Trade Center.

Fig. 1.1. The words "The Port of New York Authority Inland Terminal Number One" are still visible below the Google sign on 111 Eighth Avenue.
(Photograph by Scott Roy Atwood, June 2013. Courtesy Wikimedia Commons, CC BY-SA 3.0.)

As the Port Authority marked its centennial in 2021, few would have disputed its significance to the region. Its facilities permit the (usually) effective circulation of millions of people and a more than a million tons of goods every day.[2] It is a crucial actor, and often leader, of major infrastructure development projects across the region. The Authority has emerged as a critical voice in regional planning and has unquestionably operated on an epic scale—orchestrating the construction of monumental infrastructure such as the George Washington Bridge across the Hudson River (the world's busiest motor vehicle crossing), consolidating the management of three of the nation's busiest airports, and constructing (and then reconstructing) the World Trade Center. As an organization, it has frequently proved masterful at achieving its goals—often in the face of daunting opposition.

However, the organization has also faced its share of challenges. To say that the modern Port Authority has been immersed in controversy in recent years is an understatement. In September 2013, a Port Authority staff mem-

Introduction

ber created a traffic jam at the George Washington Bridge because a local mayor refused to support New Jersey Governor Chris Christie's reelection bid. This incident, known as Bridgegate, exposed the infiltration of politics into the Port Authority's once touted independence and rational decision-making processes. Three years later, the Port Authority opened a magnificent train station at the World Trade Center; but at a cost of $4 billion, it has been widely regarded, even within the Authority itself, as wasteful and excessive. The Authority has faced repeated calls for reform, and it has been subject to an ongoing critique of its handling of some high-profile projects. It is worth noting that in the last fifty years, the Port Authority has not attempted to execute as many projects that have rivaled the accomplishments, scale, and impact of its earliest efforts. Whatever its faults, the Port Authority is an organization with an important legacy and a central place in the future of the New York metropolitan region.

This is a book about an organization that has done big things—won big but also failed big—in one of the most complex and dynamic regions in the world. It can be read as a reflective history of this organization and its significant moments building the infrastructural foundation for the New York metropolitan region. However, we also use the Port Authority's experiences to develop a better understanding of the internal attributes that help or hinder an organization's ability to execute its vision. The Port Authority's success in this respect is tied to its ability to construct supportive coalitions around projects and to counter opposition from multiple quarters. Our analysis shows that four factors (internal resources, autonomy, culture, and leadership) all contribute to an organization's ability to generate supportive coalitions.

The Port Authority, the nation's very first public authority, now has more than 35,000 copycats in the U.S., alone. These authorities provide a wide variety of services such as building and operating parking facilities, convention centers, low-income housing, and hospitals.[3] While our book focuses on a very particular organization—a bistate infrastructure development entity that has had an uncommon degree of autonomy and a powerful reputation—we believe the lessons revealed in this book are relevant for any organization that needs to balance the interests of its individual members against its collective mission. In short, we offer both a fascinating story about an organization that has shaped a modern metropolis as well as insights to guide it, and other organizations, to a bright future doing big things.

The Rise of a Modern Metropolis and the Origins of the Port Authority

New York was transformed from a regional hub into a center of world commerce thanks to one of the nation's most successful infrastructure projects. In the early 1800s, the Port of New York was the nation's fifth busiest behind Boston, Baltimore, Philadelphia, and New Orleans.[4] In 1825, after the Erie Canal was built to connect the Hudson River with the Great Lakes, Manhattan's piers began handling more goods than the next three cities in the United States combined.[5] New York became the North American hub for materials and goods from the Caribbean, Europe, Midwest, and the entire Eastern Seaboard. The city's rise as a global trading hub spawned the city's prominence as the nation's center for manufacturing. When the nineteenth-century railroad tycoons built their lines, they all wanted to connect with the nation's busiest port and manufacturing center. By 1900, eleven different railroad companies carried goods and passengers to New York's port. Most of the railroad terminals were located in New Jersey on the west side of the Hudson River. To get across the river, passengers took ferries while railroad box cars crossed on barges.[6]

In the late nineteenth and early twentieth centuries, the port became not only the gateway for goods traveling by water and rail but also the entry point for millions of immigrants from Europe. Many of the new Americans made their homes in New York's neighborhoods where they could continue speaking their native languages and attending familiar houses of worship. The city's government and business leaders encouraged the rapid growth by building streetcar lines and elevated railroads that transformed farmland into densely populated neighborhoods. Between 1800 and 1900, New York City's population soared from less than 80,000 to more than 3.4 million.

In the early twentieth century, New York City was an industrial and economic powerhouse with nearly 900,000 people employed in the manufacturing sector. Most of the nation's furs, hats, leather goods, women's clothes, pipes, and pens were made in New York City, along with more than 40 percent of the nation's jewelry, umbrellas, and men's clothing.[7] The insurance and banking industries grew along with the shipping, trading, and manufacturing sectors. Exchanges for trading commodities and stocks prospered as well. Corporations across the country chose to locate their headquarters in the city to be near each other and to be close to law firms and other business services that catered to their needs.

Introduction

An early twentieth-century visitor's guide to New York described the Hudson River waterfront along Manhattan's west side "as the great shipping section with one long succession of steamers, ships, piers, docks and ferries." Practically the entire foreign fruit trade of the country was conducted in just a few blocks. Steamships and railroads brought in their produce and meat including apples from Oregon, grapefruit from Florida, pineapples from Hawaii, and cattle from Nebraska. Visitors were amazed to watch how thousands of barrels and hundreds of tons of perishable goods were removed almost immediately after they were delivered to make way for the next train and ship. "One can hardly realize that lemons in lots of twenty-five thousand boxes are frequently disposed of in a few moments."[8]

By 1915, only one U.S. state, Pennsylvania, had more residents than the New York metropolitan area's population of 7.1 million people, and nearly half of the nation's international commerce passed through the Port of New York. Calling it the "Port of New York" was actually a misnomer because it was not a single waterfront nor a single waterway but rather nearly 2.000 piers, wharves, and quays along 650 miles of waterfront in two states.[9] Ships came into the city's five boroughs (Brooklyn, Bronx, Queens, Staten Island, and Manhattan) on the New York side, and into New Jersey's industrial cities (including Newark, Elizabeth, Hoboken, and Jersey City). As the volume of goods increased, moving goods to and from the waterfront became increasingly congested and chaotic (fig. 1.2). Businesses throughout the region were concerned because they depended upon reliable and inexpensive transportation services to move their goods. Military leaders added to the clamor for improvements to the port, after experiencing major backups moving troops and supplies through the port during World War I.

To fix the port's problems, New York and New Jersey needed more extensive and ongoing cooperation. In 1921, the two states established the Port Authority as a quasi-independent corporation because the governors and legislatures in both states understood that the residents and businesses of the 105 municipalities located near the port would be best served by working together. The Authority could spur economic development and reduce the cost of transporting goods by improving the infrastructure and facilities for ships and trains. Over the course of the next one hundred years, the Port Authority's mission evolved from improving rail freight to building motor vehicle crossings, seaports, airports, heliports, bus stations, office towers, industrial parks, and truck terminals (including the one on Eighth Avenue). The Port Authority saw government action as a way to moderate the ineffi-

Fig. 1.2. Traffic along the Hudson River, circa 1920.
(Photograph by Irving Underhill. Reprinted by permission of the Museum of City of New York.)

ciencies of untrammeled competition and fill gaps in services that the private sector could not provide. The Authority relied on scientific expertise and rational planning as a route to solve problems, improve transportation facilities, and enhance the region's economic strength.

One thing that most of the Port Authority's initiatives have had in common is that they involve facilities and networks that can be used cooperatively and efficiently by individuals and multiple firms. Numerous truckers and shippers use the airports and seaports where goods are gathered, sorted, and dispatched to their destinations. Two dozen different bus carriers use the Port Authority's Midtown Manhattan bus terminal, while more than seventy different airlines serve John F. Kennedy Airport. From the Port Authority's perspective, it did not make much sense for each airline, bus company, railroad, and trucking firm to build its own airport, bus terminal, rail terminal, or river crossing. Even the Port Authority's justification for building the World

Trade Center fit this model, since the complex was designed to serve as a center for the efficient sharing of information about importing and exporting products and services.

The Port Authority still bears many of the hallmarks of its Progressive Era origins (discussed in detail in chapter 2). Although it never achieved the degree of political and financial autonomy that its architect, Julius Henry Cohen, envisioned, the Authority's institutional design came as close as any of its vintage to enshrining the Progressive Era principles of nonpolitical and professionalized agencies and bureaucracies, vigorous executive action by competent leaders who were appointed on merit, and adherence to principles of scientific rationality and efficient practice. The Port Authority Compact, signed in 1921 and approved by Congress, created an organization with a broad mandate to manage mobility in the region, though its authority was limited to the specific areas designated by the two states.

Through this mandate, it has built and operated transportation facilities throughout the metropolitan area and raised revenues by charging fees to use its assets and floating bonds to finance future projects. This has provided the Port Authority with a measure of fiduciary independence that has proved crucial to its infrastructure development ambitions. However, the organization has been limited in important ways—it cannot tax, use eminent domain without explicit state authorization, veto local plans that contravene its own, or create regulations outside its own facilities. These limitations are designed to ensure that the organization cannot trample over the powers of local counties, cities, and towns. In practice, this has meant that the Port Authority has had to muster all its creativity and organizational assets to change minds, diffuse opposition, and build coalitions to support its initiatives.

An Organization Apart but Not Sovereign: Coalitions and Capacity

Political organizations and partnerships can rarely act unilaterally. Even if they have considerable power and capacity, they still must operate in environments that typically will not be unanimously supportive of their goals. Even when they are designed to have a significant measure of autonomy, they will still have to consider the positions of external constituencies and political masters. As such, an organization's ability to mobilize coalitions at various scales to overcome opposition is a crucial factor in its capacity to get things done.

The Port Authority is one of the most powerful infrastructure governance agencies in the world by many measures—the significance of its portfolio of assets; the number of passengers, vehicles, and goods that pass through its areas of influence; the scale of the projects that it has completed; its influence on state and national policies, and on private firms; and even occasionally its role in shaping global trends. Yet, as the previous section demonstrates, while its architect had hoped to invest the Port Authority with as much autonomy as possible, at its foundation it was firmly bound to its bistate political masters. As such, despite its size and significance, the Port Authority faces many of the same constraints that all intergovernmental and collective organizations do: it cannot act alone and its ability to accomplish its goals depends on its capacity to mobilize and maintain a supportive coalition.

This book develops this argument by focusing on noteworthy initiatives—successful, less successful, and still uncertain—from the Port Authority's more than one hundred-year history. Where the organization was able to construct a viable supportive coalition, it was able to implement a version of its agenda, and where it failed to, the Authority's projects fell short. In some cases, this required compromise. In almost all, it required creativity to navigate the complex political waters and muster support against the inertia of opposition.

One important point about coalitions is that they do not merely *exist*, but rather they must be *constructed* and then they can be leveraged. Groups and individuals who share common goals may be coordinated and unified, but often they are not formally organized. Astute leaders recognize the constellation of actors who share interests and objectives and use them to support their mutual policy goals. Coalition participation can be passive or active. In some cases, leaders will point to groups that share their interests to demonstrate the breadth of support for a cause and highlight the political consequences of failing to deliver. In other cases, leaders will more actively organize interest groups to put direct pressure on decision-makers from various quarters. Additionally, coalitions can be expanded as those most centrally interested seek to convert others to support their goals. Any political outcome can be understood as the result of a struggle between interests, and many of those outcomes are the results of the concerted efforts of coalitions. But coalitions are neither permanent nor transferable. Those that support an organization's actions in one sphere may not in another, or the next time. As a result, collaborative organizations must constantly work to build and maintain support.

Despite the New York and New Jersey statehouses' relatively strong general support for the Port Authority in principle, and confidence in its utility to the region, when it comes to major projects the Authority has had to mobilize coalitions to overcome resistance. This has become particularly important when projects appear to benefit one state over the other. One of the interesting aspects of cooperative organizations like the Port Authority, which are constructed and to a certain degree controlled by their members, is that their objectives can be at odds with the interests of their membership. Consider how the goals of the United Nations oftentimes conflict with the goals of its individual members.

The Port Authority's membership consists of only two states, but each state does not necessarily speak with one voice because the governor, state senate, state assembly, and the men and women serving on the Port Authority's board of commissioners do not necessarily have the same interests. Since cooperative organizations are dependent on the funding and political support of their members, conflict between those members can undermine organizational aims.[10] In such cases, it is often necessary to convince not just the organization's leaders (such as board members) but also officials in both state capitols who have the power to block projects in various ways.

In this introductory chapter we focus in on three examples of significant Port Authority initiatives to help illustrate the mechanisms and factors that influence its ability to build coalitions supportive of its goals: (1) the conceptualization and construction of the George Washington Bridge; (2) the Port Authority's acquisition of the region's three major airports; and (3) the Authority's bid to dominate maritime shipping through developing the region's ports. While we develop these cases in more detail in chapters 2, 3, and 4, these summaries provide both a preview of what is to come and demonstrate how the factors that influence coalition-building capacity function and interact.

The Bridge

The construction of the George Washington Bridge connecting New Jersey with New York City across the Hudson River remains one of the Port Authority's most monumental and enduring accomplishments. In fact, Jameson Doig in his book about the Port Authority, *Empire on the Hudson*, paints this early accomplishment as particularly decisive for the fledgling organization, one that consolidated its position as the preeminent bistate Authority and, crucially, provided a financial foundation for future projects through the tolls it would collect from motorists.[11]

The construction of the bridge is an important story of coalition-building because it is an example of how the Port Authority managed to seize an opportunity largely of someone else's making and maintain control of the project through potentially disastrous political challenges. In fact, the plan by the bridge designer, Othmar Ammann, for a trans-Hudson motor vehicle span was originally in competition with the Port Authority's own plans to construct rail tunnels between New Jersey and Manhattan. However, the Authority astutely recognized that crossings for cars and trucks would be crucial to the future of the region and, after detailed study of alternatives, pivoted to adopt the bridge plan and its designer and engineer.

Ammann himself laid much of the groundwork for the political approvals of the bridge plans in 1925 before he joined the Port Authority by relentlessly promoting his initiative to local politicians, business communities, and state legislatures. These supportive constituencies were instrumental in securing political buy-in for the project and would come in handy again once approvals had been secured. As work on the bridge began, political battles brewed between the two states and threatened to derail the project and the construction of three other bridges in the region that were proceeding in parallel. Factors related to the bridge's construction and design provoked a movement in New Jersey to give the legislature approval power over all Port Authority contracts. This sparked an arms race of sorts between the two state governors, both of whom sought a veto power to ensure that they had the final word on Port Authority matters. A decisive political communication strategy was needed to overcome these hurdles. In a bold maneuver, the Authority's leadership suspended construction activities on the four interstate crossings in progress while the political battle raged. Halting work produced the desired effect, resulting in widespread protest from business interests and local politicians who argued that the shutdown threatened economic growth. The offending legislation in New Jersey was repealed relatively quickly and both states had passed laws limiting veto authority over the Port Authority's actions to the governors. Work on the crossing resumed, and the George Washington Bridge opened successfully in 1931.

The Airports

One of the most significant elements of the Port Authority's current portfolio of infrastructure is the region's three major airports—Kennedy, LaGuardia, and Newark Liberty—which serve more than 140 million passengers annually. Today, the Port Authority's role as steward of these crucial assets is taken for granted, but airports were not initially included in the organization's domain. For one, when the Authority was created commercial aviation was not a pressing concern, and once airports started to be seen as important economic engines, cities regarded them as valuable local government assets. As such, when in the 1940s the Port Authority leaders wanted to gain control over the region's airports, they faced an uphill battle.

A formidable group of interests arrayed against the Port Authority's airport ambitions, including local officials in Newark and New York City who wanted to retain control of their respective airports and had plans of their own to modernize facilities. Robert Moses, who at the time headed up many of New York City's infrastructure authorities, had his own imperial eye set on the prize of air infrastructure. New York's state legislature and its governor, Thomas E. Dewey, supported Moses's effort by enacting a law creating a competing authority to modernize what is now John F. Kennedy Airport. This is a notable example of where the Port Authority's ambitions were opposed by one of its members, namely the state and governor of New York. As such, this case demonstrates how the organization prevailed despite strong opposition, highlighting the power of building and activating strong external coalitions as a strategy for organizations that find themselves at odds with their political masters.

In order to overcome these significant challenges, the Port Authority mobilized an equally impressive coalition of supporters, including the Regional Plan Association (a highly regarded civic organization), the region's business community, the press, airlines, and investment banks, among others. The narrative that finally won the day was that the Port Authority "had far greater financial resources and staff expertise, and a strong general reputation, than the patronage-riddled city agency of the new Airport Authority."[12] In broad strokes, the Port Authority leveraged some unique organizational resources to bring together a supportive coalition that turned public opinion and exerted sufficient pressure on its "enemies" to achieve a total victory on the matter of airport control. Its use of its financial resources, internal expertise, and skillful deployment of data were critical in winning over a variety of coalition members.

The Ports

Ironically, the Port Authority did not gain control of the actual *ports*, shipping, or waterways of the New York metropolitan region until it had been in existence for nearly two decades. While the bulk of the ships entering the New York region's ports now dock in New Jersey, for much of the region's history the piers along the Manhattan and Brooklyn waterfronts processed most of the region's freight. During the Port Authority's early years, New York City jealously guarded control of its port facilities along with the valuable revenues and political constituencies that they represented. So while the Authority made several bids to take over control of maritime freight assets in New York, they were repeatedly thwarted by mayors and dockworkers' unions.

Where New York was resistant, cities in New Jersey were open to dealing away their languishing docks that were expensive to maintain. Eager to gain a toehold in the region's shipping industry and recognizing both the weaknesses in existing port infrastructure and technological changes on the horizon, the Port Authority moved aggressively to secure its piece of the waterfront. In 1947, the same year Newark handed over control of its airport, Newark also concluded a lease agreement for its docks, which were promptly improved and modernized by Port Authority investments. In the late 1950s, New Jersey ports expanded to include the nearby Elizabeth facility and began cutting ever deeper into New York's market share. The mayor of New York City, Robert Wagner, began looking to the Port Authority as a potential partner to help revive the city's ports and also deal with increasing traffic congestion along Manhattan's waterfront. But political factions within the city prevented any deals from going forward. Meanwhile, the Port Authority, convinced of the future of containerization, took steps to further upgrade its New Jersey facilities in expectation of a massive increase in transoceanic traffic. By the time the Port Authority gained control of marine terminals in Brooklyn, shipping trends had already begun to shift toward containerization, which favored vast mechanized ports like Newark and Elizabeth. As New York City real estate interests found better and more lucrative uses for properties near the waterfront, its ports fell into disuse, leaving the Port Authority the undisputed master of the region's ports.

In this case, the Port Authority was successful due to a combination of organizational skills and external factors. Its actions in the decade preceding containerization secured the region's role as the dominant port on the east coast of the United States. This period of investments in the ports and Newark airport was also notable for initiating a new era of diversification in its infrastructure portfolio where projects tended to occur within one jurisdiction or another rather than explicitly linking the two states as many of the bridges and tunnels had done. This set up a dynamic where each project *appeared* to benefit the host partner more than the other (even if there was clear regional benefit). In such a context, generating support for projects became ever more a political game and one fraught with pitfalls—particularly in the case of the development of New Jersey port facilities where the Authority was in direct competition with New York City's ports.

These examples illustrate a fundamental principle of organizational analysis: even the most powerful organizations are not monolithic. They face challenges from both within and without and securing the support of key actors and overcoming opposition is a crucial element of any organizational successes. The following section unpacks this logic.

Organizational Capacity and Coalition-Building

This book helps us understand the Port's Authority's successes and failures by examining both its internal and external environment, how they relate to each other, how they have changed over time, and how the organization has been able to leverage these to its advantage. It begins from the observation that organizations do not function in a vacuum—they are constrained and enabled in their missions by the environment within which they must function and by their own internal attributes.

We recognize that the concepts of "internal" and "external" conditions set up a bit of a false dichotomy. Internal factors can be affected and constrained by the external environment and that external environment is not immutable to change by the actions of organizations themselves. That said, this conceptual division does serve an important purpose. It allows us to focus our efforts on understanding the mechanisms that help organizations, like the Port Authority, function and flourish irrespective of the environments in which they are embedded.

While external constraints and opportunities are certainly very important explanations for organizational success, emphasizing them too much risks overlooking the importance of attributes that permit organizations to effectively respond to their shifting environments. As such, throughout the book we will draw out the external factors that shaped the sociopolitical landscape within which the Authority sought to implement its agenda, but we will focus more firmly on the groups of actors and interests arrayed in support and against the fulfillment of that vision and, by consequence, the range of resources that the Port Authority was able to marshal to build effective coalitions.

We focus primarily on four internal factors that impact organizational capacity to mobilize coalitions: (1) resources, (2) organizational autonomy, (3) culture, and (4) entrepreneurial leadership. It is important to note here that we treat these factors as a lens through which to understand the Port Authority's successes and failures, and not as a theory intending to demonstrate the combination of factors that will predict certain outcomes. Furthermore, we acknowledge that this list of factors may not be exhaustive. However, it represents a cross-section of some of the attributes that are usually necessary, if not sufficient, for effective coalition mobilization and that have had demonstrable impacts on the initiatives that we profile in this book. Below, we discuss each of these factors in turn with reference to the examples in this chapter. The significance of these factors is developed in more detail in the following chapters, and we return to them with lessons learned in the concluding chapter.

(1) Resources

Internal resources are one of the most obvious factors that organizations can leverage to achieve their aims and build coalitions. Organizations that can marshal certain types of resources that are of value to others increase their ability to influence external actors and mobilize supporters to their cause. Two important points are worth making: first, resources come in a wide variety of forms and, second, resources are inert until deployed or leveraged by leadership. While we tend to think of resources in financial terms, the stock of organizational resources can include a wide variety of things, including, but not limited to, personnel and expertise, information, technology, and tools. Any and all of these can be used in the service of coalition-building or maintenance as well as for project implementation.

Another organizational advantage not often discussed in this context, but well worth noting, is *creativity* in assessing and deploying these internal resources. In her work on productivity in firms, the British economist Edith Penrose noted that resources are not always decisive in and of themselves. That is, firms can have identical resources and experience wildly different outcomes.[13] While many factors play a role in different outcomes, Penrose's contribution to economic theory was to highlight that it was the utility that managers and leaders interpret their resources to have and how they are used that matters. As we shall see, the Port Authority leaders have at times been extremely canny in securing support and extracting cooperation by leveraging resources and creatively interpreting the value of their internal resources.

Introduction

FINANCIAL RESOURCES

Organizations with significant financial resources can accomplish things that others cannot. Financially secure organizations attract more partners and can use their money to obtain other resources, such as expertise and information. The Port Authority has access to a stable source of income through its ability to issue bonds and raise the tolls and user fees levied on its infrastructure holdings. Many public authorities that rely on rents and tolls have this asset, as do some that rely mainly on legislative funding.

Financial resources played an important role in the construction of the George Washington Bridge. Many of the project's political supporters preferred that the bridge be owned by the public yet financed with private funds to minimize the public's risk. Given the Port Authority's bistate nature and its ability to raise private capital, the newly established Authority was a logical choice to lead the bridge project. In short, a supportive coalition came to the Port Authority due to this internal asset and the Authority did not need to do much work to maintain this support as a result. In the case of the airports, the Port Authority's superior financial position not only made its plans for modernizing air facilities credible with supporters but also helped to choke off funding to competitors. Investment banks supporting the Port Authority's venture stated publicly that they would accept Port Authority bonds for airport development while simultaneously implying that the bonds of competitor agencies would not find buyers.

EXPERTISE, SKILLS, AND TECHNOLOGICAL MASTERY

Organizations with access to expertise and skills that others lack can be attractive partners and policy leaders. A considerable degree of organizational influence is derived from specialized technical knowledge, training, and experience that is not immediately available to other actors.[14] In some cases, an organization is seen as the best qualified to take on a given task and is therefore ceded authority. In others, the influence of expertise is more reputational. Even when an organization might not have ever acted in a specific area before, it can leverage its reputation for excellence or adaptation to win over skeptical stakeholders.

Before taking on the George Washington Bridge project, the Port Authority had not yet proved its mettle in infrastructure development. Yet it was viewed as an agency with the appropriate degree of internal expertise to evaluate the project and weigh it impartially against its own originally preferred tunnel alternatives. Later, the Port Authority internalized crucial design and engineering skills by hiring the bridge's designer, Othmar Ammann. As the leader of the coalition of political and business interests that had supported the project before it was invested in the Port Authority, Ammann had a good deal of credibility and was instrumental in maintaining support by deploying reasoned arguments when choices of building materials generated political heat.

In the Port Authority's bid to wrestle control of airports from local governments it deployed an impressive array of skills. From a planning perspective, its modernization plans were ambitious, backed by impressive data, and professionally presented. However, in this case, the Port Authority's mastery of public relations and the media was a skillset that was enormously powerful in swaying public opinion and the views of powerful stakeholders, such as the business community and airlines.

CONTROL OF DATA AND INFORMATION

Knowledge is power. An organization with data or information that no one else has can wield it persuasively to control narratives and build coalitions or counter-coalitions. The strategic uses of information include "solidifying coalition membership, arguing against an opponent's policy views, convincing decision-making sovereigns to support your proposals, and swaying public opinion. Stakeholders often spin or even distort information to bolster their argument."[15]

Leaders at the Port Authority wielded data decisively to take over management of the region's airports. Their production and analysis of travel trend data was professional and scientific, and bought the organization greater credibility with stakeholders (such as funders and airlines) than its competitors were able to muster. In the example of the ports, the Authority's canny analysis of shipping trends was among the factors that enabled them to foresee shifts in infrastructure needs and convince shippers to defect from New York facilities.

(2) Organizational Autonomy

Organizational autonomy and organizational capacity, in general, are frequently linked.[16] Autonomy refers to an organization's ability to make its own decisions, while capacity refers to its ability to marshal resources and achieve its goals. In general, agencies with more autonomy are less constrained in

Introduction

pursuing their preferred goals and *in adjusting strategies* to secure winning coalitions.

Autonomy can be interpreted in a variety of ways. Its most typical manifestation is institutionally rooted. Organizational bylaws and state statutes confer various types of powers (either legally or informally) that can insulate an entity from outside interference. For instance, the Port Authority has a protected right to raise funds using a variety of mechanisms elaborated in its governing statutes. It also has the exclusive right to build and operate motor vehicle crossings across the stretch of Hudson River within its jurisdiction. No other agency can build a crossing within twenty-five miles of the Statue of Liberty, which is why the New York State Thruway Authority built its three-mile-long Tappan Zee Bridge a few feet north of that line, even though it was at one of the river's widest spots where the bridge's foundations could not be supported by solid rock.[17]

Organizations such as the Port Authority, despite some early efforts, will never be (nor were they meant to be) completely autonomous. But they can derive autonomy from other sources that can help them implement their agendas and build supportive coalitions. For instance, organizations can secure autonomy by being thought leaders or policy innovators. Autonomy exists when "agencies can make the decisive first moves towards a new policy, establishing an agenda or the most popular alternative, which becomes too costly for politicians and organized interests to ignore."[18] Authorities can also transform the preferences of elected officials, organized interests, and the general public.

Throughout its existence, the Port Authority has wrestled with institutional limitations on its autonomy, which have often functioned as a double-edged sword. For example, before the Port Authority can build a new Hudson River crossing, it needs approvals from both state legislatures. Ironically, this bistate structure has helped insulate it from several attempts to bring it under more restrictive state control. During the political conflicts that erupted as bridge contracts were being awarded, the bistate structure also protected it from the threat of political meddling. As Doig notes, "Because the agency was accountable to two masters—the two states—it was less accountable to either. What one state wished to do, its partner could resist; and so the bistate agency might retain much of its independence against the slings and arrows of politicians and advocates of localized democracy."[19]

And so, ironically, the very features that some might have described as a weakness of the Port Authority's organizational structure function equally as bolsters to its autonomy. Furthermore, this feature was important to various members of the coalition that supported the George Washington Bridge project as well as key allies for any project—financiers. The Port Authority's autonomy has also given it a time advantage over other public organizations. For instance, since it is not subject to the same civil service and procurement rules as other public agencies, the Authority has been able to hire workers, employ consultants, purchase parts, and begin construction projects faster than other public entities such as the state departments of transportation. Likewise, the Authority is not subject to the whims and calendars of state legislatures when it needs to obtain funds.

(3) Organizational Culture

The culture of an organization has an important effect on its ultimate capabilities. Generally, an organizational culture refers to the shared beliefs and values that inform and constrain its actions.[20] Several dimensions of culture are relevant to our analysis. First, they determine the degree to which an organization is interested in, sees the value of, and is willing to engage in coalition-building activities. Second, in organizations with long histories (such as the Port Authority) it is highly likely that there has been a degree of cultural change, which could be observable in its activities. Similarly, certain cultures may also be remarkably durable over time. Moreover, different divisions of a large organization (and the Port Authority certainly qualifies) might have different internal cultures that can affect internal cohesion.

The political scientists Michael Barnett and Martha Finnemore make an interesting point about how internal cultures can operate counter to one another to produce unexpected outcomes.[21] They argue that organizations have cultures, but they are not monolithic. Internal cultures may diverge or come into conflict at times as they evolve over time. Indeed, while the Port Authority originally enshrined Progressive Era values that promoted organizational efficiency and principles of scientific rationality, which were reflected in its internal culture and external reputation, the organization has seen several important shifts during its existence. What have emerged are norms of quid pro quo between the states that do not always allow the organization to pursue the most efficient strategies either for itself or for the region.

Although the Port Authority was a brand-new entity when it embarked on the George Washington Bridge project, it already had a very strong internal culture and reputation, which meant that a good many political actors were willing to place their confidence in the organization's ability to execute such an ambitious project. That confidence was not only apparently well-placed, but the widespread acclaim for the Port Authority's early endeavors only served to augment this reputation and consolidate its internal culture. By the time the bridge opened in 1931, the Port Authority, according to Doig, "was regarded as a premier example of the advantage promised by the Progressive Era doctrine of independence, expertise, and entrepreneurial energy."[22] The city of Newark cited its confidence in the Port Authority's commitment to managing infrastructure for the benefit of the broader region and to high standards of management and execution in its decision to hand over its port and airports to the organization. Similarly, in the airport case, the Port Authority's culture of political impartiality sharply contrasted with its competitors, which were viewed as unreliable and subject to political forces, rendering the Authority the more attractive organization with which to invest with control of the region's air infrastructure.

Organizations are not simply creatures that fulfill the vision of their creators precisely and accurately, but they are also the tools of their members, leaders, and bureaucracies. As such, internal conflict can be a factor in achieving organizational aims when different factions work against each other.[23] Internal conflict over identities, aims, and/or processes can blunt an organization's ability to effectively mobilize external support.

No organization is completely immune to internal conflict, but how it is managed and manifests to the outside world can have important consequences for coalition-building and sustaining capacities. The case of the George Washington Bridge was an interesting early test in this regard. The Authority's original Comprehensive Plan for the region favored a series of trans-Hudson rail freight tunnels, and well into 1924 the organization actively resisted the idea of adding bridges to its plans. However, the Port Authority's leadership recognized that political winds were shifting to support Ammann's bridge proposal and their own work suggested that motor vehicle crossings would be a priority for the region. Relatively quickly, the organization assented to study the potential of a bridge crossing and then embraced bridge building as its central mission during its early period. Any elements within the organization that might have been disgruntled by this change were kept neatly in check as the Port Authority moved forward bringing the full brunt of its collective resources to bear on the problem of bridging the Hudson.

(4) Entrepreneurial Leadership and Vision

Entrepreneurial leaders can be critically important in both shaping inspiring goals for their organizations and bringing together external coalitions to support their organization's efforts. They combine all the previously identified determinants of organizational capacity. That is, they use a wide range of resources in creative manners, take advantage of their autonomy to initiate new programs and move their organizations in novel ways, encourage the development of skills and expertise that helps them embark on new initiatives, and instill a culture of innovation and promote cohesion with effective leadership strategies.

In short, entrepreneurial leaders build and deploy the internal assets of an organization in order to achieve that organization's goals. While leaders manipulate and should ideally augment many of the factors discussed in previous sections, we include them here on equal footing to other organizational assets. As this book reveals, leadership is not the feature of a single executive but can emerge to important effect from many places within an organization, sometimes simultaneously. As such, we prefer to study this feature as one that is not predictably vested in key executives but as an asset that can be cultivated and used from anywhere within the organization.

Leadership was key in the execution of the George Washington Bridge project. Ammann's legwork convincing public and private actors around the region, particularly on the New Jersey side of the project, established a relatively durable coalition of supporters who not only backed the political approval of the project but rallied to put an end to the interstate bickering that emerged around key materials contracts. The significance of this leadership to the future of the Port Authority should not be understated. According to Doig, "Ammann utilized his technical abilities and administrative skills to press ahead with all four bridges at a surprising pace. And as each new bridge foundation was dug, each tower raised, each span completed, the press drew attention to the accomplishment, adding to the reputation of the bistate agency and her Swiss-American engineer."[24]

While internal resources made a critical contribution in the airport control case, the role of the Port Authority's leaders should not be underestimated. Austin Tobin (the Authority's executive director between 1942 and 1972) and his team crafted a narrative, brokered connections with key supporters, and effectively deployed organizational resources. Tobin was also crucial in seizing the opportunity to develop port infrastructure in New Jersey.

The Structure of the Book

Taken together, these four factors (resources, autonomy, culture, leadership) help us understand how the Port Authority was able to build some of the most iconic structures in the world and continue to innovate across its diverse portfolio for over a century to keep the metropolis moving. This is the story of the challenges (and there were many) that the Authority faced in shaping and implementing its agenda and how it either overcame opposition through effective coalition-building or cannily adapted to adversity to accomplish its vision in other ways. We reveal how the Port Authority has responded to and influenced public sentiment, and the ways in which its priorities have anticipated and addressed the region's needs.

It is also the story of how advantages, such as the ones discussed above, can erode and evolve over the lifespan of an organization. The Port Authority of today is a very different entity than the one formed in 1921. Arguably, it has seen the diminishment of all the internal endowments that fueled its successes and adaptability, and an increase in bistate political friction. And while we are clear-eyed in our assessment of the weaknesses that have become apparent over recent decades, we also see opportunities to reinvigorate the characteristics that have enabled the Port Authority to plan and develop truly regional infrastructure while balancing these with accountability, transparency, and oversight appropriate to modern public authorities. The lesson for the Port Authority and other organizations is that understanding the power and limitations of this constellation of internal endowments, developing them and leveraging them to generate supportive coalitions, is crucial to organizational success. The example of the Port Authority proves that even in a fragmented and complex political context, progress is possible. It is not always easy, nor is it guaranteed, but collaborative organizations can transform regions, and themselves, in the face of shifting external conditions.

The book proceeds semi-chronologically emphasizing important moments, projects, battles, and turning points in the Port Authority's history. Chapter 2 sets up the Authority's early accomplishments, describing the establishment of the Port Authority and the construction of the tunnels and bridges between New York and New Jersey. It highlights the challenges faced by the business leaders and government officials who gathered support for ceding control over major transportation projects to an independent regional authority, while others opposed those efforts to undermine local sovereignty. These crossings did no less than bind the two states into a partnership that has persisted for more than a hundred years and established critical cornerstones that provided a foundation for the Authority's later development capacity. Where these foundations were strong, the Authority has been able to flourish.

The next two chapters track the Port Authority's role in airports and ports. Chapter 3 explores the battle to take over and expand three of the nation's busiest airports: Kennedy, LaGuardia, and Newark. Keeping them up-to-date and expanding their capacity, however, has been a perpetual challenge. The Authority's attempt to build another international airport in New Jersey, less than thirty miles from Manhattan, was thwarted by a nascent environmental movement, and its airport about sixty miles north of New York City has not yet lived up to its potential. Chapter 4 explores how the Port Authority took over and expanded the region's port facilities and became a leader in developing container ship traffic. Most of the innovation in maritime commerce has taken place on the New Jersey side of the harbor, generating some envy and hostility toward the Port Authority by mayors and other New York City officials. The chapter describes how the Authority had to be creative to overcome challenges and to maintain the port's competitiveness after containerization became widespread. Its efforts had global significance, literally reconfiguring international trade routes to the New York region's advantage. More recently, the Port Authority has relied on building networks to improve the efficiency of flows through its port facilities and to increase resilience to unexpected events.

By the 1980s, building major new bridges and tunnels was no longer feasible for both political and environmental reasons. Chapter 5 describes how one creative Port Authority official, Lou Gambaccini, built effective coalitions and new member-based organizations by leveraging resources that were just as relevant as money. He jumpstarted ferry services, created a regional traffic and transit operations center, set up a groundbreaking transit program, and nurtured a coalition-building culture that led to the development of the E-Z-Pass electronic toll system now used between Florida and Maine.

In chapter 6 we pause to reflect on the evolution of the organization in the 1990s and describe a key turning point for the Authority. For its first seven decades the Port Authority resisted patronage and political influence, relying on managerial expertise and rational planning to solve problems. In the 1990s, however, its senior executives started focusing more on the political priorities of the governors, while its board of commissioners increasingly became a rubber stamp for decisions made in Albany and Trenton. After the

Authority slashed both its staff and portfolio, two fiefdoms began to form at its headquarters, with each faction reporting to a different governor. As a result of these changes, a clash between the two states threatened the viability of the region's marine terminals and the Authority itself.

By focusing on three bridges between New Jersey and Staten Island, chapter 7 reveals how the Port Authority has responded to and influenced public sentiment, and the ways in which its priorities have anticipated and addressed the region's needs. In recent years, the Port Authority spent more than $3 billion to raise the deck of its Bayonne Bridge by sixty-four feet (because its height threatened the viability of the region's marine terminals) and replaced the Goethals Bridge. To complete these two megaprojects, Port Authority officials and their stakeholders navigated an extraordinary set of political, regulatory, financial, and engineering challenges.

In the early 1960s, as described in chapter 8, the Port Authority hoped that its audacious plan to build the world's two tallest buildings would create a global center for international trade and secure New York's role as the nation's leading port. Instead of achieving these two goals, the Port Authority stretched its mission, diminished its credibility, and created powerful enemies. On September 11, 2001, a terrorist attack destroyed the entire World Trade Center complex killing more than 2,600 people including 84 Authority employees. The Port Authority not only lost its largest real estate investment and headquarters, but also suffered extensive damage to its rail network. The Authority's efforts to rebuild the center in an emotionally charged and politically fraught atmosphere revealed the limits of its autonomy, ambitions, and resources in the twenty-first century.

Chapter 9 assesses the Authority's experience with political scandal and institutional constraint. More than a century ago, the states of New Jersey and New York created an entity that could take vigorous action in an effective manner without worrying about the day-to-day concerns of political leaders. The states ceded control and accountability to an Authority that identified the region's problems, proposed projects to address them, and then prioritized its priorities over local concerns. In its early years, the commissioners combined political independence with self-confidence, choosing staff executives and shielding them from short-term political demands. Although the Port Authority has never been immune from political influence, the Bridgegate episode marked a low point for the Authority's independence. In recent years, the Authority has struggled to maintain its independent and professional approach to regional challenges as governors have sought to use the

Authority's financial strength and region-wide reach to meet their own political needs. This chapter tracks the Port Authority's institutional evolution and delves more deeply into how and why its capacity has changed over time.

The Port Authority's successes and failures reveal lessons for the future of the New York metropolitan area, many of them applicable to other regions in the United States and beyond. In chapter 10, we reflect on what our analysis offers the Port Authority as it looks to the future and draws out lessons for other organizations. Our critical retrospective of the Port Authority's experience allows us to describe the myriad ways that the organization has affected the region, for better and for worse. However, we go beyond description by making an argument about how, as an organization, the Port Authority managed to accomplish its goals, often in the face of impressive opposition. While the Port Authority is a unique organization and its experiences are regionally specific, there are important lessons in its experiences that are relevant for any organization that needs to balance the interests of its individual members against its collective mission.

About the Port Authority

Leadership

The governors of New York and New Jersey each appoint six members to the Authority's Board of Commissioners for overlapping six-year terms. The board establishes the Authority's policies and adopts its strategic plans, capital plans, and budgets. An executive director reports to the board and manages the Authority on a day-to-day basis.

Major Facilities

Airports: John F. Kennedy, LaGuardia, Newark Liberty, Stewart, and Teterboro.
Motor Vehicle Crossings between Manhattan and New Jersey: George Washington Bridge, Lincoln Tunnel, and Holland Tunnel.
Motor Vehicle Bridges between Staten Island and New Jersey: Bayonne Bridge, Goethals Bridge, and Outerbridge Crossing.
Bus Stations: Midtown Bus Terminal and George Washington Bridge Bus Station.

Introduction

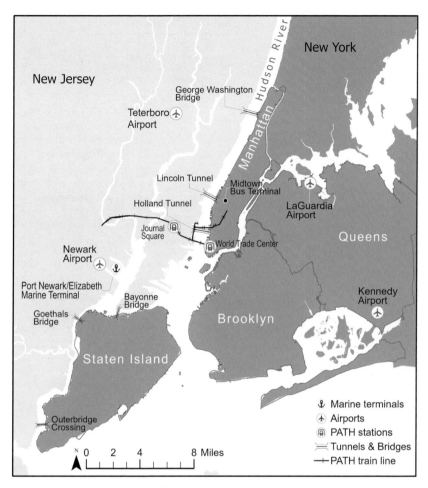

Map 1.1. Major Port Authority facilities.
(Map by Md. Shahinoor Rahman.)

Marine Terminals: Port Newark, Elizabeth, and Howland Hook.
PATH: Passenger rail service with six stations in New York and seven in New Jersey.
Real Estate: World Trade Center, Teleport (business park on Staten Island), industrial parks in Elizabeth (NJ) and Bathgate (Bronx), and Newark Legal & Communications Center.

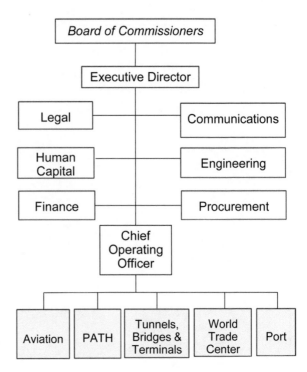

Fig. 1.3. Key Port Authority officials and departments.

Organization Structure

As shown in figure 1.3, the Port Authority currently has five departments that manage its airports, bridges, bus stations, PATH train, tunnels, ports, and the World Trade Center. The Authority also has departments that provide centralized functions such as communications, engineering, human resources, and legal services. Approximately 8,000 are employed by the Port Authority.[25]

CHAPTER 2

Creation and First Triumphs

Much has been written about the Port Authority's early days. This is not surprising as some of its most iconic and enduring assets—soaring bridges and technologically sophisticated tunnels—were constructed in the organization's infancy. This chapter provides a broad overview of some critical moments in the Authority's formation and early life, highlighting how an organization with an experimental design (that had the great fortune of being born at an auspicious moment in American political development) managed to develop, consolidate, and flourish. While the stories here refer to some topics and themes that are discussed in later chapters, we feel it important to cover this foundational period separately.

While the New York metropolitan region now takes the Port Authority's accomplishments for granted, neither its success nor its endurance was ever guaranteed. Despite its active and entrepreneurial leadership, and the fact that it enjoyed enough political support to get it off the ground, the Authority was contested, and tested, from the outset. Yet it survived the Great Depression, political change, and World War II, and retained its capacity and reputation for effectiveness and vision. The thesis of this book is that much of the Authority's success is attributable to its ability to build and sustain coalitions to support its agenda in the face of (sometimes hostile) opposition from the various interests that control its fate. The foundations for the resources that it has been able to draw on in order to fulfill its ambitions were largely laid in the Authority's crucial first decade of operation and through projects that remain, to this day, its flagship accomplishments.

This chapter begins with an overview of the Progressive Era in American politics and its significance in the formation of the Port Authority. It then explores the border-spanning issues that necessitated a bistate, regional solution. We next turn to the three most significant projects and events in the Port Authority's first two decades—the construction of the Holland Tunnel,

George Washington Bridge, and Lincoln Tunnel—before reflecting on how through these projects the Authority grew and established itself, exiting its early era as an organization uniquely placed to tackle emerging, and challenging, regional infrastructure issues.

The Progressive Era: A Unique Nursery for a Unique Organization

The Progressive Era in which the Port Authority was created had an indelible influence on the shape and emergence of the organization. Not only did it heavily influence the individuals that ultimately designed the organization, it created a policy window within which political decision-makers at various levels of government were uniquely receptive to the principles of a professionalized bureaucracy upon which the Port Authority was based. In his book *Empire on the Hudson*, Jameson Doig notes, "to its creators and champions in the business world and beyond the Port Authority was stamped with the Progressives' coin of optimism."[1] So important were these principles to understanding the early genesis of the Port Authority that a brief overview of them, and their influence, is appropriate here.

Roughly spanning from the turn of the century to the early 1930's, the Progressive Era and Movement emerged as a response to the political corruption and excessive inequalities of the Gilded Age in the United States. Large businesses had used their powers to corrupt governments and the rise of unregulated monopolies perpetuated dangerous working conditions and vast inequalities. The costs of public works projects were frequently bloated because governments awarded contracts to their political cronies. Moreover, the government workers who oversaw those contracts were often appointed and promoted based on their political connections, not their abilities.

While the social movement, and the political movement it spawned, had several core missions, one of the most central was a reform agenda aimed at promoting efficiency, professionalism, and business-like government that should create policies based on rational and scientific thought. Doig identifies four themes of American political development that particularly influenced the Port Authority's emergence and evolution: a movement toward depoliticized bureaucracies shaped by expert analysis; a public willingness and encouragement of vigorous executive action; a belief that the government should support the instruments of capitalism for economic development;

Creation and First Triumphs

and a deep optimism that the American political and social system, and the energies and ingenuity of its people, could overcome the complex problems of the day.[2] Each of these values enabled the emergence of the Port Authority and shaped its agenda in different ways.

The principles of and faith in rational planning—the practice of examining problems and then systematically evaluating policy alternatives—were entrenched in the Authority's ethos from its inception. This manifested as a strong deference to expertise, analysis, and an ideal of impartiality. Innovation and experimentation were also encouraged both in the technical approaches to complex problems and in organizational process and design. This deference to expertise was tested on numerous occasions as the early Port Authority faced political pressures to take specific decisions—on contracts and materials, for instance—only to repeatedly support the judgment of its engineers.

After all, this was an organization designed and then led through its first fifty years by engineers, planners, and creative lawyers, not by politicians. Its architect, Julius Henry Cohen, and a succession of early leaders were committed to action and took as many steps as they could to insulate the Authority from political interference and corruption. Doig refers to this effort as a "heroic search" for "government without politics."[3] As this book will demonstrate, they were only partially successful in this aim. Although complete organizational autonomy was never a possibility, the Port Authority was created with a notable and unprecedented degree of separation from its political masters. In recent decades, the Authority's erosion of autonomy has diminished its ability to draw upon resources, facilitate coalition-building efforts, and achieve its goals. That it had such formidable resources in the first place, however, is in part due to the fact that it came of age in a period that insulated it from the full brunt of bistate political interference.

The spirit of capitalism and individualism was another important driver of the Port Authority's creation and early successes. In the Progressive Era, business interests were particularly active in identifying grand challenges facing their enterprises (such as traffic congestion) and framing them as matters that affected both efficient operation of commerce and the common good. This activist mindset provided ample justification of government intervention as well as the broad support necessary for decisive action—such as the creation of innovative and semi-autonomous organizations like the Port Authority. The region's business community was supportive of the Port Authority in the hopes that it would improve commercial vitality, individual mobility, and the efficiency of public infrastructure. This narrative of capitalism, in which government intervention to help businesses would support the greater good, helped overcome local objections to grand regional projects that were the hallmark of the era.

Three of the Port Authority's ambitious early projects (Holland Tunnel, George Washington Bridge, and Lincoln Tunnel) captured the entrepreneurial and optimistic spirit of the era and fueled the enthusiasm of the Port Authority's leaders and its supporters. In its early days, the Port Authority was driven by the "energetic optimism" of its creators and leaders. Overcoming daunting engineering and political obstacles with dramatic and unprecedented results—for instance, the George Washington Bridge was the world's largest suspension bridge when it opened—only increased the Authority's optimism and the confidence of the region's stakeholders in its legitimacy and mission.

That the Progressive Era had a significant influence on the creation and development of the Port Authority cannot be denied. Had the idea of creating the Port Authority been seriously attempted earlier or later, it is highly likely that the outcome for the Authority and the region would have been dramatically different (though how is an open question). While we give this contextual dimension of the Port Authority's history its due, we want to be careful not to give the impression that its formation during, and its subsequent embodiment of the values of, this unique period of American politics explains the entirety of its early successes as an organization. Rather we contend that the particularities of these beginnings allowed the organization to consolidate the resources that it used to execute on its expanding agenda in subsequent decades. Exploring these beginnings is a crucial first step to understanding the evolution of this groundbreaking organization.

A Barrier as a Catalyst: The Regional Problem that Spawned a Regional Solution

Just as the social and political environment contributed important elements to the birth of the Port Authority so too did other less obvious factors, such as the geography and patterns of urban and economic development in the region. For instance, if the Hudson River had not been so formidable a geographic obstacle, it is unlikely that the Port Authority would have emerged when and in the form that it did. In the very simplest terms, the Hudson River was the regional problem to which the Port Authority was the solution.

Figures 2.1 to 2.4 illustrate the crux of the problem facing businesses and policymakers in the region at the time. Half of the nation's imports and exports flowed through the bustling piers along the Hudson and East Rivers in Manhattan and Brooklyn. These centers of industry and commerce were located on two islands—Manhattan and Long Island (where Brooklyn is located). While the islands were connected to the mainland by several rail lines radiating to the north and east, most of the transcontinental railroads terminated across the Hudson River in New Jersey (shown in figure 2.1 as a cluster of railroad terminals on the left shore). In the absence of a freight line across the Hudson, cargo had to be floated at great expense on barges across the river.[4] Ports existed on the New Jersey side, but only seven shipping companies landed there while seventy used docks on the New York side.

If that were all there was to the issue it is likely that this problem would have resolved itself. Freight would begin to bypass New York City's ports in search of options that required less travel time and expense. The problem was the Interstate Commerce Commission (ICC), which set freight rates across the nation. The ICC had concluded that the railroads should charge the same fee to carry freight to New Jersey's terminals as it did to New York, even though the railroad's *actual* cost was far lower to New Jersey. Municipal officials in New Jersey advocated for the ICC to lower rates to New Jersey. This change would have had a significant impact as railroads and shipping companies would have looked to build modern marine terminals along the Hudson River's western shore, leading to expanded commercial activity throughout northern New Jersey.

In May 1916, New Jersey's state commerce agency, joined by Jersey City and three other municipalities, filed a complaint with the ICC, arguing that railroad rates for New Jersey destinations should be lowered. In response, the New York Chamber of Commerce, alarmed by the possible impact on New York businesses, asked Julius Henry Cohen (an attorney and political reformer) to take the lead in countering the New Jersey position. Cohen decided not only to oppose the change in freight rates but also to argue that both sides of the Hudson would benefit if they would cooperate in improving rail and water transportation across the bistate area. The ICC rejected the New Jersey argument and embraced Cohen's position. "Cooperation and initiative," the ICC concluded, not hostile litigation, would "eventually bring about the improvements" needed to improve efficiency in freight movement throughout the region.[5]

The governors of both states soon convened a meeting with Cohen and several business leaders. Cohen suggested that a "study commission" be

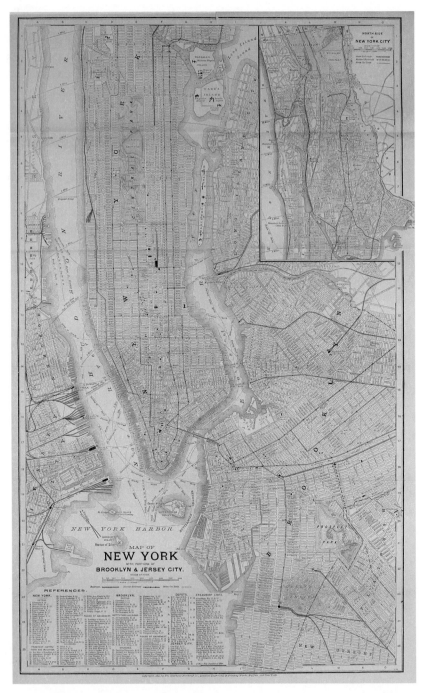

Fig. 2.1. New York Harbor in 1893 showing (*left to right*): Jersey City railroad yards, Manhattan bristling with piers, and Brooklyn.
(Illustration © D. Appleton and Co.)

Creation and First Triumphs 33

Fig. 2.2. Aerial view of Manhattan in 1927.
(Photograph reprinted by permission of the Air Photo Archives, UCLA Department of Geography.)

created and charged with developing a binding plan for cooperation, together with a specific set of engineering proposals to improve freight movement across the harbor. The governors readily agreed, a bistate commission was established in March 1917, and Cohen was named the commission's counsel. While the ICC challenge was a central catalyst for the creation of this commission, both Cohen and the business community saw the challenge of managing the New York region's ports as greater than just resolving a freight pricing issue. Traffic congestion, the deteriorating condition of port facilities, and intraregional competition were all eating into the overall competitiveness of the region's port system and the bottom line of regional enterprise. The private sector proved incapable of raising funds to pursue its own solutions, and so it fell to the states to find a way to keep the region moving. While the 1917

Fig. 2.3. Hudson River piers in Manhattan, c. 1905. *(Photograph from the George P. Hall & Son Photograph Collection, New York Historical Society, reprinted by permission.)*

commission began as an exercise to develop cooperative processes and technical solutions around the interstate freight issue, its deliberations ultimately led to a far more wide-ranging proposal. But it all began with the river.

Founding the Port Authority

After twenty months of study, the commission led by Cohen drew up a detailed proposal that recommended the two states join in creating a new governmental agency, "The Port of New York Authority," to be established via the Compact Clause of the U.S. Constitution. This clause allows states to enter into agreements subject to U.S. congressional approval, although it had never been used to create a permanent agency. Cohen had studied the history of earlier attempts to cooperate across local and state boundaries, using parallel commissions, and he found that conflicts among various local interests often led to disruption. New mayors and governors replaced board members with their own allies, and sometimes they abolished "cooperating" agencies.[6] Tying the new body to the Compact Clause would anchor it in firmer ground.

Creation and First Triumphs

Fig. 2.4. Railroad yards along Jersey City waterfront in 1941.
(Photograph from the Collection of the New York Historical Society, reprinted by permission.)

The word "authority" had never been used in the title of an American government agency, although it had been employed in creating the Port of London Authority, which chose the name simply because the Port Compact, as the law creating the agency was known, had many paragraphs that began "Authority is hereby given." After 1921, the term became widely used throughout the world, in part due to the success of the Port Authority.[7]

Cohen's study of England's experiences also convinced him that the new Authority should have a high degree of independence, so its multiyear planning and construction efforts would not be halted by political disputes. Embedded in his draft legislation were important measures to institutionalize its autonomy. A more detailed discussion of these measures appears in chapter 9 in our analysis of the Port Authority's institutional evolution.

Three measures bolstered the insulation granted by the Authority's creation through the Compact Clause. First, the Authority was granted access to a relatively stable source of funding since it could issue bonds secured by tolls and fees levied on users of its (then nonexistent) infrastructure. This undercut the ability of legislators to withhold funds if they disagreed with the agency's plans. As we demonstrate in this chapter, that the Port Authority was able to develop (or acquire) so many revenue generating assets in its early years was one of the factors that secured its future sustainability.

Secondly, the governing board was constructed to minimize political interference from or co-option by the two states. The Port Authority's commissioners (originally three from each state) would be appointed by each governor for five years, which was longer than the terms of the appointing governors.[8] Furthermore, the commissioners would receive no salary. British port officials had advised Cohen that he "would get better commissioners if they were not paid" because they would be viewed as "posts of honor." If the commissioners were salaried, the port officials warned, the positions would most likely be used as "political patronage."[9]

Finally, the Port Compact enshrined decisions taken by the commissioners as binding and did not initially include any measures for state governors to meddle with outcomes after the fact. This again was meant to insulate the Authority politically to preserve its ability to conduct its business with integrity. Not all of these measures would survive the ensuing decades. However, that the Authority was born with a relatively high degree of autonomy certainly facilitated much of the activity that it undertook in its early years.

In part because of this institutional design, the Port Authority was not welcomed everywhere with open arms. The proposal to create a bistate authority was challenged by New York City and New Jersey local officials. For example, New York City's mayor, John Hylan, denounced it as "the greatest deal ever attempted to be put over on the city. It's simply another method of grabbing the Port of New York."[10] But Cohen was anxious to insulate his offspring from any local quarrels, and he persuaded officials at the two state capitals to view the Port Authority as a wide-ranging agency that would require a multistate regional vision, not limited by narrow local perspectives. He won that battle. The Port Compact was approved by both states in April 1921, and despite the demands of local officials that they make appointments to the Authority, the two governors would choose all members of the Port Authority's board of commissioners. The unique governance configuration of this distinctive quasi-independent authority was possible because of the vision, creativity, and efforts of Julius Henry Cohen exercised within a political moment supportive of these fundamental values.

Creation and First Triumphs

Cohen was appointed counsel to the new authority, and he served in that position from 1921 until he retired in 1942. Notably, the original plans proposed by the Port Authority, which involved the creation of new rail freight lines across northern New Jersey and under the Hudson, ran into vehement opposition from the railroads and were finally scuttled. That failure meant that Cohen and the Port Authority's railroad engineers had very little to show for their efforts beyond a new bistate organization. However, building from a solid organizational foundation the Port Authority adapted a broader agenda and followed a path envisioned by neither Cohen nor the Port Authority's first commissioners.

Early Successes Establish the Port Authority as a Regional Power

The plan to build a rail freight link across the Hudson River, a key component of the Port Authority's original mission, died a slow death in the 1920s. Although freight mobility was a perennial topic of bistate discussions, it took on a very different tenor with the increasing use of cars and trucks. Between 1920 and 1925, the number of registered motor vehicles in New York City more than doubled from 223,000 to almost 500,000.[11] The economic need to facilitate truck traffic and the political desire to accommodate cars for personal use, led to a public outcry for new and improved motor vehicle facilities. While the rail initiative faltered, the Port Authority took advantage of an opportunity to take on significant and dramatic projects, demonstrating the power of coalition-building and laying the foundation for many of the Port Authority's subsequent successes.

The story of the Port Authority's early projects is often tackled in a fragmented fashion—focusing on one great bridge, tunnel, or plan at a time. In reality, as shown in figure 2.5, these projects overlapped substantially such that the Port Authority's early years were a flurry of activity on different fronts, each of which influenced the others.

So while this chapter proceeds through a separate, and chronological, discussion of each of these foundational projects, the metanarrative of how these stories weave together deserves some attention here. In 1927, the Holland Tunnel was the first Hudson River motor vehicle crossing to be completed, and it went on to become one of the Port Authority's most important assets. However, the project was neither planned nor completed by the Port

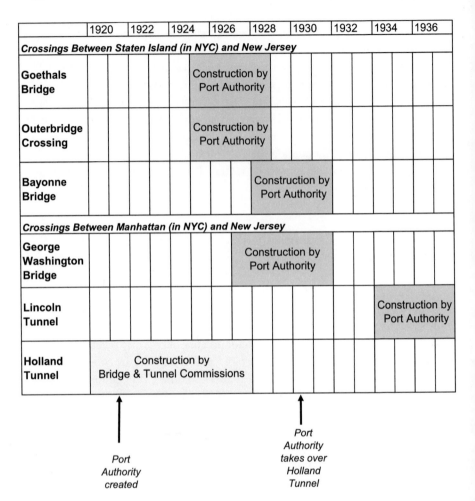

Fig. 2.5. Timeline of major Port Authority construction projects.

Authority, but rather by the two state bridge and tunnel commissions (New Jersey Interstate Bridge and Tunnel Commission and the New York State Bridge and Tunnel Commission). The Authority's success completing two bridges between New Jersey and New York's Staten Island in 1928 led state leaders to support the Port Authority's ultimate capture of the two bridge and tunnel commissions in 1930. The Port Authority, unlike the two commissions, had constructed its crossings ahead of schedule, with little controversy, and at a cost less than originally estimated.[12]

The relative confluence of the Port Authority's completion of the George Washington Bridge and a third Staten Island bridge in 1931, the Authority's acquisition of the Holland Tunnel, along with the revenues from all of these crossings, marked a series of successes that both bolstered the reputation of the fledgling organization and filled its coffers, enabling its next phase of public works and organizational expansion.

This chapter summarizes these early projects with a focus on highlighting their significance for the Port Authority's development and particularly on its early efforts at coalition-building. Given the structure of this book, we fully acknowledge that we will not do justice to the rich and fascinating stories that led to the construction of what are still some of the most dramatic and important transportation facilities in the New York metropolitan region. For much more comprehensive and vibrant histories of the construction and lives of these Hudson crossings, see Donald Wolf's *Crossing the Hudson*, Angus Kress Gillespie's *Crossing Under the Hudson*, and of course Jameson Doig's *Empire on the Hudson*.

The Holland Tunnel

At the dawn of the twentieth century, the problem of crossing the Hudson River had taken on increased urgency. The issue of rail freight and passenger mobility ultimately led to the creation of the Port Authority in 1921, but even before the Authority's inauguration, work had begun to span the Hudson River. The federal government granted a ten-year charter for the construction of a suspension bridge as early as 1890, and two private passenger rail tunnel networks were completed and in operation by 1910.[13] Still, with the rapid increase of vehicle traffic, and the continued failure of leaders to sort out a solution for rail freight, the region faced an acute challenge to improve commercial and private vehicle mobility in and out of Manhattan. The first such crossing to be constructed was the Holland Tunnel, which opened to traffic in 1928.

The Port Authority's early relationship with the Holland Tunnel was complex. Initially, the two state bridge and tunnel commissions and the tunnel they built were competitors to the Authority's plans to span the Hudson with a suspension bridge. After the tunnel opened in 1927, however, a large portion of its revenues were funneled to Port Authority projects and then in 1930, the Authority took control of the tunnel. The absorption of the Holland Tunnel represented a triumph for the Port Authority and the recognition of

Fig. 2.6. Officials from New Jersey and New York shaking hands before the opening of the Holland Tunnel. *(Photograph from the New Jersey Interstate Bridge and Tunnel Commission, courtesy New York Public Library Digital Collections.)*

its preeminent status as the go-to organization for regional infrastructure initiatives. But there was nothing inevitable about that outcome.

To tackle the thorny issue of cross-Hudson travel, both states established their own interstate bridge and tunnel commissions in the early 1900s. The initial solution was to strike parallel but collaborative (in theory) commissions to explore the problem. As their names indicate, the type of span—bridge or tunnel—was still under debate at the time. A series of reports issued by the commissions themselves and various consulting firms agreed that a tunnel would be much more economical to build, though their estimates differed substantially. In March 1918, the New York commission released a report in support of the immediate construction of a tunnel, and in 1919 the two states signed an agreement to jointly build, construct, operate, repair, and maintain a motor vehicle toll tunnel, funded by tolls, between the two states (fig. 2.6).

As with all big projects—and particularly expensive and groundbreaking bistate ones—the Holland Tunnel sustained all sorts of conflicts over leadership, design, construction methods, and location of entrances. Gillespie evocatively summarizes the tensions of the time in *Crossing Under the Hudson*:

> The debate involved greed, bureaucracy, personal conflict and power politics. . . . With professional engineers in disagreement, there was no clearcut path to a decision; it would be a political one. But it would not be easy, because there were two decision-making bodies, two commissions: one for New York and another for New Jersey. All this debate was taking place before

Creation and First Triumphs

the creation of the bi-state Port Authority. The two commissions would have to reach a voluntary consensus; neither could force its will on the other. The commissioners were community leaders and men of influence, but they were laymen rather than engineers or traffic experts or contractors.[14]

Cohen watched this debate play out publicly in 1919 and 1920 as he was designing his approach to bistate political cooperation. The tension highlighted some of the issues—political divisions, personal interest, and the perils of inexpert decision-makers—that would have to be considered when designing the Port Authority's organizational structure.

One major conflict between the two commissions centered on tunnel construction techniques proposed by competing bidders, pitting George Goethals's single concrete tube design against Clifford Holland's twin cast-iron ring tunnels. The design stalemate was eventually broken by the influential chair of the New York commission, General George R. Dyer, who favored Holland's approach, in part, because two tubes would create less traffic congestion on local streets. Construction finally began in 1920.

Although the tunnel was frequently lauded as the eighth wonder of the world upon completion, the arrival of the Port Authority on the scene in 1921 contributed to the demise of the two tunnel commissions a decade later. The bickering between the commissions in the lead-up to and during construction of the Holland Tunnel had irritated both state governors. In 1923, New York governor Al Smith joined his counterpart in Trenton (New Jersey governor George Silzer) to urge that all future bridges and tunnels between the two states be constructed by the Port Authority. Smith appreciated the Port Authority's wider mandate and its record, unlike the tunnel commissions, of financing its crossings without tapping into state revenues.[15] Only months later, Smith argued that the Port Authority should take over the Holland Tunnel project and, after failing that, orchestrated a scheme to devote part of the New York share of toll revenue to the Port Authority for construction of the Staten Island bridges. The success of the tunnel, once it had opened, and the realization that it would reach capacity sooner than expected, prompted a new round of discussions about additional tunnels despite the fact that the George Washington Bridge was then under construction and expected to soak up some cross-Hudson demand. The bistate tunnel commission partnership was, to some, the obvious choice to complete these additional projects, but the Port Authority had other ideas. Fearing that additional spans north of the Holland Tunnel could siphon traffic from its new bridge and cut into its profits, the Port Authority tabled a plan in 1928 that authorized it to spearhead new tunnel projects.

In its quest for a monopoly on bistate bridge and tunnel construction, the Port Authority faced not only competition from the existing tunnel commissions but also had to defend itself against calls for its dissolution—all the while finishing four simultaneous bridge construction projects (George Washington, Bayonne, Goethals, and Outerbridge). In waging its campaign to take over the tunnels, the Port Authority relied on the support of a powerful coalition—notably the New York City business community, the New York State Chamber of Commerce, and the leading news media. Arrayed against them were the Republicans who controlled the legislatures in New York and New Jersey. They preferred private operation of tunnels and bridges, and they feared the potential slippery slope of governmental bodies eroding legislative powers. As various bills related to the governance of future Hudson River projects were dueling in the New York and New Jersey legislatures, the new governor of New York, Franklin D. Roosevelt, finally proposed merging the tunnel commissions with the Port Authority.

This was a victory of enormous significance to the Port Authority. The income generated by the Holland Tunnel stimulated confidence in the bond market and fueled the Authority's later enterprises. The "wedding" between the agencies was, in actuality, a funeral for the tunnel commissions, which were abolished with six commissioners added to the Port Authority's existing six-member board.[16] This left the Port Authority unopposed in the development of major bistate bridge and tunnel projects and consolidated its status as *the* sensible steward for a variety of other infrastructure functions that would evolve over time. The Port Authority prevailed through the tenacity of its leadership—specifically Cohen—to be sure, but also because of the demonstration effect of its first set of projects. The George Washington Bridge (and other concurrent projects) showed that the Port Authority *worked*. It got things done. Chambers of commerce, the business community, and crucially the financial industry were convinced of the merits of the "Port Authority method." The Authority was described as having "the most efficient staff of engineers and experts dealing with transportation and terminal problems ever organized in one body" and lauded for its ability to "resist political interference."[17] And so demonstrated expertise, resources, organizational autonomy backed by a culture dedicated to supporting progressive values, and entrepreneurial leadership won over the external and political coalitions necessary to secure the Holland Tunnel and, more crucially, its unassailable status as the region's infrastructure authority.

Creation and First Triumphs 43

The George Washington Bridge

If the capture of the Holland Tunnel consolidated the Port Authority's status in the region, it was only possible on the back of the George Washington Bridge project. As the only bridge in New York City that crosses the Hudson, it remains one of the most dramatic and iconic of the Port Authority's many infrastructure projects, both because of its colossal and graceful presence and for its immense significance to regional mobility. The project was also extraordinarily important to the reputation of the fledgling Port Authority, proving itself equal to the task of planning and managing monumental public works and, perhaps more crucially, demonstrating that it possessed organizational qualities above and beyond what its competitors could muster—namely a singularity of purpose, an internal culture that sought to uphold the pillars of progressive governance, the organizational autonomy that permitted it to hew to those principles, and the expertise and resources to execute on its agenda.

The idea of a cross-Hudson bridge had its origins, as the Holland Tunnel did, in the region's rail and passenger freight problems. In 1890, Congress had granted Gustav Lindenthal (designer of the Hell Gate Bridge) and his North River Bridge Company, a federal charter to build a rail crossing at 23rd Street in Manhattan. With progress on the Holland Tunnel rekindling interest in a bridge, Lindenthal revamped his original design and added space for vehicles, this time proposing a crossing at 57th Street. His revised design featured sixteen lanes of motor vehicle traffic and ten rail lines, and it was expected to cost at least $200 million.[18] (In comparison, the cost to build the four-lane Holland Tunnel was less than $50 million.) As resistance to the cost and location of this bridge mounted, Othmar Ammann, Lindenthal's more junior partner, offered up a competing alternative: a lighter and less expensive bridge located further north between 170th and 185th Streets. The plan caused a bitter rift between the two men, which only worsened as their mutual friend, New Jersey governor George Silzer, threw his support behind Ammann's plan.

The Port Authority was still a newcomer to the region as various bridge design schemes and locations were being debated. Yet, because rail transportation was within its purview, the Authority considered Lindenthal's 57th Street bridge as part of its blueprint for vast new rail and freight-terminal investments across the region.[19] However, the Authority's 1922 Comprehensive Plan rejected Lindenthal's bridge partly on the basis of sound planning and engineering considerations—notably issues related to traffic congestion, the number of buildings that needed to be demolished, and the difficulty of providing enough rail service from that far uptown to the city's commercial center in Lower Manhattan—as well as the shrewd understanding that, for many of those reasons, the business community would not support the design.[20]

Interestingly, although the Port Authority was eventually picked to lead the bridge project, records show that through 1923 Authority staff were not terribly interested in building a bridge. A trans-Hudson bridge was not in the Comprehensive Plan and, as Doig points out, "during most of this period it was reasonable to foresee that the Holland Tunnel would be followed by a series of other tunnels under the Hudson built by the joint commissions, possibly with one or two others financed by private investors."[21]

The construction of the bridge was the result of some canny coalition-building for the Port Authority. It managed to leverage an opportunity largely of someone else's making and maintain control of the project through potentially disastrous political challenges. In fact, Ammann's plan for a trans-Hudson motor vehicle span directly competed with the Authority's own plans to construct rail tunnels between New Jersey and Manhattan. However, the organization astutely recognized that motor vehicle crossings would be crucial to the future of the region and, after a detailed study of alternatives, pivoted to adopt the bridge plan and its designer and engineer.

The entrepreneurial Ammann personally played an important role in securing political approvals for the bridge plans before joining the Port Authority by relentlessly promoting his initiative to local politicians, business communities, and state legislatures. In the early 1920s, he was tirelessly writing letters to media outlets, giving public speeches and "campaigning with the vigor of a politician running for office, describing the virtues of his bridge."[22] These supportive constituencies were instrumental in securing political buy-in for the project and were a critical and borderless counterbalancing force in subsequent bistate political struggles.

As work on the bridge began (fig. 2.7), conflicts erupted between the two states that threatened to derail the project as well as the construction of three other Port Authority bridges. Factors related to the bridge's construction and design—specifically construction techniques and which contractors would be tapped to provide materials—provoked a movement in New Jersey to give the legislature approval power over all Port Authority contracts. This sparked a "veto power" arms race of sorts between the two state governors, both of whom wanted to ensure that their states had the final word on Port Authority matters.[23] In response, the Authority's leaders audaciously suspended

Creation and First Triumphs

Fig. 2.7. George Washington Bridge under construction.
(Photograph reprinted by permission of the New York State Archives.)

activities on the four interstate crossings in progress while the political battle played out. The gambit paid off, resulting in a broad outcry from business interests and local politicians who argued that the shutdown threatened economic growth. Shortly thereafter New Jersey repealed its legislation and both states had signed bills limiting veto power over the Port Authority's actions to the governors. Work on the crossings resumed, and the bridge opened successfully in 1931.

The bridge was a significant and enduring accomplishment, but the project had other important legacies. First, it built a strong foundation and reputation of competence that established the Authority, once and for all, as the organization of record for regional transportation infrastructure projects. As Doig notes, the Port Authority and its engineering department "served as an exemplar of the Progressive theme—demonstrating what government could do, if individuals of talent were brought together, given a clear mission, and insulated from the uncertainties of politics while they carried out their assigned tasks."[24]

The conflict over veto power would have long-lasting consequences that both institutionalized and undermined the Authority's political autonomy (see chapter 9). The result was a curtailing of organizational autonomy through the enactment, in both states, of clauses granting gubernatorial vetoes. Ironically, the episode also legitimized the Port Authority's model to the extent that it entrenched the fact that the Authority could not be controlled as if it were any other state agency and it could, at least for a while, "retain much of its independence against the slings and arrows of outraged politicians and advocates of localized democracy."[25] All in all, the construction of the George Washington Bridge served to consolidate the Port Authority's position as the best instrument to solve regional projects and to shore up political support in the region, so much so that even its detractors were forced to concede rather than risk being seen as running counter to the waves of pro-Port Authority sentiment.

The Lincoln Tunnel

The success of the George Washington Bridge endeavor was also an important precedent for the Port Authority's first tunneling project. The Lincoln Tunnel, connecting Midtown Manhattan and New Jersey, emerged as the Port Authority's bridge-building efforts were well underway, and the acquisition of the Holland Tunnel was in progress. The construction of the Lincoln Tunnel's first tube represented another important step in the consolidation of the Authority's dominion over regional transportation infrastructure projects (fig. 2.8). Recall that, at the time the tunnel was first being discussed seriously by the two states in the 1920s, various Port Authority projects and initiatives were in motion but had not yet been decisively completed. The decision to vest the new tunnel project with the Port Authority came just as the Authority took over the Holland Tunnel and as it was completing the George Washington Bridge project. In particular, the selection of the Port Authority to lead the Lincoln Tunnel project, and not the bridge and tunnel commissions, secured the Authority's role in the region.

Creation and First Triumphs

Fig. 2.8. The second tube of the Lincoln Tunnel opened in 1945.
(Photograph reprinted by permission of Port Authority of New York and New Jersey.)

However, this project proceeded less smoothly than the two previous cross-Hudson endeavors. The Lincoln Tunnel was to be the first major beneficiary of the Authority's model of consolidating revenues from all of its properties to finance new projects. Except timing did not work in its favor. The Great Depression beginning with the stock market crash of 1929 reduced traffic on the Port Authority's other properties, constricting revenue just as financing for the Lincoln Tunnel project was required. And the collapse of the bond market meant that despite the Authority's mounting reputation and good credit, it could not secure funding at reasonable interest rates. Instead the project was scaled back from two tubes to one and the Authority sought, and secured, a $4.8 million loan from the New Deal's Public Works Administration to complete the first tube, which opened in December 1937 to great fanfare.

While the first tube of the tunnel was completed successfully, it was not the immediate success that its planners had hoped. The disappointingly low number of crossings (in its first full year of operations it was used by 1.8 million vehicles compared to the Holland's 12.4 million[26]) did not bode well for expected revenues, just as they were badly needed to pay for construction of the second tube. In fact, the Authority announced in 1938 that completion of the north tunnel then under construction would be postponed and would not resume again until 1941. Due to the advent of World War II, the completion of the project was further delayed, and the second tube did not open until 1945. By the time the third and final tube opened in 1957, the Port Authority had evolved significantly as an authority and political force in the region.

Reflecting on the Significance of the Port Authority's Early Successes

Three major crossings—three distinctive and iconic pieces of infrastructure—marked the early years of the Port Authority. While they remain as some of the most heavily trafficked and enduring links between New York and New Jersey, their legacy was, and is, far more significant than their continuing contribution to the functioning of the region. These structures did no less than bind the two states into a partnership that has persisted for more than a hundred years.

While due credit should be given to the entrepreneurial individuals who led the Authority and its projects—Cohen and Ammann—and the governors who struggled to shape its identity from the state capitols—Smith, Silzer, Roosevelt, and others—the legacy of these early projects was both the product of the collective toil of the Authority and its leadership. Most significantly, they established three critical cornerstones that laid a foundation for the Authority's later development capacity. First, a reputation for excellence and efficiency in project design and execution; second, the institutionalization and political acceptance of independence and organizational autonomy; and third, the revenue streams that would enable it to raise resources outside normal public funding processes.

As the Authority evolved over the course of the ensuing decades and engaged with real estate, rail, port, and airport operations, these foundations proved fundamental to enacting its agenda in the murky and complicated world of bistate politics. Where these foundations were strong, the Authority was able to flourish, and when they faltered the Port Authority also struggled. The Port Authority's first two decades were crucial to setting it on a trajectory along which it would change the face of the region and in many ways serve as a model for regions across the globe.

CHAPTER 3

Grappling with Capacity Problems at the Airports

As the United States economy became increasingly reliant upon trucks and cars in the 1920s and 1930s, the governors of New York and New Jersey encouraged the Port Authority to build bridges and tunnels. In the 1940s, the Authority muscled its way into another growing transportation field, the aviation business. The Port Authority's airport experience reveals a wide range of behaviors and attitudes when trying to build coalitions for its projects, from persistence and foresight to uncompromising arrogance in the face of widespread opposition.

In 1942, the Port Authority's board of commissioners was so impressed by Austin Tobin's leadership skills that they selected the thirty-nine-year-old to serve as the Authority's executive director.[1] As the Authority's assistant general counsel, Tobin had led a nationwide effort to preserve the tax-exempt status of municipal bonds after President Franklin D. Roosevelt's administration proposed eliminating their exemption. This was a critical issue for the board. When the Authority issued bonds to raise money for its projects, investors were willing to accept lower interest rates because the payments paid by the Port Authority to the bondholders were not subject to income tax. The Port Authority was able to embark on major construction projects that might have been financially disastrous for a private firm because its interest payments were lower.

In Tobin's first twelve months as executive director, he worked with the Authority's chief planning official (Walter Hedden) on a 1943 confidential report about regional problems. Tobin and Hedden identified numerous activities the Port Authority could pursue, once World War II ended, to maintain the region's preeminence as "the gateway for world commerce." These initiatives included building a bus terminal in Manhattan, operating marine terminals, creating truck terminals on both sides of the Hudson River, and taking a leading role in air transportation. Tobin argued that the region's

49

three major airports would "not be adequate" to meet the region's passenger and air cargo demands. At the time, the City of New York owned and operated LaGuardia Field and Idlewild (later renamed John F. Kennedy) Airport while the City of Newark owned and operated Newark Airport in New Jersey. Tobin proposed that the Authority help finance, construct, and operate additional airports.[2]

Tobin epitomized the characteristics of entrepreneurial leadership discussed in the first chapter. He used a wide range of resources in creative manners, taking advantage of his autonomy to initiate new programs and move the organizations in novel ways. He instilled a culture of innovation and encouraged the development of skills and expertise that helped the Authority embark on new initiatives.[3] Over the next thirty years, Tobin masterfully leveraged the Authority's assets to build support for his ambitions.

Tobin sought approval from his board of commissioners in 1943 to fund detailed studies in various transportation fields. Since the Port Authority's board chair was hesitant about taking on costly new initiatives, Tobin went around him by meeting with business leaders, civic groups, and federal officials to discuss postwar needs related to the marine and air industries. The board members subsequently decided to replace their chair with someone more in synch with Tobin's ambitious vision.[4]

As Tobin considered potential areas of investment, his staff assessed consumer demand and market factors. To avoid being perceived as overreaching, he encouraged civic groups and elected officials to seek the Port Authority's assistance. It was a strategy Tobin used effectively before initiating major projects such as taking over the three major airports and building the world's two tallest towers. After receiving requests from outside groups, Tobin liked to put together a panel of experts, have them study a proposal, and then issue a well-informed report. Even if the Authority did not pursue a potential project, a study itself had side benefits—the possibility of building a popular project alleviated political pressure on the Authority to reduce its tolls or spend its surplus funds on unprofitable ventures.[5]

In 1943, Tobin and Hedden started putting together a staff to assess trends in the air transportation industry. They estimated the costs of developing airport facilities and potential revenue sources. Working closely with airport experts in government and civic organizations, the Authority issued a report in 1944 titled "Types of Airports Needed in the New York Area."[6] The Authority's planners determined that the Authority could modernize the region's airports and then generate sufficient revenue from passengers and airlines to properly maintain the airports' facilities. The results of the financial analysis were important because Tobin did not want to undertake any endeavors in which he thought the revenues would not eventually meet ongoing costs. As the Authority's planners considered the region's needs and opportunities relating to air transportation, they created an important asset for the Authority—credibility and leadership in the aviation field.

Port Authority officials recommended improving airports, encouraging more airline services, and providing "for the swift and ready interchange of cargo and passengers between air, rail, ship and motor-truck carriers."[7] The Authority also advocated for the New York region's interests before the federal officials who designated airline routes and regulated municipal airports.[8] Tobin made sure that the Authority's expertise was widely known by hiring a talented and experienced public relations expert (Lee Jaffe) and then paying her well. Jaffe enhanced the Port Authority's reputation by keeping editorial writers and newspaper reporters informed of the Authority's activities, research results, and accomplishments.[9]

Given its extensive knowledge of passenger and freight transportation by road, rail, sea, and air, the Port Authority was in a strong position to help local governments develop and implement economic development plans. Encouraged by Port Authority officials, in December 1945 the City of Newark formally requested that the Port Authority consider expanding and operating Newark's seaport and airport.[10] New York City officials resisted the Port Authority's interest in taking over LaGuardia and Idlewild, even though the city did not have sufficient funds to build modern airport facilities (fig. 3.1). New York City had too many other priorities including building new highways, upgrading school buildings, providing affordable housing, and fixing up its subways. In 1946, the city established its own public authority to operate the airports, under the direction of the famed power broker Robert Moses. However, Tobin convinced airline executives, investment bankers, and other business leaders that the Port Authority was in a better position to upgrade and operate the city's airports because it could issue bonds and then pay them off by tapping into its toll revenues. Here the financial autonomy afforded by its access to toll revenue and bond raising capacity was crucial to solidifying the perception of the Port Authority's superior capability.[11]

In 1946, after the Port Authority completed its study of Newark Airport that had been requested by Newark officials, the Authority offered to take over the airport and triple its capacity. Tobin's maneuvering with the business and financial community to support its acquisition of New York's airports,

Fig. 3.1. LaGuardia Field in 1948.
(Photograph reprinted by permission of Port Authority of New York and New Jersey.)

coupled with the Authority's by then strong reputation for professionalism and excellence in building and managing infrastructure paid off. Prompted by the Port Authority, New York City's newspapers encouraged elected officials to consider a regional approach to developing three major airports. A *New York Times* editorial subsequently concluded, "It is time New York City invited the Port Authority in to do the same thing for its airports that it has done for Newark. As a bi-State authority, taking not only a regional but a world-wide view of the New York region's air future, it could hardly decline to do for Idlewild and LaGuardia Fields what it has agreed to do across the river. It is obvious that we need the Port Authority's help, its wisdom and skill in financing large enterprises."[12]

The next day, New York's mayor, William O'Dwyer, asked the Port Authority to conduct a study of taking over the city's two airports, saying the Authority could "relieve the city of a tremendous burden of future airport financing and at the same time make the terminals available without cost to the city's taxpayers."[13] In April 1947, the Port Authority took over New York City's airports in a fifty-year lease agreement.[14] Six months later, the Port Authority leased both Newark's airport and marine facilities for fifty years. In 1949, the Authority added a small airport in northern New Jersey, Teterboro Airport, to its portfolio.

During his thirty-year tenure as executive director, Tobin transformed the Authority from a bridges and tunnels authority into a powerful regional organization with a leading role in transportation via plane, helicopter, ship, car, truck, train, and bus. Thanks to Tobin, by the end of the 1950s the Port Authority not only had four airports under its control but also a heliport, two truck terminals for consolidating freight, six marine facilities, the Midtown Manhattan bus terminal, and offices to promote trade through the Port of New York in Chicago, Pittsburgh, Cleveland, and Washington, D.C., as well as in Brazil, England, Switzerland, and Puerto Rico.[15]

The three major airports helped the region maintain its global economic preeminence at a time when immigrants were no longer fueling the city's population growth and manufacturing facilities were moving west and south where land and labor costs were lower.[16] In previous generations, New York's unparalleled port and rail facilities had transformed the region into the nation's economic powerhouse. In the 1950s, the airports experienced phenomenal growth as business and leisure travel shifted from trains and ships.[17] Between 1949 and 1959, the number of passengers at the Port Authority's airports increased from 4.1 million to 15.6 million. A similar shift took place for high-value and time-sensitive goods with the volume of air mail and air cargo more than tripling.[18] By the late 1950s, the three airports were accommodating most of the nation's international flights, and remarkably about one-fourth of all U.S. airline passengers.[19]

The availability of rapid, frequent, and reliable air service to all parts of the nation and world helped New York maintain its position as America's financial, commercial, and cultural center. Corporate executives and their sales force flew out to meet customers, and buyers came from around the world to purchase goods as well as accounting, legal, and advertising services. Manufacturing and distribution companies in the metropolitan area were becoming increasingly reliant on airport services to ship out and receive products. Aviation, as Port Authority consultants pointed out, was "increasingly bringing the peoples of the world—as visitors, students, artists, politicians, businessmen—to enjoy and take advantage of the culture and economic resources of the region."[20] They helped the region prosper by spending their money at hotels, restaurants, theaters, schools, shops, and nightclubs.

Great Swamp

Although building new infrastructure often harms neighborhoods and their natural resources, in its earliest endeavors the Port Authority managed to overcome local opposition by building effective regional coalitions. However, during the 1950s and 60s, the Authority's experience trying to build an airport (sometimes referred to as a jetport) in New Jersey's Great Swamp was a comeuppance to the organization's ambitions and exposed the limits of its powers.

The United States entered the jet age in 1958 when Pan American World Airways began the first commercial nonstop flights between New York and Paris. Jet planes could travel faster and farther than propeller-driven aircraft, and since they were more economical to operate, airplane travel became more affordable.[21] Because the three airports did not appear to have sufficient capacity to accommodate the expected growth in air travel, the Port Authority's Aviation Department, under the direction of Tobin, had begun studying potential sites for the region's fourth major airport.[22]

Similar studies were underway in other cities. For example, federal officials were studying potential locations for a new airport in the Washington, D.C., area. President Eisenhower selected a 10,000-acre site, twenty-six miles west of downtown. Dulles Airport, as it would be named, would have four runways and buffer space to protect its neighbors from increasingly noisy aircraft.[23] Port Authority officials also wanted to build a four-runway airport on a 10,000-acre site with a buffer area to protect neighbors.[24] The land would have to be reasonably level and the surrounding area free of mountains, tall buildings, and other obstructions. Ideally, it would be less than forty-five minutes by car from Manhattan, so it was easily accessible to potential passengers. The site, however, could not be too close to Newark or New York City, otherwise it would interfere with existing air traffic corridors. Since two of the region's three major airports were located in New York, and because the planners were expecting population and passenger demand to grow faster west of the Hudson River, the Authority officials preferred locations in New Jersey.[25]

Finding available land to accommodate a new airport was not easy because post-World War II prosperity and new highways were rapidly transforming rural areas into suburban communities. The Port Authority's bridges, tunnels, and bus terminal had contributed to this trend. Building a new airport near New York City was especially challenging because the area was the most densely populated part of the country. While approximately two million people lived in the Washington, D.C., metropolitan area, nearly 12.4 million lived in the New York City and Newark metropolitan areas.[26] Finding suitable locations for relatively undesirable facilities such as power plants, incinerators, and garbage dumps has always been challenging. Tobin's task was considerably more complicated because a modern airport required so much more land. A 10,000-acre site is the equivalent of more than fifteen square miles. By comparison, LaGuardia Airport is 680 acres, and Kennedy Airport is less than 5,000 acres. The Port Authority was seeking a site more than twelve times the size of Hoboken, a New Jersey city with about 50,000 residents at the time.

In 1959, the Port Authority's aviation department completed its analysis of fifteen potential sites. Only one site met its criteria—the Great Swamp area of Morris County in New Jersey,[27] located about twenty-six miles west of Manhattan. The Authority considered this swampland area to be "undeveloped." At the time, few people appreciated or understood the importance of wetlands in reducing flooding, absorbing pollutants, improving water quality, and protecting wildlife. The New York metropolitan area had long filled in wetlands for commercial uses. In fact, landfill had been used along the Flushing Bay, Jamaica Bay, and Newark Bay to build LaGuardia, Kennedy, and Newark airports. In March, behind closed doors, the Authority's board endorsed the proposed airport site and New Jersey' governor, Robert Meyner, offered his tentative approval. The Authority continued studying site conditions and began talking with airlines about the location's benefits.[28]

In November 1959, Edwin Wilson, the Port Authority's director of community relations, drove out to Morris County. He stopped at the local chamber of commerce office and a women's club to learn more about the area and identify the names of influential residents, especially those with ties to financial institutions and corporations. He wanted to reach out to these individuals to help generate support for the new airport. Wilson reported back to Tobin that the area had numerous estates owned by some of the nation's wealthiest families.[29] The communities near the Great Swamp were rapidly changing with a wave of middle- and upper-middle-class families moving to Morris County's new suburban developments. In the previous ten years, the county's population had grown from approximately 164,00 to 261,000.

Most of the new homes near the proposed airport site were priced between $30,000 and $60,000[30] at a time when less affluent New York suburban communities had new two-story colonial homes selling for less than $20,000.[31]

News Leak

Tobin wanted other organizations to highlight the need for the new airport and tout its economic benefits. Local officials and business leaders championing the Great Swamp site could help secure the approvals needed from both state legislatures to proceed with the project. Tobin also needed more time to convince the airlines that the costs to staff and equip a fourth major airport in the region were in their best interests.[32] The airlines' support was critical. While the Port Authority was responsible for the infrastructure (such as runways, utilities, roadways, and parking garages), most buildings at its three major airports (including the terminals) were paid for and built by the airlines.

The Port Authority planned on keeping its proposal for the Great Swamp secret until it had time to generate support from influential business and civic leaders. But on December 3, 1959, front page articles in the *Newark Evening News* broke the news about the Port Authority's plan. The reaction in both the newsroom and the area was one of shock and disbelief. Authority officials moved fast to bolster support for their airport proposal, setting up a briefing for December 14 with state legislators and reporters. At the meeting, Tobin talked about the project's economic benefits, its proximity to New York and Newark, and the extensive precautions the Authority would take to minimize noise to nearby residents.[33] He released a preliminary report that showed the number of airline passengers in the region would increase from fourteen million in 1958 to twenty-five million in 1965, and then forty-five million in 1975. The capacity of the region's existing airports would be reached by 1965 at the latest.[34]

The Port Authority was able to persuade elected officials, business leaders, and reporters that the region needed a fourth major airport. But the Authority's vaunted public relations team was unable to garner much support for the Morris County site. A December 1959 editorial in the *New York Herald Tribune* said the need for the additional airport is indisputable, and so were the economic benefits that would come. However, the editors noted—more than a decade before the acronym NIMBY (Not in My Back Yard) was coined—"People are generally all for progress, but they want the improvement in someone else's backyard."[35] Likewise, a *New York Times* editorial argued, "An airport in the jet age, especially, is a blessing and a bane. Everybody wants it and nobody wants it."[36]

Within days of the December 3 news story, Governor Meyner received 951 letters about the proposed airport with only five supporting it.[37] He would not undermine the Authority, though. The Democratic governor appreciated how a new airport would create tens of thousands of jobs. Moreover, he had close friends on the Authority's board and the Port Authority had paid for some of his overseas business trips including a ten-day trip with his wife to Europe and trips to Brazil and Venezuela. In December 1959, the governor said about the Great Swamp proposal, "It's the kind of thing everyone should study" and "it is much too early for people to make snap judgments about this."[38]

Although local residents were enraged that the Authority would have to knock down about 700 homes and several churches to build the airport, this was not a shocking number for the Port Authority.[39] In 1959, the Authority was completing construction of the George Washington Bridge's lower level, a project that required relocating 1,824 families and 109 businesses.[40] To build the third tube of the Lincoln Tunnel two years earlier, the Authority had relocated 817 families.[41]

The Authority would soon learn that taking apartments from working-class residents was easier than clearing land for an airport near prized country estates and upper-middle-class homeowners who were concerned about threats to their property values and way of life.[42] One corporate executive living near the proposed airport site said, "If the Port Authority could have picked an area with more large, expensive estates, I don't know where."[43] The *Newark Sunday News* calculated that within a mile of the site sat thirty-five estates owned by well-known residents, including a 480-acre farm owned by John Jacob Astor III and estates owned by Donald C. McGraw, Jr. (the book publisher) and William H. Moore II (the chair of Bankers Trust Company.)[44]

The opponents of the airport had a formidable task because they were trying to stop a project before numerous laws and regulations had been enacted to protect the environment and ensure public participation in a government agency's decision-making process. In the 1960s, the Port Authority was not required to hold public hearings or identify the environmental impacts of its projects. Likewise, it did not need to worry about extensive federal regulations relating to endangered species, biodiversity, historic preservation, or water quality. The Morris County residents had to sway public opinion and ensure that the state legislature and the governor were on their side. While Tobin was trying to enhance the mobility of the metropolis, community leaders living near the Great Swamp were mobilizing the masses.

Opposition at the Swamp

Local elected officials organized a public meeting at a Morris County high school on December 18 to discuss the Port Authority's plans for a jetport.[45] Advertisements for the event asked, "Do We Want a Jetport (Twice the Size of Idlewild) in Our Backyard?" More than one thousand people showed up to answer with a resounding "No." State legislators promised their constituents that they would fight the Port Authority's proposal in Trenton, but they did not minimize the challenge. A state senator declared, "We are going to put all our Christmas energies behind the fight," and a state assemblyman told the crowd that a plan of opposition required time, talent, effort, money, and organization.[46]

Peter Frelinghuysen, Jr., a Republican congressman, promised to take the fight to Washington, D.C. The congressman owned 312 acres of land[47] near the Great Swamp and he was a member of one America's most fabled political dynasties. His family had settled in the area in 1720 and four different Frelinghuysens had served as U.S. senators. Frelinghuysen was accustomed to working with legislators on both sides of the aisle, and it did not take him more than a few weeks to get the entire New Jersey congressional delegation to announce its opposition to the new airport.[48] Frelinghuysen helped establish a new nonprofit organization, the Jersey Jetport Site Association (JJSA), to oppose the Port Authority's proposal.[49] JJSA's leadership included the influential people that the Port Authority's director of community relations had been seeking out for support just a month earlier, such as the president of Bell Labs, a retired state Supreme Court justice, the former New Jersey Chamber of Commerce president, and the heads of local financial institutions.[50]

The Port Authority had a highly paid and talented staff with a wide range of expertise. Remarkably, they faced volunteers who could counteract them on every front. By the end of December, JJSA had already set up eight committees including those focused on finance, public relations, and institutional, technical, and conservation issues. The organization quickly raised enough funds to hire an energetic full-time paid director, a realtor whose business dried up after news of the airport had first leaked.[51]

JJSA retained a public relations firm led by two men with extensive media and political experience in New Jersey. They told JJSA's leaders, "The Port Authority maintains perhaps the greatest public relations and propaganda machine in the nation per capita." To counteract the Authority, the firm prepared a plan with a three-pronged approach: secure statewide public approval, obtain legislative support, and attack the Port Authority on every vulnerable point. Among other ideas, they recommended putting the Authority on the defensive by demanding a legislative investigation and full access to the Authority's records, establishing liaisons with groups who wanted an airport in south Jersey, and setting up a speakers' bureau. The firm went on to prepare news releases, arrange press coverage, and collaborate with the volunteers on their newsletters, brochures, bumper stickers, and lapel buttons.[52]

Both the Port Authority and JJSA sent out representatives to speak with community organizations, clubs, elected officials, political party leaders, and service groups. Between the middle of December 1959 and the end of January 1960, Port Authority officials made approximately two dozen presentations in northern New Jersey, touting the economic benefits of an airport to the region and to the local economy.[53] The Authority claimed that a major airport not only created jobs for 80,000 people but would also support 680 restaurants, 90 drug stores, 110 automobile dealers, 440 clothing stores, and 350 doctors.[54] Meanwhile, between December and the end of February, a JJSA speakers' bureau signed up 106 volunteers to refute the Port Authority's arguments and make forty presentations.[55] Volunteers circulated petitions, mailed out newsletters, reached out to local organizations, passed out leaflets, and created fact books comparing the Port Authority's statements with JJSA's analysis, legal opinions, and technical information.[56]

JJSA, working with the local municipalities, hired consultants to study the Great Swamp's physical characteristics, determine whether another major airport was really needed, and assess the airport's social and economic impacts.[57] To pay its expenses, JJSA raised money in a highly organized fashion—soliciting funds by mailing letters to thousands of homes, placing posters in stores, distributing leaflets to commuters, and placing articles in the local newspapers.[58] Committees were set up in all the communities near the Great Swamp, and they were each assigned fundraising targets.[59] Volunteers were given materials and scripts they could use to explain JJSSA's efforts and encourage donations. Within a year, JJSA raised more than $111,000,[60] a substantial sum considering that a postage stamp cost only four cents.

The New Jersey state legislators from the Morris County area (who were mostly Republican) put together an effective coalition with Democrats who supported building a new airport in the southern part of the state.[61] Airport opponents also tapped into a resentment among many New Jersey legislators that the Port Authority was not using its surplus revenues to help the financially ailing private railroads provide essential train services. In January 1960, the New Jersey state Senate voted twenty to one on a resolution opposing a new major airport in Morris County area, calling it "a nuisance and a public health hazard that would decrease residential property values."[62] The vote in the state General Assembly on a similar resolution was unanimous.[63] Even after the votes, the governor was still hesitant to criticize the Port Authority's proposal, though, stating he could not "make a reasoned decision" and "any announcement of my feeling at this time would be premature" because the Port Authority was still analyzing the Morris County location and the feasibility of other sites.[64]

According to a Port Authority commissioner, the board expected that the "emotional outburst" would subside over time. He said the Authority hoped that a new legislature "may take a different point of view."[65] But the Port Authority found itself in the unenviable position that few government agencies ever encounter—a simultaneous attack by local, state, and federal legislatures.

Brooklyn congressman Emanuel Celler, the chair of the U.S. House Judiciary Committee, had long been concerned that federal and local officials did not have sufficient oversight over the Port Authority. With the encouragement of Frelinghuysen and then the rest of New Jersey's congressional delegation, Celler initiated a federal inquiry into the Port Authority's operations.[66] Even though the Judiciary Committee issued subpoenas to Tobin, he refused to hand over any materials except for published reports and other documents that were typically made available to the public.[67] At the time, transparency was a foreign concept to Port Authority officials. The board met behind closed doors and the states had yet to pass laws that would subject the Authority to freedom of information laws. In August 1960, the full U.S. House of Representatives passed a resolution citing Tobin for contempt of Congress (for his "contumacious conduct"), which carried a sentence of up to one year in prison.[68] Although the U.S. Court of Appeals later reversed the contempt citation, Celler's hearings proved embarrassing by exposing costly entertainment expenses and favoritism when selecting financial institutions and insurance firms.[69]

In September 1960, the New Jersey state Senate unanimously voted to pry information from the secretive Authority by conducting its own investigation.[70] Tobin was much more conciliatory with state senators, though, whose support he needed to move forward with major projects. He arranged facility tours and provided them with internal records.[71] After years of pressure from the legislators to provide funding for commuter railroads, he also offered to take over the bankrupt Hudson & Manhattan Railroad as part of the World Trade Center project.[72]

Port Authority officials had not been prepared to take on Congressman Frelinghuysen; nor did they anticipate having to face the opposition of one of the nation's wealthiest men. In the first months of 1960, unbeknownst to the Port Authority and JJSA, Marcellus Hartley Dodge led his own efforts to protect the Great Swamp. Dodge and his wife (Geraldine Rockefeller Dodge) owned not one but two sprawling estates in the area. He was an ardent conservationist who had been a trustee of the North American Wildlife Foundation, a nonprofit conservation organization.[73] Dodge had powerful friends in Washington, D.C., including U.S. president Dwight Eisenhower, who had been a frequent overnight guest at Dodge's home.[74]

To prevent the Port Authority from building its airport, Dodge and likeminded conservationists discussed ways to turn the Great Swamp into federally protected land. They settled on a plan to purchase land and donate it to the North American Wildlife Foundation. The nonprofit organization would then transfer it to the federal government to ensure that it was protected from development. Contributions to the foundation would not only protect the land but they were also tax deductible, an appealing feature at a time when the top income tax rate in the United States was 91 percent.

Dodge pursued his plan quietly for two reasons. First, if word got out, land costs might skyrocket. Second, some airport opponents wanted the Great Swamp to remain in private hands so that the town could continue collecting real estate taxes on the property.[75] Thanks to Dodge's financial contributions and his phone calls to fellow landowners, in September 1960 the Wildlife Foundation signed papers that would turn over nearly 1,000 acres of land to the U.S. Department of the Interior for use as a wildlife sanctuary.[76] The Port Authority was undeterred, though. After all, both Kennedy Airport and Washington's National Airport were located near lands protected for wildlife.[77]

In the spring of 1961, dueling reports were released. JJSA's consultants concluded that an airport would not be needed for another quarter-century, and they identified numerous negative impacts associated with the Great Swamp location such as traffic jams, flooding, threats to water supplies, air pollution, and noise.[78] Meanwhile, after evaluating seventeen potential sites, the Port Authority reported that the only one close enough to population centers with sufficient physically suitable land was the Great Swamp area.[79] When Tobin had first proposed the Great Swamp in 1959, he was working

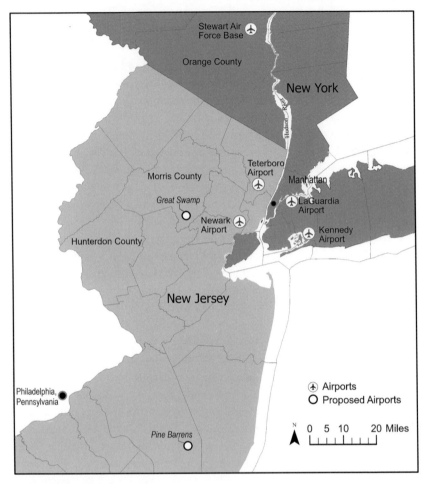

Map 3.1. Map showing the three major airports along with Stewart Airport, Great Swamp, and the Pine Barrens.
(Map by Md. Shahinoor Rahman.)

toward a "definitive recommendation" that would be submitted to the governors and legislatures.[80] But his 1961 report treaded more carefully, pointing out, "Of course, the Port Authority has no power whatsoever, and therefore can have no plans whatsoever, to construct another major airport."[81]

In June 1961, the state legislature overwhelmingly passed a bill prohibiting an airport in the Morris County area, but Governor Meyner vetoed it, arguing that the Great Swamp was the most logical site for a new airport.[82] He said, "We shall have to deal with the jet age in more realistic terms. We cannot legislate it out of existence."[83] Meyner was the last supporter of a Great Swamp airport to live in the governor's mansion. At the end of 1961, JJSA began winding down its work[84] because the governor-elect, Richard Hughes, opposed the airport.[85]

Further Evaluation and Additional Sites

Throughout the 1960s, the Port Authority continued evaluating alternatives to the Great Swamp site including new locations recommended by the two governors. But the Authority concluded, again and again, that none of them were feasible. Governor Hughes continued to oppose sites "where the community would be disrupted by such a development," and the Port Authority continued to insist that the airport be close enough to Manhattan to attract enough passengers.[86]

As soon as JJSA was established in December 1959, Congressman Frelinghuysen began promoting an airport site in southern New Jersey's Pine Barrens region. "The best defense is a good offense," he said.[87] South Jersey's elected officials strongly supported the airport because it would spur dramatic increases in economic activity, property values, and population.[88] Since the Pine Barrens were sparsely populated, a 20,000-acre airport could be built that would be surrounded by 75,000 acres of rural land acting as a noise buffer.[89] The problem was that the Pine Barrens were located too far from New York City. In fact, the airport would have been closer to Philadelphia's Liberty Bell than to New York's Empire State Building.

The conservationists with the new governor's support continued their efforts to protect the Great Swamp from development. In May 1966, the Great Swamp was named a national natural landmark, an important designation but not one that would prevent the Port Authority from building an airport.

Tobin was not accustomed to losing battles. He had withstood challenges from Congress on the Port Authority's autonomy. He had wrestled control of the airports from Robert Moses, New York's ultimate power broker. In 1966, he had overcome opposition from New York City's mayor to begin constructing the world's two tallest towers at the World Trade Center. From Tobin's perspective, no amount of wishful thinking could make an unsuitable site workable. Building an airport in the Pine Barrens would not serve the people and businesses of New York and northern New Jersey; instead, he argued, it would be a waste of public funds.[90]

The Authority issued yet another report in December 1966. This time, the Authority's planners looked at twenty-three sites. The Authority said that twenty-two of the sites did not meet the criteria for providing "adequate, dependable, and essential air service" for northern New Jersey and New York. The Authority still deemed the Great Swamp as the best choice, despite the fact that the New Jersey governor opposed it and the U.S. Secretary of the Interior said he would fight it.[91] After confirming all its previous conclusions about the suitability of the Great Swamp and the flaws with all of the alternatives, the Port Authority warned that the consequences of the region's "continued inability to provide for its future air transport needs would be an economic catastrophe for its people and commerce."[92]

In 1968, President Lyndon Johnson ended all the Port Authority's hopes for the Great Swamp when he signed the Great Swamp Wilderness Act. The president said, "by establishing a wilderness close to millions of people, a departure from the usual concept of wilderness, Congress has seized a rare opportunity to provide an island of solitude for those who truly need it."[93] The Great Swamp National Wildlife Refuge would eventually protect nearly twelve square miles (7,768 acres) of wetlands, streams, and forests (fig. 3.2).[94]

A few weeks before President Johnson signed the 1968 legislation, the Port Authority's aviation director, John Wiley, told a congressional panel that the Great Swamp was the best site to serve the region, but if it was unavailable then the Port Authority could purchase and expand the small family-owned Solberg Airport in New Jersey's Hunterdon County.[95] It was now, according to the Port Authority the "only remaining practicable site for construction of the urgently needed new facility."[96] The Federal Aviation Administration and the airline industry both supported the Port Authority's efforts to build a new major airport in Hunterdon County.[97]

The Great Swamp would have been forty-four minutes[98] from the Lincoln Tunnel while the Hunterdon County site would have been an hour and six minutes away.[99] Because of those additional twenty-two minutes, the Port Authority had previously ruled it out, concluding that it was too far from the "region's traffic generating center and would not attract enough air passengers."[100] If Tobin had not so stubbornly insisted on the Great Swamp site and pivoted to Hunterdon County earlier, he would have faced less resistance and might have succeeded in building the region's fourth major airport. Instead, the events of 1961 repeated themselves in 1969.

During the 1961 gubernatorial campaign, Richard Hughes had promised to oppose the Great Swamp Airport and he kept his word after he was elected. In 1969, a new airport was still a prominent campaign issue and the Republican candidate, William Cahill, made his position clear: "New Jersey

Fig. 3.2. The Great Swamp National Wildlife Refuge
(Photograph by Jesper Rautell Balle, March 2008. Courtesy Wikimedia Commons, CC BY 3.0.)

doesn't need another jetport. New Jersey doesn't want another jetport."[101] A week after Cahill was elected, Tobin announced that the Port Authority was abandoning its hopes of building a new airport in Hunterdon County.[102]

In a 1969 speech to the New York Chamber of Commerce, Tobin lamented the region's inability to build another airport. He said, "The concern which people have about putting an airport in their community is understandable." He continued to argue that noise impacts would be minimal, and that air and water pollution would not be a problem at a properly located airport. Tobin warned, "In a region such as ours, nothing gets built without putting it some place where some people don't want it. But millions of our people need that airport and the jobs and the business that it will support. So far, the problem of locating a fourth airport has been answered by not putting it anywhere. Such a course—such a default—must inevitably lead to an economic catastrophe for all of the people of Northern New Jersey and New York."[103] Tobin had thrown in the towel and the Authority would not seriously consider creating a fourth major airport for the next three decades.[104]

Catastrophe Averted

When the Port Authority recommended building an airport in the Great Swamp, Authority officials claimed, "It will be utterly impossible for the existing major airports to handle the air traffic of 1975, even if technological improvements should result in some increase in capacity."[105] Despite the Port Authority's repeated warnings in the 1960s, the region's failure to build a fourth major airport did not lead to an economic catastrophe. Instead the aviation industry adopted new technologies and the Port Authority reluctantly agreed to use its airports more efficiently.

In the 1950s and 1960s, aviation officials estimated future airport capacity by calculating the number of planes that could take off and land during an airport's peak hour under inclement weather conditions. Claims about future capacity were predicated on numerous assumptions about how many planes would use the airports, the number of passengers in each plane, and future technologies.

The most basic assumption was the number of passengers taking off and landing. In 1959, the Port Authority estimated the number of passengers would more than triple from less than fourteen million in 1958 to more than forty-five million in 1975.[106] Considering the difficulty of their task, the estimates prepared by the aviation officials were fairly close—the number of passengers at its three airports increased to thirty-nine million in 1975. The airports could accommodate many more passengers than expected, though, because newer airplanes carried more passengers than older ones. In the 1950s, the widely used Douglas DC-6 carried up to 89 passengers. In the early 1960s, the first jets flying from New York could carry up to 179 passengers. In 1968, Boeing introduced its 747 airplane, the world's first jumbo jet, which could accommodate 374 passengers.

Since only one plane can be on a runway at any one time to avoid collisions, the Port Authority desperately wanted to add more runways to accommodate more planes. In 1959, the three major airports had a total of eight runways. By 1975, the airports had only added one more (at Newark Airport in 1970). Nevertheless, the airports were able to increase capacity by upgrading their existing runways. They also added and upgraded taxiways that helped clear the runways faster, allowing more planes to land during peak periods. Moreover, new air traffic control systems at the airports and navigational systems on airplanes increased the number of planes that could operate safely during inclement weather conditions.

Although the Great Swamp set off intense opposition, few people in the region questioned the need for another major airport. The general public, the media, and business leaders all expected airplane travel to continue growing. They did not realize, however, that the Port Authority could easily improve the efficiency of its airports to accommodate more passengers. In the late 1950s and early 1960s, when Authority officials publicly discussed the future number of takeoffs and landings, they rarely mentioned how most of the growth was associated with "general aviation" rather than scheduled commercial flights. General aviation refers to corporate planes, charter flights, and air taxis that accommodate mostly business and wealthier fliers. For example, a Madison Avenue advertising executive could fly on a chartered plane from LaGuardia Airport to Procter and Gamble's headquarters in Cincinnati. Likewise, a vacationing couple could take an air taxi from a local airport near their Connecticut home to Kennedy Airport and then board a commercial flight to Paris.[107]

From Tobin's perspective, the region's economy relied upon accommodating small planes even during the most congested times of the day. A survey in August 1966 found that these general aviation planes constituted more than half of the planes using LaGuardia Airport between 5:00 pm and 8:00 p.m., even though they only carried about 5 percent of the passengers.[108] The Port Authority's position was the equivalent of claiming that the bus terminal was at capacity because limousines were parking at half the bus gates.

The gross inefficiency of the airports was not only the Port Authority's fault. Until the late 1970s, the federal government set all routes and fares. Airlines could schedule their flights for any time of the day, once their routes were approved. Since every airline charged the same fares, one of the ways they differentiated themselves was by offering more flights during peak periods. That might have been good for an individual airline, but it exacerbated delays at the Authority's airports during peak periods. Since fares were the same no matter the time of day, passengers had little incentive to fly at off-peak times.[109]

The airlines had a vested interest in reducing the number of small planes because their commercial jets would then be subject to fewer delays, and they could avoid building expensive new facilities at a fourth airport. In 1965, a coalition of ten major airlines prepared a report indicating a new airport would not be needed until 1980 at the earliest, if half of the small business and private planes were diverted to other airports including the Port Authority's Teterboro Airport in New Jersey.[110] The Authority challenged the airlines' analysis, though, claiming that only 15 percent of the private planes flying at the three airports were "relocatable" and referred to the coalition's technical study as "specious, unrealistic and unworkable."[111]

According to federal regulations, the Authority was not supposed to give large planes carrying hundreds of people higher priority than an air taxi with two passengers.[112] The Port Authority did have an important tool to shift general aviation to other airports, but it chose not to use it until 1968. That summer, with flight delays causing a public uproar, the Port Authority raised the minimum landing and takeoff fees it charged airlines from $5 to $25. As a result, general aviation usage declined by approximately 40 percent and half as many planes were subject to lengthy delays.[113] The Port Authority also began upgrading its general aviation facilities at Teterboro Airport and precluded the airport's use for any scheduled commercial airline flights.[114]

The Port Authority issued reports about a fourth major airport in 1959, 1961, 1963, 1964, 1965, 1966, 1967, 1968, and 1969. Every one of the reports had the same flaw—claiming that a new airport was needed without providing the public and elected officials with any understanding of the fundamental problems with the existing aviation system and how it could be made more efficient. In the 1960s, Tobin repeatedly tried to use media stories about airport delays to press his case for a fourth airport, rather than advocate for reforming the aviation system.[115] He certainly knew how to lobby for systemic changes. Tobin had been promoted to executive director because he had successfully created a national coalition in the 1930s to preserve the tax-exempt status of governmental bonds. In the 1940s, he created a national alliance of airports to share information and break the monopoly power of the airlines.[116] Thanks to Tobin's relentless pressure in the 1950s, aircraft manufacturers redesigned their jets to minimize noise impacts.[117]

In 1959, the Port Authority thought it could continue expanding its facilities to accommodate everyone who wanted to fly during peak periods. But New York could never build enough airports to accommodate every corporate executive. Tobin's vision for airports in the 1960s was similar to his plans relating to ground transportation. Under his leadership, the Port Authority encouraged the construction of new highways to accommodate as many cars as possible, despite the environmental and social costs of knocking down homes, plowing through neighborhoods, and exacerbating suburban sprawl. The Authority resisted efforts to develop an integrated regional transportation policy, one that considered how to use its resources in a manner that would more efficiently move people and goods via roads, rails, and air.

Tobin's successors at the Port Authority understood that it was impossible to accommodate every airline passenger who wanted to land at Kennedy at 6:00 PM just as it could not build enough crossings for every car owner who wanted to drive into Manhattan at 9:00 AM. Port Authority's subsequent leaders have also not been as independent, ambitious, and stubborn as Tobin, who served as executive director from 1942 to 1972.

An Opportunity in Orange County

In the 1960s, with New Jersey balking at the Great Swamp Plan, New York governor Nelson Rockefeller pressured the Port Authority to build a fourth airport on onion farms in Orange County. Tobin repeatedly rebuffed the governor, however, because he considered a site eighty-seven minutes from the Lincoln Tunnel too remote.[118] Rockefeller decided that the state would proceed without the Port Authority though when U.S. defense department officials determined in 1969 that they no longer needed Stewart Air Force Base in Orange County. The governor had ambitious plans to turn the airport into the region's fourth major airport along with a high-speed line connecting the airport with midtown Manhattan.[119] In 1971, the 2,500-acre airport was turned over to New York's Metropolitan Transportation Authority (MTA) and Rockefeller obtained legislative support to purchase an additional 8,000 acres to accommodate new facilities and serve as a buffer to minimize noise for the airport's neighbors.[120]

Unlike the reaction the Authority faced in northern New Jersey, most of the residents living near Stewart Airport supported its expansion.[121] Orange County was located well beyond New York City's suburban communities, and it was not dotted with the country estates of millionaires. The county's population density was only 273 persons per square mile, compared to more than 18,000 in Queens County (where LaGuardia and Kennedy were located) and more than 7,000 in Essex County (home to Newark Airport).

Port Authority officials had been wrong in the early 1960s when they said the metropolitan area needed a new airport by 1975. However, they were correct about Orange County's suitability for a major airport. The MTA consistently lost money on Stewart Airport, and it was unable to attract regular passenger service or afford the planned train connection.[122] In 1982, Governor Hugh Carey transferred control of the airport to New York State's Department of Transportation. Although he hoped that his transportation department leaders could do a better job attracting more airline service, that did not prove to be the case.[123]

After George Pataki was sworn in as New York's governor in 1995, the Republican governor set up a commission to study the privatization of state facilities.[124] Pataki was convinced that private firms could operate services more efficiently than the public sector.[125] In 2000, New York became the first state to privatize a publicly owned commercial airport when it leased Stewart Airport to the National Express Group for ninety-nine years. State and local officials expected the transportation firm to improve air travel services, attract new businesses, and increase the local tax base.[126] National Express was optimistic that it could attract more passengers to Stewart Airport because its nearby highways were rarely congested, and airport parking was inexpensive and a short walk to the terminal.

After National Express took over Stewart Airport, Bill DeCota, the Port Authority's aviation director, referred to the airport's challenge as a chicken and egg dilemma.[127] Passengers were not using Stewart Airport because it had minimal airline service, while the airlines were not providing much service because the airport did not attract enough passengers. Airline customers preferred airports with frequent flights to the same destination in case their flight was canceled or delayed. Since Stewart Airport had few passengers, airlines were hesitant to schedule numerous flights because that would require them to lease more planes, build larger facilities, and hire additional staff. Likewise, attracting air cargo service to Stewart was problematic because most shippers wanted to be located near the three major airports where they could ship goods in the bellies of commercial aircraft.[128]

Stewart Airport failed to grow despite the capacity constraints at the Port Authority's airports. In 2005, nearly one hundred million[129] passengers used the Port Authority's three major airports, a remarkable number considering they accommodated fewer than fourteen million in 1958. However, the three airports had trouble accommodating all these passengers, which is why they consistently held the dubious distinction of having among the nation's worst on-time performance (fig. 3.3). The number of reported flight delays did not reveal the full extent of the congestion-related problem. Longer flights times and more expensive fares placed the New York metropolitan area at a disadvantage with its competitors. Airlines were increasing the time of scheduled flights to improve their on-time-performance results, a measurement that was widely reported. They were also increasing the scheduled time between flights that added to their costs and ultimately to passengers' costs. The major

Grappling with Capacity Problems at the Airports

Fig. 3.3. Planes queued up at Kennedy Airport in 2007.
(Photograph by Giorgio Montersino, July 2, 2007. Courtesy Wikimedia Commons, CC BY-SA 2.0.)

cause of delays at the region's airports was not enough capacity on the runways and in the region's airspace, two problems that were exacerbated by the region's frequent inclement weather conditions.[130]

Looking for a Fourth Airport, Again

In 2005, DeCota and other senior Port Authority officials began seriously considering creating a fourth regional airport. The *New York Times* wrote that it was not an original idea, "just one that few public officials have dared broach for about 30 years."[131] The airports were approaching what DeCota expected to be their maximum capacity of 130 million annual passengers.[132] The Port Authority's chair, Tony Coscia, said "you don't need to be a genius to realize that air travel is growing at a very fast pace."[133]

The Authority's aviation department dreamed of building an airport like the one twenty-five miles from downtown Denver that had opened ten year earlier. Denver International Airport covered about 34,000 acres (fifty-four square miles), more than three times the size of the coveted Great Swamp site. It was larger than the island of Manhattan and the City of Newark combined.

Building a brand-new airport near New York City had become virtually impossible, though. An aviation consultant said in 2005, "You can't build a 'green-field airport' because there is no green field. There is no place within 100 miles of New York City where you can buy land for less than a bazillion dollars."[134]

That is why the aviation department looked at the possibility of diverting future growth to an existing airport in New York, New Jersey, and even eastern Pennsylvania.[135] One of those potential airports was Stewart Airport in Orange County. In 2005, the airport served fewer than 400,000 passengers, which was less than the airport had ten years earlier under state control. Even though National Express received federal and local funds for marketing efforts and financial incentives, the airport was having limited success attracting new air services.[136]

In 2006, George Pataki's term as governor was ending and the state attorney general, Eliot Spitzer, was the frontrunner to succeed him. Spitzer's transportation advisor, Lee Sander, heard that National Express Group wanted to give up its ninety-nine-year lease on Stewart Airport. Deciding to make a match, Sander called up the Port Authority's aviation director (DeCota) and then the board chair (Coscia) and told them about National Express's plans. All three of them were excited about the once-in-a-generation opportunity to obtain an airport at a bargain price. Stewart Airport had two runways, and its aircraft did not fly close to the planes departing and landing at the Port Authority's airports. DeCota was hopeful that the Port Authority could use its resources and know-how to solve the airport's chicken and egg dilemma.[137]

Sander next reached out to Tim Gilchrist, a New York senior transportation official, to gauge the state's interest in having the Port Authority take over Stewart Airport. Gilchrist reported back that Governor Pataki would not support it. The privatization of Stewart Airport had been one of the governor's significant achievements and he would not want to admit that it had been a failure.[138] Coscia talked to a National Express executive and urged him to hold off on selling the airport's lease to another private company. The executive told the Port Authority chair, "you'll never get the governor to agree." Knowing that he had Spitzer's support, Coscia responded, "that's my problem not yours."[139]

In recent years, as described in chapters 7 and 8, the Port Authority has been woefully slow in its ability to secure approvals for some of its projects such as replacing the Goethals Bridge and rebuilding the World Trade Center. But in a matter of weeks after Spitzer was elected governor on November 7, Coscia obtained the support he needed to lease Stewart Airport.

On November 16, the Port Authority board authorized a review of the legal and financial issues associated with taking over the Stewart Airport lease. Tony Shorris, Spitzer's choice for the Port Authority's executive director position, was excited about the takeover because Stewart was located in one of the fastest-growing parts of the region and had great long-term potential. Compared to the other major projects on the Authority's plate, it would not be very expensive. Moreover, Shorris thought that adding the Authority's first major new facility in more than a quarter century would boost employee morale[140] and revitalize an agency that had been, in his words, "socked in the stomach, politically and emotionally" when terrorists destroyed the Port Authority's headquarters along with the entire World Trade Center complex five years earlier.[141]

At Governor Spitzer's request, Shorris made numerous trips to Orange County to alleviate any anxieties local officials might have about the Port Authority takeover. Spitzer told Shorris, "I don't want a lot of trouble." Shorris found that the business community was equally excited about the Port Authority's plans to improve the airport's facilities and services.[142] The area around Stewart Airport was economically distressed, or in Coscia's words, "sucking wind."[143] Port Authority staff worked closely with government officials in Orange County, reviewed legal issues, and prepared a plan to upgrade the airport's facilities and attract new airlines.[144] The aviation department found dealing with local officials a refreshing change. They were not accustomed to residents, business leaders, and elected officials clamoring for more flights at one of its airports.

Two days after his inauguration, on January 3, Governor Spitzer proclaimed, "we must have the vision to expand Stewart Airport to become the fourth major airport in the downstate region and to serve as an economic engine for the Hudson Valley."[145] On January 25, the board voted to acquire the lease for the operation of Stewart Airport at a cost of $78.5 million,[146] which was less than the amount it had authorized to build a 1,500-car parking garage at Kennedy Airport.[147] The Port Authority commissioners understood the capacity constraints at its airports. A year earlier, they had authorized DeCota's study of regional aviation capacity and Stewart Airport appeared to have the potential to accommodate the most passengers.[148] DeCota was enthusiastic about taking over the lease and the commissioners trusted his industry acumen.

Since Stewart Airport was located outside the Port Authority's jurisdiction that was defined in its original compact, both state legislatures needed to sign off on the Authority's lease. Coscia did not have to worry about getting approval from the New York State legislature because the state had already adopted a law—forty years earlier—allowing the governor to designate an additional airport the Authority could operate. Now Coscia needed the same exact legislation to pass in Trenton. He recruited Congressman Steve Rothman to help him gain support from key New Jersey legislators. Rothman represented the residents who lived near Teterboro Airport, and for the past five years he had been advocating for greater use of Stewart Airport because it could help reduce noise levels near his constituents' homes. As a member of the House appropriations committee, Rothman had even put a provision in the federal budget that prevented federal aviation officials from lifting the Port Authority's restrictions on aircraft weight and scheduled passenger service at Teterboro.

Coscia and Congressman Rothman worked the phones to promote the legislation. Convincing New Jersey's governor and legislators that the region needed another airport was relatively easy because virtually every single person in the New York metropolitan area understood that the airports were getting more crowded. Airplane trips had once been associated with glamour and excitement, now they conjured up visions of traffic jams, expensive parking lots, long security lines, and delayed flights. Many New Jersey officials, however, were initially skeptical about the Port Authority's proposal, because New York seemed to be getting all the economic benefits of a fourth airport. "What's in it for New Jersey," they wanted to know. Not many elected officials knew about the Great Swamp episode, so Coscia and Rothman had to explain that New Jersey residents did not want a large noisy airport near their homes. They told the legislators, "We found a place that does." Rothman remembers, "It was a political no-brainer. The legislators could do the right thing and be heroes. There was no political price to pay for supporting this. We were handing them the baton one foot from the finish line. They could do press conferences and talk about how they were supporting local communities [by reducing noise near Teterboro and Newark] and expanding air travel."[149] In early 2007, legislation sailed through New Jersey's Assembly and Senate that matched New York's 1967 New York law.[150]

Gilchrist (New York's transportation official) briefed Governor Spitzer right before the ceremony commemorating the Port Authority's takeover of Stewart Airport. Gilchrist told the governor, "When I was a young analyst, I worked on transferring the airport from the MTA to the DOT [Department of Transportation], then I worked on transferring it from the DOT to

National Express, now we are transferring it to the Port Authority. And, I promise you that I'll keep on working on it until I get it right."[151]

Operating Stewart Airport

In 2007, Coscia claimed the Authority could do a better job managing Stewart Airport than National Express because "We had the money to invest. We had the relationships with the airlines. We could be in it for the long haul. We could wait for a return. We could be the patient investor."[152] Patty Clark, the Port Authority's former chief aviation strategy officer, said, "recruiting airlines takes years of courting and building relationships. We mentioned Stewart Airport at meetings with nearly all the airlines we met with." Staff at numerous levels (including the executive director and aviation director) promoted Stewart with their airline counterparts whenever they had discussions about upgrading terminals, providing more parking spaces for airplanes, and adding gates at Kennedy, LaGuardia, and Newark.[153]

In the first year the Port Authority took over Stewart Airport, it invested about $25 million, which was more than National Express's total investment over the seven years it operated the airport. Security was enhanced, four hundred parking spots added, roadway access improved, seating areas renovated, and runways modernized. The Authority also set up an incentive program that waived landing fees, security charges, and terminal fees.[154] As the Port Authority's aviation director, DeCota had an air service development team who studied economic and demographic changes, airline industry trends, and airport catchment areas. The team analyzed airline pricing, routing, service frequency, passenger loads, and capacities. They understood the airlines' businesses and opportunities. They knew how to develop financial incentives and marketing strategies to retain and attract airline services.

All that expertise and experience did not help attract much new service, though. In 2008, DeCota told the Port Authority commissioners that he hoped to attract a low-cost carrier to Stewart. These airlines were price sensitive and typically served remote airports that charged low fees. Stewart Airport, a no-frills facility where the only dining options were a sandwich shop and a café, was a perfect fit for a no-frills airline. DeCota thought Stewart could entice more passengers from communities north of New York City as well as from Connecticut and northern New Jersey. Residents of these areas had taken eleven million flights at the Port Authority's three major airports in the previous year.[155] Although Orange County was semirural, the airport was located within an hour's drive of two million people.[156] To reach these potential customers, the Authority promoted Stewart Airport on nearby billboards and local cable TV stations.[157]

Referring to Stewart Airport's potential, DeCota told the commissioners, "It takes the little spark that lights the kindling that then sets the fire."[158] His goal, he said, was to have three million annual passengers by 2015.[159] DeCota was overly optimistic. A year earlier, the Port Authority had collaborated with federal and New York State transportation officials to forecast future demand at Stewart. They had estimated the airport would serve fewer than 800,000 passengers in 2015.[160] In fact, the actual number of passengers using the airport in 2015 was 282,000, less than 10 percent of DeCota's goal.[161] Eight years after the Port Authority took over Stewart Airport, it handled fewer passengers than when the state of New York and National Express operated it. Despite the Port Authority's financial resources and aviation expertise, the airport could not catch its spark.

In 2015, the Port Authority hoped that Edmond Harrison, an entrepreneurial leader, could turn things around. Harrison had helped the Authority bring retail stores back to the airports after the September 11 terrorist attacks. He had also worked in the Port Authority's port commerce department and was inspired by the way that his boss, Lillian Borrone, enhanced the port's business by collaborating with shipping companies, terminal operators, unions, and many other groups that relied upon the ports.[162] When Harrison was appointed Stewart Airport's general manager, he asked himself, "what would Lillian do?" His answer was to engage Stewart's stakeholders and market the airport. Harrison decided that the airport would not thrive by focusing only on suburban customers. Instead, he said, "we need to serve New York City."[163]

Marketing Stewart Airport to the millions of people who lived, worked, and visited New York City seemed daunting, but he told his staff, "We're not selling corn flakes to the world." He focused on twenty-five people—the chief executive officers of airlines who might be interested in the airport. Harrison started sending letters and updates to the airline executives. After receiving one of his letters, Norwegian Airlines sent out a team, unannounced, to tour the airport. A few months later, Norwegian decided to offer Stewart Airport's first-ever scheduled international service with fares between Norway and New York as low as $225 roundtrip.[164]

Harrison also convinced a bus operator to provide direct service to and from the Port Authority's Midtown Manhattan bus terminal, based around

Norwegian's schedule. The ninety-minute-long bus ride, like the flights, was geared toward budget conscious travelers. In 2017, Stewart Airport grew faster than any of the nation's seven hundred other airports with scheduled service, thanks to Norwegian's flights on Boeing 737 Max jets to Ireland, Norway, and Scotland.[165] That did not mean Stewart was busy, though. A British travel writer wrote that year, "Stewart International is no bigger than a motorway service station. In fact, it's probably smaller. And most of the time it's deserted." She warned that "a taxi ride is not an option, unless you want to pay as much as your airfare."[166]

Harrison wanted to change the airport's name since few people outside the area knew where it was located. However, Orange County business and political leaders had long resisted rebranding the airport because the Stewart name honored a prominent local family.[167] When the Port Authority was getting ready to take over the airport in 2007, the Authority's executive director, Tony Shorris, announced at a local economic summit that the Authority had no plans to ever change the airport's name. Orange County's newspaper, the *Times Herald-Record*, reported, "His audience went wild at the announcement, causing Shorris to remark that he suddenly knew how it felt to be a rock star."[168] Undeterred, Harrison persuaded local elected officials and three Orange County civic organizations of which he was a board member that an airport that included the words "New York" would help attract more airlines, passengers, and businesses.[169] In 2018, the Port Authority officially changed the airport's name to the New York Stewart International Airport.

Harrison's entrepreneurial inclinations and the Port Authority's extensive aviation resources were not enough to overcome Stewart Airport's shortcomings and unexpected events beyond its control, though. The next year, the airport lost its most prominent carrier when Norwegian Air suspended service after Boeing grounded its Boeing 737 Max jets following two fatal crashes.[170] A few months later, the airport took an even bigger blow when the COVID-19 pandemic forced airlines to cut services across the globe.

The Continuing Constraint

When taking over Stewart Airport in 2007 and the four airports in the 1940s, the Port Authority generated supportive coalitions because of the four factors identified in chapter 1 (resources, autonomy, leadership, and internal culture). The Authority's entrepreneurial leaders marshalled their ability to finance improvements and their expertise in the aviation industry. Since the organizational culture valued data and analysis, its decisions and strategies were based upon long-term considerations, including aviation industry trends and expected revenue from airlines, airport shops, and parking lots. The Authority helped secure its autonomy by developing a popular plan that transformed the preferences of elected officials, organized interests, and the general public. Business leaders and the media welcomed the Port Authority's participation because of the organization's reputation and skills.

The Great Swamp episode revealed the limitation of the Port Authority's autonomy. Although the Port Authority in the 1960s had sufficient resources, aggressive and entrepreneurial leadership, and the appropriate culture needed to build a new airport, Austin Tobin never created a supportive coalition to counter local opposition. Instead Morris County residents outmaneuvered the Port Authority. The Port Authority might have been a powerful organization, but the governors and legislatures never gave it free reign to bulldoze communities and fill in every swamp.

Although the bistate region has continued to thrive, capacity constraints at the Port Authority's three major airports remain a critical issue because the New York metropolitan area's economy (including its financial, business services, and tourism sectors) continues to rely upon frequent air travel to and from numerous destinations. Stewart Airport has the potential to supplement the three major airports, but even if it could attract several million annual passengers that would still be only a small percentage of the region's overall air traffic. Although the Port Authority and the airlines have invested billions of dollars to build state-of-the-art terminals at Kennedy, LaGuardia, and Newark, these improvements have limited effect on accommodating more planes and reducing flight delays.

The three airports have been able to accommodate more passengers in recent years because airlines have been swapping out some smaller jets for larger ones and flying with a higher percentage of their seats full. Improvements on the drawing boards will help clear runways faster and allow more planes to land during peak periods.

Although the Port Authority has successfully figured out how to squeeze more capacity out of its airports, at some point it will not be able to add many more passengers. Inevitably, this will result in some combination of higher fares, frustrated passengers, recurring delays, and fewer airline service choices—all of which will make New York a less desirable place to live, work, and visit.

In the same way that Austin Tobin encouraged outside groups to seek the Port Authority's help, the Port Authority has encouraged others to advocate for airport capacity expansion projects. For example, the Authority provided the bulk of the funding for recent airport studies conducted by the Regional Plan Association (RPA), an urban research and advocacy group. Patty Clark, the Authority's former chief aviation strategy officer, said, "The RPA is independent, and we needed a third party to examine all the issues and look at all the alternatives. If we had conducted our own study, its recommendations would have been seen as self-serving. The RPA has credibility among business leaders, media, and elected officials. It has gravitas."[171]

The RPA warns, "Intercity travel is at the core of an increasingly interconnected and competitive global economy. Without the ability to efficiently transport business and leisure travelers and time-sensitive cargo, both domestic and international business would grind to a halt."[172] The RPA reflects the Port Authority's thinking. Improvements, such as new technology to track airplanes and service expansion at Stewart Airport, would help accommodate more passengers, but New York and northern New Jersey are only delaying the inevitable. To maintain a world-class aviation system, one that could accommodate more passengers with fewer delays, the Authority needs to start planning for additional runways at one of the three major airports.

Neither the Port Authority nor any government agency is actively promoting the construction of a new runway, however, because the airports are constrained by environmentally sensitive lands, highways, commercial uses, parks, and residential areas. Every time the Authority has assessed the possibility of constructing additional runways, it identifies insurmountable political, financial, and environmental issues such as the need to take land from Newark's marine terminal, encroach into the federally protected Jamaica Bay, or move the New Jersey Turnpike. That is why the airports have not added any new runways since 1970.

Building new runways would require approvals from the cities of Newark and New York, as well as well as from state and federal officials. Right now, elected officials are clamoring for less airplane noise not more flights, while the media has ignored the airport's long-term needs. To build a new runway, the Port Authority needs the type of local support it had in Orange County. When the Port Authority was ready to take over Stewart Airport, a supporting coalition of public officials, civic groups, and private businesses was in place with welcoming arms. Without support from elected officials, regulatory agencies, business leaders, and the public, the Authority cannot mobilize the metropolis on any more major airport capacity expansion projects for the foreseeable future.

As shown in the next chapters, airports are very different than most of the Port Authority's other facilities. New York and New Jersey are usually eager for Port Authority investments and the economic development benefits that go along with them. Numerous times, when the Port Authority has decided to pour investments into one side of the river, conflicts have erupted and slowed down the Authority's efforts.

CHAPTER 4

Ports Competing on a Global Scale

In a typical year, cargo ships including those carrying containers, oil, and chemicals transport the equivalent of one and a half tons of goods for every person in the world. Since ships carry approximately 90 percent of all world trade, the shipowners trade association likes to say, "Without shipping, the import/export of affordable food and goods would not be possible—half the world would starve and the other half would freeze."[1] This lifeblood of global trade launches from and makes landfall at ports, from whence goods make their way—through complex and expansive networks of intermodal freight systems—from their origin to their ultimate destinations, be they businesses, shops, or your front door. Many people do not recognize the importance of maritime freight and the infrastructures that support it. In her book *Ninety Percent of Everything*, Rose George marveled at the degree to which the world of shipping remains hidden:

> These ships and boxes belong to a business that feeds, clothes, warms, and supplies us. They have fueled if not created globalization. They are the reason behind your cheap T-shirt and reasonably priced television. But who looks behind a television now and sees the ship that brought it? Who cares about the men who steered your breakfast cereal through winter storms? How ironic that the more ships have grown in size and consequence, the less space they take up in our imagination.[2]

Port facilities, often hidden on urban margins, are scattered around the New York metropolitan area. The most heavily used docks are tucked away on industrial lands in Elizabeth, Newark, and Bayonne in New Jersey. But the observant traveler can see shipping containers and the cranes that move them from vantages on the New Jersey Turnpike, the Bayonne and Goethals Bridges, from rail lines on the Northeast Corridor, and from Newark Airport.

Smaller cargo facilities continue to operate in Staten Island and Brooklyn as well. Visitors to Manhattan can still see vestiges of Manhattan's shipping infrastructure. The High Line and parks along the East and Hudson rivers have sprung from the piers and docksides that fueled the region's growth until the mid-twentieth century and cemented New York's significance as a global city.

In the same way that consumers are oblivious to the supply chain that fills their refrigerators and gas tanks, most residents in the New York region are unaware of the port's economic benefits. In 1946, Howard S. Cullman, then chair of the Port Authority, introduced an article about the twenty-fifth anniversary of the organization with a similar sentiment: "Most of us accept New York Harbor—and New Jersey's harbor—as something that has always been there and is here to stay. Few of us give thought to its far-reaching influence. We hardly realize that it is a bulwark of prosperity not only for metropolitan New York and New Jersey but for the nation itself."[3]

Cullman's observations are just as true today. The Port of New York and New Jersey complex[4] is still a vital element of the region's economy. It is the largest port on the East Coast of the United States and the third largest in the country (behind the ports of Los Angeles and Long Beach in California). The Port Authority estimates that 75 percent of ships carrying goods destined to the East Coast make the Port of New York and New Jersey their first port call.[5] Every day, these facilities handle thousands of shipping containers;[6] a single forty-foot shipping container can hold approximately 100,000 bananas, 800 televisions, or 8,000 boxes of shoes.[7] Because they come in standard sizes, containers can be moved by cranes very quickly between ships, trains, and trucks. As a result, shipping has become so efficient that under normal circumstances moving goods via the sea adds little to the cost of products.

Even if the maritime history of the city is evident all along the waterfront and active port facilities still operate on New York City's shores, many observers likely perceive these activities as remote or separate from their daily lives if they notice them at all. Nevertheless, the port generates considerable economic value for the region. The North Jersey Transportation Planning Authority and the New York Shipping Association estimate that port activities support half a million jobs related to logistics, transport, administration, finance, insurance, warehousing, and other functions across New York, New Jersey, and eastern Pennsylvania.[8] The port benefits from a dense and diverse economic hinterland, the area from which the port draws its customers and those businesses, in turn, benefit from their proximity to the port through shorter connections to supply chains and international customers.[9] Seen from a broader vantage, ports affect the competitiveness of local and regional businesses and, as a result, increase the attractiveness of regions.

All told, the New York and New Jersey ports generate an impressive return on investment considering their facilities only encompass about 3,000 acres. However, in operationalizing its impact on and connection with the region's economic fortunes, the port is heavily reliant on the transportation infrastructure in its surrounding region. The millions of shipping containers loaded or offloaded at Port Authority facilities must get to and from the docks somehow—by truck or train—adding congestion, noise, and wear and tear to the infrastructure and communities through which they travel.[10] As a result, the port has an important stake in regional infrastructure decisions over which it typically has little direct control. Similarly, since the port is a significant source of traffic, those entities that make infrastructure decisions have a great deal of interest in developments at the port and their broader implications for regional mobility.

This chapter joins the chorus of literature, from Robert Albion's *The Rise of New York Port* to Steven Erie's *Globalizing L.A.*,[11] in stating emphatically that there is nothing inevitable about a port's, or a region's, success. While amenable geography and luck may have dictated harbor locations and early commercial significance, their continued salience and competitiveness is closely linked with that of the economies within which they are embedded and the infrastructure upon which they rely. Improvements to port facilities generate crucial benefits, but those benefits cannot be effectively realized if surrounding infrastructure creates bottlenecks that constrain the flow of goods—one way in which port capacity can be throttled.

Port competitiveness, therefore, relies on functioning effectively at the nexus of trends in global trade and regional economic mass and the transportation and logistics infrastructure that dictate potential flows and capacity. This requires long foresight, to identify opportunities for and barriers to growth, and the capacity to act nimbly to acquire the investment necessary to institute improvements in time to retain, or gain, competitive advantage. Failure on any of these scores can have dire consequences as tales from the New York region's own port development attest. The decline of maritime freight activity on the previously bustling shores of Manhattan was primarily due to weak coordination of and investment in port facilities. While this development was not a deathblow for the region because the Port Authority's efforts in developing container facilities in New Jersey (see below) kept shipping business in the region; the episode demonstrates the steep price of failing to compete.

As in its other spheres of operation, given the constellation of actors and interests involved in port and associated infrastructure development, much of the Port Authority's success in maintaining the competitiveness of its port assets has depended on its ability to bring together a broad coalition to support its agenda. Port strategic documents list no fewer than fourteen different groups of stakeholders,[12] none of which can be characterized as having homogenous interests. This chapter explores the Port Authority's relationship with its port facilities, highlighting how its ambitions rely on coalition-building and how this intersects with other regional infrastructure under its jurisdiction. It begins by explaining how the Port Authority established control over the ports (in much the same way as it took over the airports) and then consolidated the competitiveness of its facilities by placing them at the forefront of the containerization movement in maritime shipping. The chapter then turns to how the Port Authority has maintained the competitiveness of the ports by effectively capturing freight traffic and engaging in critical infrastructure improvements, such as channel deepening, as well as its role in catalyzing and developing intermodal transportation infrastructures. Finally, it investigates how in the twenty-first century it increasingly relies on supply chain coordination and how these relationships are helping to plan for the port of the future. As in other chapters, the thread that binds these episodes is the Port Authority as master coordinator, the source of entrepreneurial vision that required the buy-in and collaboration of a wide variety of actors to execute effectively.

Putting the "Port" in Port Authority

Today, the Port Authority manages and oversees operations at a network of warehouses and intermodal freight infrastructure that process cargo such as imported automobiles, dry and liquid bulk, and containers. The ports also service cargo ships and provide marine support services. Importantly, while the Authority "manages and oversees" operations, it does not own or directly control any of these activities. Rather it owns the port lands and leases dock, warehousing, and cargo processing space to terminal operators who, in turn, have their own arrangements with carriers, logistics, and shipping entities.[13] This relationship is particularly important as it highlights the Port Authority's role in providing land and water access, optimizing land use, and otherwise coordinating the activities of what are, for the most part, private actors in order to maximize port capacity and efficiency. As this chapter explains, sometimes this involves large and expensive infrastructure projects (for instance, dredging) and at other times it requires interventions in process and practice. Because the Port Authority does not have direct control over the private actors that use these facilities, almost everything it does has to take a wide variety of interests into consideration and rely on the cooperation, buy-in, support, and ultimately action of its tenants and other relevant links in the supply chain.

When the Port Authority was first established, it was at an even greater disadvantage in exercising its mandate to manage maritime affairs. This section discusses the evolving relationship of the Port Authority as an infrastructure agency and its ports. It outlines the story of how it was able to take advantage of evolving changes in the shipping industry to seize control of and develop the region's existing port infrastructure into modern facilities that now generate annual revenue in excess of $300 million for the agency.[14]

A Maritime Mandate without Control

In the exercise of its mandate to develop the "terminal, transportation, and other facilities of commerce" of the region, the compact that created the Port Authority granted it "full power to purchase, construct, lease and/or operate any terminal or transportation facility" in the port district, to make changes for its use, and to borrow money secured by bond or mortgage to do it.[15] However, the same document strictly forbade it to "impair the interests" of local or private property or enterprise, and delegated it no powers to control the use of private or city-owned property.[16] It was thus established as a planning agency with little formal power other than those of "study, analysis, persuasion, and petition on the one hand, and . . . acquisition, construction, and operation of terminal and transportation facilities [that it acquired or built] on the other."[17]

As in other areas of its jurisdiction, this governance arrangement created significant incentive for the agency to build and acquire assets in order to exert more control over critical infrastructure and activities in the region. Its ambitions for the ports were no exception. Harmonizing rail links, harbor transport, and lighterage (barging) issues was its initial raison d'être, and the agency continued to try to ease mounting congestion and increase the region's competitiveness even after its early proposals with the railroads failed. What ensued was a protracted campaign by the agency to gain control over the area's international shipping infrastructure, then located primarily in Manhattan and Brooklyn. Its eventual monopoly over maritime commerce was not the product of shrewd acquisitive deal making, as was the case with the airports, but of a controversial strategy to develop its own facilities even though that meant competing with ports owned by the city of New York. The Port Authority succeeded due to a combination of foresight and boldness, the resources to act decisively, the agility to seize opportunities, and fortuitous timing. The outcome was ultimately for the best, for the region, the maritime industry, and arguably the city as well, since the iconic public parks and tourist attractions that now stud the Manhattan waterfront (and have driven up real estate values) on repurposed piers rose from the ashes of New York's decimated shipping industry.

Early Efforts to Tackle the "Port Problem"

The challenge that the Port Authority was created to address was at once easy to articulate and difficult to solve. Most of the marine terminal and cargo facilities were east of the Hudson River and most of the rail lines were on the west. But railroads were obliged by federal regulations to charge the same rates to transport goods across the river to New York City as to the western shores in New Jersey. Moving freight to where the major marine terminals were, the coasts of Manhattan and Brooklyn, caused congestion, added expense (to the carriers), and generated conflict between companies and complaints that the fee structure was unfair. At the time of its creation in 1921, the situation dockside had been described as disgraceful and "costly and inefficient beyond all comparison."[18] To drive the point home, shortly after its creation the Port Authority commissioned a short film to explain, in concrete terms, why its efforts were so desperately needed. It depicted the journey of a weary potato weeping about how long he had been sitting on a train in New Jersey before being dumped onto a barge to Manhattan and transferred to a truck that crawled through traffic to a West Side merchant and then onto the Bronx. The journey from New Jersey to its final destination, a distance of just over fifteen miles, took nine and a half hours, the film proclaimed.[19] There were three potential solutions: move the ports to where the rails terminals were (i.e., New Jersey), extend the rails to where the ports were, or cooperate to figure out how to harmonize the whole operation. In 1948, the Port

Fig. 4.1. Trucks lined up for the ferry in Hoboken (c. 1918–1919). *(Photograph reprinted by permission of the Hoboken Historical Museum.)*

Authority moved toward the first option and began what ultimately became its (controversial) core strategy to acquire and build port capacity in New Jersey in direct competition with New York's piers.

The organization started with a more conciliatory approach that sought to link up and harmonize port and rail facilities on both sides of the Hudson. The Port Authority's 1921 Comprehensive Plan was an ambitious proposal that involved connecting and building new railroad lines near port facilities,[20] establishing cooperative barging arrangements,[21] constructing cross-Hudson rail tunnels, and building massive inland freight terminals[22] to reduce congestion along the waterfront. The plan was approved by both states in 1922, not without strong opposition from New York City,[23] but ultimately disintegrated after more than a decade of maneuvering as railroads refused to cooperate and the Authority failed to gain control of key rail lines and real estate.[24] By the time the plan lost momentum, the Port Authority had evolved as an agency and had furthered parts of its mission to mobilize the metropolis through the construction of motor vehicle crossings while pursuing (mostly unsuccessfully) various Comprehensive Plan infrastructure projects independently during its next decade. While the Authority continued to address port congestion, it largely abandoned large-scale, rail-focused solutions by the mid-1930s.

The Authority was not, however, idle on port matters. Through the 1930s, it completed some small rail projects, attempted to secure key waterfront properties for ferries and passenger ships, built one of Manhattan's largest buildings to consolidate freight, engaged in court cases to protect port competitiveness,[25] and pursued some waterway improvements. Initiatives that improved the efficiency of barge operations and consolidated rail terminals on the Manhattan and Brooklyn piers[26] demonstrated the Port Authority's tenacity and capacity to extract agreements to coordinate activities from otherwise recalcitrant railroads. Moreover, the considerable coalition of actors that needed to be convinced and brought into these arrangements showcased its growing role as a broker of port matters. However effectively many of these projects were executed, they were incremental and were mostly overwhelmed by increasing freight and passenger traffic. They did not significantly improve either the issues of port congestion in New York or challenges with the transfer of freight rail in New Jersey. The construction of the motor vehicle crossings did alleviate some of the concern over rail freight as more goods began to move by truck, but this just created more vehicle traffic in Manhattan on and around its chaotic piers. Two decades later, the Port Authority once again invoked the travails of a potato (now "Mrs. Jones' potato") from origin to destination through a series of terminal and trucking operations to demonstrate the need for increased efficiency.[27]

The Port Authority Acquires a Port

Throughout this period the Port Authority had a fine line to tread. It wanted to accomplish its goals of harmonizing operations but did not control any of the actors involved. In the process of proposing and negotiating it frequently ran afoul of New York City politics, in which interested parties were resistant to outside interference in their port facilities, even if those interventions might benefit them. Since 1942, the New York ports had been managed under the aegis of the New York City Department of Marine and Aviation,[28] and fear of loss of control was a constant impediment to coordinated port development. Tensions became even more pronounced as the Port Authority mounted its ultimately successful bid to take over the city's airports. However, in the 1940s, governors from both states began to see the Port Authority as a tool to manage issues that were apparently beyond the capacities of local authorities. In 1944, the state of New York transferred ownership of the deteriorating Gowanus Grain Terminal in Brooklyn, giving the Port Authority its first marine freight property.

The beginning of Austin Tobin's three-decade reign as executive director in 1942 marked a period of intense entrepreneurial and portfolio expansion activities. While the airports and other infrastructure projects typically received more attention in this period, the ports were no exception. By the end of his tenure, the intensely fragmented ports, characterized by the "imaginary dividing line"[29] between the states, were united, modernized, and prospering.

Ironically, this process began (as discussed in the previous chapter) with an airport. In 1945, on the advice of its Central Planning Board, the city of Newark requested that the Port Authority study the problems of and come up with a proposal to improve the municipally owned Newark Airport and Port Newark marine terminal. Both the airport and the seaport were burdens on the city's finances and risked falling into disrepair. A report by the city's consulting engineers had concluded that "since the location and the traffic of both the seaport and the airport are so completely integrated with the remainder of the New York metropolitan area, it is unwise for Newark to attempt to further the development of these facilities by itself. Their greatest usefulness and the maximum volume of traffic to be expected will be attained only through their coordination with other facilities in the New York metropolitan area."[30] For Newark, fiscal necessity and the spirit of regionalism coincided, and the city and Port Authority reached a deal to transfer ownership and responsibility for the facilities and to begin extensive modernization and expansion initiatives in 1948.

Although the city of New York had long maintained a competing view, business groups and civic organizations also pushed it to consider a regional approach to New York's airports and seaports.[31] Facing financial constraints of his own and a growing need to accelerate waterfront improvements, in October of 1947, Mayor William O'Dwyer requested that the Port Authority survey the municipally owned piers and waterfront facilities.[32] The proposal that the Authority presented in 1948 to the city for leasing, financing, construction, rehabilitation, and operation of its port assets was ultimately rejected. The reasons were political and convoluted, hinging on factors such as lease rates and the lure of a competing proposal; but the main problem was that the city did not want to relinquish control over its marine terminals. While it is likely that the sting of losing the airports fueled some resentment toward the Authority, the reality was that industry and local political blocs associated with pier ownership and labor groups had strong incentives for the retention of local control and were successful at doing so even as the Port Authority proposed alternative plans over the next several years.

The fact that both New York City and Newark had turned to the Port Authority to consult on their port problems was not insignificant. The Authority's perceived expertise and financial capability was central to these decisions as well as continued confidence (if not always full support) in the benefit of a regional approach. While it did not operate any port terminals, as we have described above, the Port Authority had been deeply involved in port affairs from logistics management and legal initiatives to channel improvements. Through these actions, it had developed a reputation for excellence and disposed a professional staff capable of undertaking complex studies of the regional context. The city of Newark's consulting engineers concluded that the Port Authority was in a better position to operate Newark's airport and seaport given the Authority's resources and transportation experience.[33] The planners wrote:

> If a new local port commission were created, it would take many years to create a staff of equal competence and experience and the overhead expense would amount to a substantial sum annually. The Port of New York Authority, at present, has very large financial resources because of its exceptionally fine credit rating and issues bonds at very low interest rates. . . . It would be illogical to create a new metropolitan or state agency for this would be a duplication of the functions of the Port Authority.[34]

And so, the many years of patiently coordinating and brokering port affairs on behalf of the two states and their cities had paid off. Officials on both sides of the Hudson considered the Port Authority a legitimate and capable steward for their expensive and burdensome infrastructure and subscribed at least in principle to the idea that these were assets of regional significance. As a result, as the 1950s dawned, the Port Authority had managed to establish itself in the port development business, if only on the Newark side of the harbor, and was poised to expand its influence as a port operator.

It was also, however, in the complex position of developing and operating terminals in direct competition with New York City. It took another twenty years to fully gain control of marine freight facilities in the region. As with many of the Authority's triumphs in this period, much came down to Tobin's ability to leverage the Port Authority's financial resources and know-how to underpin his entrepreneurial agenda. However, when it came to the ports, his mission to establish domination over New York's facilities was helped enormously by the coming revolution in transglobal shipping: containerization. Here, as with many other cases, the Port Authority effectively recognized and was able to seize opportunities to further its agenda and mobilize the region.

The Box That Killed Manhattan's Ports

While the decline of New York City's ports could be said to have many causes, the ascent of the shipping container was the most decisive one. Until containerization, shipping largely relied on a breakbulk model. Goods were loaded and stowed and then unloaded by manual labor according to weight, size, and shape, characteristics of the freight (perishable or durable), and the configuration of the ship.[35] In this context, shipping was an urban industry where manufacturers and merchants clustered close to the docks, which were their primary sources of supply and trade, as did the people who worked in and relied on those industries. Figures 4.2 and 4.3 give a sense of the bustle and chaos of this era of shipping. In its heyday, the island of Manhattan[36] bristled on all sides with busy piers, and its shape and geography permitted, at least for much of its operation, certain advantages of density and operational efficiency. For a while the southern tip of Manhattan was one of the most significant economic and physical gateways in the world.

Containerization changed everything. The shipping container, so familiar and ubiquitous to us today, was a revolution in its time. First introduced in Port Newark in 1956, "the box" permitted a different mode of shipping that drastically reduced costs and accelerated the flow of goods enabling a shipment to be transferred from ship to truck, train, or storage in a single secure and trackable container. Mark Levinson's account of the rise and significance of container shipping in *The Box* covers the origins and transformative effect of this innovation in great and enjoyable detail, some of which we summarize in this section. However, the most fundamental fact of container shipping is that it requires *space*. The configuration of piers, storage, and transportation infrastructure needed to be completely reimagined to accommodate this new

Fig. 4.2. Unloading freight on a Manhattan pier in 1910.
(Photograph by the New York City Dept. of Docks and Ferries, reprinted by permission from the Ports & Terminals Collection, New York City Municipal Archives.)

mode of shipping. Docks in dense, residential, and spatially constrained urban areas could no longer effectively serve. Even if New York had the resources, expertise, and political will, it would have been difficult for the city to create the space required to support a modern shipping industry. As it happened, it had none of those things anyway and many more problems besides—a set of contexts that could have spelled doom for the metropolitan area's economy and competitiveness had the Port Authority not developed its New Jersey assets (which had ample space, at the time) with containerization in mind.

By the early 1950s, the Port Authority was in the process of redeveloping the Port Newark terminal facilities while New York City had elected to maintain local control of theirs. Over the next twenty years, the development strategies of these two actors diverged significantly. New York City continued to rebuff Port Authority proposals to redevelop its piers and ultimately adopted a municipally led program of port modernization. The Port

Fig. 4.3. Manhattan's Banana Docks in 1906.
(Photograph reproduced courtesy of the Detroit Publishing Company photograph collection, Library of Congress Prints and Photographs Division.)

Authority spent more than $11 million on improvements to the Port Newark facilities, channel dredging, and transportation links, and created an internal office for port promotion activities. The Authority's efforts paid off as more steamship lines were attracted by ongoing investments, including Waterman Steamship Company for whom the Port Authority designed and built a large new terminal. Waterman moved from Brooklyn to the new facilities, the largest of any company to do so to that point. Port Newark was a competitive force. But it still was not large enough for the Port Authority's ambition.

In 1953, the Authority leased terminal space on the Newark waterfront to a trucking company—McLean Trucking. This was an unusual move at the time, but the port facilities provided space for truck loading and turning operations close to where cargo was being discharged as well as access to rail.

Fig. 4.4. Crane placing containers on the 1956 maiden voyage of the *Ideal X* in Port Newark, New Jersey.
(Photograph reprinted by permission of Port Authority of New York and New Jersey.)

What soon became apparent was that McLean had bigger ideas than just trucking freight off docks. In fact, it was designing the first container ship and planned to use Port Newark as one of its first staging areas. On April 26, 1956, the first container ship, the *Ideal X*, sailed from Port Newark to Houston (fig. 4.4). The Port Authority reported this development with modest fanfare, noting it its 1956 annual report that "the new shipping method, inaugurated . . . at the Waterman wharf, has proved so successful that the line has already put two additional ships into operation, bringing the total number of container ships to four."[37]

Even before the *Ideal X* sailed, the Port Authority was developing a vision for how containerization might change marine shipping. In 1955, it purchased 450 acres of tidal marsh property in Elizabeth, New Jersey, to develop additional port facilities. By this point, the fate of New York's ports was essentially sealed. Levinson notes that New York City's planned port upgrades were state of the art for 1950. Meanwhile, what the Port Authority and McLean had planned for Port Newark and Port Elizabeth were laying the foundations for the future. Even if New York City had understood the significance of McLean's experiments in New Jersey, the city's disadvantages were nearly insurmountable.

The city, however, continued to plan and spend to support the faltering industry and its politically important labor force. After purchasing Port Elizabeth, the Port Authority largely ceased its attempts to acquire the New York City piers, turning its attention instead to serving the growing demand for container shipping. It did acquire piers on the Brooklyn waterfront but understood that even these larger areas would never have the space to support large scale container shipping.[38] Over the next decade, the Port Authority was relentless in expanding and upgrading its New Jersey port facilities and captured the overwhelming majority of shipping in the area, now trading largely in containers. The world's first dedicated container terminal opened in Port Elizabeth in 1962. By the 1970s the Port Authority presided over the largest container terminal in the world.[39]

A 1972 *New York Times* article reflecting on the impact of ten years of container shipping lamented, "Manhattan, once the hub of the port's commerce does not fare too well in the modern scheme.... Prospects for attracting new maritime business to the Manhattan waterfront appear dim because of lack of land and the kind of super highway system that enables the Elizabeth piers to handle up to 15,000 trucks a day."[40] By the middle of the decade, New York's marine terminals were "largely a memory."[41] Some port activities limped along under municipal control, but the city no longer developed its facilities. What remains of the legacy of New York City's proud shipping heritage are a handful of still-active Port Authority controlled properties in Brooklyn and Staten Island, and a passenger terminal on the west side of Manhattan. Most piers and terminals have fallen into disrepair or been demolished. However, the waterfront land and facilities in good repair have been turned into pleasing parks (such as the four-mile-long Hudson River Park and the Little Island park in figure 4.5) and other recreational venues such as the Chelsea Piers sports complex.

There is little doubt that transforming Manhattan's waterfront from industrial to recreational uses has been a boon for the city's residents and tourists. But the transition was painful and resulted in a significant economic shift away from logistics and manufacturing through the 1970s. At the same time, the Port Authority effectively consolidated its grip on shipping infra-

Fig. 4.5. Little Island, a park along the Hudson River, replaced an old Manhattan pier. *(Photograph by Jim Henderson, May 21, 2021. Courtesy Wikimedia Commons, CC BY-SA 4.0.)*

structure and rode the wave of containerization to maintain its position of East Coast shipping supremacy. However, being at the forefront of the container shipping revolution did not guarantee that it would remain there. The following decades showed how crucial it was to maintain vision, focus, and drive innovations in port development to maintain competitiveness.

Maintaining Competitiveness

The ports of New York and New Jersey obey different logics from other Port Authority infrastructure assets. Bridges and tunnels, for instance, are fixed assets that require maintenance and improvement but whose relevance and revenue streams are virtually guaranteed as long as people and goods have a reason to cross them. Airports serve vast local and regional markets and within their catchment areas do not typically compete with similar facilities in neighboring regions. In fact, New Yorkers have long complained of conditions at major airports, but that has not significantly dampened air travel demand. By contrast, because of the variety of alternative routes and forms of inland transportation, ports on the same continent compete to handle cargo from around the world. This competition has been particularly fierce on the Eastern Seaboard, where there are several other credible contenders for primacy. While the Port Authority had an advantage in the early days of containerization its dominance was not assured, and the Authority has had to be aggressive in planning for the future and responding to, and staying on top of, shifting trade and shipping patterns.

The competitiveness of modern ports hinges on a complex and multidimensional array of factors, many of which highlight the degree to which ports must be keenly attuned to global as well as local and regional contexts. As the Port Authority and its port infrastructure faced the evolution of container shipping, it struggled with challenges on multiple fronts as costs escalated and competition increased, while at the same time physical infrastructure and navigation (or shipping) channels required additional development and investment.

This section explores these challenges and the Port Authority's responses through the 1980s and 1990s. It also highlights how important broad vision is to maintaining market share, not only in understanding the evolving needs of the industry and enacting (comparatively) nimble capital programs, but also understanding the port's role in shifting global markets and ensuring that it is as optimally positioned in trade networks as possible. The port's future is also tied to continuous improvements in the efficiency of goods moving through the port facilities and along the rail and road network it relies upon. We show how the Port Authority sometimes quietly, sometimes loudly, laid important foundations for port competitiveness into the twenty-first century. Each case highlights how important building coalitions and partnerships, within the region and beyond, was for achieving its agenda.

Responding to Shifting Trade and Rising Competition

The Port Authority's greatest challenge is maintaining competitiveness in an increasingly crowded and sophisticated market—a struggle that became particularly acute by the 1980s. As trade from Asian markets increased and then exploded, Los Angeles supplanted New York's long-held position as the nation's busiest port. Geographical location and nautical accessibility put

New York ports at a disadvantage as ships brought Asian cargo to West Coast gateways (such as Los Angeles and Long Beach) where containers were transferred by rail to the rest of the country. The containers traveled on routes known as "land bridge" routes because the trains bridged the continent by land. The innovation of double stacking containers on trains headed inland further reduced the costs of moving goods from California.[42]

The economic downturns in the 1970s had also shaken New York's economy and the Port Authority was acutely aware of the precarity of the port's, and the region's, position, noting in 1984, "Our port faces tough new competitive pressures at a time when a few ports are likely to emerge as pivotal cargo centers and other ports may lose a significant amount of shipping. The Port Authority is taking steps to protect the competitive position of the port."[43] At the time, costs of shipping in and out of the New York ports were quite high and inefficient operations constrained capacity and impeded growth.

In response, the Port Authority engaged in traditional activities such as ensuring that shipping channels could accommodate evolving larger ships and promoting port activities through its world trade department. However, the work that the port department did during the 1980s and 1990s to mitigate geographical and nautical accessibility disadvantages vis-a-vis Asian trade was instrumental in maintaining its competitiveness and status as the shipping giant on the East Coast. While the threat to the port and the region may seem relatively benign in hindsight, the cost of failing to maintain market share could have had extreme consequences, as a 1992 newspaper article recognized:

> In a trend that threatens to push the New York metropolitan region's maritime industry further onto the sidelines of international trade, half or more of the imports destined for the East Coast arrive not on the great merchant fleets that once crowded the docks of New York and New Jersey, but stacked two deep on high-tech railroad flat cars, hauled by trains often a mile in length that dash in from the West Coast in three days.... It is a trend, experts say, that rivals the impact of the development of containerized cargo three decades ago, which eliminated the jobs of thousands of longshoremen by ending the need for the handling of cargo by people.... The land bridge means that millions of tons of products are arriving annually into the region without ever crossing a Port Authority pier, without providing work for the cargo handlers and without paying for taxes, insurance and dockside warehousing that creates much of the port's wealth.[44]

Ports Competing on a Global Scale

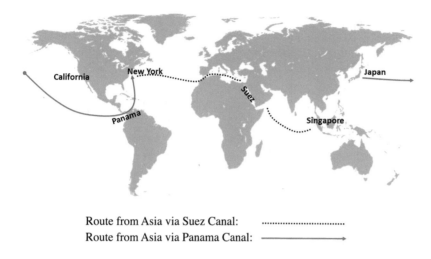

Route from Asia via Suez Canal: ....
Route from Asia via Panama Canal: ─────────▶

Fig. 4.6. Trade routes for shipping between Asia and New York via the Panama Canal and the Suez Canal.

The port director at the time, Lillian Borrone, stated that "as this landbridging evolved and took hold, we began to understand that we were faced with a different and new reality. . . . We are not going to change the basic nature of that reality."[45] While New York's location relative to Asia was immutable, its location relative to trade routes was not. The answer to this threat involved remaking world trade routes to bring Asia closer to New York. No small feat. Borrone[46] reflected that one of her first challenges was to understand the magnitude of the problem. In the late 1980s, the Port Authority board approved studies into where cargo was going and how it was being directed. These studies suggested that if trade from Japan and Korea shifted to Southeast Asian countries (e.g., Singapore, Vietnam, Thailand), then shipping goods through the Suez Canal directly to the East Coast would be competitive with the land bridge route (fig. 4.6). Borrone recalled that consultants "looked at every single carrier that could provide service through the Suez [Canal] and figured out what that route would have to look like and what would be required to sell it to carriers."[47]

Armed with a data-driven sales plan, Borrone and her team toured Asia to find carriers willing to try the new route, first securing Neptune Orient Lines (a Singapore-based shipping company) in 1991. Neptune brought in Asian goods to the United States by sailing through the Suez Canal to the

Mediterranean Sea and then across the Atlantic Ocean.[48] With more manufacturing moving to Southeast Asia, Singapore became the world's busiest port and the all-water route through the Suez Canal to the New York area saved at least three days of transport time over the Pacific route.[49] By the late 1990s, seven carriers were using the Suez Canal route and the Port Authority had entered into a marketing alliance with the Egyptian Suez Canal Authority to publicize its success.

While the total contribution of Southeast Asian trade was initially relatively small compared to the port's total volume, it had significant long-term impacts[50] and important symbolic value. Inaugurating this new trade route was a meaningful signal of the Port Authority's intention to aggressively pursue new business on behalf of and in partnership with its terminal operators. These marketing efforts were also combined with equally aggressive initiatives to reduce costs, which were among the highest in the world at the time. Borrone worked closely with terminal operators, labor organizations, shippers, logistics firms, and others to identify points of weakness, extract additional operational efficiency, increase reliability, and exploit opportunities for port improvements beyond capital plans. These collaborative initiatives collectively helped to increase port competitiveness through the end of the twentieth century and laid strong foundations for more deeply institutionalized port partnerships.

Of course, capital improvements are crucial to port competitiveness, and major investments made in the 1990s and 2000s maintained the region's port among the world's biggest and most significant. The goods moving through the Port of New York and New Jersey has grown at a remarkable rate. In 1995, the Port handled the equivalent of 2.5 million twenty-foot containers and in recent years that number has exceeded 7.5 million.[51] As the examples below demonstrate, it takes years of planning and work to execute capital programs, but each has been vital to ensuring competitiveness and resilience.

Dredging to Accommodate Larger Ships

Without question, deepening shipping channels by dredging is the most basic, important, and expensive capital improvements undertaken at the Port of New York and New Jersey. As a matter of course, about six million cubic yards of sediment needs to be dredged annually from the harbor because fresh water from the Hudson, Passaic, and Hackensack rivers constantly carries in silt, sand, and muck. Maintaining navigable depths in shipping channels is critical to waterborne commerce, just as roads need to be paved, potholes filled, and snow cleared on the region's highways. As ships get larger, the approaches and channels that are continuously silting also need to be deepened. If a port cannot accommodate a carriers' largest ship, it is quickly passed over for those that can, and losing that business can be fatal. Consequently, channel deepening and maintenance is a perennial issue. An excerpt of a description of channel improvement projects from 1930 would not be alien to port planners today:

> Year after year the work of digging invisible roadways to connect different parts of the port goes on. Only pilots and ship masters know where these trails are. But when on rare occasion a great ship strays off the track their importance is dramatized. More material has been dug out of the Ambrose Channel [the Port's main shipping channel] than was excavated in the digging of the Panama Canal. Today, with the growing size of ocean ships constantly growing, the need for deeper and wider channels is particularly pressing.[52]

Since its creation, the Port Authority has worked continuously with the U.S. Army Corps of Engineers to maintain the shipping channels within the port area. After a long fight to win congressional authorization, the two agencies began a program in 1987 to deepen the port's major shipping channels, which were less than thirty feet deep in some sections,[53] down to forty feet so that the largest container ships could navigate through the New York harbor.[54] Environmental issues and changes in the shipping industry, however, jeopardized the project's success.

Nearly all the harbor's dredged materials had long been disposed in the Atlantic Ocean, six miles east of the Jersey Shore, in an area known as the "mud dump." In the early 1990s, though, federal officials instituted new testing protocols that determined only about one-third of the harbor's dredged materials were "clean" enough to be deposited in the ocean. Dredging was suspended until safe solutions for disposal of sediment (including those contaminated with PCBs, dioxins, and heavy metals)[55] could be devised. Complicating the problem was the Port Authority's need to accommodate even larger ships than first anticipated. That meant disposal sites were needed for more dredged materials so that contractors could deepen the channels to at least forty-five feet not just forty feet deep.[56]

Under pressure from New York's governor, George Pataki, to quickly reopen a Staten Island container port in 1995, the Port Authority sent 150,000 cubic yards of contaminated dredged material from Staten Island to Utah. Normally, the cost to dump it in the ocean would have been $750,000. Sending the materials on an 1,800-mile journey via barges and trains cost nearly $18 million. A Port Authority official said, "We can't stay competitive without an economically and environmentally sound method to dispose our material." He warned, "when you have to go to Utah, it's a crisis."[57]

Assemblyman Steve Corodemus, who headed a task force set up by New Jersey governor Christine Todd Whitman to address the issue, warned that the port was facing a "slow death" because its shallow channels could not accommodate newer and larger container ships.[58] Behind closed doors, Lillian Borrone told the Authority's commissioners and the governors' aides that unless the Authority could make firm commitments about dredging, it would soon lose two of its shipping lines.[59] Although the Port Authority still controlled the East Coast's largest containerized cargo facilities, it was losing business to faster-growing ports in Philadelphia, Charleston, Baltimore, and Norfolk.[60] Because of the shallow channels, carriers had to lighten their vessels before entering New Jersey's ports. In 1996, approximately 90,000 containers were diverted to ports with greater depths such as Halifax.[61] This hurt New York area's shipping-related companies as well as businesses waiting for their imported goods. With carriers around the world making long-term plans, the president of Maher Terminals, Brian Maher, said, "once set in motion, diversion of cargo from the Port of New York and New Jersey may be impossible to stop."[62] And time was of the essence. While debates raged over how to dispose of dredged materials, ship dimensions continued to increase leading the Port Authority to request that channels be deepened even further to fifty feet.

Doing nothing was not a reasonable option and, in addition to the regulatory, logistical, and cost challenges associated with dredging, the Port Authority faced heavy opposition from civic groups seeking to block any activity that might be environmentally harmful. The Environmental Defense Fund became a leading opponent, arguing that toxic materials could not be safely disposed of on water or land. Fisheries and recreational groups also raised concerns about any toxic leakage that would impact their industries. Public debates were often heated, port leadership, dredging experts, and environmentalists were divided on how to treat the contaminated sediment.

The issue was ultimately resolved not with a bang but a whimper. While many options (such as building a manmade island[63]) were considered scientifically viable, they carried price tags that would render the work prohibitively expensive. In 1996, an agreement was reached after negotiations that involved the Port Authority as well as both state capitals, congressional delegations, and then Vice President Al Gore. The plan outlined new decontamination techniques and permitting processes along with the creation of submerged pits in Newark Bay, and the use of decontaminated mud along the shore.[64]

In the process of developing and implementing plans, the Port Authority had to manage complex negotiations and juggle numerous competing interests. But not all its efforts involved political actors. During this period, it became a leading environmental advocate in the region, initiating activities to control the source of contaminants and recover damages from past polluters. Port officials realized the best long-term solution was to stop new pollution from entering the harbor and they advocated for more investments into water treatment facilities and aggressive law enforcement. It was a key actor in what became the Harbor Estuary Program[65] and it commissioned funds to distribute to environmental groups for pollution mitigation efforts. The Authority also worked with local government officials, labor groups, and industry leaders, as well as other ports across the nation to revise legislation and regulations.

Dredging resumed and two decades later, in 2016, the U.S. Army Corps and the Port Authority celebrated the completion of the $2.1 billion project that deepened thirty-eight miles of shipping channels down to fifty feet. A senior Army Corps official noted, "it was the most important and influential project related to modern day economics in the Northeast."[66] This episode in the Port Authority's long experience with the crucial but mundane business of dredging is notable for several reasons. First, the environmental issue marked a turning point in port operations where a tedious and sometimes logistically challenging, but relatively uncontroversial task, became a major point of contention and put the port's future at risk. Delays in accomplishing the deepening not only lost the port business (through diverted traffic) but shook the confidence of shipping companies in the long-term viability of the port for their existing and expanding fleets. Secondly, as discussed in chapter 6, it occurred at a moment of acute interstate conflict that held up the port's capital improvements.

Finally, it demonstrated the considerable capacity and determination of the port department and its leadership to handle politically sensitive and logistically challenging crises. In this, the agency was helped by the coalitions that Borrone built through the early parts of the decade. Terminal operators, logistics companies, and labor organizations were publicly supportive and privately influential in making sure that political actors understood the magnitude, and urgency, of the dredging problem. The local business community was also important in pressing for a resolution. Dredging manager Tom Wakeman reflected on the many monthly meetings that he attended and how that outreach was critical for working out what everyone needed to walk away happy and, significantly, how much they were willing to pay for it.[67] This collaborative approach to problem-solving, backed by the Port Authority's considerable engineering expertise and experience, was a major asset to resolving a challenge that could have sunk the East Coast's preeminent port at the turn of the twenty-first century.

Developing Intermodal Transportation and ExpressRail

Not all important port capital programs involve ships. Many improvements in operational efficiency are possible with land-side investments that help goods move faster through port facilities. For shippers, these improvements are important because they affect the overall time that it takes goods to reach their final destination. However, logistics and the flow of goods to and from the piers is where the port, which for many people exists as kind of a remote and abstract facility, intersects most obviously with the region. It is a gateway that disgorges goods that must then travel through the region somehow, contributing to congestion, pollution, and taking a toll on transportation infrastructure. The development of effective inland distribution networks is therefore an important dimension of port activities and competitiveness.

The growth in container ships threatened to put significant pressure on land-side and inland distribution capacity even as the dredging battles raged through the 1990s. Larger ships meant more containers would need to be shifted at every docking, which risked overwhelming existing facilities and networks. To put this in perspective, the largest modern vessels can carry more than 20,000 containers. As recently as 2001, the maximum was around 6,000.[68] While this was most acutely a problem felt by terminal operators, who were the ones in charge of managing flows through their facilities and faced high fixed costs, the Port Authority recognized that failure to address the issue for all tenants could threaten everyone's capacity to handle increasing volumes and affect its revenues. As with many challenges during this period, port leadership opted to work with its coalition of partners to devise solutions. The first initiative was to streamline and expand dockside cargo handling capacity for moving containers.

The terminals in New Jersey had long had the advantage of a location close to major rail lines. However, until the 1990s goods had to be moved by truck to regional rail terminals before they could be loaded onto rail cars. In 1991, Maher Terminals in Elizabeth constructed and opened the first direct ship-to-rail and rail-to-ship service. While this infrastructure was privately developed, it involved collaboration between the Port Authority and numerous actors to put into place. On its side, the Port Authority had been exploring the potential for expanding rail capacity to the ports. Frank Caggiano, deputy port director in the 1990s, described his role at the agency as a problem-solver who helped to drive the dockside rail project, known as ExpressRail. He noted that one of the key challenges to constructing the service was that the best place to locate it was at Maher Terminals, which would service eleven ocean carriers. But that meant that many tenants would not have the same advantages, including Sea-Land and Maersk.[69] Caggiano and Borrone managed to convince the other terminal operators that this was a proof-of-concept project, and that service would be expanded to others in the future. In the meantime, they guaranteed Sea-Land and Maersk access and negotiated with Conrail to extend its operations to Maher Terminals.

As promised, in 1992, the Port Authority announced the planned construction of a new permanent ExpressRail facility that would be able to handle 100,000 containers a year in conjunction with improvements to Conrail service that would use double-stacking to reduce rates for Midwest and Canadian service.[70] The first ExpressRail terminal expansion was completed in 1995 and immediately began to handle a significant percentage of shipments through Elizabeth[71] and a new, even larger facility opened in 2004. The Authority later extended the ExpressRail network with new rail on or near dock terminals in Staten Island, Newark, and Elizabeth. By 2006, the Port Authority estimated that its ExpressRail infrastructure was eliminating more than 500,000 truck trips annually from state and local roads.[72] One port official described ExpressRail as "our landbridge," noting that it provided access to the Midwest market, eastern Canada, and New England, which enabled it to increase reach and market share.[73] While the rail network did serve those markets before, it did so at a much smaller scale due to the time and cost of putting containers on trucks to drive to off-terminal railroads. Overall, the Port Authority has invested more than $600 million in the ExpressRail network, which now has the capacity to handle 1.5 million containers per year.

These were not capital investments in the traditional sense. While the Port Authority invested in constructing the terminal facilities, it was not the

Fig. 4.7. Thousands of shipping containers at Port Authority's marine terminal in Elizabeth, New Jersey.
(Photograph by Captain Albert E. Theberge, courtesy of the National Oceanic and Atmospheric Administration.)

one that built the train tracks or supplied the lifting equipment to service the ships. Instead it relied on its ability to convince, or enable, terminal operators and railroads to make those investments. Even if infrastructure costs were unevenly distributed, ExpressRail provided widespread benefits—more volume through terminals, on rail cars, and through the port generated increased revenue for nearly everyone. The Port Authority did its part to offset some of the capital costs.

The development of ExpressRail illustrates an important feature of port development in the New York and New Jersey region that has strong parallels with the challenges that the Port Authority also faces as an organization. While it can spearhead large infrastructure projects, it is rarely able to act alone. In the port, the agency functions as a landlord and its fortunes are inherently tied to the decisions of the port terminal operators, shipping lines, trucking firms, rail companies, and many others. It can influence these decisions, through its own infrastructure investments, but must also rely on

Fig. 4.8. Ships loaded with containers in Elizabeth, New Jersey. *(Photograph reprinted by permission of Port Authority of New York and New Jersey.)*

its ability to bring these actors together to see how their own investments can magnify the benefit for everybody. The Port Authority's ability to play that leadership and convening role, to build coalitions and convince them to support a common agenda, is one of the foundations of its success and of the port's continued, and by no means assured, dominance (figs. 4.7 and 4.8).

The Port in the Twenty-First Century: Developing Resilience by Building Networks

The port of the twenty-first century faces many of the same challenges as it always has. Dredging continues, ships continue to get larger, and traffic congestion is an ever-present threat. Competitive pressures from competing ports on the East Coast and in Canada are unrelenting. Joining these are evolving changes to the shipping industry and port operations driven by security measures, environmental concerns, and climate change, as well as increasing threats from extreme weather events. Black swan events with severe consequences for the shipping industry, like a global pandemic, have also threatened port performance. Under these circumstances, the Port Authority continues to look to the future in its capital programs but has also focused significantly on strengthening resilience to maintain its competitive advantage. In this process, it has invested significantly in developing its leadership role and institutionalizing governance structures to drive collective initiatives to improve port performance. Three episodes illustrate the challenges that can arise to affect port operations and how these contributed to cooperative relationships that have enabled it to retain its competitive advantage.

Hurricane Sandy provided stark lessons about the vulnerability of the port to an unexpected crisis and highlighted the value of establishing mechanisms to coordinate the responses of all the actors affected to restore operations. When the storm hit in 2012, it took everyone by surprise. Rick Larrabee, the port director at the time, remembered that:

> [Sandy] was one of those events—you're always thinking about what's the worst thing that could happen? Of course we had plans for hurricanes and storms but Sandy was different in the sense that we were anticipating a much lesser impact and it wasn't until that Sunday afternoon in late October 2012 when we were on a call with the National Weather Service and the guy we were talking to was like I don't want to be dramatic but this storm is going to have dire consequences. With storm surges of 9 to 12 feet, everything in the port at that level would be covered in water. By the time it passed the next morning we had devastation everywhere. For example, we lost 40,000 brand new cars sitting on the docks that we couldn't move. A large number were hybrids and the batteries spontaneously combusted. We had fires and floods. It was like Armageddon.[74]

Long-term recovery took some time, as it did at all the Port Authority's facilities. But the port was open within four days due to the resourcefulness of the port director's team. Tom Wakeman reflected, "I will give Rick [Larrabee] and Bethann [Rooney] credit—they got out there on the phones and got it done. They only had one cell phone and were prepared,"[75] devising plans to get everyone back in business that even required tracking down gas so that employees could get to and from work.

However, one thing that interested him as he observed the port's recovery was that social networks were so crucial for coordinating an effective response and the Port Authority was not able to as effectively leverage those resources as other actors in the area. The New York Shipping Association (NYSA)—which is the membership organization that represents the terminal operators, ocean carriers, stevedores, and marine related businesses that operate the ships—had spent a lot of time building these networks between members, and so their collective response was relatively swift. Wakeman noted that "they knew each other. If you don't know each other's names then it's trickier. NYSA had created this 'social infrastructure' amongst the terminal operators and their shipping lines because they'd had lunches. They knew each other by first names and so could call each other up . . . people who had already established the communication models and friendships were ready to do what was necessary to get back into business."[76] This meant that coordination on the "water" side, in managing the movement of goods from ships to terminals, got back to business as usual more quickly than on the "land" side of the port, where ground transport and goods movement was snarled by debris and delay. This realization was not lost on the port leadership as they contemplated how to improve resilience following the next crisis of a very different nature.

In August 2013, service at one of the terminals in the port nearly ground to a halt for weeks due to a computer glitch that affected cargo routing. This episode demonstrates how something that seems relatively minor can have enormous consequences across the entire region. An outage, which occurred at Maher Terminals as they launched a new computer operating system, meant that incoming goods could not be matched up with ground transportation nor could outgoing shipments be routed to the correct vessels. This affected the entire port complex as trucks awaiting deliveries backed up for hours and ships had to be diverted. While the glitch was confined to one terminal, because the port relies on efficient movement of goods through the facility, the sudden inability of one of its terminals to do just that created congestion and confusion that affected every other terminal on the property. Furthermore, the thousands of containers that were stuck in the port impacted supply chains and retail operations throughout the region.[77] Bethann Rooney, the security manager at the time who eventually became deputy port director, used the same analogy that Wakeman had used to depict the hurricane, describing the computer problem as "a mess. Armageddon."[78] What was unfortunately disastrous for Maher Terminals highlighted a weakness for the entire port: if one link in the chain was lost, if cargo backed up for one tenant, everyone's business was at risk. As the port was managing the fallout from this disruption the foundation was being laid for a mechanism that would help to mitigate future challenges. As Rooney recalls:

> All of the business that operate in and around the port have been staunch competitors and operated in silos. And the whole supply chain is so interconnected that when one aspect of it got messed up everything is impacted. So [we thought] let's bring together a coalition of executives in the supply chain to not represent their business or employer but to represent their *sec-*

tor. [That would help us] understand where we were going wrong and set ourselves on a path for resilience [and give us the] ability to withstand any kind of disruption.[79]

A 2013 white paper prepared by the Port Authority analyzing the source of inefficiencies zeroed in on the issue of interdependencies in the system:

> Many of the problems experienced this summer were system problems involving multiple stakeholders. For example, delays at terminal gates were compounded by the unavailability of chassis [wheeled structures used by trucks to move containers]. As a result, no one entity could fix the problem. There needs to be a collective effort if some of these issues are to be addressed. If there is anything good to come of the summer's meltdown, it is the fact that all of the stakeholders appear to believe that we have real problems and that those problems can only be addressed by a collective effort.[80]

The white paper proposed the creation of a task force for constituents to identify challenges to port efficiency and service reliability, and to recommend potential solutions and key performance indicators.[81] What became the Council on Port Performance initially included representatives from the Port Authority, NYSA, terminal operators, vessel owners, labor, railroads, trucking companies, shippers, beneficial cargo owners, warehouse owners, and logistic companies.[82] While the Council itself has no formal power, as a forum for discussion and deliberation it has had an important impact on building relationships and seeding collaborative projects. One was the launch of an information portal that compiles information from all six container terminals and makes that data available in a single Internet portal for qualified users on a near real-time basis.[83] While this initiative may appear modest, it requires competitors to share what would normally be proprietary data. Terminal operators stress that they are still fierce competitors but have through institutions like the Council developed trust to share information and pool resources when there's a potential for collective benefit.[84] Other projects that have spun out of the Council include the implementation of radio frequency identification tags for trucks to improve gate security, improve truck turnaround times, and gather data that can be used collectively to optimize performance.

As the port faced the immense challenge at the start of the COVID-19 pandemic in 2020, the Council and its networks proved particularly valuable. During the initial stage of the crisis, the group decided to meet weekly instead of quarterly and added ad hoc meetings on certain issues. One huge collective focus was acquiring personal protective equipment (PPE) for their workforce in order to be able to keep the port open. Rooney remarked that "we needed to pull out all stops collectively to get PPE. We pooled resources to get PPE for the supply chain partners because if the longshoreman community went down with high rates of cases it would all fall apart. We had calls with other ports that didn't have coalitions and they were flailing. Meanwhile, we were able to deal with the problem and stay ahead of it."[85]

In April 2020, when lockdowns were being mandated across the world, cargo was still coming in. Fearing that the influx would cripple operations, the Port Authority used the Council and its own networks to identify property owners with available warehouse space and then brokered short-term marriages between those with storage capacity and shippers (or ocean carriers) that needed it. Rooney noted that this was an important proactive measure that was only possible because they were meeting regularly, talking proactively about potential problems, and collectively working on solutions.[86]

In 2021, the ports of Los Angeles and Long Beach were facing a crisis as weeklong delays forced container lines to look for alternate ports.[87] While New York and New Jersey terminals experienced some delays they were minor in comparison. This proactive stance was crucial. Wakeman commented, "If you can't move goods in an international connected supply chain then you're off the list. If businesses don't get back into business in three to five days then you lose the customers. In logistics, loyalty is everything. If you lose your customers, they're gone, and then you're out of the business."[88]

These three crises—Hurricane Sandy, the Maher Terminals computer glitch, and the COVID-19 pandemic—all emphasized the degree to which the port functions, and must be conceptualized, as a system. In its governance of the ports, the Port Authority has developed and leveraged this understanding. From Lillian Borrone's efforts to build communication and collaboration to reduce costs in the 1990s to the more formal partnership crystallized in the Council, the Port Authority has become increasingly active in convening activity up and down the supply chain to improve port competitiveness and resilience. These networks will be crucial for executing the agency's long-term visions on the capital side, including dredging of the channels to accommodate even larger vessels and developing sustainable and resilient solutions in response to climate change.

Conclusion

The ports are among the Port Authority's most enigmatic assets. At once invisible and utterly crucial to the regional economy, they have periodically come close to disaster and decline, as this chapter demonstrates. New York's dominance of East Coast shipping was neither inevitable nor assured. Rather its relative consistency is the result of aggressive and at times visionary action by leadership within the port and the agency.

On the waterfront, as elsewhere in its portfolio, the Port Authority is not sovereign. It began its stewardship of New York region shipping in 1921 with no direct control over any of the actors in the supply chain but built credibility as a convener, a reliable source of engineering expertise, and as a regional agency capable of managing the complexities of what were surely regional assets (even if that view was not universally shared). These qualities, as well as its steady stream of revenues from its tolls and bond-raising abilities, made it the logical choice for managing Newark's air and seaport infrastructure. Even if the Port Authority failed to gain control of the New York City piers, the New Jersey terminals proved enough to establish the Authority as more than just a convener of maritime interests. Even with its own facilities it needed to work with a wide variety of public and private interests to achieve its vision for port development. But reliance on these partnerships was also an advantage. Its willingness to work closely with McLean to develop custom terminal facilities put it at the forefront of the container revolution that wiped out New York City's shipping dominance. One could argue that this was partially luck. The Port Authority was in the right place at the right time and, flush with resources, could afford to take some risks. However, its leadership took this advantage and pressed it with investment after investment and developed what was, at the time, the world's largest and most significant container port. It worked with ports around the world to promote containerization, was a model for infrastructure development, and drove business to its facilities with proactive policies that enabled it to ride the wave of containerization.

When shifting global trade and transportation innovations such as land bridging threatened its competitiveness, the organization yet again drew on its extensive resources and expertise to study and sell new routes to recapture market share lost to West Coast gateways. This initiative was combined with cost reduction measures and improvements to operational efficiency that were only possible because of the strong collaborative relationships the Port Authority built with port stakeholders across the spectrum. These efforts, in turn, led to other problems associated with rising cargo volumes and pressures on port capacity. Good problems to have in the port business. As the relatively routine task of channel deepening turned into a regulatory nightmare and resulted in costly delays, the Port Authority worked with political actors and opponents drawing on its expertise and networks to devise innovative solutions to finally execute its vision. Anticipating increasing volumes, it convened rail and terminal operators to build the ExpressRail system and ensure reliable connections to inland markets.

When disaster struck in various forms in the opening decades of the 2000s it relied on a strong foundation of partnerships to respond. The lessons of the importance of networks between stakeholders throughout the supply chain that became obvious post-Sandy led to the creation of the Council on Port Performance and an officially coordinated approach to port governance and planning. During the COVID-19 pandemic, this network was instrumental in dampening the blow of supply chain disruptions and keeping the port open and operating as efficiently as possible while its competitors struggled.

As the Port Authority explores port development through the middle of the twenty-first century, the lessons of a hundred years of port governance are deeply engrained in its planning process. It has been consultative, proactive, and visionary and should provide a foundation to face the challenges of a rapidly changing and deeply uncertain world. As the Port Authority as an organization appears to be institutionally and politically weakened, financially constrained, and operationally restricted, the ports perhaps provide an important example of how ambitious agendas can be sustained through partnership and collaboration.

CHAPTER 5

Fostering Regional Mobility through Enduring Partnerships

Decade after decade, the Port Authority built new Hudson River crossings to accommodate more cars and trucks. In the 1920s and 1930s, it constructed the George Washington, Goethals, Outerbridge, and Bayonne Bridges. In the 1930s, 1940s, and 1950s, the Authority built three separate tubes of the Lincoln Tunnel, and then in the 1960s added six more lanes to its eight-lane George Washington Bridge. By the late 1970s, however, the possibility of building another motor vehicle crossing into Manhattan was completely out of the question. The mayors of New York City and their constituents wanted fewer people driving in from New Jersey, not more. The city was no longer interested in any new highways or even parking facilities that would attract more vehicles in or through Manhattan. Preserving neighborhoods and protecting the environment had become far more important priorities. Likewise, the New York metropolitan area could no longer afford major expansions of its rail network because neither the cities nor the states had enough money to adequately maintain and modernize their existing train lines.

These are challenges that persist to this day where the Authority's mission to keep the metropolis moving, an objective with broad regional benefits, comes up against understandable local opposition to property takings, land clearance, construction disruptions, and environmental consequences associated with infrastructure improvements. As the Port Authority began to face increasing constraints to its capital ambitions it had to find alternative ways to facilitate mobility. Chapter 3 demonstrated how the Port Authority's ingenuity could go a long way to solving airport capacity challenges once it acknowledged that building a fourth major airport was impossible. Beginning in the 1970s, that spirit of adaptation permeated Port Authority strategy as it experimented with programs to encourage people to drive on alternate routes, travel at less congested times, and take buses or trains rather than drive.

The strategic shift away from solving mobility problems with large-scale capital projects required a broad set of partners in both the public and private sector. This chapter introduces four initiatives that exemplify the Authority's flexibility in the face of complex transportation challenges, and the enduring coalitions that it built to sustain those ambitions: the reinvigoration of ferries, the creation of a regional traffic coordination center, the establishment of a public-private partnership to promote transit, and the launch of the nation's largest electronic toll payment program.

One man played a central role in designing these programs. The Port Authority senior official, Lou Gambaccini, had a keen awareness of the region's political and financial constraints, but he was committed to improving the capacity and the reliability of the transportation system. Working with state and local agencies across the region, he developed new programs and created new organizations by transcending parochial concerns. Gambaccini built successful coalitions by leveraging resources that were just as relevant as money—the Authority's credibility and talented staff, as well as his own professional network and reputation as a policy innovator.

Gambaccini had high standards and ambitions for the Port Authority, an important element of the Port Authority's culture nurtured by Austin Tobin, the Authority's executive director from 1942 to 1972. Not only did the Port Authority attract bright and ambitious people (with its relatively high salaries and generous benefits compared to other public sector organizations) but it also established highly regarded management training programs and encouraged staff to further their education, take on new responsibilities, and engage with other transportation professionals in the nation.[1] Gambaccini relished the opportunity to work with other transportation leaders, and while he was at the Port Authority testified before Congress, led national transit committees, and helped create the American Public Transportation Association to advocate for federal funds and protransit policies. The Port Authority's culture, benefits, and opportunity to work on exciting projects helped him attract other talented people who he inspired to build and lead their own coalitions.

Lou Gambaccini: Architect of Adaptation

Gambaccini had a long and distinguished career at the Port Authority and left a legacy that is often described reverentially by his contemporaries. He was a leader who was inspired by the Port Authority's mission and had a rare insight about the way that bureaucratic silos stood in the way of providing more efficient transportation services. This perspective enabled him to see transportation problems differently and to propose innovative solutions that worked with existing infrastructure, creating a whole new toolbox for the Port Authority to draw on as it faced increasing constraints to construction.

Gambaccini started working at the Port Authority in 1956 after receiving a master's degree at Syracuse University's Maxwell School of Citizenship and Public Affairs. He never forgot the oath inscribed on the graduate school's wall that called on citizens to make the world a better place. Those words would be a source of inspiration for his entire career, and he inculcated in his staff the importance of public service.[2] Gambaccini said he decided to work at the Port Authority because it was a dynamic organization that combined the best of the public and private sectors. He thought its requirement to be financially self-supporting encouraged innovation and attracted highly qualified people.[3] Gambaccini remembered, "When they recruited me, they picked me up at the airport in New York by helicopter and gave me a grand tour of their facilities, which was pretty exciting."[4]

Since drivers pay to use the Port Authority's roads, the agency's officials have always felt an obligation to operate and maintain them to the highest standards. Gambaccini appreciated this emphasis on customer service. Compared to the way that the cities in the New York metropolitan area took care of their bridges, the Port Authority did a far better job paving its roadways, repairing potholes, removing graffiti, updating signage, painting steel, and clearing accidents.

Gambaccini's first job after graduate school was as a management trainee at the Port Authority, a position that involved rotational assignments and classroom activity. He was subsequently asked to help plan for the Authority's 1962 acquisition of the privately owned Hudson & Manhattan Railroad that the Authority renamed the PATH system (a thirteen-station rail network that provides 24/7 train service between six Manhattan stations and seven New Jersey stations.) Gambaccini was later promoted to the position of PATH general manager. While New York City's subway cars and stations were covered with graffiti and subject to frequent breakdowns, the PATH system continuously improved from the decrepit conditions that existed before the Port Authority took it over. Gambaccini was adept and persistent at obtaining resources for the money-losing transit system. He had to fight for operating and capital funding because Authority officials preferred investing its resources into profitable ventures, such as new parking garages at the airports.

The PATH system would never be able to break even. For example, in 1976, the PATH system lost $27 million while the airports had a profit of $69 million, and the tunnels and bridges earned $76 million.[5] Gambaccini argued that rather than looking at profits and losses, policy makers needed to look at the overall benefits of transit systems. Since transit conserved energy and environmental resources, offered a safer mode of travel than driving, and helped alleviate the isolation of residents, he said trains and buses were "more analogous to police and fire protection, vital public services that have to be sustained substantially from the public treasuries."[6]

The Port Authority's culture suited Gambaccini's entrepreneurial spirit. Linda Spock, his one-time executive assistant, said he was "like Pigpen from Charlie Brown. Instead of dirt, he was surrounded by all these ideas."[7] The Authority allowed Gambaccini to pursue many of his creative initiatives, even at the risk of failure. Thanks to Gambaccini, today's commuters across the country are less likely to get stuck in traffic and more likely to use public transportation. Jerry Premo, a transportation industry executive, said, "Lou was a lion in the world of public service. Where others were cautious and too often accepting of the average, Lou aspired to and expected excellence in service to the public, both for himself and for those who worked under his leadership. His legacy is wide and deep."[8]

A Focus on Coordination

One of Gambaccini's ideas in the late 1970s was to centralize information about the metropolitan area's trains and buses. Before the Internet, travelers had much more difficulty figuring out how to get from one place to another via public transportation. The extensive transit network in the New York metropolitan area could be overwhelming to those who were not familiar with its options. For example, northern New Jersey residents heading to Manhattan's Upper East Side could take a commuter railroad train to Hoboken, board a PATH train to the World Trade Center, and then take a subway uptown. They had a bewildering array of other options, including riding a bus to the Port Authority's Midtown bus terminal, and then taking one subway to the east side and another uptown.[9] Trying to figure out how all the transit services related to each other (and whether they could park their cars at a station near their homes) was no easy task because it involved sorting through a shoebox full of printed schedules and maps, and making numerous calls.

Gambaccini wanted residents and visitors to be able to call just one phone number to obtain schedule, fare, and status information about all the transit services.[10] At the time, transportation operators were receiving more than 20,000 phone calls a day from people seeking transit information.[11] Gambaccini reached out to the other transit agencies (including the Long Island Rail Road and the New York City Transit Authority), and he assigned one of his staff members, Robert Kelly, to determine the feasibility of setting up an office with agents who could provide callers with region-wide information.[12] Since no one had ever created such a system, Kelly collected information from a wide variety of sources. He learned how utility companies managed their electrical grids and he visited California to learn about their transit services. Kelly and Gambaccini were stymied in their efforts, though, because the transit operators and the transit unions resisted ceding their customer information responsibilities. The two men were not deterred from pursuing other efforts to improve regional coordination, however. They worked for an organization that, at the time, was willing to take risks in pursuit of potential opportunities. Kelly said the attitude at the Port Authority was, "If it would benefit the region and people, let's explore it."[13]

On Saint Patrick's Day in 1978, New Jersey's newly elected governor, Brendan Byrne, offered Gambaccini (widely known for his transit expertise) the position of state transportation commissioner, and the Port Authority gave him a leave of absence to lead New Jersey's transportation department.[14] While most commissioners had focused on the state's highways, Gambaccini recognized the urgency of fixing the state's transit crisis. New Jersey was the nation's most densely populated state and many of its residents relied upon trains and buses to access jobs in large cities (including Newark, Jersey City, New York, and Philadelphia). At the time, the state's rail facilities and buses were subject to frequent breakdowns because of decrepit and poorly maintained equipment. As commissioner, Gambaccini spearheaded the creation of New Jersey Transit, the nation's largest statewide public transit system, and he served as its first board chair. He also developed important partnerships. For instance, he formed and led the Northeast Corridor Commuter Rail Agencies Committee to address common railroad issues, coordinate efforts with Amtrak, and enhance New Jersey's influence on federal transportation policies.[15]

After Gambaccini returned to the Port Authority in 1981, he was responsible for all the Authority's bridges, tunnels, and transit facilities including

Fostering Regional Mobility through Enduring Partnerships

the PATH system. Matt Edelman, who worked closely with Gambaccini, said, "Lou realized that the Port Authority could not fulfill its regional mission without cooperation from other transportation agencies."[16] The Port Authority was well-positioned to lead regional efforts because it had a mission that transcended one state or city. Its officials had always been concerned about how its own facilities connected with other highways and rail lines in both states. Furthermore, the Authority had resources to embark on new initiatives thanks to its profitable airports, bridges, and tunnels.

Gambaccini's stint as transportation commissioner and head of New Jersey Transit helped him better understand the transportation problems in the New York City metropolitan area and ways to solve them.[17] He also gained valuable experience setting up new organizations and generating widespread support for his ideas. He saw the Port Authority differently after serving as transportation commissioner. The Authority attracted talented staff, and its training programs created one of the most highly regarded public sector management teams in the country, but the organization had a somewhat insular character that was resistant to change because many of its employees had never worked outside the Port Authority.[18] In the state capital, Gambaccini worked with a wide range of stakeholders, which gave him greater confidence and insight into the transportation problems facing the metropolitan area and his ability to overcome them.[19]

Transportation patterns in the New York metropolitan area were in the midst of dramatic changes while Gambaccini was on leave from the Port Authority. In 1978, New York City was just beginning to recover from the economic and social upheavals associated with the flight of its middle-class families to the suburbs. In the 1970s, the number of people living in the city fell by more than 800,000, which was more than the entire population of most American cities, including Boston, San Francisco, and Washington, D.C. Employment levels in New York City also plunged. When Gambaccini returned to the Port Authority, New York was beginning to prosper once again, and the Authority was experiencing rapid growth on its facilities. Between 1978 and 1983, the number of vehicles crossing the Hudson River into Manhattan increased 16 percent and the average wait to enter the Holland Tunnel at 9 a.m. on a weekday rose from fifteen minutes to thirty-seven minutes.[20]

Gambaccini was frustrated by the lack of coordination that he witnessed among the government agencies that were responsible for building, operating, and maintaining transportation facilities. Spock said, "He understood how important it was to get agencies to work together. He believed in breaking down barriers between agencies."[21] Gambaccini was concerned about two different types of coordination. The first related to capital improvements. He wanted transportation agencies to think about how they could address regional goals and not just focus on their own needs when they planned and designed their projects. The second related to the day-to-day operations of the transportation system; he wanted all the transportation and law enforcement agencies to communicate with each other so they could prevent and minimize severe traffic conditions.

In 1984, Gambaccini set up a multiagency Trans-Hudson Task Force to address the ongoing and anticipated growth in commuting from New Jersey to Manhattan. A champion of public transportation, he urged the task force members to identify ways to get more people out of their cars. He explained that if only 1 percent of commuters stopped driving into the city, the rush hour queues at the tunnels would go down to ten minutes.[22] Chapter 7 discusses how the task force and the Authority coordinated the planning of long-term capital projects such as a new Staten Island bridge and a passenger railroad tunnel. Gambaccini was anxious, however, to implement shorter term measures that could increase the region's transportation capacity.

Expanding Transit Modes: Reinvigorating the Ferry System

Gambaccini understood the importance of treating the region's transportation bus, rail, and motor vehicle facilities as one single network. Using tolls to subsidize transit use, he explained, reduces traffic on roadways and increases the network's efficiency. His staff referred to this as the "gospel according to Gambaccini."[23] Although Gambaccini advocated more transit use, he was concerned that the PATH system would not be able to accommodate many more riders. Between 1978 and 1983, the number of PATH passengers increased 33 percent, and during rush hour most passengers could not find an empty seat.[24] The Authority's planning department expected the number of passengers would continue to rise because more people were choosing to live in New Jersey and work in New York, and new residential development projects were planned near New Jersey's PATH stations. In addition, more women were entering the work force and they tended to use transit more than men.[25]

PATH had only three practical ways to increase capacity during peak periods. All of them would be costly and disruptive to commuters. Gambaccini expected the most expensive option—a new passenger rail tunnel between New Jersey and Manhattan—would take at least fifteen to twenty years to build (the region is still waiting for this long-promised tunnel).[26] The second option would be to upgrade the signal system that directed the movement of trains (PATH would eventually complete this project in 2018 at a cost of more than $500 million.)[27] The third option would be to increase the length of PATH trains from eight cars to ten (that project is still on the drawing boards).

Given the capacity constraints of the motor vehicle and rail crossings, Gambaccini saw only one feasible short-term option to accommodate more commuters. "The river," he declared, "cries out to be used."[28]

Ferries had once been the only way commuters and long-distance travelers could cross the Hudson River. In 1920, ferries carried 260,000 passengers and 12,000 vehicles a day across the river.[29] Ridership plummeted after the Port Authority built its bridges and tunnels, with the last of the ferry services ending in 1967.[30] In the 1980s, a maritime official said, "If you look at an old picture of the river, there are so many boats it looks like you could have walked across. Today, you could fire a cannon up the river and not hit anything."[31] The only commuter ferry service that survived in the metropolitan area was the one operated by the city of New York between Lower Manhattan and Staten Island.

Gambaccini thought the Port Authority could get new ferry services up and running in a relatively short time. If the ferries attracted enough riders, service could be expanded, and if the service failed to attract enough passengers, the Authority could cut its losses without spending hundreds of millions of dollars. In 1985, he put together an internal task force to conduct a feasibility study of ferry services. Although Gambaccini thought ferry services had great potential, he was not sure of the best way for the Authority to initiate them.[32]

One option would be for the Port Authority to build ferry facilities and then work with private operators to provide transportation services. That was the Authority's model for many of its other facilities. For instance, the Port Authority built bus stations and airports, but did not have its own bus company or airline. Under a second option, the Authority could operate its own ferries as it did with the PATH train. The Authority's experience with PATH, however, was a cause of concern among its staff. Even though PATH fares had increased from 30 cents in 1983 to 75 cents in 1984, the railroad's expenses still exceeded its income by more than $62 million in 1985.[33] The members of

Gambaccini's ferry task force worried that if the Authority operated its own ferries, then future New Jersey governors would insist on setting low fares and then resist increasing them, just as they had long done with the PATH.[34]

Gambaccini asked Martin Robins, the head of the Port Authority's planning department, to estimate the potential ridership for new ferry services. Based on Robins's analysis, Gambaccini decided the best route for a ferry service would be between Hoboken in New Jersey and Battery Park City in Lower Manhattan. One ferry terminal would be located next to New Jersey Transit's busy Hoboken train station and the other would be built within walking distance of the World Trade Center. This ferry route would serve the most customers and provide redundancy in case of a failure at the nearby Holland Tunnel and PATH train station. Since Robins was forecasting rapid growth in PATH ridership between Hoboken and the World Trade Center, he thought the ferry would allow the Port Authority to absorb additional growth without having to undertake very costly and complex rail expansion projects.[35]

Gambaccini overcame skepticism among many Port Authority staff members who thought the Authority should prioritize PATH improvements rather than invest in ferries.[36] The executive director, Stephen Berger, thought ferries would be expensive, impractical, and never attract enough people to relieve traffic or PATH congestion. He liked, respected, and trusted Gambaccini, though. Berger remembers thinking, "I could be wrong. If I'm right, we'll close the motherfucker down. It's not that big of an investment."[37] The board members were willing to encourage ferry operations even though it could potentially lower the Authority's revenues from bridge, tunnel, and PATH users. However, most of the board members had the same concerns as the task force members: they did not want the Authority to subsidize an ongoing money-losing operation. The board did agree, however, to set aside more than $100 million to build permanent ferry facilities in Manhattan and New Jersey, if the service proved successful.[38]

Task force members visited cities with thriving ferry services including San Francisco and Vancouver. Following the recommendations of the West Coast cities, the Authority decided it would obtain all the necessary government approvals and then have a private company build temporary ferry terminals and operate service. Cutting through the red tape to start ferry services was not an easy task, though. The Authority had to complete an environmental review, ensure historic structures would be protected, and address community resistance in Battery Park City.[39] The Authority also had to overcome opposition from New York officials who preferred other Lower Manhattan ferry sites.[40]

The Authority's attorneys determined that Congress would need to change an existing federal law so that a ferry facility could be built in Battery Park City. Paul Bea, the Authority's lobbyist in Washington, D.C., worked with the New Jersey and New York congressional delegations to incorporate language related to the ferry terminal into 1987 legislation. When the Port Authority realized that the new law incorrectly referred to the area "south" of Vesey Street rather than "north" of Vesey Street, the Authority had to go back to Congress the next year for an amendment.[41]

After issuing a request for proposals—Port Authority officials said they were looking for a "ferry godmother"[42]—the Authority awarded a contract to New York Waterways. Its owner, Arthur Imperatore, had started a modest ferry service between Weehawken, New Jersey, and Midtown Manhattan in 1986, as a way to increase the value of waterfront property that he had purchased. The Port Authority's Hoboken to Battery Park City ferry service began operating in 1989 and it spurred a ferry revival. In recent years, ferries have been carrying more than 35,000 passengers between New Jersey and Manhattan on a typical weekday.[43] The ferries have also taken pressure off the PATH system, which has been carrying more than 270,000 daily passengers,[44] 50 percent more passengers in recent years compared to 1985.[45] Ferries have also played a vital role during PATH shutdowns most notably after the September 11, 2001, terrorist attacks that destroyed the World Trade Center station, and in October 2012 when Hurricane Sandy caused such extensive damage that PATH service did not operate on a normal schedule until March of the following year.[46]

The ferries were an important accomplishment, but Gambaccini left an even greater mark when he brought together transportation and police agencies from across the region.

TRANSCOM

In the New York City area, traffic was, and still is, extremely sensitive to all sorts of "incidents," such as inclement weather, construction, accidents, breakdowns, and large events. These incidents can have domino effects across the entire transportation system. For instance, vehicles approaching closed or severely congested roadways can overwhelm local roads and create hazardous conditions. As a result, the response time slows down for emergency vehicles, crossing streets can become dangerous for pedestrians, and people shift from buses to already crowded trains. Problems that seem localized can oftentimes impact huge segments of the transportation network because the region's roads are frequently congested, cross thousands of communities, and connect to highways up and down the Northeast corridor.

In 1980, Port Authority officials created near gridlock conditions in Manhattan after they closed the George Washington Bridge because explosive gas was leaking from a truck carrying 9,000 gallons of propane. Highways and local streets near the Lincoln and Midtown tunnels were jammed on both sides of the Hudson River, and eight-mile backups were reported at the river crossing north of New York City. With traffic moving at a pace of ten minutes per block, drivers in Midtown Manhattan got out of their stalled cars to commiserate with each other and pick up snacks from street vendors. Because the city's traffic officers could not keep all the intersections clear of vehicles, a trip from the east side to the west side that usually took ten minutes turned into a two-hour crawl.[47]

When traffic incidents occurred in and around New York City, the transportation agencies and police departments did not have adequate procedures or systems in place to provide real-time information with each other, let alone to the city's drivers. The impacts of the bridge's shutdown and other incidents could have been mitigated if the agencies had shared accurate, relevant, and timely information. In the 1980s, transportation and law enforcements agencies had several tools they could use if they expected a surge in traffic. They could curtail ongoing construction at key points, as well as add more traffic officers and toll plaza staff. The transportation agencies could also change the timing on traffic signals and the messages on electronic signs to alert travelers of potential delays while they were far enough away to consider alternate routes or modes.

In 1984, Gambaccini oversaw PATH as well as the Port Authority's tunnels, bridges, and bus stations. His ability to improve their services relied upon numerous government agencies working together. For instance, the George Washington Bridge sat at the intersection of fifteen major roadways operated by six different jurisdictions.[48] Gambaccini was convinced that many traffic problems could be avoided if the agencies would simply talk to each other. While he was New Jersey's transportation commissioner, he saw how the agencies that controlled the Garden State Parkway and the New Jersey Turnpike failed to coordinate their construction schedules. Since both highways ran north-south along the entire state, many drivers could switch from one to another if they knew about a problem. However, the Parkway and Turnpike periodically undertook construction projects, simultaneously, along nearby parallel sections of their highways, which exacerbated the traffic impacts on both highways.[49]

Gambaccini was spurred to coordinate the agencies' efforts on a day he was "trapped in traffic that easily could have been avoided with proper knowledge, signage and information about detours."[50] As he sat in his car for three hours, he realized that the highway should have had a variable message sign warning people about traffic ahead.[51] One of his aides later explained that the goal of integrating agency information was to intercept people before they got "into the trap."[52]

Gambaccini's experience at both the New Jersey Department of Transportation and Port Authority gave him insight into better ways of managing incidents. On most of the region's highways, the transportation agencies did not work effectively with the state and local police departments to solve problems. While the transportation officials constructed and maintained roadways, the police responded to accidents, enforced motor vehicle laws, and assisted disabled motorists. A lack of coordination between law enforcement and transportation officials was less of an issue on the Port Authority's facilities because the Authority had its own police department that worked together as a team with the operational managers and emergency dispatchers, even using the same radio system to communicate with each other.[53] Gambaccini also appreciated the benefits of having people work together in one central location because PATH had built a new control center under his leadership.[54]

In 1984, Gambaccini contacted the heads of fifteen transportation-related agencies in New York, New Jersey, and Connecticut. He asked them to send a representative to a meeting to discuss how sharing information could help them solve some of the region's traffic woes. Gambaccini called his friends and acquaintances at the other agencies to encourage their participation. His longtime aide, Deborah Wathen Finn, said, "He knew everyone, and he could talk to anybody."[55]

At the 1984 meeting, Gambaccini talked about how the region's agencies should work together to prevent problems and improve coordination when unexpected incidents arose. He asked the other participants, "How can we let each other know what's going on and not wait until an hour after something happens?"[56] Marygrace Parker, who represented the New York State

Police was struck by Gambaccini's vision and passion. She said that Gambaccini envisioned something that did not exist at the time—integrated traffic management. Parker said, "Agencies with different responsibilities were not talking to each other. Police would control traffic at intersections, transit agencies would run buses, everyone did their own piece. Even nationally, there was no model of understanding traffic management from a multi-agency, multi-jurisdictional concept." The people Gambaccini invited to the meeting, she said, "created it."[57]

Parker remembers that everyone at the meeting responded politely to Gambaccini. "When you are sent by your executive, you don't say no to someone's ideas," she said. Parker reported back to her superiors that Gambaccini was an "amazing and forward thinker" who convinced her that "the lack of coordination was a puzzle that needed to be solved." But, she told her supervisors, "I don't understand how he could possibly do it."[58]

Gambaccini continued reaching out to other agency executives and they all agreed to send staff members to ongoing meetings at the World Trade Center. Not every agency was enthusiastic, at first. He recalled, "I was getting really stonewalled by the New Jersey Turnpike Authority, who didn't want to cooperate with our efforts." The Turnpike Authority, he said, "opposed everything that wasn't their creation." So Gambaccini reached out to a friend at Governor Thomas Kean's office, who had the governor personally intervene and tell Turnpike Authority officials that they needed to work with the other agencies.[59]

None of the transportation and law enforcement agencies wanted to be responsible for continuously updating all the other affected agencies as well as all the media outlets whenever unexpected incidents occurred. The agencies came to a consensus, over the course of several months, that the best way to share information was by creating a central hub. Instead of contacting every other agency, the agencies would make one call to a central location that would disseminate information.

Gambaccini provided the idealism and vision to create a coalition, and then the resources to launch its work. He offered to set up an operation center that would collect and share information. Gambaccini assigned Robert Kelly to help manage the interagency committee's efforts and set up the center. Even though Kelly had not been able to set up a regional transit information center, Gambaccini had a great deal of faith in him. The two men coined the name "Transportation Operations Coordinating Committee" (TRANSCOM) for the sixteen participating agencies.[60] Not surprisingly, TRANSCOM selected Gambaccini as the committee's first chair.

Fostering Regional Mobility through Enduring Partnerships

Fig. 5.1. TRANSCOM's operations center in the 1980s (the room appears distorted because of the fisheye lens).
(Photograph © TRANSCOM, reproduced by permission.)

Kelly and his two staff members visited the other agencies to learn how they collected and used traffic and transit data. Kelly's team also asked the agencies what types of information could help them perform their jobs better. Kelly then took some unused Port Authority office space in Jersey City and turned it into an operations center where traffic agents collected information from a wide variety of sources including phone, radios, fax machines, computers, and closed-circuit video feeds (fig. 5.1). The agents monitored road conditions and shared information about the severity of incidents, such as how many lanes were closed and how long until they could be reopened.

Kelly's team figured out how the operations center could distribute information to TRANSCOM's members, affiliated agencies, and the media using the latest 1980s technology. Agents typed messages about incidents, up to twenty characters long, that were sent to pocket-sized pagers. One of the team's earliest tasks was developing a set of protocols to provide each agency with the appropriate amount of information. They wanted to provide as much detail as possible without bombarding agencies with data irrelevant to their needs.

In 1986, the agencies signed a formal agreement delineating TRANSCOM's responsibilities and financial agreements. The agencies agreed to share information, meet regularly to coordinate their construction activities, and help pay for the operation center's expenses by either writing a check or sending a staff member to work at the center. Ever since, federal highway officials have held up TRANSCOM as a model of regional cooperation.[61]

TRANSCOM's biggest challenge was convincing the transportation agencies to give up some of their autonomy. They were accustomed to operating independently when it came to sharing information about incidents and determining construction schedules. They had to implement new reporting procedures and consider the regional impacts of their construction plans, which meant possibly delaying projects, paying penalties to contractors, and even risk forfeiting grant money to avoid parallel roadway closings.[62]

TRANSCOM succeeded in four important areas. First, sharing information helped agencies respond to incidents faster and more effectively. Second, the public was privy to more accurate information on electronic signs as well as from radio and TV stations. Third, the agencies met regularly to coordinate their construction schedules, which helped minimize region-wide traffic impacts and avoid simultaneous construction work on parallel roads. Fourth, TRANSCOM's annual meetings of the agency's top officials led to even greater cooperation and better working relationships among the agencies.

Matt Edelman, who served as TRANSCOM's executive director between 1987 and 2015, expanded TRANSCOM's responsibilities, geographical reach, and technological capabilities. He worked with the agencies to create "off-the-shelf plans" they could jointly implement in case a bridge was closing or a storm approaching.[63] Edelman and the Port Authority's lobbyist Paul Bea developed a close relationship with U.S. senator Frank Lautenberg's staff, which helped TRANSCOM obtain federal transportation grants. Since Lautenberg had owned a technology company and served on the Port Authority's board before his election to the U.S. Senate, he appreciated TRANSCOM's efforts to use technology to solve regional transportation problems.

TRANSCOM transformed the region's transportation system even though it was only a small unit within the Port Authority that had no operational jurisdiction of its own. A key feature of the organization was its independence from the Authority and its governing structure. All of TRANSCOM's policy decisions had to be approved unanimously by the coalition's sixteen-member agencies. Decisions could be difficult to make, but its voting system ensured that agencies supported those decisions. Tom Batz, TRANSCOM's longtime deputy executive director, noted that the coalition has thrived and stayed together because one transportation agency's success depends on the services of other agencies. He said, "what's good for the region is good for the agencies and vice versa."[64] Ken Philmus, a former Port Authority executive, said, "When I had a major incident, turning it over to TRANSCOM for the media and public was a godsend. Particularly in a region with so many agencies, TRANSCOM is essential. I don't know what we would have done without it."[65]

In 1995, when George Marlin became executive director, TRANSCOM's days at the Port Authority were numbered. As discussed in the following chapter, Marlin wanted to slash the Authority's work force and TRANSCOM did not meet his definition of a transportation service that was core to the Authority's mission. Convinced that it played an important role, he agreed to keep TRANSCOM intact, but to spin it off.[66] The TRANSCOM staff and its members recreated themselves into a nonprofit organization, but it was a time-consuming process that diverted their energies. The nonprofit also found it harder to recruit staff when it was on its own. For most people, working at a nonprofit focusing on traffic operations was not nearly as appealing as starting a career at the Port Authority, an agency with myriad responsibilities and opportunities. Because the other agencies shared the cost of TRANSCOM's direct and overhead expenses, the only real benefit to the Port Authority was reporting a lower headcount.[67]

In 2001, Marygrace Parker became a program coordinator at the I-95 Corridor Coalition. This organization took TRANSCOM's model of regional coordination and scaled it up to cover traffic and transit conditions from Maine to Virginia.[68] Now, when a major incident occurs on the George Washington Bridge, real-time information is relayed to electronic signs and online services so that drivers across the northeast United States can be alerted to problems. They can then make informed decisions about their travel plans and alternate routes, well before they reach the New York metropolitan area. Parker said that Gambaccini's vision and the Port Authority's willingness to commit its resources spurred a new way of managing traffic. "Bringing the agencies together," she said, "is not a Port Authority or TRANSCOM story, but a national story."[69]

In this case, Gambaccini and others developed a vision that got at the heart of one of the region's thorniest transportation challenges. However, cooperation was neither easy nor guaranteed. Its success relied on a combination of coalition-building, organizational design, and technical expertise that demonstrated the value of collaboration and, crucially, did so in a way that effectively managed risk for the individual partners. While new technologies have reduced the importance of the information dissemination aspects of TRANSCOM's mission, its function as a hub that coordinates transportation decisions—such as preparing for maintenance work, major events, and extreme weather—continues to generate dividends for its partners and keep the region moving. The Port Authority adopted this model of bringing together a wide coalition of actors to launch and then spin out initiatives in other contexts as well. In each case, the Authority built the coalitions to get things going by providing leadership, resources, and a safe space to experiment with new approaches and processes. Furthermore, the trust built between agencies through TRANSCOM fueled future interagency coordination.

TransitCenter

In 1984, as part of Gambaccini's Trans-Hudson Task Force, the Port Authority's planners conducted extensive research on travel patterns in the region. They found that 64 percent of commuters driving into Lower and Midtown Manhattan received some type of parking subsidy from their employers—most of the drivers were given a free parking spot that had an average value of $200 per month.[70] Under the federal tax code, employers could write off the parking space as a business expense while employees did not have to pay income tax on its value.

Port Authority officials and their colleagues at New York's Metropolitan Transportation Authority (MTA) wanted employers to provide a similar benefit to transit users. Using their congressional contacts, they convinced the Internal Revenue Service that if employers gave workers $15 worth of transit services, the value should be considered a "de minimis benefit." That meant employees would not have to pay income taxes on the $15 benefit, in the same way they did not get taxed on other items of small value such as using an office photocopying machine for personal use or attending a company-wide holiday party.[71]

When the Port Authority's Larry Filler learned about this de minimis provision, he suggested to his supervisor, Martin Robins, that the Authority educate employers about this benefit. Robins liked the idea and appointed Filler to head the planning department's employer liaison unit and its three-person staff.[72] The employer liaisons had been having some success promoting alternative work schedules to employers. In fact, the Authority had become one of the nation's leaders in organizing, promoting, and managing a staggered work hours program.[73] The Port Authority had begun this program as a way to ease peak hour traffic on its Hudson River crossings.

Filler had much more ambitious ideas for his group. He wanted all the region's transit operators to work together to promote the $15 transit benefit to employers. Coordinating efforts would be quite a challenge. Just finding the appropriate person to talk with at each of the transit agencies was difficult. The list of transit providers ranged from three dozen[74] relatively small private bus companies to the MTA, which was the nation's largest public transportation organization. Filler was in an ideal position to bring the transit agencies together, though. He worked at the Port Authority, which operated the PATH train and two bus stations, and he had numerous connections with staff at the region's other transit agencies. After helping Gambaccini establish New Jersey Transit in the late 1970s, Filler had directed a department at the MTA in the early 1980s.[75] This gave him both the professional network and the credibility to entice key people from different agencies to work together.

Filler invited transit operators to a meeting at the World Trade Center where he shared his concept of jointly promoting transit use and providing employers with $15 worth of transit benefits. At Filler's urging, the transit agencies agreed to set up a working group that would explore opportunities and determine the business community's interest. Filler realized it would be too cumbersome for employers to distribute all the various fare media that was used by the region's transit agencies. For example, subway riders purchased tokens and PATH riders used coins, while passengers on the commuter railroads purchased tickets for one-way, round-trip, and unlimited monthly rides. The railroad tickets were the most complex because the fares were based on the length of the trip and varied by time of day. Filler knew that a transit benefit initiative in San Francisco had failed because employers did not want to deal with numerous transit providers. Filler said, "The lesson was, if you don't have a simple way, it won't work."[76]

Filler suggested that the agencies provide employers with vouchers that could be exchanged for $15 worth of trips on any of their services. At a series of meetings, the agencies identified some administrative hurdles associated with this idea. They asked how could the vouchers be validated, who would track payments, and how would transit operators get reimbursed? The agencies identified some other constraints. For example, a voucher could not be much bigger than a dollar bill; otherwise, it would not fit into a ticket booth's cash drawer.[77] A transit agency's chief financial officer (who had a Wall Street background) suggested that the voucher be a negotiable financial instrument that transit operators could deposit, like a check, at banks.[78] Based on feedback from employers, the transit agencies decided that these vouchers should be issued in $15 denominations and made interchangeable, so that companies did not have to assign specific checks to each participating employee.

Filler suggested that the transit agencies form a center for the innovation of transit that would work together with the business community. He called it TransitCenter for short.[79] Not every transit agency was eager to participate in TransitCenter, though. Some of the smaller bus carriers were leery that the Port Authority would try to collect proprietary information or interfere with their operations. Over time, however, they all began to understand how Filler could help them attract more passengers without adding to their costs.[80]

TransitCenter needed a home. The MTA seemed to be the logical choice since it carried more riders than all the other transit operators in the region combined. Although Bob Kiley, the MTA's chair, was very supportive of TransitCenter's goals, he thought the MTA would be too bureaucratic to foster an organization that needed to be flexible and creative. Moreover, the MTA did not have sustained relationships and communications with business leaders. The Port Authority was in a very different position because it promoted world trade through its port and seaports, operated industrial parks, owned the nation's two tallest buildings, and worked with private bus companies at its bus stations.[81]

The other transit operators also thought the Port Authority was the logical place to serve as TransitCenter's home in part because the Authority was subject to less political interference than the region's other large transit agencies.[82] One other thing made the Port Authority the leading candidate, and it was not insignificant. When agency representatives came to the Port Authority for TransitCenter or TRANSCOM meetings, they all appreciated the free lunches that the Port Authority served its guests.[83]

Gambaccini was enthusiastic about TransitCenter's potential and how its goals complemented TRANSCOM's efforts. He convinced the Port Authority's executive director, Stephen Berger, to provide financial support for its efforts and house the program at the Port Authority.[84] Gambaccini set up TransitCenter in a similar way to TRANSCOM, as a Port Authority unit with its own board of directors. The Port Authority and MTA agreed to provide TransitCenter's initial funding,[85] and Kiley agreed to cochair TransitCenter's board along with the president of New York's Chamber of Commerce. The two cochairs gave the organization a high profile and credibility in both the public and private sectors.

Richard Oram, a consultant who worked in the Port Authority's planning department, helped Filler develop a voucher program. Oram had worked at the federal transit agency, and he suggested that Filler seek federal funds to help get the program started. Given his contacts in Washington, Oram was confident that he could help the Port Authority obtain a $75,000 federal grant.[86] Lou Gambaccini had even better contacts in Washington, D.C., though, and he set up an August 1986 meeting with Alfred DelliBovi, the federal transit agency's deputy administrator. DelliBovi instantly understood TransitCenter's potential. He had grown up in Queens and attended colleges in the Bronx and Manhattan. DelliBovi thought Gambaccini's proposal was an ideal candidate for a federal demonstration grant program.[87]

The transit agencies submitted an application for a grant that would be used for three components: setting up TransitCenter, jointly promoting transit services with the business community, and developing and marketing a new transit voucher. Thanks to Gambaccini, the Port Authority was not awarded $75,000 but rather a two-year grant for $1.5 million. The Port Authority then provided TransitCenter with office space as well as administrative services, such as legal and human resources.[88]

At an October 1987 event covered by numerous TV stations and newspapers, TransitCenter launched the voucher program with twenty-one companies participating.[89] New York City's mayor, Ed Koch, used one of the first vouchers (named TransitChek) at a 42nd Street subway station while DelliBovi looked on. By the end of 1987, 148 employers were participating.[90] The next year, more than 400 companies were giving $15 monthly TransitCheks to their employees, and DelliBovi pointed to TransitCenter as the only group in the United States that was aggressively selling the tax-free transit benefit to employers.[91]

The transit agencies and the Chamber of Commerce realized that a $15 transit benefit might not encourage many people to shift from their cars to transit. It was a rather negligible benefit compared to a free parking spot in Manhattan. That is why Filler and his team worked with the region's congressional delegation on federal legislation to raise the tax-free cap on transit vouchers. They argued that the tax code was favoring drivers over transit riders and they wanted to even the playing field. By the time TransitCheks were launched, New York's two U.S. senators had already sponsored a bill to increase the limit to $60.[92]

Fig. 5.2. A poster advertising TransitCenter's TransitCheks.
(Illustration © TransitCenter, reproduced by permission.)

One step at a time, sometimes unwittingly, Filler created a constituency and a national coalition that would lead to the expansion of the tax-free benefit program. Filler and the TransitCenter team provided technical assistance to transit operators in other cities who were interested in developing transit voucher programs. In 1990, Richard Oram, who had worked for Filler, formed his own private company that took TransitCenter's model and replicated it in San Francisco, Philadelphia, Boston, and Denver.[93] As TransitCenter expanded and other cities adopted Filler's model, more U.S. Congress members supported increasing the $15 monthly tax-free benefit.

On Capitol Hill, TransitCenter had support on both sides of the aisle. Democrats pointed to the unfair aspect of the tax code. An executive driving a luxury car did not pay a penny in taxes for a company-supplied parking space, but a secretary had to pay taxes on a benefit for a monthly bus pass that was worth more than $15. Republicans who might have been loath to increase funding to transit agencies supported a tax cut that would help increase transit use. After Gambaccini retired from the Port Authority he continued to promote expanding the benefit. In 1992, while he was head of Philadelphia's public transportation authority and chair of the American Public Transportation Association, Gambaccini testified to a congressional committee that raising the $15 cap would equalize the benefits between income groups, stimulate the economy, reduce oil imports, improve air quality, and reduce traffic congestion.[94]

In January 1993, a new federal law went into effect that raised the tax-deductible amount to $60 a month. "At $60, you're talking about real money," Filler said. "That's a month's free ride on the subway, or the bus, or the PATH train."[95] The legislation also capped the tax benefit for parking at $155.[96]

The new law accelerated TransitCenter's sales. In 1991, 379 new companies enrolled in TransitChek and in 1992 another 457 new firms enrolled. In 1993, a remarkable 1,579 new companies enrolled.[97] Congress spurred even more sales five years later, when it amended the tax code so that employees could have money deducted from their paychecks for transit services without having to pay taxes on it.

Under the direction of Larry Filler, TransitCenter did more than just sell TransitCheks. It also hosted forums about the transit system geared toward the business community. TransitCenter provided employers with relevant information about transit services and printed "The Manhattan Traveler," the only map that provided details about all the region's transit services (fig. 5.3).[98] By bringing the transit agencies together, TransitCenter identified synergies that led to improvements, such as enhancements to the underground concourse between the Port Authority's George Washington Bridge Bus Station and the MTA's subway.[99] Filler also worked with the Chamber of Commerce on a service that tied together TRANSCOM's data network with TransitCenter's network of employers. For $750 per year, businesses were notified about major transit and highway delays that could affect their employees. This service was especially valuable when winter storms were approaching and employers were not sure if and when they should send their employees home early. TransitCenter provided valuable information about the status of transportation services and when transit operators would begin running extra trains.[100]

In 1995, TransitCenter met the same fate as TRANSCOM when the Port Authority decided to slash headcount and eliminate functions that were not considered core to its mission. The two nonprofits had very divergent paths, though. While TRANSCOM has continued to rely on the transportation agencies to pay for its ongoing expenses, TransitCenter created a lucrative and growing revenue stream. In 2012, TransitCenter sold its assets and operations to an employee benefits company for approximately $58 million.[101] The proceeds transformed TransitCenter into a national research and transit advocacy organization.

E-ZPass

Within the Port Authority, Lou Gambaccini was known as a fanatical supporter of ferry services, and he promoted the concept across the agency from the planning department to the executive director's office and the Authori-

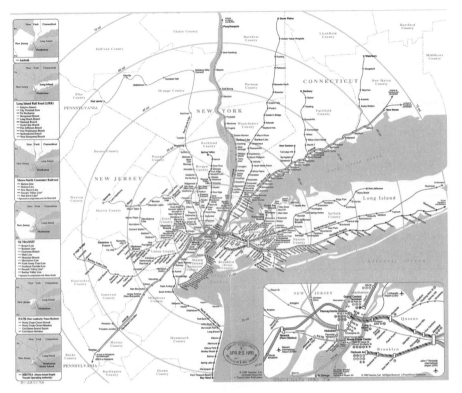

Fig. 5.3. TransitCenter's 1990 Manhattan traveler commuter rail map.
(Reproduced by permission of TransitCenter and the Library of Congress.)

ty's board of commissioners. TRANSCOM was also Lou Gambaccini's baby. He came up with the idea and nurtured it. Although TransitCenter was not Gambaccini's brainchild, he embraced it and obtained the support and funding that were needed to get it off the ground. Gambaccini never said, "let's create the world's largest electronic toll system," but his legacy inspired people inside and outside the Port Authority to do so.[102]

In 1971, the Port Authority began testing a new way of collecting tolls. Electronic tags were affixed to buses and communicated via radio frequency with readers installed at a Lincoln Tunnel toll booth. Mounting these tags on small vehicles was problematic because they were five times the size of modern electronic tags issued by transportation agencies.[103] The Authority would have to wait until the technology evolved and costs came down before they could be widely used.

Fostering Regional Mobility through Enduring Partnerships

In 1986, after Robert Kelly had successfully established TRANSCOM, Gambaccini assigned him the task of evaluating the feasibility of installing an electronic toll system on all the Authority's crossings. Kelly determined that collecting tolls electronically was not only feasible but offered widespread benefits. The Authority could reduce its considerable cost of collecting tolls, processing cash, and preventing employee theft. Drivers with tags would no longer have to fumble for change. He predicted, "the day of the electronic license plate is coming."[104] Because an electronic toll lane could handle more than three times as many vehicles as a typical toll lane, drivers would no longer have to endure toll booth backups that typically lasted thirty minutes at peak periods.[105] A *New York Times* reporter wrote, "the region may see some relief from the time-wasting, fuel-depleting, spirit-wilting toll-booth lines that are as dismal a part of motoring life in metropolitan New York as changing lanes without warning and honking at the car ahead when the light turns green."[106]

Initially, the Port Authority worked on its own, testing the technology and getting ready to select the one that best suited its needs. The first test was at the Lincoln Tunnel. In 1989, 1,500 buses from twenty-three different carriers used electronic tags at the toll booths on a typical weekday morning.[107] As testing was underway, Larry Yermack (the Triborough Bridge and Tunnel Authority's chief financial officer) suggested that his agency and the Port Authority coordinate their electronic toll efforts. The Port Authority and Yermack's agency (which operated seven bridges and two tunnels within New York City) collected more tolls than any other organization in the nation. Yermack was one of TRANSCOM's most enthusiastic supporters and he recognized the benefits of a regional electronic toll system. The Port Authority quickly agreed and Yermack started working closely with the Port Authority's Linda Spock, Gambaccini's former executive assistant. Spock had been inspired by Gambaccini's goals of leaving the world a better place and breaking down barriers between agencies.

The Port Authority decided to slow down its installation and potentially incur additional expenses so that its system would be compatible with other toll agencies in the region. The two agencies tested the same electronic tags, first at the Goethals Bridge and then at the Verrazzano-Narrows Bridge. Spock remembers, "this was an important first step in interagency cooperation."[108] Spock and her team slept during the day and drove back and forth through the toll booths at night to test the accuracy of the readers using different Authority vehicles.[109]

As a result of the two agencies' ongoing cooperation, the top officials at seven toll agencies in New York, New Jersey, and Pennsylvania decided to work together on electronic tolls. Most of them had gotten to know and trust each other through TRANSCOM's executive committee. The agency officials realized that drivers would be more likely to sign up for the electronic toll system if they could use the same tag at all the region's facilities. Moreover, the agencies were concerned that the radio frequencies from multiple tags could interfere with each other, and they knew the state motor vehicle departments were unlikely to allow car owners to place multiple tags on their windshields.[110]

Even though the Port Authority collected about twenty times as much toll revenue as the agency that operated the Atlantic City Expressway, the seven members of the Interagency Group agreed to follow the same procedures as TRANSCOM. Each agency would have one vote and all decisions would be made unanimously. Gambaccini was retired from the Port Authority by 1989, but his legacy lived on through Linda Spock and TRANSCOM. Spock remembers, "TRANSCOM was a really important milestone in showing that agencies could work together. The Interagency Group looked to TRANSCOM as a role model."[111] She realized that the seven agencies could create the world's largest electronic toll system that would collectively serve more than one-third of all toll traffic in the United States. The Port Authority dedicated resources to the Interagency Group with Spock chairing its policy and marketing committees and assigning her staff members to work with its three other committees.[112]

Spock helped resolve the most controversial issue, one that almost tore the group apart. Initially, the Port Authority planned on installing a technology that determined the toll whenever a vehicle passed through a toll booth area. This technology had been used in other areas of the country. However, three of the agencies (New Jersey Turnpike, Pennsylvania Turnpike, New York State Thruway) insisted on a different system. On their highways, drivers were charged based on the distance they traveled. These agencies wanted a system where tags would record both the entry and exit points on the highway and then calculate the distance traveled. The other agencies resisted, at first, because this technology was bound to add to the complexity, risk, and expense of the installation.[113] Even though the Port Authority's staff thought the simpler and proven technology could be adapted to meet everyone's needs, the Port Authority and all the other agencies agreed to implement the more complex and expensive system.

The Interagency Group overcame numerous legal hurdles. Port Authority lawyers helped draft bills in the two states that addressed privacy concerns and allowed the toll agencies to take pictures of license plates and assess violations against drivers using electronic toll lanes without tags.[114] The attorneys also helped figure out how each agency could purchase equipment that was compatible with the other agencies yet remain consistent with laws and regulations that required procuring equipment in an open and competitive manner.

The Interagency Group had numerous discussions about developing brand awareness and promoting the electronic tolls. In 1991, the group selected the name E-ZPass for the electronic toll system; the name is still a registered trademark owned by the Port Authority. Selecting the color for its logo was more complicated than expected. Federal guidelines specify the colors that can be used on highways. For example, black is used for regulatory signs, blue for tourist information, and yellow for warnings. Thanks to the Interagency Group, the color purple that is used in the E-ZPass logo became the standard color for electronic toll lanes across the country.[115]

Some of the tasks were extraordinarily complicated and required ongoing compromises and collaboration. For example, the toll agencies had to agree upon standards and procedures to test equipment on a wide range of vehicles. Since drivers paid different rates depending on a vehicle's type, the readers and associated cameras had to distinguish between cars, motorcycles, buses, cars pulling a trailer, trucks with two axles, trucks with four axles, and so on.[116] Equipment testing was an engineering, policy, and financial issue with each of the agencies having their own needs. For example, the Port Authority's toll lanes had heavier traffic with toll lanes closer to each other than some of the other facilities. When the E-ZPass Interagency Group tested manufacturer's equipment, they demanded at least 99.96 percent accuracy. The Port Authority had found the technology to be 99 percent accurate in the early 1970s, but this was not precise enough for all the Interagency Group members because the difference between 99 percent and 99.96 percent accuracy could be millions of dollars in lost revenue. In the final stages of testing, the Interagency Group tested the system's accuracy under a variety of conditions, such as a small car traveling on a rainy afternoon, a tractor-trailer carrying its cargo on a windy night, and a pickup truck pulling a boat on a foggy morning.[117]

Between 1993 and 1997, the three largest New York toll agencies (Port Authority, Triborough Bridge & Tunnel Authority, and Thruway Authority) installed E-ZPass readers at all of their toll booth areas. By the end of 1998, a remarkable 46 percent of vehicles on the Port Authority's facilities were using E-ZPass on weekdays.[118] By the end of 1999, E-ZPass had more than two million customers in the region. Most importantly for customers, many of the traffic queues at toll plazas that had averaged twenty to thirty minutes had been cut down to twenty seconds.[119] With the widespread use of E-ZPass, TRANSCOM's Matt Edelman initiated a project using the tags. E-ZPass readers were installed along hundreds of highway miles in the region to monitor traffic conditions. By measuring the times that vehicles passed from one reader to another, TRANSCOM's computers were able to calculate the speed of vehicles along these roadways and then share that data with the media and other transportation-related agencies.[120]

The E-ZPass Interagency Group, which started as an independent organization with seven member agencies in three states, now has more than three dozen members in nineteen states with about fifty million tags in circulation. Many of the original agency participants have remarked how they increasingly put the region's interests ahead of the individual and parochial interests of their own agencies. Larry Yermack noted, "I have often thought we should have been eligible for the Nobel Peace Prize."[121]

Advancing the Region's Interests Ahead of Its Own

This chapter demonstrates how resources, culture, autonomy, and leadership all contributed to the successful creation and nurturing of the TRANSCOM, TransitCenter, and E-ZPass coalitions. The Port Authority took a leading role because of its talented staff, reputation, transportation know-how, and financial resources. The Authority's culture encouraged innovation, and Gambaccini and his team were given leeway to make things happen. Clearly, Gambaccini's vision and his inclusive leadership style were critical to the success of the programs. As a young man, Gambaccini was attracted to the Authority's culture and he shaped it to encourage multiagency initiatives, promote public transportation, and emphasize public service.

The Port Authority implemented ferry services, TRANSCOM, TransitCenter, and E-ZPass in a manner that benefited the region, not necessarily to bolster its bottom line. For example, TRANSCOM encouraged drivers to use bridges north of New York City when the Port Authority's bridges and tunnels were severely congested. Likewise, TransitCenter encouraged commut-

Fostering Regional Mobility through Enduring Partnerships

ers to use New Jersey Transit trains rather than drive through the Authority's Lincoln and Holland tunnels. The private ferries lured both drivers and transit riders from Port Authority's facilities. The Authority also slowed down the deployment of electronic tolls and installed the more expensive E-ZPass technology to help achieve broader regional goals.

When the Port Authority set up TransitCenter, the Authority did not even directly benefit because the PATH stations did not have clerks who could accept vouchers (riders used coins or dollar bills at the turnstiles). Filler remembers, "It was very embarrassing. The home of TransitCenter was asking companies to give their employees TransitCheks, but they wouldn't be able to use them on PATH."[122] PATH's customers did benefit indirectly though, since most of them also used trains operated by New Jersey Transit or the MTA.[123] PATH trains did not begin accepting TransitCheks until 1993, three years after it introduced a magnetic fare card.[124]

E-ZPass, TRANSCOM, TransitCenter, and ferries symbolize Gambaccini's commitment to improving the region's transportation network. He brought people and institutions together to address congestion problems by leveraging the Port Authority's credibility and resources along with his own personal reputation. He hired and rewarded talented people such as Martin Robins, Linda Spock, Larry Filler, Robert Kelly, and Matt Edelman. Then he gave them all a great deal of autonomy.[125] Gambaccini's accomplishments are neither widely known nor appreciated. When Port Authority officials celebrated their organization's centennial in 2021, for obvious reasons they highlighted the bridges, tunnels, and bus stations they have built, operated, and improved. Those are the accomplishments that millions of New Yorkers see every day. Gambaccini's achievements, largely done behind the scenes, profoundly improved the flow of vehicles and people by building durable bridges between institutions, not between states. With relatively small budgets, he set up collaborative organizations that continue to make notable accomplishments and he inspired others to work together, such as the way that the TRANSCOM model led to E-ZPass. Thanks to Gambaccini, transportation officials are still coming to the New York area from around the world to learn about traffic management, transit vouchers, the world's largest compatible electronic toll system, and a regional ferry system.

The next chapter reveals a darker side of the Port Authority's history. There are no lessons about how to build successful coalitions or heroic characters like Lou Gambaccini. Beginning in the mid-1990s, power began to shift, from the Port Authority's headquarters at the World Trade Center to the governors' offices in the two state capitals (Albany and Trenton). As a result, political priorities, not regional needs and objective data, emerged as the fundamental building blocks for developing plans and making decisions. With diminished autonomy, a damaged culture, more constrained resources, and fewer entrepreneurial leaders, the Port Authority became an unfamiliar and unwelcome place to Gambaccini's admirers.

CHAPTER 6

Turning Point

A Strike at Autonomy and a Blow to the Culture

In the early 1990s, the Port Authority's reputation as an organization that resisted patronage and political influence was still intact. For the most part, it had relied on managerial expertise and rational planning to solve problems during its first seven decades. Its commissioners were considered to be independent minded[1] and most of its top officials were employees who had moved up through the ranks based on their performance and expertise. The Authority conducted original research, helped form coalitions, and promoted the region's economy.

That all changed within a few years. The Authority's senior executives became political appointees who focused on the short-term priorities of the two governors, while its board of commissioners increasingly became a rubber stamp for decisions made in Albany and Trenton. After the Authority slashed both its staff and portfolio, two fiefdoms began to form at its headquarters, with each faction reporting to a different governor. As a result of these changes, a clash between the two states threatened the viability of the region's seaports and the Authority itself. These events were a major turning point for the Authority and exposed the corrosive and lasting effects that can occur to an organization's culture and resources when its fate is controlled by others and its senior officials do not share a common vision. They also demonstrate how these internal dynamics can be intensely affected in a very short time by political climates and how the choice of organizational leadership can undermine decades of reputation and practice. While the Port Authority survived the interstate duels, it has been fundamentally changed, and the uneasy alliance between the two states became more apparent than ever. This chapter digs into this important and transformative era for the Port Authority, while chapter 9 situates how these and other institutional changes

143

have impacted the organization and its effectiveness at coalition-building during its hundred-year history.

An Unusual Selection

The transformation of the Port Authority's organization and mission began with the election of three moderate Republicans over incumbent Democrats and illustrates how the ideologies and personalities of elected officials can profoundly impact the trajectory of public authorities. In his 1993 race for New York City mayor, the former federal prosecutor, Rudy Giuliani, was seeking to become the first Republican to win a New York City mayoral race since the 1960s. Because the city was much more liberal than the rest of the country, if Giuliani wanted to win, he had to run on a platform that supported gay and abortion rights.[2] That left an opening for George Marlin, a Wall Street bond portfolio manager and right-wing ideologue, who campaigned to Giuliani's right as the Conservative Party candidate. Marlin never had a chance to defeat his two opponents, but he could siphon off enough votes from conservative voters to help the Democrat win the race. Marlin was a thorn in Giuliani's side, since he appealed to both cultural conservatives and those who supported slashing the size of the city's government. Nevertheless, on Election Day, Giuliani was able to defeat his challengers from both his left and right.

In 1993, Christine Todd Whitman was elected governor of New Jersey, and the next year she campaigned for her fellow Republican, George Pataki, in his underdog race for New York governor. But Mayor Giuliani did not offer his support for Pataki. Instead of campaigning for his fellow Republican, Giuliani questioned whether Pataki was indeed the best candidate. Two weeks before election day in 1994, Giuliani stunned the political world by endorsing the Democratic incumbent, Mario Cuomo, a slight that George Pataki never forgot.[3] After defeating Cuomo, the new governor used the Port Authority to retaliate for Giuliani's endorsement.

Less than a week after Pataki took office, former Port Authority chair, Richard Leone, presciently warned that the two Republican governors would pressure the Port Authority to cut staff and sell assets so they could fulfill their campaign promises to reduce taxes. Leone said, "The Port Authority may be the metropolitan area's last remaining public institution that can think

Turning Point—A Strike at Autonomy and a Blow to the Culture

and act beyond the next political campaign." He said the executive director's position "must not be treated as a juicy political plum," because someone is needed with "exceptional leadership" skills. Leone suggested the two governors should "let the board chairmanship rotate between the two states and institute a nonpartisan selection process to find the best available public servant" to serve as executive director.[4] Although Leone's recommendations fell on deaf ears, they are still relevant today.

While the Port Authority's commissioners officially voted for the board chair and executive director, the two governors continued the decades-long tradition of the New Jersey governor selecting the chair, and the New York governor choosing the executive director and the vice chair. Governor Pataki recommended George Marlin for the executive director position, a decision not well received at the Authority's headquarters or across the Hudson River. The position had always been filled by highly regarded public administrators, but Marlin had neither management nor public sector experience. He had never even managed a small staff. Marlin did have two things going for him, though. First, the state's Conservative Party leaders had helped the governor get elected and now he was paying them back by appointing one of their most prominent members, Second, Marlin's selection was a poke in the eye to the governor's arch-nemesis, Mayor Giuliani.[5]

Unwittingly, Pataki upset the delicate balance between New York and New Jersey. Whitman was annoyed that Pataki did not consult with the New Jersey governor's office before announcing his selection, as previous governors had done.[6] Whitman refused to support Pataki's choice, until Marlin met with her and the six New Jersey commissioners.[7] Henry Henderson, a commissioner who had been appointed by a previous New Jersey governor, did not think Marlin was prepared to take the executive director's position. He said, "I am certain that if we had prepared a written set of job qualifications, his background and our requirements would not match."[8]

Whitman insisted that the Port Authority bring in one or more deputy executive directors with strong financial and public management experience who could supplement Marlin's deficiencies.[9] Consequently, John Haley, a public transportation executive with close ties to the New Jersey Department of Transportation's commissioner, was hired as the deputy executive director, a newly created position.[10] The board eventually confirmed Marlin by a vote of 10 to 2, but it was the first time in the Authority's history that the vote to hire an executive director was not unanimous.[11]

Rudy Giuliani Poisons Public Opinion

Local governments in the metropolitan area do not have any appointees on the Port Authority's twelve-member board of commissioners nor any official role in the Authority's operations. Not only is the Authority exempt from local building regulations, it even deploys its own police force. Former New Jersey governor Thomas Kean once said, "Every mayor of New York has been frustrated by the Authority because so much of it is located in their city, and they can't do anything about it."[12] New York City mayors and other local officials take advantage of their lack of power, though, by using the Port Authority as a punching bag. The Authority is a convenient scapegoat for residents who complain about tolls, fares, traffic, and airport woes.

Mayors can ask governors to help them with Port Authority issues, but Mayor Giuliani had relatively little influence with the governor's office since he had crossed party lines to support Pataki's rival. Giuliani, however, wielded a powerful tool to influence public opinion and in turn the Port Authority's agenda. New York City mayors typically get more media attention than any other public official in the region, and Giuliani was particularly adept at using his bully pulpit. With his tenacious prosecutorial style, Giuliani poisoned public opinion against the Port Authority, which he felt was undermining the city's competitive advantages by investing more heavily in New Jersey. This made it difficult for Governor Pataki to develop a consensus with his New Jersey counterpart on the region's transportation and economic development issues.

Giuliani accused the Authority of siphoning money from New York City's profitable assets (the World Trade Center and its two airports) and using them to subsidize services that mostly served New Jersey residents (PATH train and the bus stations).[13] He said, "New Jersey gets most of the services and benefits, and New York pays most of the bills."[14] The mayor wanted to create a city-state airport authority that would take over the city's two airports and then issue bonds to improve them.[15] He falsely accused the Port Authority of "Machiavellian maneuvers" and "Hollywood accounting" to reduce the Authority's annual lease payments for the city's two airports.[16]

City agencies provided the brainpower that quantified the mayor's grievances. They supplemented his theatrics with hard data that the media and New York state officials promulgated. City officials showed how the subsidies for the PATH and the bus stations had been dramatically escalating; for example, the PATH's annual operating loss went from approximately $5 million in 1962 to $70 million in 1986 and then rose to a staggering $186 million in 1993.[17] City officials also claimed that over the previous fifteen years, the Authority's capital expenditure favored New Jersey by 52 percent to 48 percent. They argued that the disparity was even more pronounced on a per capita basis with the Authority spending $485 for each New York resident in the Port Authority's district compared to $856 for each New Jersey resident.[18]

According to the Giuliani administration, New Jersey was able to upgrade its transportation system, keep its taxes low, and lure away New York's businesses because it was stealing money from New York. Meanwhile, New Yorkers were stuck with an ancient subway system and crumbling highways.[19] The city's planning department noted that Newark Airport had a new terminal with a monorail that was slated to connect with the regional rail network, while the Port Authority had studied building a train line to Kennedy and LaGuardia airports "for 25 years with nothing to show for it."[20] The mayor hired high-powered financial consultants, Rothschild Inc., who claimed the Port Authority had "grown into a vast high-cost bureaucracy of humble achievement" whose "monumental inefficiencies, excessive costs and built-in inequities" contributed to the city's economic problems. Rothschild asserted that "instead of improving the region's competitive position, the Port Authority has merely helped New Jersey to compete against New York."[21]

Few New York City politicians ever support increasing transit fares. However, in 1995, even some of the mayor's most liberal critics endorsed his call to raise the PATH fare. Supporting an increase was politically safe, since most PATH riders lived and voted in New Jersey. Moreover, they had an average household income of $70,000 compared to $36,000 for city residents. Mark Green, a Democrat who had been elected to serve as the city's public advocate, said it was very unlikely that raising the $1.00 fare on the PATH to match the subway's $1.50 fare would do much to harm PATH's riders economically or shift them onto congested highways.[22]

Giuliani's constant drumbeat about the Port Authority became the new conventional wisdom. *New York* magazine wrote, "Giuliani is the first public official in memory to take on an organization that has set breathtaking standards for incompetence and waste."[23] Likewise, a *Daily News* editorial lauded the mayor for fighting to "topple the big-spending authorities that serve themselves rather than New Yorkers, especially the Port Authority."[24] The *New York Times* called for raising the PATH fare from $1.00 to $1.50 and reducing the subsidies for buses coming into the bus stations.[25]

While the city's politicians and newspapers criticized the Port Authority, they neglected to report how New Jersey's commuters were providing tremendous benefits to the city by paying New York income taxes, and spending money in the city's shops, restaurants, and theaters. In addition, the PATH service helped New York by encouraging more firms to locate in Manhattan, which enhanced real estate values and the city's property tax revenue.

Sometimes Giuliani's rhetoric backfired. Governor Whitman withheld her support for spending billions of dollars on improvements to Kennedy and LaGuardia until it was clear whether the mayor was serious about breaking the city's lease with the Port Authority and bringing in a private management company to operate the airports.[26] Governor Whitman said, "It would make no sense for the Port Authority to make any new investments in the New York airports until their future is determined."[27] The mayor's threats also made it harder to move ahead with planned airport improvements because the uncertainty made it nearly impossible to issue long-term bonds.[28]

Marlin Slashes Staff

A few weeks after Pataki was elected in 1994, Stanley Brezenoff, the Authority's outgoing executive director, said that with a projected budget deficit of $100 million, he did not see any way to avoid raising the tolls and/or the PATH fare.[29] He thought he was doing the Port Authority and his successor a favor by preparing the public for an increase.[30] However, when Marlin was appointed in 1995, he had no intention of raising tolls or fares.[31] Marlin and Pataki wanted to downsize the Authority, and Whitman gave her support.[32] With the board's approval, Marlin imposed a hiring freeze, and cut travel and meal expenses for its employees.[33] The chair, Lew Eisenberg, noted that by holding tolls and the PATH fare steady, "It should now be clear it's the two governors who make these decisions, not the mayor."[34]

Bringing Marlin in to lead the Port Authority was like hiring a former coal plant manager to head the Environmental Protection Agency or a former mining company official to lead the U.S. Interior Department. Marlin was openly suspicious of the staff and his public views about the role of government were antithetical to the organization's mission. Under Marlin's direction, the Port Authority sold parts of its industrial parks and its twenty-two-story hotel at the World Trade Center. It also hired a financial firm to evaluate selling the entire World Trade Center site.[35] From Marlin's perspective, the Authority was "rooting out waste and eliminating the duplication of services and programs." He wanted to free resources for transportation and other core businesses by "stripping away excess layers of management staff and support functions."[36]

Marlin set up an early retirement program, inducing about 300 of its 9,100 workers to retire early.[37] With rumors about layoffs spreading, he encouraged people to retire who otherwise would not have.[38] Many of them, demoralized and disillusioned, left for more lucrative positions in the private industry.[39] The board gave Marlin a great deal of flexibility in deciding whose positions would be eliminated, even changing policies so that performance appraisals and seniority no longer had to be used in determining termination of employment.[40] After hiring the consulting firm, Deloitte & Touche, to help him identify staffing needs, Marlin instituted two rounds of layoffs in 1995, something that had never happened in the first seventy-four years of the Port Authority's history.[41]

Over the course of several months in 1995, one-quarter of the Authority's senior officials left.[42] The board then approved a 1996 budget with the first decrease in operating expenses since World War II. Marlin took steps to reduce the number of Port Authority lawyers, engineers, and maintenance staff and enter into contracts with private companies to provide these services instead.[43] By the end of 1996, Marlin had taken credit for cutting in excess of 1,000 jobs, which was more than 10 percent of the workforce.[44] The agency, which had long recruited top college graduates and provided them with extensive management and executive training programs, would never be the same.

Port Authority staff widely saw the cuts as arbitrary and Marlin's deputies, especially Haley, were widely seen as vindictive and mean-spirited. Paul Bea, manager of the Port Authority's office in Washington, referred to this period as a "nuclear winter." Alice Herman, a longtime senior Authority official, worked directly with board members and the two governors' offices. She saw Marlin's appointment as a turning point for the Port Authority because it was the first time an "overtly political" figure had been hired as an executive director, rather than a leading figure in the public sector who was familiar with the Port Authority's work. Before Marlin and Haley, she said, senior staff members were never considered to be aligned with one of the states. During this period, Herman noticed how the board members also started to take their lead from Trenton and Albany in a way they had never done before.[45]

Richard Kelly had a similar perspective. He said, "This was the moment it falls apart." Kelly was responsible for the Authority's vehicular crossings, bus stations, and the PATH. He was more than familiar with the Port Authority's history of encouraging professional development and promoting high achievers, since he had started his career in the Authority's mailroom. During his thirty-nine years at the Authority, Kelly had met countless people from around the world who came to New York to study the organization's structure, accomplishments, and procedures. After devoting his career to serving and strengthening the Port Authority, when Kelly saw Marlin tear it apart, he decided to take the retirement package.[46]

Kelly said Marlin did not care about the Authority's history and culture, which created tremendous resentment because the vast number of employees felt a visceral commitment to the organization. Marlin hired people, according to Kelly, who "didn't know anything or care about anything." He said Marlin became widely despised because he cut positions with little analysis or understanding of departmental functions. Kelly remembered, "Marlin would come in and say, 'You need to fire 10 people on Friday.' It was so counter to our culture."[47] No one at the Port Authority would claim that every employee was productive and the organization operated as efficiently as possible. The problem was that Marlin and Haley's cuts were rushed and haphazard. One senior official said, their cuts were "counter to good business sense. They didn't figure out how many people they really needed."[48]

Lillian Borrone, who headed the Port Authority's port commerce department, explained that before Marlin came in, the Authority's philosophy was to hire the best and brightest young people, pay them well, and provide them with continuous learning. She said, "Staff were encouraged to engage with the community and industries that we served. Austin Tobin believed that the more engaged we were, the more we could influence what was important to the region and community. We could also influence legislation, regulations, and business strategy. If you're engaged, they respect you. We pursued that strategy."[49]

Borrone had been credited with bringing businesses, labor, and governmental agencies to work together on common port issues.[50] She lamented that Marlin and Haley "wanted me to cut out engaging with the industry" and "they didn't understand what the business was about."[51] Furthermore, she said, "They cut a lot of mid-level staff who were being groomed to higher level positions. They knocked off that level of talent so they could control who would later take over and bring in their own people." Borrone had to go behind their backs to meet with people even within the Authority. When Marlin banned his line directors from meeting with each other, unless he or Haley were present, Borrone started convening meetings at restaurants so the senior staff could feed each other information about what was happening within the organization.[52]

When we talked to Marlin and Haley more than two decades after they left the Port Authority, they were proud of their accomplishments and dismissive of their critics. Marlin said "it was a lie that scientific principles guided the Port Authority" before their tenure. Pointing to certain departments such as governmental affairs, he claimed, "they were a political dumping ground."[53] Marlin might have understood New York's politics, but he did not seem to appreciate the distinction between a political appointee and someone with political experience. For example, Sidney Frigand was the press secretary for a New York City mayor before heading the Port Authority's government affairs office. Appointees with this type of political experience were appreciated for their useful experience and valuable contacts. When they joined the Port Authority, their first loyalty was to the organization, not to their political benefactors. Starting in the mid-1990s, however, many of the appointees who were hired because of their political connections were taking their orders from someone outside Port Authority headquarters.

Marlin recognized that he was deeply unpopular both inside and outside the Port Authority. He blamed his very outspoken prolife position for creating enemies in the media and his willingness to "upset the apple cart" for creating enemies within the bureaucracy.[54] When we asked Haley about whether the Authority experienced a "brain drain," he responded, "when we looked at the organization, there were people at the top who had been at the Port Authority for 25 to 30 years. At some point, my own belief, you need to roll people over. Even the best people get complacent and can't keep up with circumstances and technology."[55]

One hard-hit department was the Office of Economic and Policy Analysis, which lost about half of its seventy-member staff due to layoffs and retirements.[56] This department regularly brought together experts to assess the economic health and prospects of the New York metropolitan area. For example, the economists issued a 1994 report, based on interviews with hundreds of experts, that examined how industry trends might require the Authority to deepen the harbor, lengthen its airport runways, and widen bus terminal lanes.[57] In the early 1990s, the department had issued reports on regional demographic trends, the economic importance of tourism, trends in manufacturing, and implications of an international trade agreement on the region's economy.

Marlin's predecessor, Stanley Brezenoff, a seasoned public administrator, thought the Port Authority did not have the budget discipline that comes from a direct tie to taxpayers and a legislative budget process. He addressed some of the Port Authority's most egregious expenses such as closing the executive dining room, where senior officials were served subsidized meals by uniformed waiters. Brezenoff also put two helicopters up for sale and closed the Authority's trade office in Zurich.[58] Nevertheless, he appreciated how his economists and policy analysts provided the Authority with credibility and stature not only in the region but across the country. They helped him make more informed decisions, served as an instrument for public dialogue, and generated political support for his important priorities such as dredging the harbor to accommodate larger ships. Brezenoff said their work "wasn't that damned expensive" and with "no disrespect to the state department of transportations, we got greeted differently."[59]

Arguably the Port Authority did not need to conduct all the studies that it did, but no government agency would ever replace its ongoing efforts because the Authority had economic, surveying, and analytical skills, as well as resources that no other institution possessed.[60] Rosemary Scanlon, the Authority's chief economist in the 1980s and early 1990s, saw a direct link between the Authority's reports and regional economic benefits. For example, the Authority issued a report in 1983 that calculated the benefits of art and cultural institutions to the region's economy. As part of its analysis, the Authority calculated a wide range of benefits—such as tourists' spending on Broadway shows and hotels, and ballet companies' expenditures on lights and dance shoes manufactured in New Jersey. The recognition that arts and cultural activities were pumping more than $5 billion a year into the economy led city and state officials to revise their tax and spending policies to encourage even more of these activities. The Authority's report received attention across the globe because it was the first time that anyone had ever done this kind of analysis.[61]

The Authority also conducted research and convened conferences about specific industries and important public issues. For instance, it hosted a conference in 1987 to look at the early research on global warming and rising sea levels. Authority officials also brought together researchers, academics, and industry leaders that spurred the growth of the region's biotechnology sector. In addition, market researchers in the Office of Economic and Policy Analysis assessed how well the Authority's ports, trains, airports, bridges, and tunnels performed. The Authority's executives had long considered this research to be a critical function in understanding who their customers and potential customers were, how individuals made decisions about travel and shipping, and how they perceived the Authority's facilities and services. The Authority used this information to help assess its progress, allocate resources, hone marketing efforts, and prioritize projects. Likewise, the Authority used forecasts of future travel patterns developed by its planners to set priorities for the use of its resources. Marlin's cuts reduced the Port Authority's capacity to engage in these kinds of analytical and visioning exercises with important long-term consequences for its reputation as an innovative organization, and its ability to mobilize the metropolis.

Marlin took great pride downsizing the bureaucracy and eliminating departments and layers of management that he considered unnecessary. He also tried to privatize as much of the airport operations as he could. His major accomplishment in that realm was turning over management of Kennedy Airport's International Arrivals Building to a private firm. Marlin said he succeeded even though Port Authority employees were contacting local elected officials, spreading misinformation, and fighting his initiative "tooth and nail."[62] A 2012 report sponsored by the Federal Aviation Administration vindicated Marlin's decision, noting "the ability to operate outside of Port Authority procurement procedures, employment pay scales and contracts, and political influence allowed the private firm in many cases to obtain more advantageous contractual terms than could have been obtained by the Port Authority." The private firm, the report noted, "had a strong incentive to maximize passenger throughput, run a tight ship and sweat the asset, as it would retain any excess revenues and operational savings."[63]

Marlin faced minimal outside political resistance to cutting managerial positions, getting rid of the Port Authority's library, and slashing the number of positions in administrative departments.[64] But he met roadblocks in other avenues. He had to stay away from cutting union positions because Kathy Donovan, the chair, was concerned that it would hurt her political ambitions. Likewise, Governor Whitman's office did not want to upset PATH workers because she was afraid that one of the PATH's unions might go on strike.[65] Marlin wanted to sell the Port Authority's twenty-story Newark Legal Center building, but Trenton rejected that idea. He floated a proposal to sell its Staten Island Teleport business park, but he remembers that Staten Island's Republican leaders "killed it in five minutes." Marlin wanted to eliminate the subsidies for barges that carried cargo between New Jersey and Brooklyn, but Pataki's office told him to "forget about it" because the company had influential friends.[66] Since the governors have veto power over the Authority's minutes, Marlin argues, "they make everything political. At the end of day, they control the Port Authority. Decisions are based on whims of the day and politics of the day."[67]

One senior Authority official blamed Marlin's personality for limiting his effectiveness: "He wore out his welcome quickly. If he listened to people who had skills, maybe he could have gotten stuff done." If Marlin had developed better relationships and garnered more respect outside the Authority, the official said, "the Teleport and Legal Center could have been figured out."[68] By the end of 1996, Governor Pataki could not get rid of Marlin fast enough. The governor's senior aides, as well as the Conservative Party chair who had pushed for Marlin's appointment in the first place, had heard enough about Marlin's incompetence and lack of tactfulness.[69] Reports by the Port Authority police that Marlin allegedly used Authority resources for personal reasons were the final straw. In the words of one Pataki loyalist, "the staff had circled the wagons."[70]

Pataki Suggests Breaking Up the Port Authority

In early 1997, Pataki appointed his neighbor and friend, Robert Boyle, as Marlin's replacement. A former construction company executive, Boyle was president of New York City's convention center during Pataki's first two years as governor where he was widely praised for cleaning up corrupt practices. After Boyle was appointed, he made it clear that he would always be linked to his roots in the Pataki administration[71]

Peter Goldmark, the Port Authority's executive director between 1977 and 1985, was surprised when we told him that Boyle felt, first and foremost, that his loyalty was to Governor Pataki. Even though Goldmark had once been the New York governor's budget director, he said his "first loyalty was to the board of commissioners and the Authority." Goldmark noted, "It was hopeless to act on one governor's behalf." He remembered turning down numerous requests from the governors, including being asked to hire one of their daughters. When Governor Brendan Byrne wanted Goldmark to fire a senior official, he said to the governor, "You can tell me you don't like my direction, but if you want me to fire someone you have to get my badge on my way out the door."[72]

Even after Marlin's budget cuts and Boyle's appointment, Giuliani and the

New York media continued to lambaste the Port Authority for favoring New Jersey over New York. Boyle thought the mayor "bordered on being a little crazy sometimes." The executive director recalled that the mayor "wanted so much for the airports. He was a real pain in my side."[73] Mimicking the mayor's language, Governor Pataki accused the Authority of misusing public dollars and he asked Boyle to get back to him within a year on whether the Port Authority should be restructured to make it more efficient or broken up and replaced with a new entity. Pataki said, "In my mind, it is still an open question whether the Port Authority is salvageable. I think it's operated very fairly for the people of New Jersey but not for the people of New York."[74] Pataki suggested that each state should take over the facilities on its own land.[75] That suggestion certainly favored New York since the World Trade Center site and the air rights on top of the Midtown Manhattan Bus Terminal were worth billions of dollars.

Boyle remembers that Pataki and his top aides "thought the Port Authority staff were idiots and dopes, and that they had too many employees." Boyle quickly saw how Marlin had arbitrarily cut staff and damaged morale, noting, "It didn't take me more than two weeks to learn that most of them were smarter than me. I needed to put it back together so people would have confidence in me." He also decided that breaking up the Authority was in neither state's best interest.[76] Even if the two states could have agreed on how to separate the ownership and operations of the bridges, tunnels, and rail lines that crossed the two states, trying to allocate resources between New York and New Jersey would have been much more complicated than a divorcing couple trying to divvy up their assets.

The two sides repeatedly argued about who was benefiting more from the Port Authority's operations and investments. The answer depended on which time frame was considered, who a facility served, and whether both capital and operating expenses were included.

Charles Gargano, the Port Authority's vice chair, reiterated Giuliani's arguments that profits from the World Trade Center and airports were being siphoned off to help New Jersey.[77] New York's commissioners also repeated the mayor's complaints about the high level of subsidies for the bus stations and the PATH train. In response, Port Authority officials explained how the bridges, tunnels, buses, and rail worked together as a network.[78] The Port Authority had taken over the Hudson & Manhattan Railroad and created the PATH system for the same reason that the two states had taken over private railroads, subways, and bus lines: because no private company could run these transit services profitably.

Pataki's interests were simply not aligned with the Port Authority's goals. Although Governor Pataki was a strong supporter for improving transit services that served New York's suburbs, he had no interest in funding bus and train services for New Jersey residents. Understandably, he preferred spending taxes and tolls on projects that would benefit people who might vote for him when he ran for reelection in 1998. No one living in New Jersey was going to see George Pataki's name on the ballot.

The Port Authority did not effectively defend itself against charges that it was biased against New York because staff at its media and research department had been laid off, and its executive director was a New York political appointee. John Haley, the Authority's deputy executive director who had been selected by Governor Whitman, remembered that "every time we came up with a number, someone would say it didn't include everything or the numbers were wrong, or you didn't include operating costs."[79]

Governor Pataki's team also pointed to past inequities that had been identified by city officials. But these complaints about historical spending patterns were counterproductive, according to former New Jersey governor Thomas Kean. He said, "If you start arguing past numbers, who got more 10 years ago or 20 years ago, it only causes further disagreement."[80] Governor Pataki's predecessor saw a flaw in the way Giuliani and Pataki were looking at the Authority. Mario Cuomo said, "This bistate agency was set up as if the two states are equal, and it treats them as equal when we all know that New York is bigger, more powerful and has more of everything than New Jersey does. It's lopsided, and a totally unnatural situation in which it is tempting for New York to insist they should get more. But you just have to put that out of your head."[81]

New Jersey's former governor, Jim Florio, said, "There are some things that can be done in a rational way for both states that can't really be quantified for each."[82] Likewise, former New Jersey governor Brendan Byrne asserted, "Once we started with 'yours' and 'mine,' it became like my grandchildren with toys." He added, "The mentality now is we want to turn the Statue of Liberty around so it faces New Jersey half the time because we are tired of seeing her rear end in Jersey City."[83] By the end of 1997, Pataki talked less about breaking up the Port Authority after Boyle had come to appreciate the quality of the Authority's staff and the importance of its mission to the region.[84] But the governor remained convinced that New York was getting shortchanged.

Interstate Conflict Comes to a Head

While George Pataki was making a fuss about the Port Authority's bias toward New Jersey, Christine Todd Whitman was worried about the marine terminals in Newark and Elizabeth.[85] As discussed in chapter 4, when Whitman was sworn in as governor, major dredging projects in the harbor had been suspended because the dredged material was not clean enough to dump into the Atlantic Ocean. Governor Whitman had campaigned on a promise to stop ocean dumping, but she had come to realize that the other options were not practical. To satisfy the needs of the maritime industry, the demands of the environmentalists, and the priorities of fishing and tourism industry—Whitman did what many governors do when facing difficult choices—she set up a task force.

The Port Authority's port director, Lillian Borrone, was a key player on the task force because she was highly regarded by shipping-related firms as well as by Governor Whitman.[86] Borrone warned the other task force members that New Jersey was losing business to other East Coast ports because the harbor was not deep enough to accommodate larger ships. She was armed with valuable data produced by the Authority's Office of Economic and Policy Analysis. The analysis, prepared just before Marlin decided that his economists were superfluous, showed the economic impact the port industry had in the region.

Outside the task force, the New Jersey Chamber of Commerce took the lead obtaining congressional support for solving the ocean dumping problem and securing federal funds to dredge the harbor. The chamber brought together a wide range of groups (including the Port Authority) whose livelihood depended upon the port. Joan Verplanck, the chamber's president, said "keeping everyone on the same page was like a dance." She made sure that her members expressed their sensitivity to environmental issues when discussing the port's economic importance. "One loose cannon," Verplanck said, "would have set us back months." The chamber had extensive ties with all the state and federal legislators. But no one on the team knew the halls of Congress better than Paul Bea, the Port Authority's longtime Washington, D.C, lobbyist, who helped the team set up meetings with key congressional members and their staffs.[87]

Industry groups, unions, local government officials, and the Port Authority all lobbied elected officials about the need to dredge the harbor. Manufacturing firms were worried the dredging slowdown would eventually increase their cost of raw materials. Even though they tended to pay higher wages than their competitors in other parts of the country, proximity to the port helped lower their overall costs. Petroleum related firms were especially vocal because the refineries and oil terminals surrounding the harbor served as the northeast hub for crude oil, gasoline, diesel fuel, heating oil, and jet fuel.[88] Meanwhile, longshoremen were worried about their jobs and the threat to the retirement checks of their union's 8,000 pensioners, and municipal officials were concerned that losing port-related businesses would decrease their property tax revenues.[89]

Although the Port Authority, Whitman's team, and high-ranking federal officials ultimately resolved the dredging issue, they left one aspect unresolved: would the users of the port have to pay for higher dredging costs associated with constructing underwater pits for highly contaminated materials and deepening the channels and berths? Typically, federal funds paid for a portion of dredging costs and the Port Authority passed along its share of the costs to the terminal operators in their leases.[90] The New York Shipping Association, which represented seventy-five companies employing waterfront labor, thought it was unfair to pass the costs onto shipping companies and terminal operators because they were not the ones who polluted the harbor in the first place. The association said, "pricing dredging into the stratosphere and expecting the shipping industry to pick up the tab will sink this port just as surely as if dredging is banned outright."[91]

At a 1997 golf outing, Nick Taro, a Sea-Land executive, had a conversation with Robert Boyle (the Port Authority's executive director) that left Taro unnerved. At the time, Sea-Land and Maersk had a partnership at the New Jersey marine terminals that employed about 1,000 employees and handled approximately one-quarter of all the containers moving through the New York harbor.[92] Taro told Boyle that he expected the two men would spend a lot of time together as the terminal operators negotiated with the Port Authority on leases that would expire during the next three years.[93] "There won't be any negotiations," Boyle responded, "We'll give you a price and you'll sign."[94]

Port Authority officials had developed an ambitious construction and dredging plan that would allow the port to accommodate larger vessels and triple the number of containers it served. The plan included a new terminal for Sea-Land and Maersk[95] and doubling the capacity of the railroad connections between the marine terminals and the nearby freight rail lines.[96] The Port Authority proposed a new lease that would immediately increase the terminal operators' rent from $19,000 per acre to $36,000 and would continue rising until it reached $106,000 at the end of thirty years.[97] Boyle thought the increase was justified because "the container port hadn't had an increase in their lease in 30 years."[98]

Lillian Borrone and her colleague, Chris Ward, negotiated directly with Sea-Land and Maersk. They thought that they were offering a more than generous package considering the Authority's costs and the other leases at the seaports.[99] But James Devine, Sea-Land's general manager in Elizabeth, realized he could get a better price with a few phone calls to Trenton and reporters. He argued, "They're coming at us for the historic pollution and siltation of the New York harbor."[100] Not only did the shipping lines complain about the rental increase but they also did not want to pay any maintenance fees. The Port Authority was at a disadvantage with some other ports along the East Coast because it could not use taxes to subsidize its services. It relied on tolls, fares, rents, and fees to pay for its expenses.[101]

With the Port Authority showing little flexibility, in May 1998 Sea-Land and Maersk announced a competition for their business.[102] They requested proposals from seven major ports that were interested in serving as the East Coast hub for the two shipping lines. The ports would have to accommodate the world's largest ships and provide sufficient land-side connections.[103] In a brilliant publicity stunt, Maersk sailed the two-year-old *Regina Maersk* to Port Newark in July 1998. This vessel was the first container ship longer than three football fields and the first one that could handle more than 6,000 twenty-foot containers.[104] Maersk highlighted the need to dredge the New York harbor because a fully loaded ship could not be brought into the marine terminals. The crew had to unload much of its cargo in Halifax, Canada, and wait for high tide before entering Newark Bay.[105]

Whitman Installs Loyalist and Tensions Ratchet Up

Since 1921, New York and New Jersey had worked together to compete with other regions. But that sense of cooperation evaporated by 1998 because Governor Whitman did not trust Governor Pataki and his friends at the Port Authority to work hard enough to keep the two shipping lines. She was right; Pataki was not taking the threat to the ports seriously and he was willing to use Sea-Land and Maersk's threats as leverage in his bid to revamp the way the Port Authority allocated its resources. To protect her state's interests, Whitman decided that she needed someone inside the Port Authority. As tension ratcheted up between Trenton and Albany, the Port Authority's projects slowed down in a tit-for-tat that lasted for the next eighteen months and threatened the port's future.

When Governor Pataki selected George Marlin to serve as executive director, Whitman insisted that Marlin hire a deputy to help him manage the sprawling organization. Even after Marlin left, Whitman claimed that she had the right to continue selecting a deputy executive director. In 1998, Whitman selected Ron Shiftan as Robert Boyle's deputy; he was an attorney with extensive financial background, who was also a neighbor and longtime friend of the Port Authority chair, Lew Eisenberg.[106] Governor Whitman told Shiftan that his number one priority was to make sure that the two shipping lines chose New Jersey as their major East Coast container hubs.[107] Shiftan's selection was the beginning of a new period at the Port Authority. The Authority was on its way to becoming an organization with two fiefdoms, each having their own priorities, with one reporting back to Albany and another to Trenton.

At the end of 1998, Sea-Land and Maersk announced three finalists in their East Coast hub competition: New Jersey, Halifax, and Baltimore.[108] With Maryland governor Parris Glendening promising to take any "reasonable action" to win the competition, the president of the New Jersey Chamber of Commerce, Joan Verplanck, said, "Maryland is just short of paying them to come."[109]

While Governor Whitman was nervous about the economic impacts associated with losing Maersk and Sea-Land, Governor Pataki's confidants at the Port Authority (Boyle and Vice Chair Gargano) did not think shipping firms would move to another port because so much of the cargo brought into New Jersey was destined for the New York metropolitan area.[110] At the time, depending on the commodity, between 30 percent and 70 percent of items shipped into the port were consumed in the region, with the rest shipped to the Midwest and eastern Canada.[111] Boyle and Gargano, however, did not realize that the shipping firms were in fact dead serious about evaluating alternatives to New Jersey. The companies were not considering completely moving out of New Jersey, but they were prepared to move a significant amount of their shipping operations. Maersk and Sea-Land reviewed detailed proposals they received from the other ports (including engineering drawings, rail connections, and freight travel time to Chicago, St. Louis, St. Paul, Louisville, and Memphis). They even conducted a risk assessment that considered community opposition and environmental impacts associated with future expansion of port facilities.[112]

Turning Point—A Strike at Autonomy and a Blow to the Culture

At the December 1998 Port Authority board meeting, Chair Eisenberg raised questions about the Port Authority's plans to improve Kennedy Airport where American Airlines was planning to invest approximately $1 billion of its own funds.[113] Vice Chair Gargano accused Eisenberg of holding up projects in New York unless the deal with Sea-Land and Maersk was approved.[114] In retaliation, the commissioners from New York threatened to hold up improvements at Newark Airport where Continental Airlines was also planning to spend about $1 billion to expand its terminal.[115] No final decisions about the airports were made in December, and the board decided to cancel the following month's meeting because of the disagreement. Canceling the January meeting was highly unusual since the Port Authority board typically met every month except for August.

Chair Eisenberg and Vice Chair Gargano eventually brokered a deal in February 1999. The Authority would subsidize the shipping lines by reducing the lease payments by $120 million. In exchange, the Authority would allocate $120 million toward a project in New York, such as integrating the old Farley Post Office with Manhattan's Penn Station. Eisenberg and Gargano also agreed to move forward with privatizing the World Trade Center, an initiative that was important to Gargano.[116] Unbeknownst to Gargano, Eisenberg, and Governor Whitman's office, Pataki wanted a second opinion. The New York governor asked Robert Boyle what he thought of the deal that Gargano had negotiated. Boyle could have followed the direction of his chair and vice chair, which would have allowed the Authority to move forward with its critical projects. Instead Boyle sabotaged the deal because he was concerned that the agreement would turn the profitable port facility into another financial drain, and he thought that New York could do better. He told Pataki two things: "you can't kill the goose" and Whitman isn't offering you enough.[117]

Gargano had to go back to Eisenberg and explain that the deal was rescinded because he was not "speaking for the governor" at the time.[118] The Pataki administration had new demands based on Boyle's suggestions: $400 million for New York projects and a restructuring of the Authority so that money earned in New York would stay in New York.[119] In response, Governor Whitman told Eisenberg "to pull everything" off the agenda for the Port Authority's February board meeting. That meant the board would not be able to finalize a deal with Sea-Land and Maersk before their first lease expired at the end of February. In the meantime, Baltimore continued to sweeten its proposal.[120]

The Port Authority had become a dysfunctional organization. With its autonomy eviscerated and its culture shattered, the Authority no longer had a clear mission. New York's governor was not looking at the Port Authority as an independent entity that could build new infrastructure to advance the region's interest. Instead he wanted to tap into the Authority's resources and use them for his own pet projects.

Negotiations between New York and New Jersey were not going well, in part, because many of the key players disliked and distrusted each other. For instance, the New York delegation had two warring factions with Boyle on one side and Gargano on the other. One Authority official who dealt with both said the drama "made Shakespeare look like an amateur." Several commissioners stopped talking to Boyle, while others avoided Eisenberg.[121] Meanwhile, Pataki's team was furious that New Jersey was enticing some of New York's most important businesses, including the Stock Exchange and the Yankees, to move across the Hudson River. Even if these iconic institutions stayed put, New York had to put together costly packages to compete with New Jersey's incentives.

Each side had its own ways of calculating the costs and benefits of the proposed lease with Sea-Land and Maersk. For example, Gargano claimed that the lease, along with the associated capital improvements, was the equivalent of a $55 million-a-year subsidy for thirty years. Shiftan made the opposite argument, claiming that the Port Authority might incur losses for the first ten years, but it would be profitable by more than $400 million over time.[122]

In March and April 1999, the Port Authority board did not hold its usual monthly meetings because of the impasse.[123] Sea-Land and Maersk expected the Port Authority to submit its final lease offer in March, but at a meeting near the Newark harbor, the Port Authority staff was not authorized to put anything on the table because the two governors still could not agree on the terms.[124] The shipping lines gave the Authority until April 13 to deliver its best and final offer.[125] With Sea-Land's deadline approaching, Whitman sent two letters to Pataki offering to allocate $250 million in Port Authority revenues to New York. Whitman also agreed to discuss raising PATH fares and restructuring the Authority, but only after the lease with Sea-Land was signed.[126] The two governors negotiated via their staffs and in formal letters addressed to each other.

Pataki floated the idea of putting Kennedy, LaGuardia, and the World Trade Center under New York control while leaving the Port Authority with its bridges and tunnels.[127] He also suggested that New York get 75 percent of Port Authority revenue since New York projects were generating most of the Authority's profits.[128] However, neither he nor his staff ever fleshed out a

Turning Point—A Strike at Autonomy and a Blow to the Culture

proposal or put together a plan to restructure the Authority.[129] Hugh O'Neill, who had worked in the governor's office for Pataki's predecessor and later as a Port Authority assistant executive director, said at the time, "You can't have a coherent discussion of all the issues that would be involved in restructuring, let alone make a commitment to doing it, within this time frame."[130]

Pataki and Whitman were making many people nervous. H. Claude Shostal, president of the Regional Plan Association, argued, "We'd better get serious about retaining this business or we're going to see a serious economic engine weakened."[131] Joan Verplanck, president of the New Jersey Chamber of Commerce, complained, "while they're duking it out on minor issues, we may see a major shipping industry literally go south."[132] Verplanck was amazed that "two governors of the same party in the same region, served by the same port couldn't get their act together."[133]

Verplanck was not the only person surprised that Pataki and Whitman were unable to resolve their differences, despite having the same ideological bent. Former New York governor Mario Cuomo said, "They are two peas in a pod. Both liberal Republicans from the Northeast." He noted something else they had in common that worked against cooperation—they both had their eyes on running for national office.[134]

The presidents of the International Longshoremen's Association and the New York Shipping Association told the governors they were "putting at risk the livelihoods of the men and women who work in the port, as well as the businesses and investments of the maritime companies by whom they are employed."[135] The longshoremen organized a rally and invited the two governors to address the union members.[136] Whitman told more than 1,000 longshoremen at the World Trade Center, "We can't let those jobs go to Baltimore." She promised, "If we can't do it through the Port Authority, then we'll have to do it on our own. I will not abandon your jobs or this port without a fight."[137]

Pataki did not attend the rally, resulting in an unusual scene in which the New Jersey governor spoke in New York about a bistate organization that they both controlled. Pataki wrote to Whitman that day, "My belief is that for at least the last decade the actions of the Port Authority have resulted in a disproportionate allocation of port resources to the New Jersey side of the river."[138] He added, "I cannot continue to allow resources generated in New York to be diverted elsewhere, nor decisions on facilities that are vital to New York's economy to be made by others."[139]

When lease discussions first began, New York Shipping Association's Greg Storey thought it was just a "simple commercial lease dispute." But, he said, "it became a gigantic monkey wrench that could have hurt the port very seriously. The governors were playing with fire." He argued, "I don't think anybody can take these things for granted. Ships can move. Other ports can make that kind of investment. New York City and New York State suffered for years because there was a sense that no one could compete with them. They woke up and their ships were gone."[140] Brian Maher, the terminal operator president, said, "It seems pretty silly" that Europe was forming a European Union, but "the states of New York and New Jersey can't agree on how to run their common assets."[141]

The Port Authority's director of port commerce, Lillian Borrone, was talking to shipping companies and ports across the country. She was nervous about the robust incentive package that Baltimore was putting together.[142] She knew Maersk and Sea-Land did not want to move their operations and headquarters but were prepared to do so if the two states were not competitive when it came to costs, harbor depths, and access to rail and highways. Tommy Tomsen, president of Maersk, said, "We're not bluffing," he said. "Baltimore has developed a real alternative. This decision could go either way."[143]

The day before the deadline, on April 12, 1999, Whitman's team told the two shipping lines it would provide them with approximately $120 million in state subsidies to keep them in New Jersey.[144] A few weeks later, Maersk and Sea-Land announced that they would remain and expand in New Jersey based on the terms of the Port Authority's latest proposal and Governor Whitman's subsidy. A decisive factor in the firms' decision to stay was their obligation to make a large payment to the longshoremen's pension fund, if they moved.[145] Whitman could not yet celebrate, though, because the Port Authority's last proposal still did not have the approval from the board or Governor Pataki.[146]

As the stalemate continued, the governors faced pressure from Continental Airlines and American Airlines, who threatened to suspend their expansion plans at Newark and Kennedy airports if the Port Authority did not expeditiously approve their projects. Whitman's and Pataki's teams were willing to play chicken when it came to improving the marine terminals, privatizing the World Trade Center, and selling air rights over the Midtown bus terminal. But they would not risk losing the two giant airlines. The governors agreed that the Port Authority board could have a special meeting in June 1999 to move forward, simultaneously, on the projects at the two airports.[147]

Throughout the summer of 1999, with Pataki still refusing to sign off on the leases for the shipping lines, Governor Whitman told the six Port Authority commissioners from New Jersey not to approve any more major board items.[148] The commissioners met behind closed doors in September, but they canceled the open session where votes are held.[149] Through the rest of 1999, the two sides did not make any headway. More board meetings were canceled and when the commissioners did meet, they only handled routine business.[150]

Whitman continued holding the rest of the Authority hostage until Pataki agreed on a lease for the shipping lines. Meanwhile, Pataki was waiting for Whitman to agree to raise PATH fares that had been $1.00 since 1987 and to increase tolls that had last been raised in 1991.[151] He also wanted the Port Authority to set up a "development bank" that would be used to help pay for non-Port Authority projects. The term was a euphemism for saying that he wanted the Authority to send a check to Albany.[152] New Jersey was not against the concept, as long as funds were also allocated for its own pet projects.[153] The idea was not unprecedented. The Port Authority had set up a development bank in the early 1980s when New York State agencies moved out of the World Trade Center and were replaced with higher-paying private tenants. Peter Goldmark, the executive director at the time, had proposed this arrangement during a period when the states were facing a severe economic downturn and the Port Authority was in a strong position to help them out. In the late 1990s, the states were having fiscal issues not because of job losses but rather because the two governors were trying to slash taxes.[154]

In December 1999, the New York delegation boycotted the monthly board meeting. Gargano said, "'I think there is a new precedent set this year by the New Jersey side in holding other projects hostage because there is one project they want approved. The consensus was not to attend the meeting. Why waste our time?"[155] No board meeting was held in January 2000 either.

Former Governors and How the Authority Had Changed

With the governors feuding, many former governors in New York and New Jersey expressed the importance of good working relationships and keeping disagreements out of the public eye. New Jersey's Thomas Kean, who had tried to meet with New York's Mario Cuomo once a month, said, "I think they ought to have regular meetings until this thing is solved."[156] He added, "The more you know each other, the more you talk, the harder it is to fight."[157] New Jersey's Brendan Byrne remembered his understanding with New York's Hugh Carey in the late 1970s and early 1980s that "the PATH fare was going to be 35 cents for as long as I was in office, and he never challenged me on it. He wanted some things that weren't necessarily the best for New Jersey, but I went along."[158] Byrne recalled when Carey was getting pressured to ban noisy supersonic jets from Kennedy Airport, "I got him off the hook and solved the problem for him by vowing to veto agency minutes and thereby stop all agency activities if the planes were not allowed."[159]

In the late 1990s, the members of the Port Authority's board were less independent than they had been in the past. Pataki and Whitman had been appointing more loyalists to the board, some of whom owed their full-time jobs to the governors. For example, the Authority's vice chair, Charles Gargano, was the head of Pataki's economic development agency.

Ron Shiftan, the former deputy executive director, noticed that the Authority had three types of commissioners, all of whom were controlled by the two governors. Shiftan said that some of the commissioners "took their time to learn about the Port Authority's mission and promoted it." The second type, he said, understood the Authority's regional mission, but "they weren't concerned about what was right or good. They didn't think it was their job to reason with the governor, but rather to do what the governor said." The third type, he said "didn't know and didn't really care."

In Trenton, Richard Mroz made sure the commissioners followed the governor's lead. As the director of the governor's authorities unit, Mroz coordinated the state's policy for about three dozen independent agencies. He interviewed potential commissioners for state authorities (including the Port Authority) and recalled, "I gave them ground rules" to make sure they were willing to follow the governor's direction.[160]

From Mroz's perspective, the Port Authority was not independent from politics but rather controlled by the two states. He said, "I see the states as two shareholders in a corporation with the shareholders making the ultimate decisions." He thought "the chairman's job was to make sure the Port Authority followed Whitman's agenda." Sometimes Mroz talked to the Port Authority chair a few times day. "On big issues," he said, "the commissioners needed to support policies that were consistent with the governor's policies. We translated those to the chair and commissioners." He admitted that the commissioners would sometimes object to the governor's instructions, but that it was counterproductive because the governor could always veto the minutes. A veto, he explained, would be "embarrassing to the governor, commissioners, and agencies."[161]

Former Port Authority officials remembered how board members and executives once had much greater autonomy. For example, Peter Goldmark, the executive director between 1977 and 1985, said, "We didn't have six to six votes on the board. They settled disputes in private with mostly unanimous votes." Most of the commissioners, he noted, were senior businessmen who wanted the region to grow and saw the Port Authority as an engine of growth. One Port Authority official recalled that the commissioners during that time were "giants of finance and insurance."[162] The governors, Goldmark said, could not tell Gus Levy, the president of Lehman Brothers, to vote a certain way. Nor could they threaten the vice chair, Robert F. Wagner, who was a former New York City mayor. Serving on the Port Authority's board, Goldmark said, was seen as more prestigious during his tenure.[163]

By the late 1990s, membership on the Authority's board of commissioners was not as attractive to top business leaders. The public had become increasingly skeptical about the government's ability to solve problems and the Port Authority was not expected to initiate any bold new ventures. Moreover, high ranking executives were less active in regional organizations because of the nationwide merger of corporations, especially in the financial sector.[164] Although some business leaders had become less connected and invested in their communities, the two governors never had trouble finding individuals willing to serve on the Port Authority's board. Plenty of people were attracted to the prestige and the opportunity to make business connections. The board was just not attracting the same level of professionals.

Paul Bea (the Port Authority's longtime Washington, D.C., lobbyist) and Lillian Borrone (who served as assistant executive director before retiring) also noticed this change. Bea recalled how the commissioners had acted as a body in the 1980s. He pointed out that the governors had always used their leverage, for example, Brendan Byrne refusing to approve any PATH fare increase. However, Bea said that starting in 1995 the Authority would not do anything without first getting prior approval from the governor.[165] Borrone said that in the 1970s, "people on the board were successful and wealthy. They saw this as a public service. Clearly, they talked to each other about business, but they weren't there to suck up to the governors. Not the case with Pataki and Whitman. They appointed people who were dependent on them."[166]

The worst stalemate in the Port Authority's history continued through early 2000.[167] The appointments made by Pataki and Whitman gave them greater control of the Port Authority, but made the conflict harder to resolve.

While New Jersey's business leaders were making a fuss, their New York City counterparts were staying quiet because they were less impacted by the maritime business, and they did not want to antagonize Mayor Giuliani. One civic group official said, "Any support of ending the impasse at the agency might be seen by the mayor as giving aid and comfort to an entity that he would just as soon see disappear from the face of the earth."[168]

Robert Boyle, the executive director was not in a position to resolve the conflict. Former governor Byrne said, "In the old days, the executive director of the Port Authority was seen as nonpolitical. For years, Austin Tobin ran the Port Authority with the respect of both states. He was viewed as a professional. And, to some extent, Peter Goldmark had that image." Byrne lamented in early 2000, "there now is an assumption that New Jersey chooses the chair and New York chooses the executive director. That makes the executive director a political appointment, which it never was intended to be. . . . If they would go back to having a professional executive director, it would solve a lot of problems."[169]

Upon the instigation of Maersk's president, two U.S. senators embarrassed Whitman and Pataki by publicly warning them that "billions of dollars of revenue from projects on both sides of the Hudson" were at stake. New Jersey's Frank Lautenberg and New York's Daniel Patrick Moynihan told the governors that "besides holding up billions of dollars in Port Authority projects and investment decisions, this dispute threatens to make the port an unattractive place to do business. It provides ammunition to our port region's competitors who would seek to draw away key port customers; creates an appearance that it is very difficult to get major public projects accomplished and endangers federal appropriations for important channel deepening projects." The two senators harkened back to the early twentieth century when "the port was being torn apart by rivalries between the two states, by the machinations of railroad tycoons, and the conflict of a hundred other interests." Lautenberg (a former Port Authority board member) and Moynihan (a scholar with a love for history) wanted the Port Authority to continue being the "leading forum for solving regional problems and making commerce more efficient."[170]

A few weeks later, at an April 2000 Port Authority board meeting, the commissioners were poised to approve the annual operating budget that was now four months late.[171] The board had been unable to take any significant action since it approved the expansion programs for Kennedy and Newark airports the previous year, but now the governors seemed ready to resolve their differences.[172] The commissioners met behind closed doors before their publicly scheduled vote. Optimistic Port Authority staffers set up the conference room where the commissioners would vote on the budget in public. Three ring binders were placed on the tables in front of each commissioner's seat.[173]

Despite all the preparations, the New York commissioners refused to vote on the budget because of three last-minute issues. First, they demanded to see how the five-year capital budget would allocate funds between New York and New Jersey projects. Second, they wanted to expedite the Authority's development bank payments to New York. Third, the New York delegation said the Authority's press release about the budget should mention the need to increase tolls or PATH fares. Without any explanation to the public, the Authority's staff members rushed around the room removing papers from each of the binders. Then the commissioners filed in, approved some minor items, and left ten minutes later.[174]

Later that day, Whitman's communications director called it a "total nuclear meltdown."[175] Whitman's counsel, Richard Mroz, said, "This has been the classic M.O. of the New York commissioners, and it has continued to befuddle us on what will settle the impasse, short of giving New York a windfall from agency revenues for no reason." He added, "It is bizarre and it is no way to do business."[176] Mroz found the standoff exceedingly frustrating and his conversations with Pataki's senior aides were fruitless. Pataki was not giving a straight answer because he was not getting involved in the details nor did he have a clear endgame. Mroz recalled, "we tried many times to hear about their priorities and figure out how to move things along. Invariably, there was no response. We would say, 'give us a counter proposal then we'd hear nothing.' That dynamic led to the hiatus. We could never figure out why they wouldn't let the lease proceed."[177] In Albany, Pataki approached the Port Authority the same way that he did his legislative deals. Everything was on the table and negotiations were done at the last minute with only a few people in the room.

Former chair Richard Leone traced the feud back to 1995. He said, "It's a crisis that results from neglect masquerading as intense interest. I don't think either governor has been paying attention, except milking the Authority for whatever money they can get. They've heavily politicized it, which is one of the consequences of the Marlin appointment." He asked, what is the point of having an independent board if the commissioners are acting as agents of the governors and don't have the authority to negotiate a deal?[178]

June 2000 Agreement

The two-year standoff between Pataki and Whitman was finally settled after a few hours of phone conversations between the governors in June 2000. The board made it official with two minutes worth of votes.[179] Their deal did not reflect even a pretense of a regional approach or advancing the Authority's mission. It certainly did not involve a rational planning process.

The governors' agreement included a new thirty-year lease for the shipping lines and $120 million for dredging that Whitman had previously offered to pay with state funds.[180] The Authority would also improve New York's port facilities in Staten Island and Brooklyn. Whitman agreed to move forward with privatizing the World Trade Center and selling the air rights over the Midtown Bus Terminal.[181] She also agreed to a future PATH fare increase, although the public announcement only said the Authority would study a potential increase.[182] As part of the deal, the Port Authority would lease space in the Farley Post Office building that would become part of the new Penn Station complex in Manhattan.[183] This was important to Gargano who was both the Port Authority's vice chair and the head of the state development corporation that owned the post office building. Robert Boyle later called this a "snake oil" deal because it disguised a grant as a lease. The Port Authority was expected to lease 250 square feet (a space smaller than the size of a typical hotel room) for $10.5 million annually for 35 years.[184] A future Port Authority chair would later call Gargano's involvement an "egregious conflict of interest."[185]

Pataki and Whitman also agreed to set aside $250 million for New York projects related to transportation, economic development, and infrastructure renewal. These funds would not be selected for their regional significance, nor would Port Authority staff select them after a thorough cost-benefit analysis. Instead the commissioners passed a resolution that gave the New York governor the power to select projects.[186] Since the Pataki administration was unable to identify suitable projects at the time, the exasperated and worn-down Whitman team agreed to give Pataki the flexibility to select them later.[187]

Conclusion

The agreement between Pataki and Whitman allowed the Port Authority to move ahead with its seaport projects in Elizabeth and Newark. The invest-

Turning Point—A Strike at Autonomy and a Blow to the Culture

ments in dredging and new facilities paid off. Shipments at the two marine terminals grew faster than they had in decades, twice as fast as the national average. By 2005, the port was handling 2.8 million containers annually compared to only 1.3 million containers ten years earlier.[188] New warehouses and distribution centers were built throughout North Jersey and firms hired more longshoremen, truck drivers, and other workers.[189]

The long feud did inhibit some of the ports' growth, however. While conducting its study of alternatives to New Jersey, Maersk learned about a promising site in Portsmouth, Virginia. Two years later, Maersk purchased the property and then created the largest privately owned container terminal in the United States. When the port complex opened, the governor of Virginia called it a "huge win" that would benefit "every city and county" in his state.[190]

The period between 1995 when Marlin was appointed and 2000 when Pataki and Whitman resolved their differences was a turning point in the Authority's history. The two governors—rather than the commissioners or Port Authority staff—began determining which of the Port Authority's major projects would be funded. Their priorities and the development bank would drain the Port Authority's resources. New York's insistence on raising the PATH fare did help bring in some additional revenues, though. In 2001, the fare was raised for the first time in fifteen years from $1.00 to $1.50, which matched the city's subway fare at the time. Future governors have since agreed to keep the PATH more or less in line with the subway fare, which has generated hundreds of millions of dollars for new initiatives favored by the two governors.

Marlin's cuts and privatization efforts also had a long-lasting impact to the organization. As the Authority's chief engineer between 1995 and 2010, Frank Lombardi deplored the deterioration of the Authority and its once-vaunted engineering department. Lombardi started in 1971 and for a quarter century worked with engineers who were revered at international engineering conferences for their expertise in a wide array of fields, such as the innovative ways they used concrete and asphalt, developed noise mitigation measures, tested suspension cables, managed traffic, and expanded runways. Starting with Marlin, however, engineers were discouraged from attending conferences, and they found it harder to stay up to date with new developments in their fields.[191] When Marlin cut the number of Port Authority engineers and shifted work to outside consultants and temporary workers, Lombardi lost some of his best engineers and then found it increasingly difficult to attract and retain top staff. Their work was less appealing and challenging because they were increasingly managing outside engineers rather than performing the work themselves.

The Port Authority's senior staff thought of themselves as dedicated public servants, but under Marlin that sense of public service deteriorated. By focusing on the short-term bottom line, Marlin's team eliminated training programs, cut employee benefits, and devalued institutional knowledge, all of which were an integral part of the organization's culture. "The social contract was broken," Lombardi said, and "they shattered the strategy and the philosophy of public service."[192]

The Port Authority would no longer be in the same position to generate supportive coalitions to promote its interests. Its autonomy was all but lost and its reputation and technological know-how were decimated. The Authority's proud internal culture was shattered while its leaders were afraid to take risks on behalf of the organization. The Port Authority would never regain its former strength; instead it would continue to be a tool for the two governors. This organizational weakness plays out in the following chapters when a New Jersey governor directed the Authority to rebuild a Staten Island bridge and the Port Authority tried to rebuild the World Trade Center site after the 2001 terrorist attack.

As the Port Authority's lobbyist between 1980 and 2005, Paul Bea witnessed what he called the Authority's "rapid change from a vigorous, highly ambitious and self-confident agency" to one that was heavily politicized with insufficient resources. Marlin's tenure and Whitman's appointment of a deputy executive director, he explained, "started the bifurcation of the executive offices of the Port Authority and more intimate levels of decision-making through the taut strings that ran back to Trenton and Albany." He said, "Patronage may have had its start with George Pataki and Christine Whitman, but what succeeding governor didn't want to put his own people in nicely salaried jobs, even if those jobs had to be created? The genie was let out of the bottle."[193]

CHAPTER 7

Moving Three Bridges from the Periphery to Center Stage

The Port Authority's Goethals, Outerbridge, and Bayonne bridges are not an iconic part of the New York skyline. Their images are not printed on many postcards, and they are more likely to be used as the backdrop for a murder scene than a romantic comedy. While the George Washington Bridge gracefully spans the mighty Hudson River in Upper Manhattan, these three Staten Island bridges are located on the outskirts of New York City and cross over waterways whose names are unfamiliar to most New Yorkers. Despite their relative anonymity, the three Staten Island bridges have reshaped the entire region. Their stories reveal how the Port Authority has responded to and influenced public sentiment, and the ways in which its priorities have anticipated and addressed the region's needs.

This chapter covers three separate time periods. In the 1920s, the two state legislatures and governors invited the Port Authority to build three bridges between New Jersey and New York's Staten Island. In the 1950s, the Port Authority had the credibility, foresight, and resources to help integrate the region's rapidly growing suburban areas via these Staten Island crossings. Just a few years ago, the Authority raised the roadway on the Bayonne Bridge (because its height threatened the viability of the region's marine terminals) and replaced the Goethals Bridge. To complete these two most recent projects, Port Authority's officials and their stakeholders navigated an extraordinary set of political, regulatory, financial, and engineering challenges.

The Staten Island Connection

The bistate study commission that recommended establishing the Port Authority more than a century ago, envisioned trucks playing only a peripheral role in moving freight, similar to the role that horse-drawn carriages played. Trucks were deemed ideal for short trips, transporting goods from railroad stations and shipping terminals to nearby warehouses and shops.[1] The Port Authority's founders initially focused on improving railroads to solve the port's problems. As the region's transportation needs changed, so too did the Authority's priorities. Fewer than 400,000 trucks were registered in the United States in 1917, the year that New York and New Jersey set up the bistate study commission. By 1923, that number had more than quadrupled to 1.8 million and by 1929 it reached 3.5 million. At the same time, cars were becoming increasingly available and affordable to the general population. Between 1917 and 1929, the number of cars registered in the United States jumped from 4.7 million to 23 million.[2]

Elected officials were under immense pressure from businesses and car owners in the 1920s to accommodate these vehicles and address rapidly growing traffic problems. Likewise, property owners, construction firms, and realtors lobbied for better roads that would spur residential and commercial construction, and their own prosperity. These forces played out throughout the metropolitan area from the most densely populated neighborhoods of Manhattan to the semirural areas of Staten Island.

Staten Island's economy and lifestyle have long differed from New York City's other four boroughs (Bronx, Queens, Brooklyn, and Manhattan). In 1920, only about 2 percent of the city's population lived on the island even though it comprised nearly 20 percent of the city's land.[3] Staten Island was isolated with its residents and businesses relying upon ferries and ships, while all the other boroughs were accessible by train, car, and foot. Geographically, Staten Island is closer to New Jersey than to the rest of New York. If you extend a line south of the Hudson River, you will see that Staten Island is west, not east, of the river.

Three bodies of water divide Staten Island from its neighbors. Along Staten Island's eastern edge, "The Narrows" waterway separates the island from Brooklyn, and it is the primary entrance for ships coming into the New York/New Jersey harbor. The island is separated from New Jersey on its north by the Kill Van Kull and on the west by the Arthur Kill. Although the word "kill" might suggest that the first European sailors were terrified of these waterways, the sailors had simply named them for the Dutch word for "creek" or "channel."

Advocates for building a bridge between New Jersey and Staten Island touted numerous benefits. Staten Islanders would no longer have to wait on

Moving Three Bridges from the Periphery to Center Stage 175

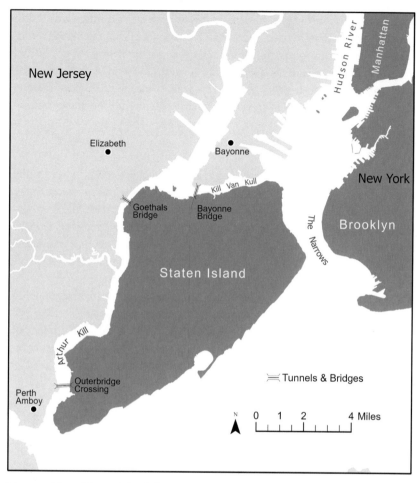

Map 7.1. Map of Staten Island showing the three bridges and the waterways surrounding the island.
(Map by Md. Shahinoor Rahman.)

long ferry lines to reach New Jersey, their property values would increase, and the cost of bringing in food and supplies would decrease. The *New York Herald Tribune* claimed that new bridges "would help to develop the island's empty areas and make it a manufacturing and shipping section, like other parts of the city which face the harbor."[4] City planners talked about the island accommodating millions of residents with new parks, roads, and potentially a train tunnel to Brooklyn.[5] Business leaders and elected officials in Perth Amboy and Elizabeth (two industrial cities located on the Arthur Kill) thought their cities would become more prosperous if bridges connected them with Staten Island. New Jersey's shore communities also supported the bridges because their beach areas would be more accessible to New Yorkers, who could ferry to Staten Island and then drive along the New Jersey coast.[6]

Three New Bridges

In 1923, after the two states authorized funding for a preliminary survey, the commissions responsible for building the Holland Tunnel began studying the possibility of building a bridge or tunnel across the Arthur Kill.[7] The commissioners thought that if they started building a Staten Island crossing, the two legislatures would be less likely to carry out their threat of eliminating the commissions and transferring their powers to the newly created Port Authority.[8] The commissions were doomed, though, because construction of the Holland Tunnel was repeatedly delayed and over budget and, as detailed in chapter 2, the Port Authority emerged as a credible alternative. After George Silzer was sworn in as New Jersey governor, he wanted the Port Authority to take over building all bistate vehicle crossings, arguing that the tunnel commissions had come to be looked at as a "political institution, much interested in the preservation of jobs for the faithful."[9]

Governor Silzer said any Staten Island bridge should be built as a "business proposition" that would only proceed if toll revenues could pay for it. He feared that the public might support building a bridge with tolls, but once it opened they would clamor to remove the tolls. "If a bridge is made free," he said, "the result is that the burden is put upon all of the people of the state of New Jersey, rather than upon those whose convenience will be served by the bridge." Silzer wanted tolls to cover the Port Authority's expenses, so that it would be able to finance even more crossings.[10] The New Jersey governor saw eye-to-eye with his counterpart in Albany. New York governor Al Smith, who had served on the Port Authority's board of commissioners in 1921 and 1922, also talked about relieving taxpayers in both states from further burdens.[11]

Organizations, just like people, can get lucky. When they are in the right place at the right time, and if they are well prepared, they can take advantage of opportunities to enter into promising new markets. When the two state legislatures empowered the Port Authority in 1924 to build two bridges over the Arthur Kill, they justified giving these projects to the Authority because the bridges were "in partial effectuation" of the comprehensive plan the Authority had developed for the region. This justification was a bit of a stretch, however, since the plan did not envision the Authority constructing its own motor vehicle crossings.[12]

In 1924, the Port Authority started planning two bridges over the Arthur Kill that would connect Staten Island with Elizabeth and Perth Amboy.[13] The Authority's commissioners engaged distinguished architects alongside notable engineers because they wanted their bridges "to combine beauty with stability and convenience."[14] They expected that construction of bridges, including preliminary studies, would require at least three to five years.[15] The two bridges would later be called the Goethals Bridge and the Outerbridge Crossing. The bridge closest to Manhattan was named after George Goethals, the Authority's consulting engineer who had previously overseen construction of the Panama Canal. Oddly enough, the name Outerbridge was not chosen because it was located further south but because the Port Authority's first chair was named Eugenius Outerbridge.

Before the Port Authority could build any of its crossings, it needed authorization from the state legislatures to proceed. Hoping for an economic windfall, many local officials and business leaders in New Jersey lobbied for their cities to be the site of a new bridge. That is why in 1925 another crossing was added to the Authority's portfolio—a bridge connecting Bayonne with Staten Island. Legislators in Trenton cobbled together a coalition by combining bills for bridges that would connect four different New Jersey counties with New York City. The three Staten Island crossings would be located in Middlesex, Union, and Hudson counties, while the George Washington Bridge would connect Bergen County with Manhattan.[16]

The Port Authority moved quickly ahead on the Staten Island bridges—acquiring property, conducting field surveys, and preparing plans for contractors. Local and federal officials approved the Authority's plans and permits,[17] and ground was broken for the Goethals Bridge and Outerbridge Crossing in 1926 (figs. 7.1 and 7.2).[18] The Authority, as it promised it would, awarded construction contracts to firms based on quality and cost, not on political connections. When the commissioners selected architects, engineers, and builders they chose what they considered "the most competent and reliable men with the right kind of organization."[19]

Silzer, who was appointed Port Authority chair in 1926 after his term as governor had ended, explained the most challenging feature of the Authority's endeavor: "The Port Authority, a body unique in the history of this country,

Fig. 7.1. Construction of the Outerbridge Crossing.
(Photograph reprinted by permission of Port Authority of New York and New Jersey.)

with no assets, no funds of any kind, an organization politically sponsored by two States, planned to build two bridges for which it needed $14 million." Silzer and other Authority officials had to convince Wall Street bankers to buy bonds issued by the Port Authority, at that point an untested organization, that would be paid back with toll revenues from the new bridges.[20]

The legislatures had helped the bond offering succeed by giving the Authority exclusive rights to construct motor vehicle crossings between New York City and New Jersey. The Port Authority was in effect a monopoly that could set its own tolls and did not have to worry about any public agency or private company competing with its crossings. Moreover, the Authority's high-powered legal team provided reassurance to investors. Former U.S. Supreme Court chief justice Charles E. Hughes told potential bond holders that the Authority's bonds would be lawfully issued, and their interest would be exempt from state and federal income taxes.[21] The Authority did not promise to remove tolls once the bonds were paid off; instead Chairman Silzer said that the tolls may be used to build future Authority projects or may be lowered to pay only for maintenance and repair expenses.[22]

Fig. 7.2. Goethals Bridge construction.
(Photograph reprinted by permission of Port Authority of New York and New Jersey.)

The Authority faced relatively little opposition in its plans to connect Staten Island and New Jersey,[23] although one tugboat captain did presciently warn at a public hearing that the Bayonne Bridge would be a menace to navigation. In response, Othmar Ammann, the Port Authority's bridge engineer, said its planned clearance would have been sufficient for about 90 percent of the traffic that passed through the Kill Van Kull the previous year. Ammann said all of those boats could have passed beneath the height of the bridge, if they had lowered their masts.[24]

When the first two Staten Island bridges opened on the very same day in June 1928, Chairman Silzer thanked the Authority's commissioners for working "unselfishly, without pay and only from patriotic impulses."[25] The Authority was widely praised for its efficiency in building the bridges ahead of schedule and at a cost lower than initially estimated.[26] The *New York Times* said that "the combination of engineering and inter-State problems baffled all attempts at solution until the creation of the Port Authority."[27] The *Jersey Journal* claimed that the Port Authority may not have succeeded in its efforts to connect railroads and build new rail lines, but "as interstate bridge builders the Port Authority has thus far scored quite a success."[28]

When the Bayonne Bridge opened in 1931, elected officials were effusive that the Port Authority now had five crossings between the states: the Holland Tunnel and the George Washington Bridge (see chapter 2), along with the three Staten Island crossings. New York's state comptroller, Morris Tremaine, said, "The commissioners who constitute the Port Authority, have rendered a public service not excelled. The skill with which the Port Authority has managed its affairs is evidenced by the fact that these bridges cost less than the very conservative estimates made by competent engineers and rechecked by bankers. This saving of money plus the great saving in time of construction would be a great credit to any private enterprise, and is proof positive that public work can be constructed efficiently when directed by the right men."[29]

These five crossings gave the Port Authority sufficient resources to take on new projects and a reputation as an organization with extraordinary capabilities and an exemplary culture. In 1931, New York's governor Franklin D. Roosevelt praised the Port Authority as a "model for government agencies throughout the land," and after he was elected U.S. president the following year, his administration promoted the use of public authorities as an effective means of building infrastructure.[30] When the Port Authority was established in 1921, it was the very first public authority in the United States. By the 1950s,

Fig. 7.3. Cars crossing the Goethals Bridge in the 1930s.
(Photograph reprinted by permission of Port Authority of New York and New Jersey.)

New York State alone had more than fifty authorities including the Triborough Bridge and Tunnel Authority, an entity set up to build river crossings within New York City.[31]

In the 1950s, the Port Authority tapped into all of its strengths—its resources (e.g., financial, credibility, technical know-how, media relations) as well as its autonomy, entrepreneurial leadership, and a highly regarded organizational culture—to undertake one of the most ambitious building programs in the history of the New York City metropolitan area.

Going around Lower and Midtown Manhattan

The Holland Tunnel, Lincoln Tunnel, and the George Washington Bridge each carried between fifteen million and twenty million vehicles in 1950.[32]

Over the next two years, thanks to rapid suburbanization and continued postwar prosperity, the number of vehicles crossing these three Hudson River facilities rose by 24 percent.[33] With motorists experiencing frequent delays, the Port Authority considering building a third tunnel into Manhattan.[34] However, after analyzing the traffic patterns of the vehicles using its existing Hudson River crossings, Roger Gilman, the agency's director of port development, thought that a new tunnel would be useful only in rush hours and would not, therefore, generate enough traffic to pay for construction and operation.[35]

Gilman figured out something else after looking at the results of customer surveys. More than half of the drivers crossing the Hudson on weekdays and almost three quarters on weekends were *not* starting or ending their trips in Manhattan. Instead of building another tunnel into the congested streets of Midtown or Lower Manhattan, Gilman realized that the region should add highway capacity that bypassed them both.[36] New highways were needed to improve connections with the city's other boroughs as well as the rapidly growing suburban communities in northern New Jersey, Long Island, and Westchester.

At the time, the new U.S. president, Dwight Eisenhower, was interested in building an interstate highway system. Gilman and the Authority's executive director, Austin Tobin, expected that federal funds could help pay for a regional highway network integrated with the interstates. In 1953, he and his staff sketched out plans, borrowing from ideas that had been kicking around for decades. They wanted to improve traffic by building new roads south and north of Manhattan's central business district.[37] Tobin would set the Authority's priorities, generate public support, and then reshape the entire region.

South of Manhattan, the Authority's Staten Island crossings had plenty of capacity to handle more traffic. In Gilman's plan, a New Jersey driver would be able to cross the Goethals Bridge to Staten Island and then drive along a new Staten Island highway (later to be called the Staten Island Expressway). At the island's eastern edge, a new bridge would span The Narrows and connect with Brooklyn. The Narrows might have seemed "narrow" to the Dutch and British sailors who sailed thousands of miles across the Atlantic Ocean, but it did not seem very narrow to the engineers as they gazed over the waterway. They realized that a crossing would be enormously expensive because it would be the world's longest suspension bridge. The bridge's towers in Brooklyn and Staten Island would have to be nearly as tall as a seventy-story building.

Using Staten Island to bypass Manhattan's business center appealed to Tobin for another very important reason. Building The Narrows bridge would boost the Port Authority's burgeoning coffers by attracting more cars and trucks to the Outerbridge, Bayonne, and Goethals. The Authority's three Staten Island bridges had turned out to be money-losers for many years because Staten Island had not grown as fast as expected.[38] For instance, the Authority estimated that 8.4 million vehicles would cross the Bayonne Bridge in 1950, but only 2.3 million vehicles crossed that year.[39]

Gilman sketched out an equally ambitious scheme north of Midtown Manhattan. In the 1920s, the George Washington Bridge was designed in a way that a lower level could be added in the future. At the time, extending the city's subway system to New Jersey was seriously contemplated, but it had never been financially viable to build and operate. Now Gilman and Tobin wanted to add a lower level for cars, trucks, and buses to accommodate more vehicles and generate additional revenue. The bridge would have a total of fourteen lanes with eight on the upper level and six more below. On the New Jersey side, Gilman's plan envisioned a new east-west highway (later to be called I-80) connecting with the bridge. In New York, the Authority would connect the George Washington Bridge with new roadways in Upper Manhattan, the Bronx, and Queens. In addition, a new bridge would be built over the Long Island Sound near the Bronx's Throgs Neck neighborhood.[40]

Tobin reached out to Robert Moses, the chair of New York's Triborough Bridge and Tunnel Authority. Tobin had a complicated relationship with Robert Moses, who had fought the Port Authority's attempts to take over the city's two airports and build the Manhattan bus terminal. Now Tobin wanted the two men to work together on The Narrows and Throgs Neck bridges and advocate for the new highways that would connect their facilities. Tobin recalled that when he went to meet with Moses, "I left the door open behind me when I went, in case I had to make a fast exit."[41] Tobin did not have to worry. Moses was excited about the possibility of building two new bridges, especially The Narrows bridge, which Tobin offered to finance. The two authority leaders agreed to conduct a joint study to flesh out the Port Authority's conceptual plan.[42] From the outset of their collaboration, they decided they would only recommend projects that would be financially self-sustaining to the authorities—which ruled out their involvement with any railroad or subway project.[43]

In 1954, the two authorities developed their plan to build The Narrows and Throgs Neck bridges and double-deck the George Washington Bridge at

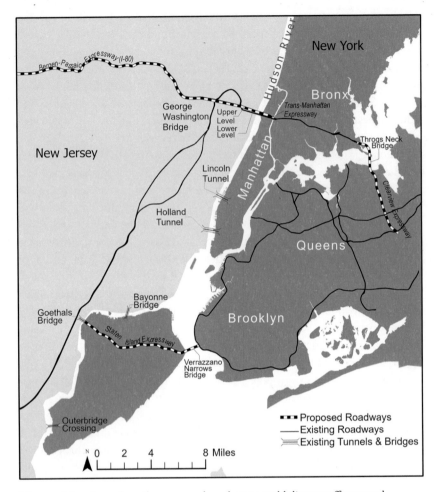

Map 7.2. Map shows how the proposed roadways would divert traffic around Midtown and Lower Manhattan.
(Map by Md. Shahinoor Rahman.)

a cost of $379 million. The region's new interstate highways, funded mostly with federal resources, would cost an additional $198 million.[44] It was an extraordinary sum considering that New York's state legislature had allocated less than $40 million a year for highway construction across the entire state during the previous nine years.[45] After the joint study's recommendations were released in January 1955, the Port Authority's media relations team helped generate widespread support for the new bridges and highways.[46] In

New York, the *Herald Tribune* called the plan "awe-inspiring" and the *Long Island Daily Press* wrote, "For Long Islanders these improvements would be no less than a godsend."[47] In New Jersey, the *Herald-News* exclaimed, the "region is in for the greatest concentration of highway and bridge building that the world, perhaps, has ever seen," and the *Paterson News* referred to the projects as "of almost staggering proportions."[48]

The authorities and states fulfilled Gilman's vision. As Tobin and Moses had expected, federal funds did pay for new roadways to connect their bridges. The Throgs Neck Bridge opened in 1961 and the George Washington Bridge's lower level in 1962 (in private, some Authority employees would playfully refer to the lower level as "Martha" and the upper level as "George") (fig. 7.4). The bridge over The Narrows took longer to build. The two authorities entered in an agreement in which the Port Authority would finance and construct The Narrows bridge and then lease it to the Triborough Authority.[49] Although the Port Authority provided temporary financing for the bridge, by 1959 the Triborough Authority was in a strong enough financial position to build the bridge on its own.[50] After the bridge (named the Verrazzano-Narrows Bridge) opened in 1964, a transportation reporter wrote, "the last link in a solid ring of roads around the congested Manhattan core has been forged." The bypass routes were widely praised for creating an extensive regional highway network, cutting travel time, and spurring even more residential and commercial development in Queens, Staten Island, Long Island, and New Jersey.[51]

The new highways and bridges improved the ability to move goods across the region, but they never did solve the traffic congestion problem. The additional roadway capacity accommodated more vehicles, but additional roads led to even more traffic because they encouraged people and businesses to move to Staten Island and the city's suburbs where cars were needed for working and shopping. The Port Authority certainly benefited financially, however. The number of vehicles crossing the Staten Island bridges increased from 8.5 million in 1960 to 23.5 million by the end of the decade. Over the same period, the number of vehicles crossing the George Washington Bridge rose from 38.9 million to 69.3 million.[52]

The visions of Tobin, Moses, and other highways builders in the middle of the twentieth century came with another cost. In the 1950s and early 1960s, elected officials and the two powerful public authorities were willing to ignore local opposition and bulldoze through neighborhoods to construct new highways and accommodate more vehicles. The resulting urban blight and environmental degradation led Congress to pass a series of laws in the 1960s and 1970s that would make it much harder to ever build a new crossing

Fig. 7.4. The world's busiest motor vehicle bridge, the George Washington Bridge, has eight lanes on the upper level and another six on the lower level. *(Photograph by John O'Connell, October 17, 2008. Courtesy Wikimedia Commons, CC BY 2.0.)*

or even replace an existing one in the New York metropolitan area. Government agencies would be required to solicit public opinion, identify the environmental impacts of transportation projects, and evaluate potential alternatives in a transparent manner. Unlike the residents living near the Great Swamp in 1959, opponents of infrastructure projects in the 1980s had legal tools they could use to slow down projects and reveal information that government agencies preferred not to acknowledge. This new way of doing business would stymie the Port Authority's efforts to build new infrastructure.

Using the Island Again to Address the Region's Needs

The number of vehicles using the Port Authority's bridges and tunnels continued to increase in the 1970s and early 1980s. During peak periods, crossings were approaching their capacity and drivers were becoming increasingly frustrated. In 1984, the Port Authority's assistant executive director, Lou Gambaccini, set up an interagency Trans-Hudson Task Force to address the traffic problems.[53] The task force members pursued a number of solutions such as setting up TRANSCOM as discussed in chapter 5. They also considered how long-term transportation improvements along three different east-west corridors (north, central, south) would accommodate future demand. The task force relied upon technical data from the Port Authority's planning department that estimated how travel patterns were expected to change over the next several decades.

The region would not be able to rely on dramatic infrastructure projects to improve transportation along the northern corridor, whose centerpiece was the George Washington Bridge. With its fourteen lanes, the world's busiest bridge was not the corridor's major bottleneck. Rather New York City's highways east of the bridge, such as the Cross Bronx Expressway, were the cause of recurring traffic delays. Unlike in the 1950s and 1960s, the city and state had no appetite for expanding these roadways because construction would have been regarded as too destructive of the city's neighborhoods.

The central corridor connected New Jersey with the core of the region's economy, the portions of Manhattan below 60th Street that are known as Midtown and Lower Manhattan. On a typical business day, about 3.4 million people entered this central business district from the suburbs and the city's four other boroughs. More people squeezed into this nine-square-mile area of Manhattan than lived in the entire states of Connecticut, South Carolina, or Colorado. Gambaccini's task force members realized they needed to focus on ways to bring in more people not vehicles, which is why the task force's signature recommendation to improve transportation services would be a new rail tunnel under the Hudson River for passenger trains.[54] That proposal, on the drawing boards for four decades, has not yet come to fruition.

While the opportunity to expand capacity was limited in the northern corridor and faced daunting challenges in the central corridor, the Port Authority could make significant improvements in the southern corridor. Adding capacity to one of its Staten Island bridges would alleviate the biggest traffic bottleneck between New Jersey and Brooklyn. Moreover, since the George Washington Bridge was the only Authority crossing that met modern interstate highway standards, upgrading one of the Staten Island bridges would entice more trucks to use Staten Island and help alleviate traffic in more congested parts of the city.[55] Addressing the southern corridor was timely because Staten Island and central New Jersey were among the region's fastest-growing areas in terms of both population and employment. An increasing number of Staten Islanders were working in New Jersey, especially in its sprawling suburban office parks. Between 1980 and 1985, traffic rose 30 percent on the Staten Island bridges, compared to 17.5 percent on the Authority's other three crossings.[56]

Gambaccini understood the challenges and importance of coordinating efforts with the region's other transportation agencies. In most segments of the interstate highway system, only one entity was responsible for operating, maintaining, and upgrading the highway. That was not the case in New York City. I-278 was the only interstate highway that touched all five New York City boroughs. Along a 35-mile stretch, it ran over nine different roadways owned and operated by the Port Authority, Triborough Bridge and Tunnel Authority, the state of New York, and the city of New York.[57]

Gambaccini's interagency task force considered combining all the agencies' proposed improvements, similar to the way that Austin Tobin and Robert Moses had merged their efforts. But that approach would be difficult to replicate because new environmental laws and regulations made it harder for the transportation agencies to add new lanes and build new roads. Instead of combining their projects, the agencies decided to coordinate their efforts. This would give them the flexibility to proceed with their own initiatives, in case one of the agencies should get bogged down in environmental issues, community opposition, or financial shortfalls.[58]

In 1985, Port Authority planners and engineers started looking more closely at the three Staten Island crossings.[59] The Goethals, Outerbridge, and Bayonne bridges had some obvious problems. Each of them had only two ten-foot-wide lanes in each direction. Because the bridges were designed when cars and trucks were narrower, they had a higher accident rate than newer roadways, such as the Verrazzano-Narrows Bridge and Staten Island Expressway, which had standard twelve-foot-wide lanes. Accidents as well as disabled vehicles were also causing frustrating traffic jams because the three bridges did not have shoulder lanes. When a vehicle blocked one lane, the other lane had to be cleared for emergency vehicles.[60]

To help the transportation planners better understand the region's existing traffic conditions, Port Authority toll collectors handed out thousands of surveys asking motorists about their origins and destinations, routes they used during their trips, and the number of passengers in their vehicles.[61] With this data and forecasts of future travel demand, the Authority's planners developed a computerized model that simulated traffic conditions based upon future conditions with and without capacity improvements.

When considering which of the three Staten Island bridges to expand, the Goethals made the most sense because it had the best connections with the New Jersey Turnpike and the Staten Island Expressway.[62] The Goethals also happened to be located closest to the Port Authority's marine terminals and

Newark Airport. Starting in 1985, the Authority looked at twenty-seven different alternative ideas, including adding a second deck on the Goethals Bridge, attaching additional lanes to the bridge, and replacing the bridge altogether.[63] By 1990, the Authority's senior executives decided that the best way to accommodate growth would be to build a new span, parallel to the existing Goethals Bridge.[64] When completed, each of the spans would carry one-way traffic and be wide enough for three standard-width lanes along with shoulders.[65]

The manager of the Port Authority's Staten Island Bridge Development Program, Peter Ciano, told Staten Island's local officials in 1990 that he expected construction on a new span to begin by 1995 with a completion date of around 1999.[66] In 1923, Ciano's predecessors at the Port Authority were accurate when they said preliminary studies, design, and construction of the original Staten Island bridges would take three to five years.[67] Ciano woefully miscalculated in 1990, however, because Port Authority officials did not have all the ingredients needed to build a successful coalition and overcome the political and bureaucratic challenges they would face.

The Island's Reaction to Expanding the Goethals Bridge

The Port Authority's planners were trying to anticipate critical needs in the same way that their predecessors had, but they worked in a much more challenging regulatory and political landscape. Elected officials were more sensitive to neighborhood concerns and the public was skeptical about the benefits of building new roads. At a series of public information sessions held on Staten Island in 1991, residents were ambivalent about expanding or replacing the bridge. The Port Authority's planners, engineers, and executives had focused on what they thought was best for their customers and the region's economy. But Staten Island residents wanted to know how the Authority's proposal would benefit them.[68] A new bridge could have meaningful transportation and economic benefits for the metropolitan area, but it might not necessarily improve the quality of life for Staten Island's residents.

Staten Island had been growing rapidly and the resulting environmental and traffic impacts concerned many of its residents.[69] After the Verrazzano-Narrows Bridge was built, the island had a dramatic surge in population. Between 1960 and 1990, the number of residents increased more than 70 percent while the population of the rest of the city *decreased* by more than 8 percent. Many of the new residents had moved to the island because of the 1960s transportation improvements, but they resented the massive increase in the number of vehicles going through Staten Island on their way to and from New Jersey. In 1960, 8.5 million vehicles crossed the Port Authority's Staten Island bridges. By 1990, that number had risen more than 500 percent to approximately fifty-five million.[70]

Compared to residents in the other four boroughs, Staten Islanders relied more on their cars and less on public transportation.[71] Although they wanted highway improvements, many motorists and elected officials (including the borough president) expressed concern that a new bridge would lead to higher tolls and might attract more traffic to Staten Island.[72] The island's busiest highway, the Staten Island Expressway, was congested every weekday and drivers did not want more vehicles exacerbating their traffic woes. On weekdays, approximately 45 percent of all vehicles (and 75 percent of the trucks) coming off the Goethals Bridge were going directly to the Verrazzano-Narrows Bridge.[73] From the residents' perspective, these vehicles were polluting their air and exacerbating traffic as they used Staten Island as a thoroughfare. Staten Islanders also resented the high tolls charged by the Port Authority. In 1993, when the hourly minimum wage was $4.25, the Port Authority charged cars $4.00 for a round trip.[74] Drivers crossing the Goethals Bridge during peak periods did not just have to pay tolls, they were often delayed fifteen to twenty minutes waiting in line to pay the toll booth attendants.[75]

Staten Islanders did not have to worry about any imminent construction because the Port Authority could not expand the bridge's capacity until it conducted an environmental review, a federal requirement that was not in place before the 1970s. Residents, elected officials, and a plethora of local, state, and federal agencies would have numerous opportunities to comment upon potential alternatives, the issues to be studied, and the methodology that would be used to evaluate environmental impacts. Then the Port Authority would prepare an environmental impact statement. Throughout the environmental review process, Port Authority staff and their consultant team would have to meet with public officials, regulatory agencies, interest groups, and the general public to solicit their input.[76] This environmental review, which began in 1993, would slow down the planning process, give time for opponents to coalesce, and reveal data that would provide ammunition to the project's enemies.

Even though the Authority's planners had looked at twenty-seven different alternatives starting in 1985, they had to start evaluating the alternatives all over again. To comply with federal regulations, they had to consider an even broader range of options, including thirty-eight different transit (public transportation) alternatives.[77] For the most promising alternatives—including building a new span south of the existing bridge—the Authority had to assess a staggering list of potential impacts, including issues related to archaeological resources, wildlife, floodplains, vegetation, water, hazardous materials, historic buildings, traffic, air quality, scenic vistas, and noise.[78] The Port Authority and its consultants had to consider so many different issues and coordinate their efforts with so many other agencies that the Authority would not issue its final environmental impact statement until 1997, more than four years after beginning its environmental review.

Staten Island residents and their elected officials repeatedly called for public transportation improvements to either supplement or substitute for a new Goethals crossing. But none of the region's agencies were interested in providing new transit services because bus and rail lines could not break even, let alone turn a profit. The city of New York provided ferry services between Manhattan and Staten Island but did not provide rail or bus services for Staten Island commuters. New Jersey Transit did not want to take on any more money-losing routes while New York's Metropolitan Transportation Authority was not interested in helping New Yorkers access jobs in New Jersey.

The Port Authority, the only agency with bistate transportation responsibilities, did not want to be burdened with ongoing operating losses associated with new transit services. Richard Kelly, the director of the Authority's Interstate Transportation Department, told Staten Islanders that it would not be cost effective to incorporate rail on the new bridge because commuters were not going to a few destinations that would be well-served by a train; instead they were heading to cities and suburban office parks all across northern New Jersey.[79] The Authority's refusal to incorporate a rail line on a new bridge was especially infuriating to Staten Islanders because the tolls paid on the Port Authority's bridges helped subsidize the Port Authority's PATH trains, but the PATH did not operate on Staten Island.

Port Authority officials understood Staten Island's frustrations and Kelly hoped that the Authority could do more. In 1994, he told the executive director, Stanley Brezenoff, "While the community's dependence on toll crossings itself is an issue, the knowledge that revenues from these crossings subsidize other transit services galls borough residents who feel deprived of adequate transit alternatives."[80] Brezenoff agreed to design a new Goethals Bridge span so that a rail line could one day be added.[81] But it was too little too late. The Authority did not have a promising track record on incorporating rail into its facilities. Back in the 1920s, the Bayonne Bridge and the George Washington Bridge were designed to accommodate future train services but were still only carrying cars and trucks.[82]

As the Port Authority worked on its environmental analysis, a coalition of fourteen environmental and transportation organizations set up a new organization, the Tri-State Transportation Campaign. In its 1993 founding document, the coalition referred to the Port Authority's plan to build a new span parallel to the existing Goethals Bridge and wrote, "Highway expansion projects are not part of the solution, but part of the problem, reflecting traditional thinking that new lane capacity will reduce congestion and pollution."[83] Tri-State quickly established itself as an influential player in the transportation policy arena. Although the Port Authority saw new highway capacity as a means to promote economic growth, Tri-State's founders thought more roads would have the opposite effect in the long run, fueling an ominous sprawl of automobile-dependent, low-density development. The Tri-State Transportation Campaign's staff organized local groups and had an enormous influence on local officials and the media.[84]

Port Authority officials sometimes referred to a new span as the Goethals Bridge's "fraternal twin."[85] Tri-State gave it an even catchier nickname—the "evil twin."[86] Tri-State criticized the lack of a transit component and the scattered efforts by various government agencies in the region to address interrelated transit and highway problems. In the summer of 1995, while Tri-State was winning the ground game in Staten Island, the Port Authority was desperately trying to build outside support by meeting with numerous civic groups and city officials.[87]

The environmentalists were more persuasive than Port Authority officials. They offered specific suggestions to promote transit use and they tapped into Staten Islanders' fears about more traffic and the public's skepticism about the Authority. Instead of expanding capacity for cars and trucks, the Tri-State Transportation Campaign and others promoted a "congestion pricing" program that involved charging higher tolls when highways were congested. This could theoretically alleviate the need to build another crossing by encouraging motorists to change their travel times or switch to carpools and public transportation.[88]

In 1995, one Staten Island elected official after another came out against twinning the Goethals. Staten Island's Republican borough president, Guy V. Molinari, said, "I told them in no uncertain terms that the proposal, as it is, does very, very little for Staten Island."[89] Although the borough president did not have the formal power to stop a Port Authority project, his opinions were influential with Albany's decisionmakers. Another powerful Republican, the island's state senator John Marchi, excoriated Authority's officials for their callousness about the island's traffic and air quality issues. He said, "The population of this borough is more than an abstract factor in a traffic engineer's computer printout. It is a living, breathing, working collection of men, women and children whose safety should be a paramount concern."[90] Staten Island congresswoman Susan Molinari, the borough president's daughter, argued that another bridge would help New Jersey not Staten Island commuters. She asked, "Where, I wonder, do Port Authority officials believe they are going to put the additional cars that are going to result?"[91]

The *Staten Island Advance* had a prominent role in shaping public opinion. It was the city's only borough-wide daily newspaper, and it dedicated a reporter to cover transportation issues. In a 1995 editorial, the *Advance* wrote, "The volume of traffic moving from the bridge onto the Staten Island Expressway and the close-by West Shore Expressway, will be more or less double what it is now. You might eliminate backups on the bridge, but you cause backups elsewhere, not just on the expressway but on local roads to which drivers flee to escape traffic."[92] Likewise, the Port Authority did not find much vocal support from Staten Island's interest groups, except from the construction industry. The project was even publicly opposed by Brooklyn elected officials, who were worried that the new bridge would increase traffic on Brooklyn's highways and residential streets.[93]

In October 1997, the Port Authority finally issued its 2,000-page final environmental impact statement associated with building a new span. Authority officials knew that the Goethals Bridge would not be expanded anytime soon, however. New York's Republican governor, George Pataki, would not support a project that was so intensely opposed by Staten Island's Republican leaders and its leading newspaper. Staten Island was an important part of his electoral base. In the 1994 gubernatorial race, Pataki received more votes than his Democratic opponent on Staten Island, but only 25 percent of the voters supported him in the rest of the city.[94] Chris Ward, a senior Port Authority official (and future executive director), told Staten Islanders in 1997, "One thing is certain, the Port Authority will not build a new structure without the participation and support of the New York and New Jersey communities involved."[95] By this time, as described in the previous chapter, the Port Authority had limited autonomy and was neither willing nor able to take on Staten Island officials. Robert Boyle was the executive director, and his first loyalty was to George Pataki, not to the Port Authority.

By 1998, the Authority had spent more than $40 million planning and designing the bridge expansion whose construction was estimated to cost about $350 million.[96] Boyle wanted to set aside $5 million to continue design work, but he changed his mind after the Staten Island borough president complained to Governor Pataki's office.[97] Guy Molinari said at the time, "Since the inception of the Goethals Bridge twin concept, I have made it clear that I would do everything in my power to block construction of the new bridge until Staten Island is provided with an extensive mass transit service from the Port Authority."[98]

Not willing to give up, the Port Authority's engineers and planners remained patient and persistent until the external obstacles that had stymied their efforts weakened. Ultimately, a new governor, borough president, and mayor came in with different priorities and perspectives. Furthermore, Authority officials made extensive efforts to enhance their own credibility with Staten Islanders, a resource that would help turn opposition into support.

Changing Island Winds

In early 2001, the Port Authority implemented the congestion pricing concept it had previously resisted. The Tri-State Transportation Campaign's arguments had helped persuade Authority officials to offer drivers lower tolls when the bridges and tunnels were typically less congested. At the same time, Peter Rinaldi, the engineering manager for the Authority's bridges and tunnels, was developing plans to rehabilitate the seventy-two-year-old Goethals Bridge, a project that would involve much more than replacing the driving surface. The bridge needed to be repainted, but since it was covered with so many layers of paint, all the old layers would have to be stripped off, a process that involved costly ventilation and dust collection equipment. In addition, some of the steel under the bridge had to be replaced because salt applied to the roadway over the years had deteriorated it. Furthermore, the engineers wanted to strengthen the bridge's structural supports to protect it against a potential earthquake.[99]

Because contractors could only close lanes for limited periods of time, construction was expected to take several years. Ken Philmus, the director of the Tunnels, Bridges, and Terminals Department, would not shut down the bridge until 10:00 p.m. and he wanted the bridge back in operation by 6:00 a.m. That meant contractors had less than eight hours to move their equipment and materials into place, perform their work, and then clear out.[100]

Rehabilitating a bridge while keeping it in service was not only costly but also disruptive to drivers.

Rinaldi's engineers estimated the construction costs for both rehabilitating the bridge and completely replacing it. They also calculated the annual maintenance costs for both options. Rinaldi summarized these life-cycle costs in a presentation to Philmus's staff. Based on the two most important criteria—cost and service to the Authority's customers—he argued that the Goethals Bridge should be replaced rather than repaired.[101] Philmus then put together a team of Port Authority staff members and consultants to revisit the Goethals project. They dusted off the old reports and drawings and began taking steps to replace the bridge. Philmus said in April 2001, "We need this today—not tomorrow. But if the states don't want it, we won't build it."[102]

On the morning of September 11, Peter Rinaldi was on vacation in North Carolina, not in his 72nd floor World Trade Center office, when terrorists crashed an airplane with 9,000 gallons of jet fuel into the Port Authority's headquarters. When he returned to New York a few days later, he worked nearly round-the-clock leading a team of engineers supervising the cleanup and providing technical support to police, fire, and other emergency personnel. Philmus was in Boston attending a transportation conference on September 11, talking about the success of electronic tolling and the benefits of congestion pricing as a means to manage traffic. Upon his return home, he had to focus on security issues since the Port Authority's crossings were seen as highly vulnerable and an attractive target for terrorists.[103]

Philmus developed a new appreciation for redundancy when he thought about the Goethals Bridge. In case of a terrorist attack, two bridges with six lanes each would be safer than one bridge with twelve lanes.[104] "When something happens," he said in 2002, "the transportation system needs to have as much flexibility as possible. We did a good job [after September 11] with what we have but a strained system became broken. Redundancy has historically been thought of as too expensive, but we now know that it is vital for our future."[105] Authority officials were increasingly optimistic in 2003 they would be able to move forward with replacing the bridge because most Staten Island elected officials and local groups now supported replacing the bridge with a more modern facility.

The Port Authority's persistence paid off. The new Staten Island borough president, James Molinaro, supported building a new, wider, stronger, and safer bridge.[106] The *Staten Island Advance* had once helped lead the charge against twinning the bridge. In a 2003 editorial, the newspaper used the Port

Authority's talking points when it wrote, "Not only is the bridge in its current condition inadequate to handle the increased traffic flow, but it is unsafe and daunting for drivers to cross because of narrow traffic lanes and no shoulders, and the heavy use, particularly by trucks, has taken a heavy toll on the bridge deck." The editorial argued that a modern bridge was "no longer merely nice to envision; it's absolutely necessary to build."[107]

Why did public opinion change about the Goethals Bridge so dramatically? Some external factors were important in overcoming local opposition. For instance, a new mayor was not as antagonistic toward the Port Authority as Rudy Giuliani was in the 1990s. Although Mayor Giuliani did not publicly oppose twinning the Goethals, he hurt the Authority's credibility by relentlessly attacking it for mismanaging resources and prioritizing New Jersey's needs over New York. The Authority's biggest nemesis, the Tri-State Transportation Campaign, was no longer an outspoken opponent. While the organization's environmental and transit advocates were against building a new bridge in the 1990s, they did not object to replacing the aging and obsolete bridge in the 2000s.[108] Two other external factors also helped the Port Authority's cause. Drivers found the narrow width of the Goethals Bridge increasingly uncomfortable with more people driving wider vehicles, such as sport utility vehicles and pickup trucks. And then in 2004, Staten Island officials wanted to increase highway capacity because they were excited about NASCAR's proposal to build a racetrack with more than 80,000 seats about a mile from the Goethals Bridge.[109]

Trust, prestige, and credibility were valuable resources. In a 2004 editorial, the *Staten Island Advance* referred to the Authority "as efficient and far-sighted public agency as there is."[110] The newspaper appreciated how in the 1990s E-ZPass tags were speeding up travel (see chapter 6).[111] The terrorist attack and the Port Authority's relentless efforts to protect its facilities also affected the public's perceptions about the island's bridges. Before September 11, project opponents focused on quality-of-life issues. After September 11, safe and sufficient infrastructure had become a life-or-death issue. New York's state assemblyman Matthew Mirones said the region lies under the "constant fear of terror attacks. We are very concerned with ingress and egress off the island in the case of an emergency."[112]

The Port Authority's earlier warnings about increased traffic were seen as prescient. In 1985, the Port Authority started planning for additional capacity before it would be needed. Since then, the number of vehicles driving annually through its Staten Island tollbooths had risen from 23.4 million to 33.2

Moving Three Bridges from the Periphery to Center Stage

Fig. 7.5. The narrow lanes and heavy truck traffic on the original Goethals Bridge made many drivers uncomfortable.
(Photograph by formulanone, July 2013. Courtesy Wikimedia Commons, CC BY-SA 2.0.)

million.[113] Because of the bridge's narrow lanes, many drivers had long felt anxious driving next to trucks, but it was getting harder to avoid that situation because of the increasing number of vehicles (fig. 7.5). Ken Philmus said in 2003, "One of the concerns we kept hearing [in the 1990s] was that if we build the bridge, the traffic would come. Well, guess what? The traffic came anyway."[114] The concern that a new bridge would exacerbate traffic congestion had abated somewhat because New York was getting ready to build a high-occupancy-vehicle (HOV) lane in each direction on the Staten Island Expressway. Along with the Port Authority's congestion pricing program, the HOV lane would encourage more people to carpool and use buses.

The Authority was also praised for an economic development initiative near the Goethals Bridge. In the mid-1990s, Staten Island's business leaders and elected officials had called on the Port Authority to revive a long-neglected and virtually abandoned 187-acre marine facility at Howland Hook. By 2004, the Authority had poured tens of millions of dollars into creating a modern marine terminal and building a rail connection so that freight trains carrying shipping containers could travel between the marine terminal and New Jersey.[115] Through its work at Howland Hook, the Authority strengthened its ties with elected officials, business leaders, and community groups. Businesses that were tied to the marine terminal's success strongly supported a new bridge because trucks were constrained by the existing bridge's narrow lanes.[116]

The Port Authority learned lessons from the 1990s and approached the community in a fundamentally new way. Instead of talking about improvements to the southern corridor, when Ken Philmus and other Authority officials talked to Staten Islanders, they emphasized the need to replace a functionally obsolete bridge. They talked about safety issues for motorists associated with narrow lanes and how the lack of shoulders was endangering emergency workers. When describing the alternatives to replacing the bridge, Philmus was not shy about scaring residents, business leaders, elected officials, and civic groups. He said Staten Islanders would have to endure years of construction with periodic closings, similar to the construction work they had recently endured, and frequently complained about, on the Outerbridge Crossing.[117]

Philmus avoided saying that replacing the bridge was his preferred alternative in 2003. Instead he talked about a transparent planning process. "There will be more public meetings than you've ever seen," he said. "What you have here is a process where the public will develop the choice, as opposed to a choice being brought into the public meeting." Rather than discounting the possibility of rail service on the bridge, he said, "Whether it's HOV, light rail, I don't know. There might not be a market for that now, but there might be in another 25 years. That's part of what the EIS [environmental impact statement] will figure out."[118]

Port Authority's representatives shared Staten Island-oriented data with community groups. When they did presentations to community groups, they used graphics to show how traffic would back up, even from a minor accident.[119] A Port Authority planner, Lou Venech, said, "we made sure there was a shared base of understanding of problems and opportunities. We worked with people on Staten Island, organized workshops, and talked about potential future conditions, and their transportation concerns."[120]

Two More Hurdles

Because the Port Authority wanted to replace the entire bridge and its 1997 environmental impact statement had never been approved by federal officials, the U.S. Coast Guard determined that an entirely new environmental impact statement would be needed.[121] The Authority began work on the environment review in 2004 and after more than six years of data collection, analysis, and extensive public review, the Coast Guard finally signed off on the environmental document in January 2011,[122] more than a quarter century after planning for a new span had begun.

Now that the Port Authority had federal approval on the environmental document and Staten Island support for the project, it still needed to overcome opposition from the other side of the Arthur Kill. The residents of Elizabeth, a New Jersey city with a population of 125,000, had just as much reason to resent the Port Authority as Staten Islanders. Elizabeth was not only the landing for the western portion of the Goethals Bridge it was also home to the Authority's Elizabeth Marine Terminal and a portion of Newark Airport.

In 1931, the Port Authority agreed to make an annual payment of $63,000 per year in lieu of taxes for its seaport and airport land. If these properties had been privately owned, by 2010 the owner would have paid more than $15 million annually in real estate taxes. Instead the City of Elizabeth's leaders made a mistake in 1931 that would haunt its future residents. They neglected to peg the Authority's annual payments to the rate of inflation or the municipal tax rate. Elizabeth's neighbor had been more farsighted. The city of Newark leased, rather than sold, its land to the Port Authority. In 2010, the Authority's comptroller issued a $63,000 check to Elizabeth and approved a payment to Newark for more than $65,000,000.[123]

Chris Bollwage was first elected Elizabeth mayor in 1992 and he was still in office when the Port Authority completed its environmental review. A lifelong resident of Elizabeth, he had thought the Goethals Bridge needed to be replaced since he was eighteen years old. At the time, New Jersey's drinking age was twenty-one but only eighteen in New York. The future mayor driving home from the Staten Island bars recognized that the lanes on the Goethals Bridge were not wide enough.[124]

Mayor Bollwage had the power to wreak havoc with the Port Authority's schedule for the Goethals Bridge project by preventing contractors from staging construction equipment on city property, and refusing to sell city-owned land the Authority needed to build a wider bridge.[125] The Port Authority could try to use its powers of eminent domain to take the city's property, but doing so might result in a court battle that would delay the project for several years.[126] Bollwage's track record revealed why the Port Authority needed a productive working relationship with the cities it served. In 1999, he had been furious when the Port Authority purchased private land that took a 177-acre property off the municipal tax rolls. In retaliation, the mayor told police officers to set up roadblocks leading to the Elizabeth marine terminal and then issue summonses for any possible motor vehicle violation, such as broken taillights, missing license plates, and bald tires. Police officers ended their traffic stops only after more than 600 summonses were issued and New Jersey's governor, Christine Todd Whitman, promised Bollwage that the Port Authority would acquiesce to his demands.[127]

As mayor, Bollwage had two concerns about the new Goethals Bridge. He wanted it expanded on its southern side because it would have less impact to taxable land. The Authority shared his preference because building the new bridge north of the existing one would have encroached on several important Staten Island commercial properties, including the Howland Hook marine terminal.[128] Second, Mayor Bollwage insisted that the highway connections be improved between Route 1/9 and the Goethals Bridge, to reduce the number of cars and trucks using the city's local streets. These improvements had been on the drawing boards since the early 1960s.[129] The mayor was able to strike a deal with Bill Baroni, the New Jersey governor's hand-picked deputy executive director at the Port Authority. Baroni told the Port Authority commissioners in no uncertain terms that the Authority would not be able to replace the Goethals Bridge unless it provided $130 million to build a new highway interchange. Baroni told the commissioners, "The governor said that the decades of this not taking place had to come to an end."[130]

After twenty-five years of planning, the Port Authority was set to build its first new bridge since 1931. One major hurdle remained, however. A $1.5 billion dollar hurdle. The Authority no longer had sufficient resources to pay for it. Since the Authority's board in 2006 had adopted a ten-year $26.1 billion capital plan that included more than $1 billion to replace the bridge, one might wonder, how could the Port Authority not have had enough money?[131] The short answer is that the Authority did not have sufficient funds to pay for all the projects in its capital plans. Sometimes the Authority just included projects in its capital plans to appease certain stakeholders or elected officials. Other times, it made overly optimistic assumptions about project costs, schedules, and funding.[132]

In 2010, the Port Authority was having financial problems because World Trade Center rebuilding costs were higher than expected and it was facing revenue shortfalls associated with a national economic recession (see chapter 8). Typically, the Authority borrowed money for its capital improvements, but in 2010 the Authority was reaching the limit for how much it could issue

Moving Three Bridges from the Periphery to Center Stage 201

Fig. 7.6. The two spans of the new Goethals Bridge opened between 2017 and 2018. (Photograph reprinted by permission of Port Authority of New York and New Jersey.)

in bonds, an amount determined by its revenues.[133] The Authority figured out a workaround by entering into an unusual public-private partnership. A private company would borrow money from the federal government and issue its own bonds that would not count toward the Port Authority's debt limit. Then the firm known as NYNJ Link would design, build, and maintain the bridge. When the Staten Island bridges were first built, the Authority was known for having some of the world's greatest bridge engineers and architects. Now it was farming out the design to a private firm. Likewise, the Authority had always been known for taking excellent care of its facilities. Now the private firm would maintain the bridge.

Building a new 1.4-mile long bridge with six lanes and shoulders was faster than completing an environmental review. Construction started in 2014 and both spans were completed four years later (fig. 7.6). As the Port Authority had expected and hoped, the traffic volumes and toll revenues increased after the new bridge opened while the accident rates plummeted.

Bayonne: A Bridge Too Low

At the same time the Port Authority was replacing the Goethals Bridge, it was addressing an issue with another Staten Island Bridge, a problem that was threatening the heart of the Authority's mission. The Bayonne Bridge project may appear to be another achievement that reflected the Authority's ability to identify economic needs; devise creative plans to overcome engineering, economic, and political hurdles; and mobilize support for its plans. But its story also reveals how one governor co-opted the agency's priorities to advance his own reelection prospects.

In the 1990s, the top of large ships, sailing along the Kill Van Kull, occasionally scraped the paint off the underside of the Bayonne Bridge's deck, about 150 feet above the water. More than once, the bridge had to be closed after ships' cranes damaged the bridge's steel supports underneath the bridge's deck.[134] A more immediate concern was making sure that the Kill Van Kull was deep enough for the bottom of the ships. The Kill Van Kull was not some minor creek filled with canoes and kayaks, it was the gateway to the Authority's major marine terminals in Newark, Elizabeth, and Staten Island. At a Port Authority board meeting in 2000, Rick Larrabee, the Authority's director of the port commerce department, briefed the commissioners on the authority's ongoing dredging efforts to accommodate larger container ships. After he finished speaking, Ken Philmus leaned over to him and whispered, "What are we doing? How are they going to fit under the bridge?" Philmus remembers that Larabee turned to him and muttered, "oh shit!"[135]

In the early 2000s, some of the larger container ships had to schedule passage along the Kill Van Kull during the low tide when the Bayonne Bridge's clearance was 156 feet rather than the high tide's clearance of 151 feet. The bridge's constraints were well known in China, Korea, and Japan and were taken into account when ships were designed and loaded. Even though ship owners installed sensors to measure their clearance under the bridge, light bulbs were still getting shattered, and antennas snapped off as they sailed underneath.[136]

By 2006, Port Authority officials had already considered several measures it could take to replace or redesign the bridge so that it would not hamper the port's viability. But the Authority's senior officials placed a higher priority on replacing the Goethals Bridge, which was a more important source of ongoing revenue.[137] Tolls on the Goethals generated $84 million in 2006, but only $23 million on the Bayonne. The Staten Island bridges, which had been money losers before the Verrazzano-Narrows Bridge was built, had become an important profit center for the Authority. The Authority's engineers were also concerned about the structural integrity of the Goethals since it was subjected to heavy truck traffic. In fact, when George Marlin was Port Authority executive director in 1995, his engineers told him that the Goethals would only last another fifteen years.[138]

The Authority's executive director in 2007 and early 2008, Tony Shorris, was not panicking about the Bayonne Bridge. He was not convinced that the benefits of fixing the clearance issue were worth the costs of replacing or rehabilitating the bridge.[139] A megaproject more than 2,000 miles from the New York harbor, however, was adding urgency to concerns about the Bayonne Bridge. In 2008, Panama began a multibillion-dollar program to expand its canal so that wider and longer ships could cross between the Atlantic and Pacific oceans. To take advantage of the expanded canal, shipbuilders were starting to construct vessels that could carry twice as many containers. Shippers, manufacturers, distributors, and retailers in Asia and the United States were excited because the crew size and fuel expenses for these larger ships would stay about the same. That meant shippers would be able to lower their shipping rates and increase their profits at the same time.

Ports all along the East Coast began projects to deepen their shipping channels and build new facilities to handle larger ships.[140] Unless the Port Authority took action, the newest ships would not be able to dock in the New York metropolitan area since they could not fit under the Bayonne Bridge. Officials in the Authority's port commerce department were eager to address the bridge problem because they knew from the Authority's experience with the Goethals Bridge that the planning, design, and construction of a new bridge could take ten years or more to complete.[141] In 2008, the Authority's engineers seriously considered three different options: replacing the Bayonne Bridge, building a tunnel under the Kill Van Kull, and raising the entire bridge.[142]

In 2009, the Bayonne Bridge's clearance issue was still an important concern but not a top priority for the Authority. Billions of dollars were allocated toward rebuilding the World Trade Center, replacing the Goethals, and funding a new passenger rail tunnel under the Hudson River. The executive director, Chris Ward, did not think the Port Authority had the resources to take on another billion-dollar-plus project and he did not buy into the conventional wisdom about the urgency of raising the bridge.[143] Ward had worked in the maritime industry and in the Authority's port commerce department before serving as executive director. After talking with industry leaders and authority officials, he concluded that the Authority had time to solve the clearance problem, and that ships trying to go under the bridge could be retrofitted at a modest cost.[144]

The media and the general public were not paying much attention to the Bayonne Bridge's problems because the bridge was the Authority's least utilized crossing, few people understood the importance of the port to the region's economy, and the problem had yet to affect anyone's livelihood. Business and labor interests associated with the ports were ringing the alarms, however. In the late 1990s, the New Jersey Chamber of Commerce had set up the NationsPort organization to advocate for port improvements. A Port Authority representative sat on its board and the Authority's lobbyist in Washington, D.C., set up periodic meetings with congressional members and their staffs. In 2009, with the channel on its way to being deepened to fifty feet, the group had no higher priority than solving Bayonne's clearance issues. NationsPort warned that unless the bridge problem was addressed, jobs would be threatened, more goods would have to be hauled in by truck, and the cost of goods would rise.[145]

NationsPort's members included shipping firms, unions, truckers, and real estate developers, as well as engineering and construction firms that would benefit from building new bridges.[146] NationsPort staff and its members had influence with every elected official in northern New Jersey. In 2009, Chris Christie, the Republican candidate for New Jersey governor, heard their message. He promised unions and industry groups that solving the Bayonne Bridge problem would be his "highest transportation priority."[147] The changes institutionalized at the Port Authority in the 1990s (as described in the previous chapter) enabled future New Jersey governors to divert Authority resources toward their own priorities. In Christie's case that meant minimizing state taxes, repairing state roads, and addressing the problem in Bayonne.

The Governor's Loyal Aide

When Christie was sworn in as governor, he continued the tradition that had started under Governor Whitman in 1995. The New Jersey governor selected the Port Authority's deputy executive director, while New York's governor appointed the executive director. Christie, poised to politicize the Port Authority to unprecedented levels, wanted a deputy whose loyalty was to the governor's office not to the Authority's bureaucracy. During his administration, the Authority's executive and deputy executive directors would each have their own priorities and their own staffs who kept secrets from each other.

Governor Christie offered the deputy executive director position to Bill Baroni, a state senator who was the only Republican to vote for a bill allowing gay couples to marry.[148] Baroni knew his socially progressive positions would prevent him from rising much further in the Republican party, so he jumped at the opportunity to gain managerial experience and work on important regional projects.[149] Christie's number one priority for Baroni was figuring out how to solve the Bayonne Bridge clearance problem. The day that Governor Christie announced Baroni's appointment to the Port Authority,[150] the senator's phone started ringing with union leaders and industry officials urging him to focus on the bridge problem.[151]

Baroni took the advice of a previous deputy executive director who told him, "You'll be inundated. It's like drinking from a fire hose. You need three or four things to focus on."[152] Baroni would spend more time working on the Bayonne Bridge project than any other Port Authority initiative and he relished the opportunity.[153] The former state senator had longstanding ties with New Jersey's unions and feared the loss of jobs to states that could accommodate larger ships. He also saw the Bayonne Bridge project as a way to burnish his credentials, by proving to people that he could successfully manage and expedite a massive project.[154]

After Baroni started in March 2010, he held a meeting where senior officials briefed him about all the Port Authority's major projects. Joann Papageorgis, a program director, spoke last and Baroni's ears perked up when she talked about her planning efforts related to the Bayonne Bridge. Baroni mentioned that he was going to a meeting on Staten Island and asked if she had any advice for him. She responded, "Don't talk about the three T's—tolls, transit, and traffic." Baroni immediately liked her blunt manner and told her that he wanted to start meeting with her on a regular basis.[155] He would later say, "Joann is maybe the single greatest employee I worked with in my 26 years of working in government."[156]

Baroni gave Papageorgis seemingly impossible instructions regarding the Bayonne Bridge: obtain all the approvals needed to begin construction as soon as possible, avoid taking any private properties, and keep at least some of the bridge's lanes open to traffic during construction.

The Authority's chief engineer, Peter Zipf, had his own ideas. After looking at various options, Zipf determined that the best plan to solve the clearance problem would be to replace the entire bridge at a cost of approximately $2 billion. Based on the life-cycle costs of construction and maintenance, this would be the least expensive solution.[157] Zipf's predecessor, Frank Lombardi, had come up with an even less expensive option. After considering the costs and benefits, he wanted to retain the Bayonne Bridge's historic steel arch and remove the roadway. Lombardi did not think the bridge was a vital element in the transportation network since fewer than 20,000 vehicles were crossing it on a typical day, compared to more than 71,000 that crossed the Goethals and 75,000 that crossed the Outerbridge.[158] Since removing the roadway would inconvenience thousands of people every day, this option was a non-starter in Trenton.

Likewise, the recommendation to replace the entire bridge was unacceptable. Papageorgis had worked on Goethals Bridge planning efforts and knew that removing the existing Bayonne Bridge and building a new one would trigger the need to conduct a multiyear environmental review. Moreover, the Authority would need to acquire more than fifty private properties to create a sufficient right-of-way.[159] Baroni, an attorney, realized that the litigation associated with property takings would have tied up the Port Authority in lengthy legal battles, and he would have also met fierce resistance from the city of Bayonne officials who were insistent that the Port Authority not take any residential property.[160]

While the engineers were evaluating alternatives, Baroni was looking around for a spare billion dollars. His opportunity came in the summer of 2010. Chris Ward, the executive director, told Baroni that the Port Authority needed to allocate an additional $1 billion to break a logjam related to the rebuilding of the World Trade Center's office towers. Ward asked Baroni whether Governor Christie would support this funding request because he knew the Port Authority's board members from New Jersey would not approve such a major budget change without Christie's blessing. After briefing the governor, Baroni reported back that Christie would agree to Ward's proposal, under one condition: the Authority would have to set aside $1 billion for the Bayonne Bridge as well.

Baroni called Papageorgis while she was on her summer vacation in Virginia. She was preparing to retire soon, but Baroni pleaded with her to stay at the Authority, promising that the Bayonne Bridge project would soon be fully funded. Since Baroni did not tell Papageorgis about his discussions with the governor and the executive director, she did not believe that he would be able to secure enough money to pay for the project. The Authority never allocated money to complete a major project until it had conducted preliminary engineering and developed a detailed scope of work, budget, and schedule.[161] Papageorgis thought that Baroni must have some magical powers when the Port Authority's board voted to allocate $1 billion for the Bayonne Bridge at its September 2010 meeting.[162]

Papageorgis decided to stay on, even though the task of building the bridge as soon as possible while minimizing traffic disruptions and avoiding any property takings seemed impossible. She pleaded with the engineers to figure out how to use the existing bridge and the existing right-of-way.[163] She wanted the Authority to build a new roadway on top of the existing roadway and then take down the existing one.[164] The Port Authority's engineers figured out a way to do it, although Chris Ward (the Authority's executive director) thought it was a "cockamamie scheme" that would be difficult to construct and overly expensive.[165]

Four days after Christmas, the Authority announced that rather than replacing the bridge or jacking it up, a new roadway would be suspended with steel cables from the bridge's arch and new approaches and ramps built above the existing ones. To perform this feat, construction workers would have to close two lanes of traffic and then lift materials and equipment sixty-four feet in the air. One irreverent reporter wrote, "I was hard-pressed to imagine how that would be done, but the Port Authority of New York and New Jersey has explained it all on a succinct Web page that uses impressive-sounding words like 'gantry' and 'constructability' and 'conceptual animation,' so apparently it's possible."[166]

Elected officials in both Staten Island and Bayonne were supportive because raising the roadway was the least disruptive option for a project that would protect port-related local jobs and businesses. The Port Authority's substantial resources helped minimize opposition in Bayonne. At the insistence of Governor Christie, in 2010 the Port Authority agreed to purchase waterfront property from the city of Bayonne for approximately $80 million more than its appraised value to help the city avoid bankruptcy.[167] Baroni also allocated money to mitigate some of the local officials' concerns. Port Authority funds were used to clean swimming pools as well as install new air conditioners and windows for residents living near the construction. The Authority also gave money to a little league and fixed up two Bayonne parks.[168] Some residents were even given hotel vouchers during very disruptive construction periods. Papageorgis referred to these programs as a "good neighbor policy," while Baroni considered them similar to the types of constituent services that he performed as a legislator.[169]

Baroni and Papageorgis could do little in response to one recurring request. Although Staten Islanders urged that a light rail line be built on the Bayonne Bridge, the Authority was still not willing to pay for train lines on any of its motor vehicle bridges. Instead Authority officials said the new roadway "would be designed with the capability to accommodate any future bus or light rail transit initiatives."[170] The answer was similar to the ones the Authority had been giving on some of its other bridges for nearly ninety years.

The Authority's engineers were excited to work on the Bayonne Bridge project. While the Port Authority entered into a public private partnership for the Goethals, the Authority's engineers would keep tighter control over the Bayonne work.[171] Peter Zipf, the Port Authority's chief engineer, said, "It's a completely challenging project, and that's an engineer's delight."[172] Steve Plate, the Authority's chief of major capital programs, said keeping the channel open to ships and two bridge lanes open to vehicles was "like performing open-heart surgery on a runner while he's running a marathon."[173] He also had deep respect for Othmar Ammann's original design of the Bayonne Bridge. "This was one of his prized possessions," Plate said. "It's like being commissioned to restore the Sistine Chapel."[174]

Even though Baroni secured project funding and spearheaded a design that met his goals, he still faced pressure from businesses and unions who wanted the Bayonne Bridge clearance problem fixed as soon as possible. The Panama Canal project would be complete within a few years and New York's competitors could accommodate the new ships under construction. In Trenton, the Republican governor desperately wanted support from construction unions for his 2013 reelection campaign.

Although the Port Authority was not building a new bridge, raising the span would still require forty-seven permits from nineteen different government agencies.[175] Baroni set up a team of Authority employees and lobbyists to pressure officials at these agencies. As a state legislator, he had worked on many controversial issues. Now he was delighted to promote a policy initiative that had widespread support among a wide range of industry, labor, and civic groups.

Baroni took advantage of all his political connections. For example, he had served in the state assembly with congressman Albio Sires and had been an election lawyer for U.S. senator Robert Menendez and congressman Rodney Frelinghuysen (whose father had led the fight against an airport at the Great Swamp). Baroni was able to recruit the state's most liberal and conservative congressmen to support his efforts and his team worked closely with Vice President Joe Biden's office, which was able to get the project identified and then expedited as one of President Obama's high priority national projects.[176] "I left nothing on the table," Baroni said.[177]

With the White House monitoring the project, congressmen pestering the federal agencies, and the U.S. Coast Guard waiving the requirement for an environmental impact statement, Baroni was able to move his project along much faster than Port Authority officials working on the Goethals Bridge. That made his "boss" very happy. In July 2013, Governor Christie joined hun-

Moving Three Bridges from the Periphery to Center Stage

Fig. 7.7. Governor Chris Christie at a 2013 rally with union workers to celebrate upcoming construction work on the Bayonne Bridge. (Photograph courtesy of the New Jersey Governor's Office.)

dreds of local construction workers to celebrate the project's groundbreaking (fig. 7.7).[178]

The executive director, Chris Ward, had been concerned that the design was rushed and overly complicated. He was not surprised when construction was delayed by two years and the cost rose (from what Baroni said would be just over $1 billion[179]) to $1.7 billion. Ward, who had referred to the design as "cockamamie," called the bridge construction work a "clusterfuck."[180] A few hundred million dollars and an extra couple of years did not spoil the celebrations though. After the construction was completed, the American Society of Civil Engineers awarded the Port Authority an Outstanding Civil Engineering Achievement Award based on its innovation, resourcefulness, and contribution to civil engineering progress (fig. 7.8).

In 2017, a containership sailed across the Pacific Ocean from Shanghai to Panama.[181] More than four football fields long, it could carry 7,200 standard forty-foot shipping containers.[182] After crossing the canal, the ship sailed through the Caribbean Sea and then north along the Eastern Seaboard of the United States. It passed under the two decks of the Verrazzano-Narrows

Fig. 7.8. Construction underway at the Bayonne Bridge to raise the bridge's clearance by sixty-four feet. The original deck has yet to be fully removed in this photo. *(Photograph reprinted by permission of Port Authority of New York and New Jersey.)*

Bridge and headed into New York Harbor toward the Statue of Liberty and the World Trade Center. The pilot then turned the ship west onto the Arthur Kill and slowed down at the Bayonne Bridge.

No containership this large had ever berthed in the New York harbor or any other East Coast port. A few months earlier, the ship would have ripped through the Bayonne Bridge's deck. But now that the deck had been raised, the crew received a hero's welcome. The ship was aptly named the "Theodore Roosevelt." Roosevelt was born and raised in Manhattan, and his family owned piers on Manhattan's west side and a farm on Staten Island.[183] As U.S. president, he had appointed an engineer named George Goethals to build a canal in Panama.

Conclusion

The Staten Island bridges reveal how the Port Authority's ability to achieve its goals became much more difficult as both its internal and external environments fundamentally changed.

In the 1920s, the Port Authority had widespread support from elected officials, businesses, and civic groups to build three bridges between New

Moving Three Bridges from the Periphery to Center Stage

Fig. 7.9. One of the world's largest container ships sailed under the Bayonne Bridge in 2020.
(Photograph reprinted by permission of Port Authority of New York and New Jersey.)

Jersey and the New York City's semirural island. The Authority overcame challenges by establishing a highly regarded organizational culture with a professional staff who secured the autonomy and resources needed to successfully complete three ambitious projects. Before building the Staten Island bridges, the Authority was mostly known for conducting studies and issuing reports. By the time the bridges opened to the public, the organization had a reputation for constructing enormous facilities on time and on budget which gave it an opportunity to take on more ambitious projects.

In the 1950s, the Authority had enterprising leaders and a sophisticated planning team who seized opportunities to redraw the region's map. They figured out how to use the Authority's substantial resources, leverage them with external funds, generate public support, and then integrate the region's rapidly growing suburban areas via the Staten Island crossings and a new level on the George Washington Bridge.

By the 1990s, Staten Island's population was greater than the city of Atlanta and the island's residents were suspicious of any claims that a new bridge would benefit them. Environmental regulations gave opponents of twinning the Goethals Bridge several years to coalesce, and by the time the Port Authority was ready to begin the project, it had neither the political support nor the autonomy to take it on. The Authority's board of commissioners were hamstrung trying to set its own priorities and allocate its own resources. But the Port Authority's patience and persistence paid off because it eventually replaced the entire bridge by taking advantage of a changed political environment and creatively building upon two key resources: credibility and finances.

The Bayonne Bridge revealed a very different set of dynamics that showed how the events described in the previous chapter had transformed the Port Authority. Even though officials were concerned about the bridge's clearance problem, it was not the Authority's most important priority. Bill Baroni had a peculiar role in this effort. He was a Port Authority deputy executive director who could wield the power of the New Jersey governor to usurp the executive director. Trying to fulfill Governor Christie's wishes, he faced an extraordinarily difficult engineering challenge and an extremely tight timeline. He created his own supportive coalitions and solved the clearance problem by combining the Port Authority's engineering know-how and its financial resources with his own connections in the political arena.

Baroni's tenure at the Port Authority did not end well for the deputy executive director or for the organization as a whole. Five months after the Bayonne Bridge's groundbreaking, his role in the Bridgegate scandal was revealed (see chapter 9). Baroni closed lanes leading to the George Washington Bridge and then blatantly lied about it to protect the governor. A few weeks after the U.S. Supreme Court reversed Baroni's conviction of seven counts of conspiracy and wire fraud relating to Bridgegate, he told us, "it breaks my heart, that I'm not defined by the Bayonne Bridge but by a different bridge."[184]

CHAPTER 8

Building and Rebuilding the World Trade Center

The World Trade Center symbolized New York City's commercial prominence and later its greatest tragedy. When the office complex was constructed in the late 1960s and early 1970s, the twin towers represented the dramatic expansion of the Port Authority's ambitions, its capacity to take on great risk, and its ability to complete massive and transformative construction projects. After the towers fell in 2001, the Authority was in disarray. Its headquarters in the north tower were destroyed, the executive director and eighty-three other employees were killed, and the institution (already weakened by the 1990s turmoil) was left with the mammoth task of rebuilding in a politically fragmented environment. The challenge of redeveloping the World Trade Center site and adjusting its infrastructure to a post 9/11 world also paralleled the Port Authority's struggle to heal and come to grips with its diminished capacity and autonomy since the upheavals of the 1990s.

A Center for World Trade

Like many of the Port Authority's other major initiatives, the initial idea of building a center for world trade in Manhattan did not originate at the Authority's offices. The concept can be traced back to an age before the Internet when the buyers and sellers of goods actually met face to face to learn about products, exchange information, sign contracts, and arrange shipping.

The world's greatest cities once celebrated technological innovations and cultural contributions by hosting international expositions. In 1939, the theme at New York City's World's Fair was "The World of Tomorrow" where RCA introduced the television, General Electric demonstrated the fluorescent bulb, and General Motors envisioned a future with interconnected expressways and vast suburbs across the United States. Fairgoers learned that

213

in the world of tomorrow, cities would have neither slums nor sunless streets, every office building would be built on a park with plenty of parking spaces, and travel across the region would be swift and efficient.[1]

Winthrop Aldrich helped organize an exhibit at the fair dedicated to "world peace through trade." Aldrich headed America's largest bank and his sister had married John D. Rockefeller, Jr., one of the world's richest men. Convinced that the interdependent cooperation of men and nations would create a free and prosperous world, Aldrich dreamed of building a permanent center for world trade in New York City. A central marketplace exhibiting and promoting the sale of goods from across the world had the potential to be an economic boon for the region, not to mention Aldrich's bank. An international trading center would capitalize on the city's port facilities and its global leadership in manufacturing, finance, and trade.[2]

The state of New York set up a World Trade Corporation in 1946 to study the feasibility of a World Trade Center, and Governor Thomas Dewey appointed Aldrich to serve as chair of the corporation's board of directors.[3] Aldrich came up with a plan to create a World Trade Center complex with twenty-one buildings including exhibition halls. The idea quickly died, though, because market research indicated there would not be enough demand for the space.[4] The Port Authority reportedly told the mayor that the corporation's concept of a World Trade Center was unnecessary and unfeasible.[5] The World Trade Corporation also vied, unsuccessfully, to take over and rehabilitate New York City's aging piers, warehouses, and terminals. The corporation was disbanded in early 1949 because it did not have the resources, technical knowledge, or experience to compete with the Port Authority in building and managing port facilities.[6] However, two of Aldrich's nephews, Nelson and David Rockefeller, would help make their uncle's dream of a World Trade Center a reality.

The Rockefellers and the Port Authority's executive director (Austin Tobin) each had their own reasons for pursuing a World Trade Center. In 1958, David Rockefeller and other prominent business leaders established the Downtown-Lower Manhattan Association to promote improvements in Lower Manhattan, and one of the association's first proposals was a World Trade Center where businesses and government officials could meet to facilitate trade. Rockefeller was vice chair of Chase Manhattan Bank,[7] the financial institution closely associated with the Rockefeller family fortune. A World Trade Center would enhance business opportunities for the bank, its customers and business partners, as well as increase the value of the bank's property in Lower Manhattan's financial district. David Rockefeller was also excited about the prospects of building a successful downtown business complex like the one his father had built—Rockefeller Center—in Midtown Manhattan.[8]

For the members of the Downtown-Lower Manhattan Association, a World Trade Center would help their neighborhood compete against Midtown Manhattan (between 34th Street and 59th Street), which had more land to build upon, newer office buildings, and direct commuter railroad service from the rapidly expanding suburbs in Westchester, Long Island, and New Jersey. Midtown was also closer to the Upper East Side, the neighborhood where the city's elite lived; and it was also more accessible by car and subway from Queens, where many middle-class families were moving.

Rockefeller's vision meshed with Austin Tobin's own goals. With the continuous growth of traffic at the Port Authority's bridges, tunnels, and airports—Tobin was looking to invest resources into new projects that could be profitable or at least revenue neutral. In 1948, the Authority's operating revenue exceeded its operating expenses by $19.9 million and that number had risen to $50.6 million by 1958.[9] In the 1950s, Tobin was under a lot of pressure, especially from New Jersey lawmakers, to use the Port Authority's surpluses to help subsidize the region's commuter rail services.[10] By the late 1950s, highways and river crossings could turn a profit with tolls, but America's remaining private railroad and streetcar companies were facing financial insolvency because of the rise in automobile ownership. These firms needed large capital investments to modernize their trains and infrastructure, as well as ongoing government subsidies to provide train services.

New Jersey's legislators viewed the Port Authority as both a cause of and potential solution to the railroads' problems. The Port Authority's bridges, tunnels, bus stations, and parking facilities had encouraged tens of thousands of people to travel by car and bus rather than train. The legislators wanted to tap into the Authority's surpluses to preserve train services that many of their constituents relied upon. Pressure on the Authority to save railroad service became even more intense in 1958 after Congress passed a transportation law allowing railroads to shed unprofitable rail and ferry services.[11]

The commissioners of the Port Authority were unanimously opposed to any legislation that would involve the Port Authority in the passenger railroad business. Led by Tobin, they argued in 1958 that taking on the commuter rail "deficit was legally, financially and contractually impossible" and that it would have "disastrous consequences for the people of the two states."[12] Tobin told the two governors that it would cripple the Authority's credit and halt the development of essential marine and inland terminal facilities, airports, and the interstate arterial system.[13] The Port Authority did not want to take any responsibility for the railroad crisis, dubiously claiming, "The private automobile into and out of Manhattan presents negligible competition to mass transportation."[14] In 1958, the Port Authority even added restrictions to its bond covenants that would make it harder for the Authority to subsidize public transportation operations.[15]

Tobin had other reasons for participating in the World Trade Center project. He hoped it would encourage more ships to use the New York region's marine facilities, since they were losing market share to U.S. ports in the south and west. The ports in New York and New Jersey were carrying more foreign trade cargo than previous years, but their volume of the nation's share had dropped from 34 percent in 1952 to 23 percent in 1960 (the year after the Saint Lawrence Seaway opened, connecting the Great Lakes with the Atlantic Ocean).[16] Tobin also hoped the project would increase trade through its three airports. By the late 1950s, New York already had the world's largest air cargo center, and new cargo buildings were under construction for Air France, Alitalia, Lufthansa, American Airlines, and KLM-Royal Dutch Airlines.[17]

Tobin was not afraid to take on a massive project. He liked to quote Daniel Burnham, the Chicago urban designer who said, "Make no small plans, for they have not power to stir the blood."[18] Tobin led a prosperous and well-respected government agency in an era of megaprojects—interstate highways were connecting every U.S. city, Americans were talking about sending men to the moon, and slums were getting cleared for new residential, commercial and entertainment centers.

David Rockefeller realized the Port Authority was the logical organization to spearhead the building of a massive project because it had both the necessary financial and human resources. With Austin Tobin as executive director, the Port Authority had entrepreneurial leadership and a culture of innovation. The Authority could also secure financing thanks to its toll revenues. Furthermore, once the two state legislatures authorized the Port Authority to build a project, it could use its power of eminent domain to acquire private properties.

The Port Authority was anticipating a rapid growth of international trade via both sea and air. Unlike many government agencies, the Port Authority had a long-term perspective; it anticipated economic, technological, and transportation changes and then designed its facilities to meet expected demand. In 1958, to accommodate more bus riders and drivers, the Port Authority was expanding its Midtown Manhattan bus terminal by 50 percent, adding six lanes onto the George Washington Bridge, and building a new bus station on the bridge's eastern end. To prepare for an expected growth in air travel associated with jet airplanes, the Port Authority was building new control towers, upgrading runways, and adding new passenger terminal buildings. In Newark and Elizabeth, the Authority was building state-of-the art marine facilities to accommodate an expected growth in container ship use.[19]

The Authority was also seen as the ideal government agency to build a World Trade Center because it was so heavily involved in world trade. The Port Authority had offices promoting the region's port facilities in London, Zurich, San Juan, Pittsburgh, Washington, Cleveland, Chicago, and Pittsburgh. Its staff worked with importers and exporters, as well as transportation and government officials across the globe.[20] The idea of tying a World Trade Center with port facilities was not a new idea. Houston established a World Trade Center to encourage port commerce in 1927, and New Orleans, Boston, and San Francisco had also created their own trade centers.[21]

As Downtown-Lower Manhattan Association members developed their proposal for a trade center, they worked closely with members of the Port Authority staff on the project's details.[22] After a meeting with David Rockefeller, Tobin wrote, "I don't believe that I exaggerate when I say that both politically and legally the prospects of Port Authority participation in this venture may stand or fall on the name of the project." Tobin liked the names Foreign Trade Center, Port Commerce Center, World Trade District, Foreign Trade District, and World Trade Center.[23]

Rockefeller hired the McKinsey & Company consulting firm in 1959 to evaluate the needs and benefits of a trade center. The consultants found that a trade center concept could be a financial disaster because there was no need for a physical space to bring trade services together. Rockefeller disregarded these findings, though, with one of his aides recalling that to get one of the consultants to publicly praise the trade center concept and extoll its benefits, "we stuck a steel rod up his fanny."[24]

In January 1960, David Rockefeller released the Downtown-Lower Manhattan Association's plan titled "World Trade Center: A Proposal for the Port of New York" that called for the Port Authority to further study a World Trade Center complex on a site along the East River. The Lower Manhattan business leaders wanted to build a 13.5-acre complex, which would be much larger than the two-acre site of the Empire State Building, but smaller than the twenty-two-acre Rockefeller Center.[25] The proposed complex included a fifty- to seventy-story building with ten floors of hotel space along with an international trade exhibit hall, securities exchange building, enclosed shopping arcade, and a large outdoor plaza. Lower Manhattan, the association claimed, was the ideal location because it was already home to the corporate offices of numerous firms involved in trade.[26]

Tobin envisioned bringing together various functions of foreign trade including merchandising, finance, insurance, and government clearing of commerce.[27] He did not want just *a* World Trade Center, he wanted *the* World Trade Center.[28] He told his senior staff that he would sell the concept of a World Trade Center as a port without water—a place to bring together people and firms who were conducting international trade.[29] In retrospect, Tobin's objective was both quaint and naïve. One office complex could not and would not serve as the headquarters for international trade where buyers, sellers, and government officials would share information, process documents, and conduct transactions.[30]

Austin Tobin ran with the idea of a World Trade Center, assigning twenty-eight staff members[31] to work on it full-time, including experts in architecture, planning, finance, real estate, and law.[32] He would not jeopardize the support he and Rockefeller had generated from the downtown business community, so when the Port Authority reported in 1961 that the World Trade Center was economically feasible, Authority officials parroted the Downtown-Lower Manhattan Association's proposal that the site along the East River was the most appropriate location for the trade center.[33] The Port Authority and the Downtown-Lower Manhattan Association convinced the media, elected officials, business leaders, trade unions, and various civic groups that the project offered widespread benefits. Leading business organizations, such as the Commerce and Industry Association of New York City, were enthusiastic supporters.[34] New York City's mayor, Robert F. Wagner, said, "This World Trade Center would be a tremendous addition to the beauty and economic welfare of our city and port."[35] The *Herald Tribune* exclaimed, "the World Trade Center means more business more jobs, more money to every part of the metropolitan region," and the *New York Times* applauded the idea of bringing together the private and public sector to promote world trade and argued that only the Port Authority could undertake such a large-scale project.[36]

To take on new projects, Tobin needed authorization from both the New York and New Jersey state legislatures.[37] He also needed the ongoing support of both governors who could block the Authority's actions at any time by vetoing the minutes of commissioners' meetings. David Rockefeller, a banker and philanthropist, had key allies who could help make the proposal a reality. Most notably, his brother Nelson Rockefeller was elected governor of New York in November 1958. A few months later, S. Sloan Colt, another banker and philanthropist who linked trade with peace, was selected chair of the Port Authority. Referring to the rising economic might of the Soviet Union, Colt warned, "It is apparent that the free world must summon all of its resources to meet and overcome this challenge." Expanding our ports, he said, is "directly related not only to the prosperity of the people of the port communities and the nations in the free world, but world peace itself."[38]

New Jersey governor Robert Meyner and the state legislators in Trenton cared little about a trade center along the East River and its potential to promote world peace. They were much more interested in having the Port Authority take over the Hudson & Manhattan Railroad, which operated service between Manhattan and four cities in New Jersey (Harrison, Hoboken, Newark, and Jersey City). The railroad had carried 113 million passengers in 1927, but by the early 1960s fewer than thirty-one million passengers a year were riding its trains. Moreover, its facilities were deteriorating because of deferred maintenance and other cost reduction programs.[39] In the summer of 1960, New Jersey's elected officials stepped up pressure on Tobin. As discussed in chapter 3, the state legislature was thwarting his efforts to build a new airport in New Jersey's Great Swamp and they were poised to begin a far-reaching investigation relating to the Port Authority's financial dealings, particularly on available surpluses.[40] The investigation intended to force the Port Authority to release confidential memos and reports[41] that Tobin was refusing to disclose to the public, state officials, and even to Congress.[42]

Tobin was facing pressure from his own planning staff to help the railroads. In July 1959, they reported that it is "necessary to face the fact" that new east-west highways under construction in New Jersey would contribute to the decline of New Jersey's commuter railroads. If the railroads were unable to provide service, the Port Authority would have to expand its bus facilities to accommodate the rail passengers. The planners determined that this would be a money-losing operation for the Port Authority because it "would be forced into same unfortunate position the railroads now occupy in maintaining oversized facilities used to capacity only during the few commuter peak hours in the week." New facilities, including a new Lower Manhattan bus terminal, would have very little utility in terms of weekend traffic and would involve heavy deficits. It was essential for the region and the Port Authority, they argued, that the existing trans-Hudson rail facilities be maintained in operation.[43]

In September 1960, at the same time that Tobin was seeking New Jersey's support for the World Trade Center project,[44] he announced that the Port Authority would acquire and operate the bankrupt[45] Hudson & Manhattan Railroad, as long as the two states would agree that the Port Authority would not get involved in any other large-scale rail program operating at a deficit.[46] The New Jersey legislature still pushed back against the plan, though, because taking over the railroad was not commensurate with the cost of building the trade center.[47] In the spring of 1961, the New York state legislature passed and Governor Rockefeller signed a bill authorizing the Port Authority to build the trade center and purchase the railroad. Governor Rockefeller's overeagerness in promoting the legislation, however, made many New Jersey legislators skeptical that their constituents would receive the same level of benefits as New Yorkers.[48]

While Port Authority staff were looking at how they could renovate the railroad's facilities on Lower Manhattan's west side, they came up with the idea of combining the two projects both physically and financially.[49] Moving the World Trade Center to a site along the Hudson River and above the railroad's terminal would make it more accessible for New Jersey residents. The Port Authority's attorneys liked the idea because it would strengthen the Authority's legal position that the trade center project would serve a public purpose and be consistent with the Authority's mission.[50] When Tobin told Richard Hughes after he was elected New Jersey governor in November 1961 about the idea of combining the two projects, Hughes said "Austin, I think I can sell that plan."[51]

In December 1961, after a meeting between Rockefeller and Hughes, another project was added to the Port Authority's portfolio. To sweeten the pot for New Jersey, the Authority offered to build a new office and transportation center in Jersey City's Journal Square.[52] Jersey City's leading newspaper reported that Hughes had engineered an historic turnaround because New Jersey had long been treated as a junior partner, rather than an equal, at the Port Authority.[53] Governor Hughes then helped sell the plan in meetings with legislators, railroads, and elected officials in Jersey City and Hoboken.[54] The Authority referred to the new west side location as "a marked improvement" because of its proximity to New Jersey rail service and six different subway lines.[55] In 1962, thanks to the Authority's successful lobbying,[56] both

Building and Rebuilding the World Trade Center

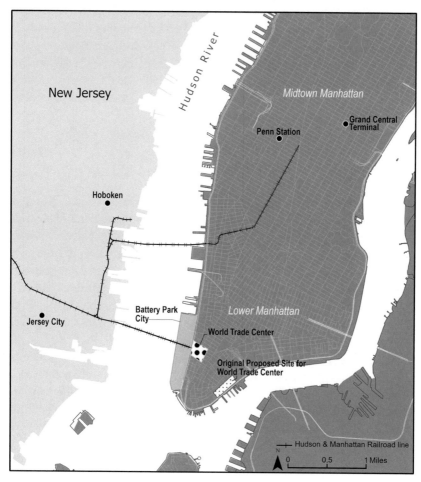

Map 8.1. The World Trade Center was designed to help Lower Manhattan compete with Midtown Manhattan.
(Map by Md. Shahinoor Rahman.)

legislatures passed identical legislation that authorized the Port Authority to proceed with a combined railroad and trade center project on Lower Manhattan's west side.[57]

The project picked up support from a wide range of organizations.[58] The Regional Plan Association, Citizens Union, and the Citizens Housing and Planning Council liked that it would create desirable jobs in a location readily accessible to public transportation.[59] The politically influential construction firms and labor unions were enthusiastic because building the trade center was expected to employ as many as 8,000 workers during peak construction periods.[60] Tobin frequently referred to President John F. Kennedy's remarks in December 1962, when he said that he was "glad to see" the Port Authority pursuing the trade center because he wanted to see American businesses sell more of their products overseas.[61]

Battling Away the Opponents

When the two states authorized the World Trade Center in 1962, they gave Tobin and the Port Authority far-reaching autonomy regarding its design, construction, and future tenants. Since the Authority was able to bypass the city's zoning, land use, and building regulations, it could determine the number of buildings, as well as their height, density, uses, and footprints. The Port Authority sought out Minoru Yamasaki, an architect from Detroit, to design the World Trade Center. The director of the Authority's World Trade Department, Guy Tozzoli, liked the serene and inviting spaces that Yamasaki had created for other clients.[62]

Yamasaki came up with the idea of building twin towers, about 80-stories high, with a huge plaza for people to gather.[63] This urban architectural style, with its "superblock" and "towers in a park," was fashionable at the time. The complex would separate motor vehicles from pedestrians by closing off thirteen small streets and putting all the parking spaces below street level. An underground concourse would provide the main access to buildings, shops, and trains.[64] His plan would accommodate about eight million square feet of office space. Tobin, though, wanted about ten million square feet of office space that could accommodate about 50,000 workers and 100,000 daily business visitors. The additional size would generate enough money for the Port Authority to more easily subsidize the Hudson & Manhattan Railroad, which the Port Authority had rechristened the PATH (Port Authority Trans-Hudson railway; fig. 8.1). Tobin liked this acronym more than the one his staff had first come up with: MOTHER, which stood for the Manhattan Operating Trans-Hudson Electric Railway.[65]

Tobin was not the only one who was thinking big. In a 1960 memo to the team studying the feasibility of a trade center, the Port Authority's influential public relations director, Lee Jaffe, wrote, "If you're going to build a

Fig. 8.1. PATH station sign replaces a sign for the Hudson & Manhattan Railroad (also known as the Hudson Tubes).
(Photograph reprinted by permission of Port Authority of New York and New Jersey.)

great project, you should build the world's tallest building."[66] Tozzoli always remembered that memo. In January 1964, the Port Authority unveiled its design for the World Trade Center with twin towers.[67] Three years earlier, the Downtown Lower Manhattan Association had proposed a 13.5 acre site with about five to six million square feet of office space featuring a tower fifty to seventy stories high.[68] In 1964, the Port Authority announced it would build the world's largest office complex[69] on a sixteen-acre site featuring two 110-story towers, taller than any other building on the planet, with a large public plaza covering nearly five acres.[70]

Commercial buildings 110-stories high had never been considered economically justifiable because the number of elevators needed would take up too much floor space. The Port Authority's engineers came up with a creative and innovative solution to the problem by borrowing an idea from New York's subways, which feature express and local train services. The engineers designed sky lobbies for the trade center where passengers could transfer between twenty-three express and seventy-two local elevators. The local elevators would be able to share elevator shafts which would increase the usable space on each floor from 62 percent to 75 percent.[71]

In 1964, the Port Authority officials did not just hang up an "Office Space for Lease" sign in Lower Manhattan. They gave presentations to firms engaged in international trade in ten cities across the U.S., and then embarked on a mission to government leaders in the capitals of eleven European nations where they were often joined by American ambassadors.[72] The Port Authority promised that the World Trade Center would offer a wide variety of essential trade services and facilities, including a hotel, exhibit space, customs offices, consulate, chambers of commerce from around the world, a research and educational institute, meeting rooms, and multilingual secretaries.[73]

Once the Port Authority released its plans for the twin towers, it had to overcome opposition from local business owners, real estate interests, the mayor, and Black leaders. The most vocal opponents were the property owners and commercial tenants whose buildings would be demolished. More than 17,000 people worked on the sixteen-acre site, an area that included numerous electronics stores in a commercial district known as Radio Row (fig. 8.2).[74] The business owners in the neighborhood banded together to fight the Port Authority in the courts, on the streets, and in City Hall.[75] Although the Authority had previously demolished hundreds of buildings to build its river crossings and bus stations, it had never faced such a well-organized opposition in New York. Tobin had lost his fight in New Jersey's Great Swamp because he had no local support. That was not the case in New York where Tobin and the Lower Manhattan business leaders had assembled a strong coalition of unions, elected officials, businesses, and unions to support the World Trade Center.

The business owners' picketing, mock funeral procession, petition drives, and lawsuit did not deter the Authority.[76] The Authority's publicity machine fought back against its opponents by portraying Radio Row's buildings as antiquated firetraps.[77] An Authority official recalled that once a decision was made to proceed with a project, "the Port Authority went gung ho, never retreat."[78] In 1963, the business owners declared victory when a court ruled that the Authority would not be able to use the power of eminent domain to acquire private parcels because not every element of the project clearly served a public purpose.[79] However, the celebrations along Radio Row were premature because the Port Authority prevailed when the state's highest

Fig. 8.2. Buildings on Radio Row (shown in April 1936) were demolished to make way for the World Trade Center.
(Photograph by Berenice Abbott. Courtesy the Miriam and Ira D. Wallach Division of Art, Prints and Photographs, The New York Public Library, and Wikimedia Commons.)

court overturned that ruling and the U.S. Supreme Court declined to hear an appeal.[80]

Many of New York's real estate industry leaders were outraged that a government agency would be competing with them. The Port Authority had an unfair advantage because it would not have to pay real estate taxes and it could obtain construction loans at lower interest rates than private firms. Property owners and developers also feared that the World Trade Center would poach tenants from other buildings leading to lower rents across the city. Lawrence Wien, who led a group that owned the Empire State Building, was especially upset that his building would lose the cachet of being the world's tallest, a designation it had held since 1931.[81]

The Authority's publicists made sure to repudiate information that could weaken public support. For example, on Valentine's Day in 1964, the *New York Times* published a front-page story about how "realty men" were starting a campaign to block construction of the World Trade Center.[82] A few hours later, the Port Authority had its architects send a telegram to the *New York Times* attesting to the safety of the towers and explaining that no building had ever been subjected to such a thorough structural analysis. The architects claimed that "The buildings have been investigated and found to be safe in an assumed collision with a large jet airliner traveling at 600 miles per hour. Analysis indicates that such collision would result in only local damage which could not cause collapse or substantial damage to the building."[83]

While most New Yorkers generally supported the concept of taking private property to build bridges and bus stations, they were much more hesitant about a government agency using those powers to build the world's tallest office buildings. As the protests intensified, the Authority increasingly came to be seen as unaccountable and out-of-touch. During this same period and for some of the same reasons, the press turned against another power broker, Robert Moses, and many of his projects, including his proposals to build an elevated highway along 30th Street and an expressway across Lower Manhattan. Tobin's speechwriter, Robert VanDeventer, realized the press was publishing numerous stories about the Radio Row's aggrieved store owners and property owners because people like to root for the underdog—not powerful government agencies. The conflicts were dramatic and the Radio Row store owners' protests were visual. The continuing news coverage fit into an ongoing narrative that sold newspapers but hurt the Port Authority's reputation. The twin towers became a manifestation of Tobin's ego and the Port Authority's arrogance.[84]

Tobin repeatedly accused Wien of distorting and misrepresenting information. The executive director told city officials that "the opposition to the trade center represented basically only the selfish interest of one man, Lawrence Wien of the Empire State Building, who was footing the bill for the entire political and propaganda effort to stop the trade center."[85] Tobin complained to construction industry leaders that Wien and his publicity agent "have applied every conceivable political pressure, every propaganda device, every distortion and every misstatement of fact that they thought would serve their narrow and selfish objectives."[86]

Wien was strategic about riling up elected officials. For instance, a group he led placed newspaper advertisements warning New Yorkers that the "gigantic trade center" would ruin television reception for millions of people in and around New York: the ads asserted, "You're going to start seeing things on your TV set you never bargained for when you bought it. Things like two second basemen. Six outfielders. And quartets where you used to see duets."[87] John Bingham, a congressman from the Bronx, did not get riled up about the Radio Row businesses or the competition between Lower Manhattan and Midtown Manhattan. But after the media publicized potential television interference issues, Representative Bingham did not want to be held responsible by his constituents for "what happened to their TV screens." He told Tobin's public affairs director, "After all, for many people in my district, TV is all they have." Behind the scenes, the Port Authority worked with construction industry officials and trade union leaders to pressure the congressman to tone down his concerns about the height of the twin towers.[88]

With the Port Authority not willing to scale back its project, influential business and property owners lobbied New York City's mayor, John Lindsay, for help. First elected to City Hall in 1965, the Republican mayor was more suspicious of large-scale projects than his predecessors had been. Although he wanted to enhance New York's role as a leading hub of world trade, he thought 110-story towers were too tall[89] and he was sensitive to the businesses being displaced. He realized, however, that it was too late to abandon the trade center, since it had strong support from the construction industry, unions, and business leaders, as well as the Republican governor in Albany.[90] Furthermore, the Port Authority had already condemned and acquired properties, started demolishing buildings, and spent $13 million on planning and design work.[91]

Nevertheless, after taking office in 1966, Lindsay withheld his support so that he could extract more money from the Port Authority.[92] By state law, the Port Authority did not need to pay any real estate taxes, although it could voluntarily agree to make payments in lieu of taxes. Tobin had struck a deal with Mayor Wagner to pay the city $1.7 million a year, which was the same amount in real estate taxes that the private property owners, including the railroad, had paid before their land was condemned.[93]

Lindsay assigned his thirty-three-year-old deputy mayor, Robert Price, to lead a committee of city officials who would renegotiate the city's deal with the Port Authority. When Price first visited the sixteen-acre site in 1966, he found much of it was underutilized and blighted. The buildings slated for demolition had been neglected, and many of the shop owners had either moved out or were going out of business.[94] City officials estimated that more than one-third of the neighborhood's firms had already left.[95]

Price learned that the city had some leverage including the power to hold up street closings and keep ownership of several city-owned parcels that the Port Authority needed for its superblock.[96] In May 1966, Price sent Tobin a memo detailing the city's position—a long list of items he wanted, including a higher payment in lieu of taxes, office space in the trade center, equal investment of port facilities in New York and New Jersey, a new passenger ship terminal in Manhattan, a containership facility in Brooklyn, and renegotiation of the airport leases.[97] Price then held up construction of the entire World Trade Center project with one simple maneuver. He refused to issue a permit allowing the Port Authority to relocate telephone cables along a street adjacent to the site.[98]

Tobin said "no" to nearly all the city's requests. He would not commit to any major pier improvements until studies determined they could be self-supporting, and he fiercely objected to the city's use of construction permits as a bargaining chip. The records from the negotiations reveal the interplay between a cast of powerful characters who were involved in numerous rounds of letters, phone calls, meetings, and the strategic leaking of information to reporters.[99]

The mayor tried to go around Tobin and negotiate directly with the Port Authority commissioners, but the commissioners sided with their executive director. Tobin tried to negotiate directly with the mayor, but the mayor would not undercut Deputy Mayor Price. In turn, Price tried to deflect responsibility for the city's hardball tactics to the mayor's negotiating committee that he led. After the chair of the Port Authority's board of commissioners reached out to Governor Rockefeller for help, the governor pressured the mayor to settle with Tobin. Rockefeller told Lindsay, "If each municipality in the area could require the Port Authority to undertake future projects not yet directed or authorized by the states as a condition to its conveyance of property on authorized projects, the Port compact would, of course, be a nullity."

The two sides were deadlocked because neither was willing to make a realistic offer—they each wanted the other to make the first move. Lindsay suggested entering into arbitration proceedings, but the two sides were unable to agree on a procedure to do so. When Tobin told the mayor that the governor's office was opposed to arbitration, Lindsay asked, "What is the governor got to do with this thing?" Tobin replied, "He has everything to do with it—he's the Port Authority's boss."

Tobin had a delicate task as he negotiated with the mayor's representatives because Governor Hughes in New Jersey was watching the terms of the agreement very closely. Port Authority commissioners from New Jersey thought the city was being parochial and would shortchange New Jersey. If Hughes determined that the Port Authority's concessions to the city were excessive, then he was ready to veto the entire World Trade Center project.[100] Hughes was able to extract one last promise before allowing the Port Authority to go ahead with construction. Tobin agreed to study how commuter railroad connections could be improved in New Jersey's Meadowlands.[101]

The stalemate between Lindsay and Tobin was not resolved until August 1966 when a Port Authority attorney (who Tobin married the following year) mentioned the ongoing stalemate to George Shapiro, a former counsel to Governor Rockefeller's predecessor. Shapiro, who was highly regarded by both the Port Authority and the city, offered to help and within days he was able to draft a deal that was acceptable to both sides.[102] The Port Authority agreed to pay a higher annual fee in lieu of real estate taxes, contribute to neighborhood infrastructure improvements, and work with the city on building a new Manhattan passenger ship terminal and redeveloping piers in south Brooklyn.[103]

Although Lindsay took credit for getting the Port Authority to undertake major initiatives, Tobin was careful not to make any commitments outside of Lower Manhattan. For example, the Port Authority did not promise to build the Hudson River passenger ship terminal but rather to make a speedy determination of its economic feasibility. Likewise, the Authority agreed to study improvements along the Brooklyn waterfront to facilitate the handling of containerized cargo. Although Tobin was pleased with the deal, he was frustrated that the conflict delayed construction work by about six months. One aspect of the agreement would benefit both the city and the Port Authority: construction workers creating the foundation for the World Trade Center would not need to take excavated materials out of Manhattan. Instead these materials would be used to create twenty-eight acres of new land west of the trade center that would be named Battery Park City.[104]

Besides the local business owners, real estate interests, and the mayor, other groups in New York raised objections to the World Trade Center. In 1966, Black leaders called on Governor Rockefeller to build office space for state workers in struggling minority neighborhoods rather than in Lower Manhattan. Instead of backing away from the World Trade Center, the governor announced that the state would build a new twenty-three-story office building on 125th Street in Harlem. Rockefeller said the new building could upgrade the entire neighborhood, just as Rockefeller Center had done for

Midtown.[105] In response to television stations' concerns that the twin towers would interfere with their broadcast signals, the Port Authority agreed to install television antennas on the north tower (and redesign the building to accommodate the additional weight).[106] Accommodating Mayor Lindsay's requests, building the the state office building in Harlem, and installing antennas were just three more ways that stakeholders extracted concessions as a condition for their support. Across the river, the Port Authority had previously agreed to take over the PATH train and build the Jersey City transportation center.

Mixed Success

The concept of a center to promote world trade was attractive to the Rockefeller brothers and Tobin. However, it was never very appealing to many of the private firms that they expected would occupy the space. That was apparent in the 1940s when the World Trade Corporation investigated it.[107] In 1959, David Rockefeller's consultants also recognized that the World Trade Center could be a financial disaster.[108] Even as Tobin was promising widespread benefits, he recognized the weakness of the trade center concept. In 1964, with the Port Authority having trouble attracting enough prospective private-sector tenants, Tobin reluctantly went to Albany seeking Governor Rockefeller's help. In his unpublished memoir, William Ronan (Rockefeller's top aide) wrote about Tobin's visit, "It was clear he had exhausted some other solutions. Now he was ashamedly looking for help. His usual bravado spirit was conspicuous by its absence." Rockefeller remarked to Ronan afterwards, "Your friend Tobin is really eating humble pie." Rockefeller agreed to save the project by announcing that the state's offices in New York City would be centralized at the World Trade Center, even though most of the offices would have little relationship to world trade.[109] Rockefeller's support for the World Trade Center was a major reason why the construction workers' unions, representing more than one-quarter million workers, endorsed him in his 1966 reelection campaign.[110]

Tobin's goals for the World Trade Center were more aspirational than the result of an analytical analysis developed through technical and specialized knowledge. Most of the businesses targeted by the Port Authority such as customs brokers, freight forwarders, steamships, railroads, and trucking firms, were simply not interested in moving into the trade center.[111] Foreign departments of major corporations were becoming obsolete while computers were changing the way that information flowed and trade was conducted.[112] In 1965, Tobin reiterated, "I want to emphasize that our policy is to make trade center space available only to firms active in world trade, or those providing auxiliary services for such tenants."[113] The following year, the Authority claimed that "many of the companies occupying space in the World Trade Center will be companies not now represented in New York City."[114]

Before the city gave the World Trade Center its final approval to close off streets in June 1967,[115] the city's newspapers were questioning the wisdom of building the project. In 1964, the *New York Times* declared, "No project has ever been more promising for New York,"[116] but in 1967 the newspaper published an editorial warning.

> The Authority has forged ahead by making sizable expenditures and promising thousands of construction jobs. It cowed the city, as it had cowed Albany and Trenton, into accepting a fait accompli. The Authority has never really demonstrated that the kind of World Trade Center it has planned is within its proper sphere of competence. It has simply declared that its gargantuan project is needed to maintain and increase the pre-eminence of the port and has gone ahead . . . In this age of almost instantaneous communication and rapid technological change, there may not be great benefit in housing all world trade services in one place . . . A center that leaves the port in its present sorry state would be a monument both to the city's former glories as a port and to the Authority's audacious ability to get its own way.[117]

The Port Authority's cost estimates for the World Trade Center rose from $350 million in 1964, to $525 million in 1965, and to $575 million in December 1966.[118] As the twin towers rose, the Authority's credibility fell. Eventually, its trade center costs would exceed $1 billion.[119] In 1973, a ribbon cutting ceremony was held at the World Trade Center with 4,500 guests.[120] Austin Tobin chose not to attend. He had resigned a year earlier and would never get the chance to work in the executive director's palatial office space.[121]

The twin towers would not receive the accolades offered to New York's early twentieth-century skyscrapers. The architectural critic, Paul Goldberger, called the towers boring and banal (fig. 8.3).[122] New Yorkers joked that the towers were so plain that they could have been the boxes the Empire State and Chrysler Buildings came in. Although the office workers had modern amenities, they did not have the city's best views from their desks. Yamasaki,

Fig. 8.3. The World Trade Center's two 110-story buildings (with Battery Park City in the foreground) in 2001.
(Photograph by Carol M. Highsmith. Courtesy the Carol M. Highsmith Archive, Library of Congress, Prints and Photographs Division.)

the architect of the world's two tallest buildings, had designed windows that were only 22-inches wide because, ironically, he suffered from acrophobia and thought that many others were afraid of heights as well.[123]

In 1971, a McKinsey consultant retained by the Port Authority realized that the Authority's approach to fostering world trade was flawed in part because it was not prepared to regularly organize programs and events that would bring together governments, associations, service organizations, and buyer groups.[124] Although the Port Authority moved its headquarters to the trade center along with more than one hundred companies involved with maritime trade,[125] that did not come close to filling up ten million square feet of office space. Port Authority officials continued to maintain its commitment to the world trade concept though, turning down hundreds of tenants who could not certify that three-quarters or more of their activity within the World Trade Center would have a direct relation to international commerce.[126] For instance, they turned down Coopers & Lybrand's request for 230,000 square feet and even a request from Chase Manhattan Bank (the bank that David Rockefeller led) for 200,000 square feet.[127]

Henry Klingman worked for the Port Authority's Trade Development Office in the 1960s, including a stint as the manager of the Authority's overseas office in Zurich.[128] He did not think Tobin really understood the mechanics of world trade. "One thing is sure," Klingman said, "He was given a lot of misleading counsel by some who stood to gain and downright bad advice by others." Klingman said that once Tobin embraced the twin towers concept, "It was too late for qualitative reflection, the Port Authority and Tobin were committed, and their energies were henceforth to be consumed in making the World Trade Center happen." Senior Port Authority officials would often claim, he said, "this thing is so big that the important players in world trade cannot afford to be outside of it."[129] According to Klingman, the trade center changed the Port Authority's culture. He added, "The Port Authority had always operated with a good deal of foresight, but with the advent of the mind-boggling World Trade Center, hard planning was put into suspension, and the hucksters had their field day."[130]

The Port Authority resisted calls for a private company to operate the complex. In 1973, officials explained that the Authority was not trying to maximize its income, but rather to facilitate the flow of international commerce through the Port of New York. An Authority official wrote,

> Any proposal for World Trade Center management by a private real estate firm would be tantamount to the Port Authority's abandoning this concept. For there could be no compromise, as there is now, between profit and public purpose if the decision maker were a management firm whose exclusive and proper motivation is the maximization of income. . . . It would be a betrayal of New York's and New Jersey's legislative mandates; and a betrayal of the Port Authority's moral and legal responsibilities toward its tenant community in the World Trade Center, and toward the international business community in the Port of New York as a whole.[131]

Soon after Peter Goldmark was appointed executive director of the Port Authority in 1977, he admitted that the World Trade Center could not rely on trade-oriented tenants. "It is time to open up the floodgates," Goldmark reportedly said.[132] His lawyers began to interpret more broadly whether a potential tenant was engaged in international commerce. State offices started moving out and were replaced by banks, insurance companies, and brokerage houses. Rents rose from about $6 per square foot in 1975 to $30 by the mid-1980s.[133] The office complex became a financial success, as annual revenue rose from $72 million in 1978 to $173 million in 1983.[134]

By the 1990s, the Port Authority could no longer hold off efforts to privatize the World Trade Center. The governors of New York and New Jersey (George Pataki and Christine Todd Whitman) were both elected by promising to trim government services and slash taxes. The World Trade Center was a successful office complex, but not a center for world trade. The governors wanted the Port Authority to get out of the real estate business and focus on transportation projects.[135] In 1998, the Port Authority's commissioners voted to pursue privatization of the World Trade Center. However, the effort stalled because New Jersey officials were afraid that selling the complex would cause PATH fares to rise in the future.[136] That was a genuine concern because many New Yorkers, including Port Authority commissioners, complained about how much the Authority was spending every year to subsidize the PATH system.[137]

As described in chapter 6, both the World Trade Center and PATH became entangled in a highly publicized feud between the two governors over which state was receiving more from the Authority. The standoff lasted until the governors finally agreed on how to divvy up Port Authority funds. They also decided to lease rather than sell the complex to simplify the financial aspects of the transaction.[138] Because of legal requirements[139] and Port Authority bond covenants, selling the site would have involved a long, drawn-out process that would have been subject to litigation. Moreover, leasing was more advantageous to potential developers for financial reasons and tax implications.[140] In the largest real estate transaction in the city's history,[141] the Port Authority finalized an agreement for a ninety-nine-year lease of the World Trade's office buildings with a consortium led by Larry Silverstein on July 24, 2001.[142] One of the initial bidders, a real estate developer named Donald Trump, decided to drop out after telling a Port Authority official, "working with government is impossible."[143]

By the summer of 2001, the World Trade Center had been a somewhat successful endeavor. The twin towers were nearly fully occupied, and the Port Authority's World Trade Center's revenues exceeded its expenses. The seventy-eight-store shopping center under the complex was one of the most profitable malls in the United States.[144] The neighborhood around the World

Trade Center was prospering with young well-educated professionals living in Battery Park City and Tribeca's old warehouses. However, the office complex could not overcome Lower Manhattan's inherent disadvantages, so commercial building owners in Lower Manhattan were still having trouble competing with Midtown office space.

The Port Authority's rescue of the Hudson & Manhattan Railroad had been crucial to strengthening the metropolitan area. By 2001 PATH was considered one of the nation's best urban rail systems.[145] The Authority had generously subsidized the rail line, pouring nearly $1.5 billion into upgrading the railroad's aging equipment and facilities. The Port Authority also covered the railroad's annual operating losses; in 2000 the cost to operate PATH was $151 million more than its revenues. (When the Authority had first proposed taking over the railroad, it had expected the annual subsidy to be less than $10 million per year.[146]) The PATH improvements and ongoing subsidies helped revitalize Hoboken and Jersey City, whose PATH stations were only a few minutes away from the World Trade Center. As a result of the Port Authority's investments, more than 74 million passengers used PATH in 2000 compared to fewer than 28 million in 1963.[147]

The construction of the trade center also led to the creation of Battery Park City, a mixed-use neighborhood that would receive international acclaim for its waterfront esplanade and a site plan that embraced rather than rejected the traditional layout of the city's streets, buildings, and parks. Other projects initiated as part of the dealmaking for the World Trade Center were neither utter failures nor highly successful endeavors, including the Harlem state office building, Jersey City's transportation center, a new Manhattan passenger ship terminal, and Brooklyn pier improvements. The trade center certainly never lived up to the promise that it would be a center of world trade or help revitalize New York's port. Although the marine terminals in Elizabeth and Newark brought in more containers, most of New York City's piers became obsolete.[148]

The 11th of September

By 2001, the twin towers had become a symbol of U.S. economic power, in the same way that the Pentagon symbolized America's military power and the U.S. Capitol symbolized the power of the U.S. government. An Islamist extremist terrorist group based in Afghanistan decided to target all three symbols. On the morning of September 11, terrorists hijacked and crashed two planes (loaded with approximately 19,000 gallons of jet fuel) into the twin towers killing more than 2,800 people.[149]

After the plane hit the north tower where the Port Authority's headquarters were located, many of the Authority's employees walked down more than 60 floors, making their way through the chaos of smoke and blinding debris. When they finally reached the plaza, they had to hustle past the bodies of people who had jumped and fallen out of the burning buildings. Shaken up and disoriented, many of the Authority's managers took ferries across the Hudson River to the Jersey City office building that had been previously designated to serve as an emergency operations center. Some of the officials were still covered in soot as they went to work at a bank of phones and computers waiting for them.[150] By the time they arrived, their former offices were a rubble of crushed building materials, smoldering office supplies, and fragments of human remains.

Ron Shiftan, the Authority's deputy executive director, had been on the New Jersey Turnpike listening to a Harry Potter audiobook when his wife called to tell him about the attacks. By noon, with the executive director missing, Shiftan became the Port Authority's acting executive director. Every day for the next few weeks, Shiftan met with the department heads at 7:00 a.m. and 7:00 p.m. One senior official said that Shiftan "steered the ship in incredibly tough times" by "gathering evidence from all the relevant people" and making decisions based on the financial, legal, and business consequence of alternatives.[151] Shiftan's priority was to help the city's search and rescue efforts. Authority employees held out hope that all their friends and colleagues would be found alive. However, only a few survivors of the attacks were ultimately pulled from the rubble. One forensic biologist said the collapse of the buildings was so destructive that "it was almost like a mass cremation."[152]

Approximately 2,000 of the Port Authority's 7,200 employees worked at the trade center, and they all knew at least one of the eighty-four Authority employees who were killed. Among the victims was the Authority's executive director, Neil Levin, who had been eating breakfast at Windows on the World, the restaurant at the top of the north tower.[153] Since few bodies were found intact, most of the victims did not have funerals at cemeteries. Instead, over the course of the next few months, Authority employees attended one memorial service after another to mark their losses.[154]

With its office building obliterated and its workforce in disarray, the Port Authority's traumatized staff had to overcome enormous challenges. The World Trade Center's PATH station was destroyed, and the Authority's air-

Building and Rebuilding the World Trade Center

Fig. 8.4. Little remained of the twin towers, seventeen days after the September 11 attacks.
(Photograph by Andrea Booher, FEMA News Photo. Courtesy Wikimedia Commons.)

ports, seaports, bridges, tunnels, trains, and bus stations were now considered among the most high-profile terrorist targets in the world. New security restrictions and alternative transportation services had to be planned and implemented. The Authority had to address skyrocketing expenses associated with stringent security measures at the same time its revenues were plummeting because of travel restrictions and sapping consumer confidence. Shiftan also had to figure out how the Authority could reconstruct all its files and engineering drawings, pay its employees, reassure its bondholders, and continue making progress on the more than 600 projects in its $9.6 billion five-year capital program.

Port Authority No Longer in Control

Given all his other priorities, Shiftan wanted other institutions to create potential concepts for redeveloping the World Trade Center site.[155] The Authority was not in the same position as it had been in the 1960s to develop a comprehensive plan. It did not have the same level of available resources, expertise, autonomy, vision, or entrepreneurial leadership. At the end of 2001, both Shiftan and the Authority's chair (Lewis Eisenberg) were planning on stepping down from their positions.[156] Moreover, the Port Authority was still reeling from the brain drain that occurred when it had slashed spending between 1995 and 1997.[157] The Authority was operating with a smaller workforce than had in more than thirty years.[158]

Developing a plan for rebuilding the World Trade Center site required bringing together a diverse set of stakeholders on a scale that was beyond the Port Authority's skill set. The Authority was accustomed to operating with minimal oversight and public participation.[159] In the 1960s, the Port Authority did not host a single public hearing nor actively solicit public input before building the trade center.[160] Compared to most government organizations, the Authority's culture was more suited to making decisions independently, quickly, and behind closed doors.

In the 1960s, the Port Authority had sufficient resources on its own to finance the acquisition of land and construction of the original World Trade Center. After September 11, the rebuilding effort would rely upon a wide range of funding sources. Three different federal agencies, each with their own rules and regulations, were administering multibillion-dollar grants, while insurance companies were expected to pay out billions more in claims. Rebuilding would also require both public agencies and private companies to raise billions of dollars from the financial markets. Complicating matters, no one even knew how much rebuilding would cost or the amount that would be available.

Because of the fragmentation of power and the intense emotions that the site generated, no single figure could drive the process. Charles Gargano, the Port Authority vice chair, referred to all the regulatory agencies, review boards, commissions, committees, geographic representatives, political groups, supervisory authorities, and organizations involved in the rebuilding as an "alphabet soup of sometime duplicative, often contradictory and occasionally outright inimical authorities."[161]

Governor Pataki was in the strongest position to control the rebuilding because he put in place loyalists to head three powerful state agencies. The state of New York set up the Lower Manhattan Development Corporation (LMDC) to coordinate activities and serve as a conduit for federal funds. The Metropolitan Transportation Authority needed to spend more than a billion dollars to rebuild and improve its Lower Manhattan subway stations. And, in

Building and Rebuilding the World Trade Center   239

December 2001, the governor named a longtime aide, Joseph Seymour, as the Port Authority's executive director. The Port Authority would not make any major decision about the trade center without first getting Pataki's approval.

New York City's mayor and a series of New Jersey governors had their own levers to influence the rebuilding efforts. Michael Bloomberg, who was elected mayor eight weeks after the attacks, appointed half of the LMDC's board members and he could offer abatements on city taxes to developers. In addition, he helped select which real estate developers could issue tax-exempt bonds that Congress had authorized for Lower Manhattan redevelopment.[162] Behind the scenes, the governors of New Jersey also played a critical role, because they could veto the minutes of Port Authority board meetings and hold up decisions.

The Battle among Stakeholders

The original trade center was the brainchild of the downtown business leaders and Port Authority officials. After September 11, numerous advocacy groups and stakeholders promoted their own ideas. For instance, many of those who lost loved ones on September 11 did not want anything to be built on what they considered "sacred ground," while Larry Silverstein (who had signed the 99-year lease only weeks before the terrorist attack) asserted that he would rebuild the World Trade Center's office buildings.[163] More than eighty-five civic, business, and community groups formed the Civic Alliance to Rebuild Downtown New York, while a coalition of architecture, planning, and design groups created their own advocacy group. The Downtown Alliance, the successor to the business organization established by David Rockefeller, brought together Lower Manhattan business and property owners, while the Lower Manhattan community board advocated for plans that prioritized the needs of residents.

Working closely with the Port Authority, the LMDC's first order of businesses was to listen to various stakeholders and set up advisory councils.[164] It was a far cry from Tobin's approach in the 1960s of releasing plans as a fait accompli. In April 2002, the LMDC announced a set of principles that would guide the development of its plans.[165] Many of these principles were not areas where the Port Authority had relevant experience, such as making decisions based on an inclusive and open public process, creating a memorial to the victims, developing Lower Manhattan as a mixed-use neighborhood, improving pedestrian experience on the streets, and preserving Lower Manhattan's historic character.[166] The Port Authority built and managed transportation facilities, not neighborhoods, and it was accustomed to fully controlling its projects.

The architects and urban planners from both the civic groups and the LMDC came to a consensus that a new World Trade Center needed to better integrate with the rest of Lower Manhattan. They would not let the Port Authority repeat the same mistake it had made in the 1960s. One of the aspects of the World Trade Center project that had appealed to Nelson and David Rockefeller was building a city within a city. Their father had created a lively oasis by integrating Rockefeller Center within Midtown's street grid, encouraging pedestrians to walk by shops, restaurants, a skating rink, and the country's most famous Christmas tree. The Port Authority had done the opposite.

In the 1960s, the Port Authority closed off streets and interrupted Manhattan's grid to create a superblock that isolated the World Trade Center from the rest of Lower Manhattan. The trade center's underground concourse was usually bustling because it had stores along with connections to the office buildings, subway, and the PATH station. At the street level, however, most of the trade center was surrounded by a wall because the Authority raised the plaza seven feet above Church Street on its eastern edge and twenty-eight feet above West Street on its west.[167] The plaza was designed to be a tranquil refuge, but since the main entrances to the buildings and transit services were below ground, few people walked up the steps to the plaza except for the occasional summer lunchtime concerts (fig. 8.5). When people did venture out to the plaza, they typically only stayed a short time because the gap between the two towers created one of the windiest spots in the entire city.[168] Anthony Robins, the author of the 1987 book *The World Trade Center*, describes how the Port Authority created a plaza the size of four football fields that was one of the "emptiest, under-used vast plazas in the world."[169]

The Port Authority's first attempt to design a new World Trade Center site did not go well. Working with LMDC in May 2002, they selected an architectural firm to develop conceptual plans for the sixteen-acre site. Governor Pataki, under criticism for the slow progress in creating a rebuilding plan, pressured the two agencies to unveil the architects' plans by July 2002. The architects did not have enough time to hone their designs, especially since they had qualms about accommodating both a suitable memorial and the Port Authority's demand for rebuilding the space it lost.[170] The Authority insisted that ten million square feet of office space, 600,000 square feet

Building and Rebuilding the World Trade Center 241

Fig. 8.5. The World Trade Center's plaza was named the Austin J. Tobin Plaza in 1978 after the death of the longtime executive director.
(Photograph reprinted by permission of Friends of San Diego Architecture.)

of retail space, and 600,000 square feet for a hotel be rebuilt.[171] The World Trade Center had generated more than $375 million in revenue in 2000[172] and the Authority wanted to maximize its revenues because it had obligations to bondholders and needed to pay for its ongoing capital program.

In June 2002, Joseph Seymour, the Port Authority's executive director, reminded a reporter, "It's our site." The chair, Jack Sinagra, reiterated the Authority's claim, saying, "It's the Port Authority's property, and the Port Authority's responsibility for what is eventually re-created on the site."[173] A few weeks later, Governor Pataki surprised the Port Authority when he announced that nothing would be built on the one-acre footprints where each of the twin towers had stood.[174] The governor had bowed to intense pressure from two groups that were receiving widespread media coverage. One consisted of organizations representing fire fighters, police officers, and other first responders who were America's heroes; these men and women had risked and sacrificed their lives on September 11. The other comprised family members who had lost their loved ones. Pataki's decision to protect the twin towers footprint was popular but costly. It affected the layout of the commercial properties and complicated the design of the below-ground utilities, bus parking lot, and a new PATH station.

When the Port Authority and the LMDC unveiled the architects' six different concepts for the trade center site in July 2002,[175] the *Daily News* blamed the Port Authority for its arrogance and disdain, writing in an editorial, "All six designs were destined to look the same because there aren't too many ways to shove 11 million square feet into a 16-acre parcel."[176] Four days later, the Civic Alliance group hosted an extraordinary public forum at the Jacob Javits Convention Center called "Listening to the City." More than 4,000 people, seated at tables of ten and staffed by trained facilitators, provided instantaneous feedback about design elements. The common themes that emerged from the participants were posted on large electronic displays.[177] The reaction to the six plans was overwhelmingly negative, especially to the Port Authority's plan to squeeze in so much office space into the site.[178]

In response, the Port Authority and LMDC held numerous discussions about ways to reduce the density. The LMDC wanted to extend the World Trade Center project area south by adding the site of a building that had been badly damaged on September 11. With the Port Authority's commissioners focusing on the financial aspect of redevelopment, Seymour was resistant to adding cost and complexity to the rebuilding efforts. Expanding the site would also give the mayor more influence since the city owned the streets and sidewalks south of the trade center. Roland Betts, an LMDC board member, convinced Seymour, who in turn persuaded his board to go along with expanding the site. Betts had tremendous influence since he was both the chair of the LMDC's site planning committee and one of President George W. Bush's closest friends.[179]

Betts led an architectural competition, ostensibly called an innovative design study, to create a master plan for the trade center site. Port Authority officials, who were accustomed to controlling designs, hated the idea of a competition, but they went along with it once they heard the thousands of comments at the Listening to the City forum.[180] After the LMDC and Port Authority culled through 406 architectural submissions from around the world, nine were released to the public in December 2002.[181] The architects who submitted their plans realized that the public would have real influence on the decision, so some of the shrewd ones hired publicists and lobbied influential civic and cultural groups.[182]

More than 100,000 people visited the finalists' designs displayed in Battery Park City and 8,000 people offered their comments.[183] A joint committee of the Port Authority and LMDC representatives then narrowed down their selection to two teams. The committee members favored a design featuring two latticework towers. However, they were overruled by Governor Pataki, who preferred a proposal by Daniel Libeskind.[184] Libeskind's plan included five office towers that spiraled down in height, and an eight-acre site for a memorial and museum, new cultural facilities, and a performing arts center. The new development would reconnect the World Trade Center site with Lower Manhattan and feature street-level retail shops and restaurants. Figures 8.6 and 8.7 shows the site plans for the original World Trade Center and the plan adopted for its redevelopment.

The tallest building, referred to as Freedom Tower and later One World Trade Center, would be the same height as the original north tower, and with its spire would soar 1,776 feet.[185] The number crunchers at the Port Authority did not like the building's height because it would become an obvious target for terrorists and would be less economically viable than a somewhat shorter office tower. Not only might the Freedom Tower lose money, but if Silverstein had to build such a costly building, he would be less likely to obtain the financing needed to construct all the other buildings on the site. One Port Authority official lamented, "We've decided that the Freedom Tower is a symbol of rebuilding. It's like building the Statue of Liberty. It's not an economic proposal. The Freedom Tower is a monument. That's what we're building."[186]

Pataki was smitten with the plan to build the country's tallest building, whose height would represent the year that the U.S. Declaration of Independence was adopted. Pataki saw the World Trade Center redevelopment as both his legacy and a way to burnish his image for a future presidential campaign. He pushed for the tower's groundbreaking to be held on the anniversary of America's independence, July 4, 2004.[187] Similar to the way that Governor Rockefeller had jumpstarted the twin towers four decades earlier by agreeing to move state offices into the complex, Pataki announced that the governor's office would be the Freedom Tower's first tenant.[188]

A separate competition took place for the design of the World Trade Center's memorial and museum. The Port Authority had little input into their design, even though it would eventually build both structures. Michael Bloomberg, New York City's billionaire mayor, would take on a leading role in the development of the memorial and museum, after he became the chair of a foundation that would eventually raise more than $450 million in private donations to build and operate them.[189]

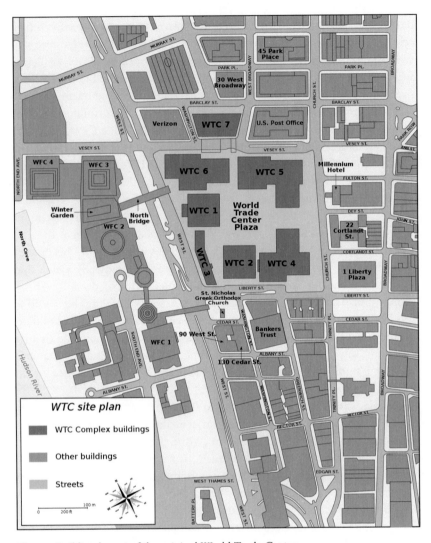

Fig. 8.6. Building layout of the original World Trade Center.
(Illustration courtesy MesserWoland, Wikimedia Commons, CC BY-SA 3.0.)

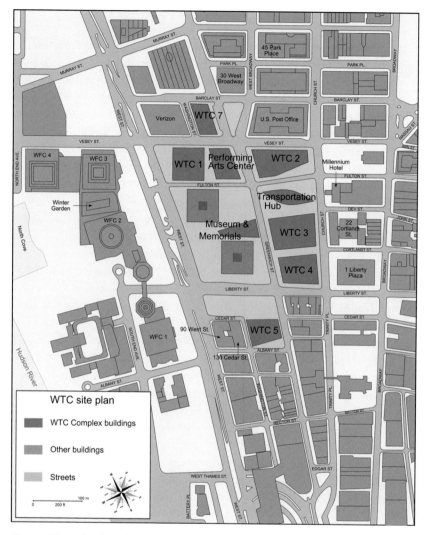

Fig. 8.7. The redeveloped World Trade Center complex includes streets that had been eliminated in the original complex.
(Illustration courtesy MesserWoland, Wikimedia Commons, CC BY-SA 3.0.)

One Delay after Another

Disagreements over design elements slowed down progress on the entire site even after Libeskind's master plan was adopted. For instance, the stakeholders argued about the location of retail stores and their entrances. Westfield America, which had a lease to operate the retail space,[190] wanted an enclosed shopping area similar to a suburban shopping mall.[191] City officials, however, wanted street-level shopping with sidewalk entrances to ensure an active street life. Meanwhile, the families of the victims did not want storefronts to intrude on the memorial or the towers' footprints. Compromise was difficult because Silverstein was trying to maximize the value of his office buildings and he was convinced that high-paying tenants would not want to rent in office buildings with shops in the lobbies or next to entrances. Eventually, the parties agreed to build five floors of shopping with numerous sidewalk entrances that faced neither the memorial nor the front of the new office buildings.

Complicating the design was the Port Authority's insistence, early on, that it create a superblock, belowground, just as it had done for the original World Trade Center. Although the site might look like separate parcels above ground, the Authority wanted the buildings integrated below street level so that it could provide more efficient site-wide services and maximize revenue from the retail space. Tying the facilities together and centralizing services was also a way for the Authority to keep control of the trade center site.

Underground concourses lined with shops and restaurants would connect the buildings, subway stations, and the PATH train. A single security center would screen all the delivery trucks before they could access underground roadways and loading docks. Security was an overriding concern not only because of September 11 but also because in 1993 terrorists had detonated a truck bomb in the World Trade Center's underground parking garage. For that reason, the Port Authority would not build any public parking spaces except those for tour buses and commercial deliveries.[192] That was something new for the Port Authority since it had long built parking facilities as a way to generate revenue at its bus stations and airports.

While architects, elected officials, and the public had vehement discussions about the buildings and the memorial, few people understood the cost and construction implications associated with creating an underground superblock. In the 1960s, the Port Authority owned the site and constructed the buildings. In the 2000s, the trade center complex had numerous ownership and leasing rights stacked on top of each other, including those held by the Port Authority, Silverstein, Westfield, the Memorial and Museum Foundation, and the Metropolitan Transportation Authority. Delays to one project had a cascading effect on all the others. Sharing underground infrastructure added to the tension between the trade center's players because its construction costs had to be allocated to all the various projects—a painful accounting process that would delay progress at the trade center and take years to settle. The costs were determined based upon numerous factors such as square footage, the weight of facilities, and the amount of water and air conditioning expected to be used.[193]

In 2005, the public as well as everyone involved in the project was frustrated that the site still looked like a seventy-foot-deep giant hole in the ground.[194] The *Wall Street Journal* reported that "the only things rising on the Ground Zero site are projected costs and tensions."[195] The rebuilt World Trade Center, which would extend seventy feet below ground and 1,776 feet above ground, became the world's largest Rubik's Cube puzzle. Since the underground structures had to accommodate the support columns and elevator shafts for the facilities above them—design and construction needed to proceed simultaneously for the office towers, retail space, memorial, museum, vehicular screening center, subway stations, tour bus parking, and the PATH terminal.[196]

While Pataki negotiated with Silverstein about financing issues, the Port Authority remained skeptical that Silverstein could raise enough money to build ten million square feet of office space. Silverstein still had not settled with his seven insurance companies on the amount that he would be reimbursed for the terrorist attacks.[197] Meanwhile, Mayor Bloomberg tried to force Silverstein out of the rebuilding process by denying him access to more than $4 billion worth of tax-exempt bonds. The mayor had support from New Jersey officials who were concerned that if Silverstein was unable to make his lease payments, the Port Authority would not have the resources to extend the PATH train to Newark Airport and help pay for a new passenger rail tunnel under the Hudson River.[198]

The *Daily News* summed up the situation in March 2006: "On one side of the negotiating table sits Larry Silverstein, single-mindedly intent on maximizing the profits he stands to make even if his planned rebuilding of Ground Zero goes bust. On the other side, there's a clown car's worth of public officials with competing agendas for the city's most important development."[199] On April 5, 2006, Governor Pataki invited Tony Coscia (Port Authority chair), Mayor Bloomberg, and Jon Corzine (New Jersey governor) to a meeting where

Fig. 8.8. Construction of One World Trade Center (Freedom Tower) in 2009. *(Photograph by Westmc9th, December 2009. Courtesy Wikimedia Commons, CC BY-SA 4.0.)*

the participants were sworn to secrecy.[200] The four men came to an agreement and decided they would deliver it to Silverstein who could either accept it or drop out of the project. Silverstein would get to build the three most profitable office towers, while the Port Authority would build the Freedom Tower and a tower on the southern site. The Port Authority would reduce Silverstein's lease payments and guarantee completion dates on its underground work so that Silverstein could proceed with his construction. Only after this agreement was finalized in September 2006 would visitors to the World Trade Center site begin to see substantial progress (figs. 8.8 and 8.9).[201]

Ballooning Costs and Yielding to the "Starchitect"

The Port Authority would not emblazon its logo on the World Trade Center's office towers, the memorial, or the museum. Likewise, the shops and per-

Building and Rebuilding the World Trade Center

Fig. 8.9. Construction of the National September 11 Memorial & Museum in 2010. *(Photograph by Derek Rose, September 11, 2010. Courtesy Wikimedia Commons, CC BY 2.0.)*

forming arts center would be associated with other organizations. The Port Authority's name, however, would be prominently displayed at the Transportation Hub, whose centerpiece would be a spectacular new terminal for the PATH train station. It would be one of the most visible and widely used features of the trade center site, and it was a project near and dear to the Port Authority chair, Anthony Coscia, who wanted to create an iconic structure, a Grand Central Terminal for Lower Manhattan.[202] The PATH terminal in the original World Trade Center had been underground, but Coscia wanted a station that would be visible from the street.

Despite its importance to the organization, the Authority failed to effectively manage the Transportation Hub project. When the Port Authority's commissioners authorized its design and construction in 2003, the Authority's engineers expected it to cost $2.2 billion with the federal government contributing more than $1.9 billion and insurance proceeds providing the remaining $300 million.[203] The final price tag for what would be known as the world's most expensive train station would eventually reach $4 billion. Costs soared because of factors that the Port Authority could and could not control.

The decision to tie all the projects together underground added to the Transportation Hub's cost since it connected underground to all the other World Trade Center facilities and buildings. Delays and changes on each of the other projects added design and construction costs to the Transportation Hub. The Port Authority ended up paying $400 million[204] for the Hub's share of the site-wide infrastructure costs. Some of that might have been avoidable; one Port Authority official divulged, "we put more of the infrastructure cost onto PATH to avoid a pissing contest with Silverstein."[205]

Accommodating Governor Pataki's priorities was also costly. Pataki insisted that the No. 1 subway line remain open through the trade center site while the Port Authority's contractors built under, over, and alongside the subway tracks. The subway line started in Lower Manhattan near the Staten Island Ferry Terminal and ran through the trade center site, above the PATH tracks. The Metropolitan Transportation Authority could have shut down the No. 1 line in Lower Manhattan, but the subway service was important for the residents of Staten Island, which was the only New York City borough that the governor won in his three gubernatorial races.[206] Keeping the subway operating during construction added more than $350 million to the Transportation Hub's cost.[207]

In the 1960s, the Port Authority sought out a relatively unknown architect, Minoru Yamasaki, to design the World Trade Center site. In 2003, the architect chosen by the Authority to design the Transportation Hub was known across the globe for his "visually striking and structurally daring" bridges, museums, and railroad stations.[208] Joe Seymour, the executive director, said the engineering department was "enamored" of Santiago Calatrava and "our people call him the Da Vinci of our time." The *New York Times* architecture critic referred to Calatrava as "the world's greatest living poet of transportation architecture."[209]

Calatrava was selected and his design approved without any public input. Anthony Cracchiolo, who headed the Authority's priority capital projects, said, "We did not want an endless public process with 5,000 public submittals."[210] Nevertheless, Calatrava's design was nearly universally praised when it was unveiled in 2004.[211] The *Los Angeles Times* architectural critic, Nicolai Ouroussoff, exclaimed that the "the structure's glistening glass shell— supported on a series of enormous, skeleton-like steel ribs—appears as delicate as a fluttering eyelash."[212] Governor Pataki and his successor, Eliot

Spitzer, fell under Calatrava's spell, who by numerous accounts was charming in at least half a dozen different languages. In 2006, Seymour's successor said, "I have become very, very fond of Santiago. . . . The guy's a genius."[213]

In the 1960s, Yamasaki made countless changes to his World Trade Center design to meet the Port Authority's needs. The architect was responsive to his client's wishes, whether or not he agreed with them. In the 2000s, Authority officials were often unable or unwilling to counter Calatrava's resistance to changes that threatened the integrity of his design.[214] The celebrity architect insisted on expensive materials such as 12,000 tons of Italian steel, cast in specialty shops, and that is what the Port Authority purchased for him.[215] The Authority's engineers acquiesced to Calatrava's impractical design elements such as white marble floors that would be stepped on by tens of thousands of dirty shoes every day. In some ways, the Authority's hands were tied. Calatrava convinced Governor Pataki that he should design not only the PATH station but other elements of the underground concourse as well. The Authority's chief engineer, Frank Lombardi, referred to Calatrava as not only a very talented architect and structural engineer but also a great salesman.[216]

After Eliot Spitzer was elected to succeed Pataki in November 2006, he selected Tony Shorris to serve as executive director. Shorris had been the Port Authority's first deputy executive director in the early 1990s and he was highly regarded for his administrative skills. He saw the World Trade Center project "as an engineering problem, wrapped in a financial problem, wrapped in a political problem, surrounded by an emotional force-field."[217]

Both Shorris and Spitzer were also dazzled by Calatrava. Referring to the architect's prodigious artistic talent, his three Park Avenue townhouses, and the exhibits of his work at the Metropolitan Museum and the Museum of Modern Art, Shorris rhetorically asked, "How could you not be impressed?" But the executive director recognized that both the schedule and budget for the Transportation Hub he had inherited from the Pataki administration were wildly optimistic. When Shorris first started, he seriously considered adding a few hundred million dollars to the cost estimate and adding a year or two to the opening date rather than be tied to seemingly unattainable expectations. But he chose to retain the budget and schedule as a way to keep pressure on the designers, engineers, and contractors. The governor, whose father was a real estate developer, agreed that Shorris needed to be tough, otherwise the project would take even longer and be more expensive to complete. Shorris remembers, "it's not like I was lying to the public. I thought I'd fight like hell to do what was promised. At some point, I might give up, but not until I did everything I possibly could to bring the project's costs back to the budget."[218]

Shorris asked his engineering team to redesign the Transportation Hub. He wanted to simplify the construction and add more retail to help pay for it. On March 7, 2008,[219] he sent a memo to Governor Spitzer that explained why the Transportation Hub's costs had risen, providing options for reducing those costs, and identifying the likely consequences of those changes. Shorris explained how the Port Authority's engineers had identified nearly $300 million in cost savings that would not affect the signature above-ground structure. The memo reveals the limited autonomy that the Authority's executive director had regarding the World Trade Center.

Shorris told the governor, "New Jersey would likely support these changes, even though they significantly diminish the experience of the PATH commuters."[220] Shorris did not know exactly what the New Jersey governor thought because he was not allowed to reach out to Trenton. At that time, only the Port Authority's deputy executive director and chair were talking with the New Jersey governor's office.[221] Shorris found this exceedingly frustrating, especially since he knew how the Authority had operated when he had been the first deputy executive director under Pataki's predecessor. Known as a skilled political figure, Shorris was accustomed to working with whomever was influential to forge compromises.[222] When Shorris did try to reach the New Jersey governor's office, he was told that he needed to work through the chair, who had been by selected by a New Jersey governor.[223]

Fearing the architect's reaction and his influence on public opinion, Shorris warned Spitzer, "It is likely Calatrava himself would oppose these changes since they so dramatically change his vision. He is a strong-willed figure and has a global reputation as one of the premier designers of our time and has never feared from protesting changes to his often over-budget designs. While we would make every effort to appease his outrage, and even appeal directly to his pecuniary interest in showing the world he can create a successful project within budget rather than another massive cost overrun, there is a very real risk he would turn to the design community to protest these changes." Although Shorris thought the cost issues would "carry the day," he warned the governor that the *New York Times* architecture critic and the chair of New York City's planning commission would take Calatrava's side.[224]

Spitzer's aides in Albany on World Trade Center issues did not consider Shorris's memo to be the sign of a weak or vacillating executive director because the governor, not Shorris, would make the choice on whether to

Building and Rebuilding the World Trade Center

scale back Calatrava's design. Shorris was known in the governor's office for writing superb memos because he succinctly provided all the information that the governor needed before committing to a decision. Spitzer and his senior staff would want to know the position of the key players and the concerns they might have. If the governor was going to be criticized in the press about the World Trade Center, he wanted to know about that in advance.[225]

Shorris did not bother discussing how the Port Authority's commissioners from New York would react to the cost-cutting proposal because they always followed Spitzer's instructions on how to vote. One senior Spitzer aide said, "The governor's office tried not to deal with the board members. We would work out our position with Tony [Shorris] and he would tell the board 'This is what the governor wants.' Tony only called me if he was having trouble."[226]

Shorris never did receive a response from Governor Spitzer to his March 8, 2008, memo because the governor got caught up in a sex scandal and announced his resignation four days later. When David Paterson was sworn in as the new governor, he faced delays and spiraling costs in every aspect of the World Trade Center reconstruction. Paterson was not wedded to unworkable elements of the project or unrealistic schedules that were tying the Authority's hands. Nor was he a micromanager like Spitzer. Furthermore, unlike his two predecessors, Governor Paterson was not dazzled by Calatrava' awe-inspiring renderings and three-dimensional models. The new governor was legally blind.

Governor Paterson replaced Shorris with Chris Ward as the Port Authority's executive director. Ward had a wide and impressive range of skills from his previous experience as Port Authority's chief planner, construction industry executive, maritime official, and New York City's environmental commissioner. He was given much more autonomy than any of the other recent executive directors. Paterson and his chief of staff simply told Ward to "do whatever you need to do" and they rarely second-guessed him.[227]

After Ward moved into the executive director's office, Governor Paterson issued a widely publicized letter calling for the Port Authority "to complete a comprehensive assessment to determine if the current schedules and cost estimates for reconstruction are reliable and achievable. If they are not, I would like an evaluation of what viable alternatives exist to get the project back on track or whether we need to alter our targets to meet the reality on the ground."[228] In fact, the governor's letter was written by Ward himself as a way to give his reevaluation efforts more clout. With this public directive from the governor's office, Ward and his team assessed every aspect of each World Trade Center project element. Given the public's frustration with the slow pace of construction, Ward thought it was necessary to set realistic milestones and then hold the contractors accountable to them.[229] Over the course of the next few months, Ward set about shifting priorities, revising schedules and budget, and adding transparency.[230]

Ward had a forceful personality that exuded confidence, and he was willing to take on many of the stakeholders including Calatrava and Silverstein. "It's a construction job now; the planning and the politics are over," he repeatedly said.[231] Ward's most important decision was to ensure that all the elements would be in place so that the memorial could open to the public by the tenth anniversary of the September 11 attacks. Meeting that milestone (even though it would be costly and delay other project elements) would restore the Port Authority's credibility, and it was a date of great importance to the mayor, the governor, and the general public.

Ward recognized that the Authority's internal processes had failed at both the staff and board levels. Although the Port Authority's engineers and construction managers had once been recognized around the world for their expertise, that was not the case in the twenty-first century's first decade. The U.S. Department of Transportation repeatedly warned Port Authority officials that they were failing to minimize risks to the budget and schedule because they did not have the technical capacity, experience, or project controls strategy needed to effectively manage the project.[232] Before Ward instituted new monitoring procedures, the Department of Transportation privately warned him that the federal funds flowing to the Port Authority for the project were in jeopardy.[233]

A cardinal rule of an effective organization is ensuring that individual board members do not interfere in an organization's day-to-day affairs. The board as a whole is responsible for setting direction, establishing budgets, and approving major contracts. Boards as a group have managerial powers, but individual board members do not. Anthony Sartor, a board member from New Jersey, crossed this line and undermined the Port Authority executive directors.[234]

The Port Authority's board of commissioners relied upon Sartor to monitor the construction work and protect the Authority's financial interests. He chaired the board's World Trade Center Redevelopment Subcommittee, a role suited him well since he had a PhD in engineering and was chief executive of an engineering firm. However, Sartor had a conflict of interest and used his board position to enrich himself. Sartor even discussed selling his company to Calatrava's partner on the project.[235] Although Sartor recused himself on hundreds of board votes that conflicted with his private engineering practice, the other commissioners knew how Sartor would have voted and approved contracts that benefited his business. They deferred to Sartor because of his expertise and his diligence monitoring the project. Sartor's relationship to the project was so intimate that he was given an office alongside the Authority's construction managers.[236]

Calatrava took advantage of Sartor's ethical faults, spending thousands of dollars in Port Authority funds so that Sartor could travel first class and stay at luxury hotels on a European tour of Calatrava's projects.[237] In turn, Sartor consistently defended Calatrava and the Hub project. Authority executives were very uncomfortable with Sartor's role and discussed it regularly. The chief engineer, Frank Lombardi, said, "Of course, he was trying to further his own business—without question."[238] Another senior official lamented, "he created a cancer inside the Port Authority."[239] Instead of directly confronting Sartor, Chris Ward and his engineers persuaded the board that their proposed revisions would reduce the Authority's costs and risks, compared to the plans advocated by Calatrava and Sartor.[240]

Opening to the Public

On September 11, 2011—ten years to the day after the terrorist attack—the World Trade Center memorial opened to the public. The memorial's centerpiece, the two largest manmade pools in the world surrounded by the names of the victims etched in bronze panels, is a moving and extraordinary monument to the victims of the terrorist attack. In 2013, the first tower on the sixteen-acre site opened and the first office workers to move in were Port Authority headquarters' staff.[241] Some of the Authority's employees decided to retire rather than return to the World Trade Center, because they were still traumatized by the terrorist attacks.[242]

In November 2014, One World Trade Center, the tallest and most expensive building in the Western Hemisphere, opened its doors to tenants (fig. 8.10).[243] The Port Authority had expected financial institutions to take up the bulk of the space, but the offices became a highly desirable location for media and technology firms. In fact, thanks to city, state, Port Authority, and federal resources, the entire neighborhood had been transformed. Rather than solely a business district, the area around the World Trade Center had become a

Fig. 8.10. The 1,776-foot-tall One World Trade Center, the tallest building in the Western Hemisphere. *(Photograph by James Tourtellotte, August 31, 2016, for the U.S. Customs and Border Protection, Department of Homeland Security. Courtesy Wikimedia Commons.)*

24/7 community where people were living, shopping, and eating, rather than just working during business hours.[244] The population in Manhattan south of Chambers Street had risen from 22,700 in 2000 to 49,000, and more than one-third of households had incomes over $200,000, nearly five times the share citywide.[245]

The World Trade Center hosted numerous events as new facilities opened. President Barack Obama and former president George W. Bush attended a

Building and Rebuilding the World Trade Center   257

Fig. 8.11. President Barack Obama, former president George W. Bush, and their wives at the September 11 Memorial on the tenth anniversary of the terrorist attacks. *(Photograph by Chuck Kennedy, White House photographer. Courtesy Wikimedia Commons.)*

solemn ceremony to dedicate the memorial (fig. 8.11). Mayor Bloomberg and Larry Silverstein cut ribbons at the opening of office towers. A ribbon-cutting ceremony marked the opening of the observatory at One World Trade Center and another ribbon was cut when a television station began broadcasting from an antenna on the building's roof.[246] However, there was only a quiet opening without any VIPs, speeches, ceremonies, or ribbons for what should have been the Port Authority's proudest moment, the opening of Calatrava's spectacular PATH terminal.[247]

When the PATH terminal (fig. 8.12) opened in March 2016, the Port Authority's executive director, Pat Foye, called it a "symbol of excess" and the *New York Times* referred to it as a "a soaring symbol of a boondoggle." Elected officials and Foye himself stayed away from the opening.[248] The architectural critic, Michael Kimmelman, wrote, "Mr. Calatrava has given New York something for its billions. But if the takeaway lesson from this project is that architects need a free pass, a vain, submissive client and an open check-

Fig. 8.12. Calatrava's soaring PATH station at the World Trade Center in 2016. *(Photograph by Anthony Quintano, August 18, 2016. Courtesy Wikimedia Commons, CC BY 2.0.)*

book to create a public spectacle, then the hub is a disaster for architecture and for cities."[249]

Conclusion

The building and rebuilding of the World Trade Center reveal two very different Port Authorities. In the 1960s, the Authority had much more political independence along with greater financial, management, and technical resources. Even though it was at the height of its powers, the Authority faced opposition that nearly thwarted its move into the world of mega real estate development. But strong leadership, its publicity machine, and friends in high places enabled the Port Authority to establish a coalition that supported its ambition to build two of the most iconic buildings the world has ever seen. Upon their completion, however, the Port Authority's reputation was somewhat tarnished because it had both underestimated the World Trade Center's costs and overestimated its benefits.

When disaster struck in 2001, the Authority was ill-prepared to handle it. Even under the best of circumstances, a strong and confident Port Authority would have struggled with the burden of planning a massive emotionally laden project under an international microscope. After September 11, though, the Authority's staff was overwhelmed and crippled. They had recently emerged from one of the most tumultuous periods of their history with an erosion in its culture, resources, expertise, and leadership. Moreover, their offices had been obliterated along with many of their colleagues, and they faced a world where demanding new security concerns imbued every asset of their portfolio. As the Authority looked to the future, the contrast with its previous experience developing the World Trade Center site could not be starker.

In the 2000s, the organization took a back seat to more powerful players and its senior officials were not in the same position to make deals and navigate political minefields. Given the costs and the numerous delays associated with reconstruction, both the Port Authority's former chair and executive director recognized the Authority's failings. In retrospect, Tony Coscia said that he would give the Port Authority a grade of "C" for its work rebuilding the World Trade Center. "With a certain honesty and humility," he said, "we ended up with the major role because we were the best." Every other organization, Coscia said, would have been a "flunking student."[250] Chris Ward said he would have given the Authority a higher grade[251] but did admit, "I think the World Trade Center straddled this divide between success and failure."[252]

The redevelopment process laid bare the Port Authority's weaknesses and highlights some of the challenges it currently faces in its role as the best of a mediocre lot of infrastructure development players in the region. As explained in the following chapter, many of these weaknesses have deep roots, even if they have only become apparent in recent years.

CHAPTER 9

The Rhetoric and Reality of Political Independence

There is no little irony in the fact that the Port Authority, created out of a Progressive Era motivation to offer business-like efficiency and integrity as a salve to the political cronyism, abuses, and corruption of the period, is now often characterized as a paragon of some of these same negative qualities. Once lauded by Franklin Delano Roosevelt as "more able and honorable" in the administration of public affairs because of its "intelligence and integrity,"[1] the Authority has recently been described as "mired in scandal" and as fostering a "culture of patronage and impunity."[2] Slightly more charitably, the Regional Plan Association notes that "political maneuvering, mission creep, and inefficient operations" have damaged the Authority, and that "its operations and credibility have suffered from political interference and the inability to finance projects."[3] The *New York Post* effectively captures the contrasts inherent in the Authority's fall from grace in an article, itself evocatively titled "Why the Port Authority is an Unmanageable Mess":

> Its originators, steeped in Progressive-era faith in technocratic management, envisioned an authority run by disinterested professionals, insulated from the pressures of day-to-day politics.... Since its founding, however, the Port Authority has proved anything but politically disinterested. It has long since become a swamp of mysterious accounting practices, patronage, favoritism, self-dealing, political retaliation and mission creep.[4]

These descriptions leave little doubt that the Port Authority has lost much of its original luster. How did an organization designed to rise above the political fray and govern with more competence and probity than the states and local governments come to merit such criticism? How did it lose some of its autonomy, integrity, capability, efficiency, and (to some) honor?

As with many thorny political questions, the answer is not straightforward. First, glowing descriptions of the Port Authority independence, autonomy, and integrity were never totally accurate. The Port Authority was never as politically insulated as its architects intended. So much so that Jameson Doig, in his book *Empire on the Hudson*, characterized what survived the political gauntlet of the bistate ratification process in 1921 as a "toothless giant."[5] However, over time, the mythology of the Port Authority's political independence has proved incredibly durable on some levels. A 2006 *New York Times* op-ed described the Authority as having "near-complete autonomy."[6] Port Authority officials and outside observers often describe the Authority as being financially independent[7] (a claim that is, to a degree, debatable), characterizing this alternatively as a source of strength, weakness, or of corruption. Yet, in practice, its autonomy has eroded to the point where political actors and observers in the region barely bother to keep up the pretense of independence. In response to criticisms characterizing New York State proposals for additional state oversight as "full-throated assaults on the independence of the Port Authority," a spokesperson for the New York governor commented in 2016 that, "By law the chairman doesn't run the Port and it's not independent; it's run by the two governors."[8]

This chapter interrogates and explores the complex evolution of the Port Authority's autonomy. It argues that although the Authority was not as unfettered as its architects hoped, it did possess some tools that enabled it to transcend interstate politics and act regionally. These institutional features were *enablers*, not guarantees, of a degree of political latitude. From this perspective, independence is perhaps best conceptualized as an asset that the organization and its leadership leveraged and protected but that, ultimately, has been neither constant nor permanent. It is an asset that has undeniably eroded over time, with important consequences for the Authority and its effectiveness.

Our conceptual framework lists autonomy as one of four factors that enable the coalition-building activities that are necessary to support the Authority's agenda and mission in the context of political constraints. By focusing on it here, we do not mean to elevate it above the others but to recognize that organizational independence has been an enduring source of conflict and debate—serving at various times as a bogeyman to be feared and tamed or a unique and wonderful strength. As autonomy has waned this has had impacts on the other factors in the framework—its resources, culture, and entrepreneurial leadership—just as these factors have at different points countered this erosion. In observing this, we reinforce the case that the institutionalization of autonomy is not a guarantee of political insulation and that to enact agendas collaborative public authorities must constantly navigate contested political waters by identifying and securing supportive coalitions. In this chapter, we demonstrate that despite the highly visible scandals that brought the Authority and its weaknesses into the public consciousness, its present predicament was not often the result of dastardly corruption. Rather a series of smaller shifts, sometimes difficult to pinpoint in time, conspired to undermine the already limited autonomy institutionalized by the Authority's founders.[9]

Finally, for all the Authority's faults, contemporary venom is probably not wholly deserved either. In previous chapters we have demonstrated that the Port Authority is still capable of delivering value to the region and, in the concluding chapter, we delve into why it is still a crucially important organization to keep the metropolis moving. However, this is an opportunity to reflect on the tensions inherent between democratic accountability and the Port Authority's autonomy and effectiveness. As such, it is important to acknowledge that in analyzing its one hundred plus years of activity and evolution, the Port Authority can and should be discussed as a profoundly political entity.

Institutionalizing Autonomy?

When the compact creating the Port Authority was signed by the two states on April 30, 1921, it was not the document that its early proponents had envisioned. The organization's principal architect, Julius Henry Cohen, had intended to create an authority with unprecedented powers and independence. He wanted it to not only be responsible for infrastructure planning and development across the entire metropolitan area but to be able to shape the activities of local and state governments and private corporations by issuing binding regulations and blocking initiatives that did not conform with the Port Authority's Comprehensive Plan. With this concentration of political power, the Authority could realize reformers' dreams of deploying a professional staff to "analyze, monitor, and shape the modernization of the Port and the economic growth of the surrounding region, guided only by principles of efficiency and the public interest."[10]

These powers, understandably, did not survive the bistate ratification process. Both states as well as local authorities objected to being bound by the proposed clauses. Through their parallel processes, the states managed

The Rhetoric and Reality of Political Independence

to reverse them entirely and require state approval for a variety of activities. As Doig notes, these changes sent a deliberate and powerful message that "the new Port Authority would be commanded by the two legislatures and the states; it would not give the commands."[11] The Port Compact ultimately protected the ability of localities to pursue their own development objectives with measures such as, "Nothing contained in this agreement shall impair the powers of any municipality to develop or improve port and terminal facilities."[12]

Despite being created with relatively constrained powers, measures to protect the Authority's political autonomy largely survived. At its inception, four key provisions insulated the Authority from "intraregional jealousies"[13]: (1) its creation via the Compact Clause; (2) its ability to raise revenue through bond issuance; (3) procedures for appointing commissioners; and (4) the lack of a state veto over the board or its decisions.

First, Cohen's innovative use of the Compact Clause as a mechanism for creating the Port Authority provided long-term stability that other types of bistate agreements could not match. The Compact Clause[14] of the U.S. Constitution provides for agreements between states subject to congressional approval.[15] Prior to the 1920s, it had mainly been used to adjudicate boundary disputes; however its use in creating the Port Authority ushered in a new era of institutionalized interstate cooperation in the development of regional resources.[16] Cohen's creative adoption of the clause was born partly of necessity and partly of shrewd strategy. The political scientists Frederick Zimmerman and Mitchell Wendell note that because the creation and activities of the Authority might have conflicted with the federal government's commerce power, Cohen wanted congressional approval via the Compact Clause as a defensive measure.[17] While this may have been a practical motivation, Cohen also saw advantages anchoring the agreement in federal statute: once approved by Congress it would be difficult for either state to withdraw. He also noted that if either of the states were to become obstinate then "a higher power, the nation"[18] could step in. So when the Port Compact was officially approved in 1921 it bound the two states into a marriage that would be hard to break and that, Cohen hoped, would be mediated, if necessary, by a reliable arbiter.

If it was to be a (nearly) unbreakable marriage, at least the Port Compact ensured that the ambitions of the newlyweds would be provided for. As a corporate and political body it was granted "full power and authority to purchase, construct, lease, and/or operate any terminal or transportation facility within said district; and to make charges for the use thereof; and for any of such purposes to own, hold, lease, and/or operate real or personal property, to borrow money and secure the same by bonds or by mortgages upon any property held or to be held by it."[19] This allowed the Authority to charge rents, fees, and tolls to pay for operational costs and modernization projects and raise bonds backed by this income. Again, necessity and strategy both played a role in Cohen's proposal to raise capital through bonds. First, given the magnitude of the projects that the Authority was created to advance (including consolidation and reorganization of rail infrastructure as well as the potential for river crossings), to be effective the Authority would need access to reliable sources of funding that would not be constrained by state rivalries. This approach had the further benefit of ensuring that Port Authority surplus revenues were retained and reinvested into regional assets and projects because they could not easily be diverted by states or cities to fund local projects.[20]

This provision was, of course, not a guarantee of financial autonomy or security. As the Port Authority initially had no assets to its name, the nascent Authority could have had difficulty securing investment and accomplishing its agenda. Fortuitously, its early leadership on the construction of the George Washington Bridge and capture of the Holland Tunnel within its first decade of existence, and the toll revenues that came with them, ensured that the Authority's financial prospects were perceived favorably by banking interests. As detailed in chapter 2, these early accomplishments were enormously significant to the reputation, and ultimately, financial autonomy of the Authority through its first half century.

With its institutional stability and independent fundraising ability codified, Cohen also hoped to ensure that the governance of the organization would not be captured by parochial interests. He proposed a board of six commissioners (three from each state) and aimed to ensure their dedication to regionalism through two mechanisms: overlapping terms and zero compensation. Staggering term expirations was meant to prevent a wholesale change in the composition at the whim of incoming governors. Forbidding a salary for their service aimed to attract commissioners committed to public service for whom civic action would be both adequate motivation and reward.[21] In a letter to the *New York Times* in 1947, Cohen cited the Port Authority as an exemplar of the "public corporate method, free of graft and politics, manned by men of public spirit and run with business-like efficiency by a staff selected solely because of their competency."[22] The practice, not codified in the Port Compact, of drawing commissioners from the ranks of business and professional elite meant that the members of the board were often well-respected and influential in their own rights in political circles and would be difficult (also ill-advised) for governors to intimidate. Hailing from a world of commerce where firms operated beyond political boundaries, these commissioners were expected to prioritize the development needs of the region over parochial politics.

Finally, while the Port Compact did state that no binding decisions could be taken without consent from a minimum quorum of two commissioners from each state, it did not initially provide a mechanism for governors to dissent and veto these decisions. The Compact, however, permitted each state to enact its own laws to establish gubernatorial veto power, which they both subsequently did. Nevertheless, the authors of the original document envisioned an Authority where governors may not need a formal veto power and were perhaps overly hopeful that politics would not intrude where professionalism should reign.

These four provisions (Compact Clause, bonds, commissioners, and lack of veto) were the bedrock upon which Cohen hoped to build an authority with unparalleled latitude, capability, and professionalism to attack the complex problems that led to its creation. While it would never achieve the degree of independence that he had hoped, with these provisions it was endowed with a set of tools that its leadership could wield to carve out the Authority's agenda for more than a century. But the Port Authority was on the defensive from its infancy as it faced various waves of political challenges. For the most part, its bulwarks did not hold. Over the years, shifts in practice, culture, and formal rules weakened, if not totally undermined the provisions designed to protect and institutionalize autonomy.

Early Political Incursions

The Veto

Perhaps predictably given that it was an element of the charter, both states moved relatively quickly to institutionalize a gubernatorial veto of Port Authority minutes. The story of how the veto was introduced demonstrates the degree to which the Authority could be vulnerable to a change in governors, the ever presence of political pressures, and how easily the day-to-day business of the Authority could become the subject of interstate power struggles and agendas.

Despite the fact that the provision for a veto had existed since the Authority's establishment, it did not become an issue for six years. The eventual enactment of veto legislation was precipitated by the very different stance of an incoming New Jersey governor toward the Port Authority and a dispute about construction materials for the George Washington Bridge. George Silzer, who served as governor of New Jersey between 1923 and 1926, supported the Authority, viewing it as a benevolent organization acting in the region's best interests. His successor, A. Harry Moore, held a contrary view, accusing the Authority of holding the powers of a "super-state," and he made no secret of his opposition to it.[23] When some complaints were made about the process used to select cables for the George Washington Bridge, Governor Moore used it as an opportunity to begin proceedings that would require New Jersey's approval of all Port Authority contracts.

The substance of the dispute was probably less important than the opportunity it presented to establish a veto provision. In any event, the Roebling Company, a New Jersey firm whose wire cables were competing against materials manufactured elsewhere to suspend the bridge deck, claimed that its solution was clearly superior and applied pressure on the governor. Moore publicly released a letter from Roebling, citing the injustice of the Authority's decision-making process and the economic impact of "depriving hundreds of our people of the work which this gigantic undertaking would supply"[24] as justification for his move to curb its autonomy. Othmar Ammann, the Port Authority's chief engineer, resisted these pressure tactics, arguing that he should choose the option that would ensure the strongest bridge, and his position was endorsed by the board. Here was a case that illustrated the importance of independence: the safety of the 4,760-foot-long span would depend on maintaining high standards of engineering judgment. Seeking to protect the Authority's integrity from Moore's demands, New York's governor Al Smith asked the state legislature in Albany to give him the power to thwart any efforts that would curb Ammann's independence. After a series of heated negotiations, which involved the suspension of work on all Port Authority construction projects, Ammann was allowed to make his own decisions on bridge design. But Moore and Smith agreed that both governors should be given the power to veto the decisions made the Authority's board of commissioners.

Doig describes this episode as the greatest challenge to "engineering integrity and general autonomy that the authority had faced in its first decade, and that it would confront during the next twenty years."[25] Perhaps he was right in this. No single episode in that period precipitated such monumental institutional change. Rather the veto was the first notable shift away from its founding principles and the beginning of a steady erosion of its lauded autonomy.

The Appointments

The six-year term of the Port Authority's commissioners has offered them some ability to resist, if the governors or others made patronage demands, and the fact that the Authority could finance its program without appealing to state legislators also secured a degree of latitude in decision-making. Occasionally, however, the board made appointments that appeared to violate its general standard to hire the best, after careful review of all available candidates. A notable case was the 1932 appointment of Morgan Larson to be a "consulting engineer" at the Port Authority, soon after he completed a term as New Jersey governor. The appointment was carried on page one of the *Newark News*, and one letter-writer responded that "things like this" lead the public to be "disgusted with politics." In response, the Port Authority defended the appointment because Larson had an "intimate contact with our plans," based on his years as governor.[26]

In the 1930s, New Jersey's governors were limited to three years in office, but they could run again after skipping one term. Moore was again elected as governor in 1931. He soon named John Milton to the Port Authority's board, and since Milton was a close associate of Jersey City mayor (and party boss) Frank Hague, it now seemed likely that Hague would have a role in staff appointments. A few patronage hires were made at lower levels in the police, real estate, and law divisions in the 1930s, but largely the Port Authority career staff maintained its professional cast.

One clear breech of the Port Authority's "nonpolitical" shield occurred in 1933, when John Galvin resigned as a New York commissioner and was at once appointed to the staff with a high salary. Galvin, who was active in Democratic party politics, was given the title of director of port development, but port issues were handled by other staff members and Galvin had no professional staff while he worked for the Authority until 1936.[27]

The Depression years sharply reduced the Port Authority's revenues, and staff members were laid off, leaving little room or taste for patronage hires. A change of leadership also rectified this potentially worrying trend. Frank

Ferguson, the chair from 1933 to 1945, was dedicated to paying off the debt incurred in constructing the first tube of the Lincoln Tunnel and the Authority became wary of adding new employees or new projects. This proved only a temporary respite from the pressure of patronage politics. In recent years, the press and public have not shied away from calling out what is now an established tradition of patronage at the Authority—albeit one that recent executive directors have attempted to resist with varying amounts of dedication and success.

While the conditions for political appointments clearly existed in the Authority's early days, the board and leadership were able to reestablish its core values at various intervals. However, the pressures of patronage were ever present. For instance, it was a challenge that one of the Port Authority's most celebrated executive directors, Austin Tobin, was quite active in calling out. During his tenure, beginning in 1942, Tobin realized that there were a few politically connected staff members at lower levels, and that a major challenge, as the Port Authority took on new duties in the fields of marine terminals, bus stations, and airports, would be to resist demands that patronage be widely applied in these new programs. So he emphasized in speeches and at legislative hearings that the Port Authority must select staff and sign contracts free from political favoritism. His authority could not be successful, he argued in a 1945 speech, "if political interference plays any part in its management or internal affairs." Interviewed by *Business Week* a decade later, he asserted, "You've got to be completely nonpolitical, or become a complete creature of the politicians."[28]

Decades later, Tony Shorris (who served as executive director between 2007 and 2008) noted that the practice of political patronage was firmly engrained and described an instance where the human resources department showed up in his early days as director to help him navigate and balance the political appointments process. Shorris reflected: "Someone once described it as the Noah's Ark of political patronage [where each position had appointees from each state]. It was totally wasteful but also inimical to the whole point of the Port Authority. It was set up by reformers who tried to insulate it from politics. Not only was it not insulated, it became a dumping ground. The human capital was completely politicized. The contracting was completely politicized."[29]

Doig noted in a 2012 op-ed on the state of the Port Authority "that outside political demands, mainly coming from the governors' offices, have generated jobs for the politically connected—initially just a handful for each state, but growing steadily over time. Their political patrons have protected these men and women from removal, and the executive director and senior staff members have had to work around these individuals, whose qualifications have in most cases been more political than substantive."[30]

The causes of this complete organizational transformation from nonpolitical entity to patronage dumping ground are not straightforward or easy to pinpoint. While the introduction of the veto and the early incidents demonstrating how easily patronage could seep into the structure tell part of the story, the Authority's contemporary permeability to political interference can also be traced to the erosion of other elements of its autonomy closer to the turn of the twenty-first century. When the Port Authority discovered the limitations of its financial arrangements, the board became an instrument of, rather than a defense against, political intrusion, and the organizational culture that had deplored such conditions was strained.

Erosion of Financial Autonomy

Having weathered the Great Depression and the challenges of World War II, the Port Authority entered a new era of development and expansion. The period between the end of the war and the early 1970s ushered in an era of growth for both the Authority and the region and, under the leadership of Austin Tobin, cemented some of its greatest successes, many described elsewhere in this book. The following decades were more tumultuous in which the burdens of growth exerted pressure on the Authority as the economy convulsed and it became an attractive tool for state governments facing severe financial constraints. These two periods could be characterized as thirty years of ascendence starting after World War II and then followed by thirty years of instability during which various practices at odds with its founding principles were institutionalized, resulting in a loss of financial autonomy, as well as board professionalism and independence. While chapter 6 details the period in the 1990s when many of these issues came to a head, forever changing the Authority's operation and public profile, this section takes a step back to explore changes to the broader institutional currents that underpinned this period of interstate friction and those that were to come.

One of the most significant impacts of the gubernatorial veto was on the Port Authority's financial autonomy. Once introduced, governors could effectively unilaterally block any board decision. From that point on, the Authority had an incentive to genuinely seek consensus on major initiatives from both states before committing or risk costly delays and uncertainty from vetoes. While this had ramifications for capital projects and other elements of the portfolio, it exerted perhaps the most constraint on revenue-raising capabilities.

So much of the Port Authority's financial autonomy stemmed from its ostensible economic independence from the two states. Because it collected revenues from its various assets, it had access to a relatively stable revenue stream to fund operations. Those revenues could be used to secure borrowing for capital projects. As a result, the Authority never had to rely on transfers from the states, which would risk embroiling it in the tit for tat of state politics. While it is technically true that, to this day the Port Authority does not rely on transfers from any level of government to fund its operations, this arrangement has not safeguarded its autonomy. The problem is that to augment its operating revenues, through toll increases on bridges and tunnels, for example, requires board approval and is, therefore, subject to gubernatorial veto.

If the Authority never needed to raise tolls or fares to cover expenses, it could reasonably claim to be financially autonomous. However, the combination of expanding portfolios, increasing maintenance and operating costs, and the effects of periods of economic instability has meant that it is reliant on a revenue source that can be incredibly politically charged, difficult to raise, and ultimately beholds the Authority to the two states. As the Port Authority evolved it constructed and acquired a wide variety of properties to operate in the interests of the region. This diversity has been a substantial asset to the region as the profitable elements of its portfolio sustained those that tend to operate at a loss. The PATH rail service, vital to residents and employers in both states, for example, is a major beneficiary of this arrangement.

Maintaining money-losing assets relies on generous margins of profitability on others. Unfortunately, as the Port Authority's portfolio expanded that balance was not always easily struck.[31] By the last quarter of the twentieth century much of the infrastructure on its books was aging and required expensive maintenance. This, combined with increasing personnel outlays at what was by then a very large Authority, increased costs and ate into its bottom line. Traffic volumes on its bridges and tunnels that had been climbing since they were constructed began to plateau in the 1990s with a predictable effect on toll revenue. A 2012 independent audit found that the interstate transportation network of tunnels, bridges, terminals, PATH, and ferry service did not have an operating cash flow sufficient to cover its own capital expenditure needs.[32] More recently, the largest Port Authority project—rebuilding the World Trade Center—has been extraordinarily expensive and became a real drain on the Authority, undercutting its ability to go forward with important projects such as the Bayonne and Goethals bridges. All of this has necessitated more frequent toll increases forcing the Port Authority to play a highly political game.

As a result, toll and fare increases became a political and politicized process, sometimes requiring years to negotiate. Because both governors hold veto power, proposed increases need to be agreed in advance of board discussions to prevent one or both states from blocking the initiative. And sometimes even that is not enough. What seems, on the surface, to be a straightforward operation is complicated by the fact that both states have strong constituencies affected by toll increases. For example, residents in some northern New Jersey communities rely upon the PATH train while others rely upon buses traveling through the Lincoln Tunnel into the Midtown Bus Terminal. Staten Islanders need one of the Port Authority's crossings to travel to most of the rest of the country, while New York businesses and consumers depend upon the constant stream of trucks coming in from New Jersey. As a result, governors are typically involved early in the toll raising process and have engaged in various episodes of brinksmanship and political theater to moderate or resist increases.[33] In one such highly choreographed instance, the governors in 2011 had the Port Authority announce larger toll increases than necessary, so that the governors could be seen as heroes by launching an independent audit into the Port Authority's finances and publicly pressuring the Authority to approve a substantially lower increase.[34]

As the revenue raising process has increasingly turned into a political game, governors have gained power and influence on the Port Authority's decisions, not always resulting in optimal outcomes for the Authority or the region. Over time, governors have also gained control over their appointees to the board in ways that Cohen never intended, further strengthening political sway over the Authority.

The Executive and the Board

Port Authority institutions were designed to encourage professionalism in its leadership and staff and to uphold a commitment to regionalism over parochial political interests. The primary mechanisms for this were the rules and practice surrounding the selection of board members and the appointment and balance of power between the Authority's executive director and chair. The Authority's 1945 annual report captured this vision in bold terms:

> From the very nature of our duties as Commissioners under a bistate commitment to the regional development of the whole Port area, it follows that we do not function as Commissioners for the development of the New Jersey part of the area alone, or as Commissioners for the New York part of the area alone. Rather, each Commissioner, from whichever State appointed, functions as a Commissioner for the development of the whole region. Any approach that attempted to match facilities, a brick for a brick, in New Jersey and New York, would be the antithesis of the regional development of the whole Port area that is intended by the Treaty.[35]

However, even by 1945 this sentiment was more rhetoric than reality. Doig argues that the practice of balancing state benefits—if not quite brick for brick, very nearly—was already firmly entrenched during Tobin's tenure. A perfect example is the Port Authority's promise in the early 1960s to take over the Hudson & Manhattan Railroad and build a transportation complex in Jersey City, so that it could get New Jersey's authorization to build the World Trade Center. Doig cites regional balance as a core guiding principle of Tobin's administration, noting that "suspicion between the two states was not abolished by waving the Port Authority wand."[36] What was at heart a pragmatic practice aimed at maintaining momentum for Tobin's dramatic expansion of the Authority's ambit and diffusing bistate bickering became engrained in its culture and infrastructure agenda thereafter. Later this division became formalized in changes to the selection of commissioners and Authority leaders as well as the political expectations attached to those proxies.

The Authority was originally designed so that neither state would permanently dominate decision-making. The Authority's leadership was originally shared, with the chair and vice chair rotating between the states. The board then appointed the executive director. This pattern changed in the late 1970s, when New York governor Hugh Carey insisted on naming an executive director from outside the career staff in exchange for granting New Jersey's governor the power to appoint the Authority's chair—a practice that persists to this day.[37] The board must still approve the choice of executive director and chair, which gives each states the power to overrule the other's selection.

The Rhetoric and Reality of Political Independence

This veto power led to yet another change in practice when in 1995 conflict between the governors of the two states (described in chapter 6) precipitated a marked increase in gubernatorial micromanagement and political control. When the New York governor named George Marlin as executive director without consulting the New Jersey governor, Christine Todd Whitman, the latter insisted on appointing a deputy executive director. Ordinarily a senior level appointment would have been made by the executive director to assist with the Authority's management. Marlin was a politically polarizing choice given both his personal politics and his lack of management experience, thus the appointment of a more qualified administrator in the form of John Haley was meant to buttress Marlin's leadership shortcomings.

A former director and deputy director of the Port Authority's planning department in 2012 characterized these appointments as politically motivated. They described a situation where the deputy acted as the internal agent of New Jersey's governor, overseeing all decisions affecting the state. The executive director's role on these matters was essentially usurped resulting in a bifurcated management structure. Governors executed their wishes through their personal representatives with the two directors translating these directly to staff, bypassing commissioners. Decisions were predetermined in Albany and Trenton before the commissioners convened. The board was increasingly a rubber stamp, not independent leaders making decisions as originally envisioned.[38]

Interestingly, even though the commissioners are characterized here as less important vectors of political control, the board too has undergone transformations that have increased the vulnerability of the Authority to political whims. As we observed in chapter 6, these modern board appointments tend to be loyalists and not the "giants of finance and insurance"[39] and independent titans of industry that used to be the preferred occupants of board seats, who Lillian Borrone observed "weren't there to suck up to governors."[40] Board members are now expected to function as instruments of Albany and Trenton.

Governors have also been more willing to openly bully members of the board who were reluctant to fall in line. Kenneth Lipper, a commissioner from New York between 2013 and 2017, recalled a tenure fraught with conflict and politics: "I am proud to say that I went through four years and came out the other end, despite incredible pressure and threats from every level of government, and that I just did what I felt was the right thing for the public."[41]

Lipper was frequently at odds with the governor and a minority of one on board votes.[42] During this period, New York governor Andrew Cuomo tried to pass legislation that would reform the organization, permitting him to dismiss commissioners before the ends of their terms.[43] Although this provision did not survive the legislative process, it is indicative of the degree to which modern governors now feel empowered to alter the Authority's institutions to increase their influence. Cuomo was not the only champion of patronage politics. New Jersey governor Chris Christie notoriously forced sixty patronage appointments as well as diverted Port Authority funds to local projects of dubious regional merit. Doig and his associate, Mary Dufree, noted that board members "either directly abetted these violations of the port agency's charter or stood by silently, unwilling to confront Christie's probable wrath by speaking out against these incursions."[44]

During his tenure as New York governor, Andrew Cuomo was slow to appoint new commissioners after terms have elapsed. For example, in 2021, three members of the New York contingent had expired terms, two from 2019 and one from 2020. This trend of allowing board members with "holdover" status exposes commissioners to a different political dynamic where they can be dismissed and replaced at any time if they fail to toe the line.[45]

As discussed in more detail in the following chapter, political interference has carried a heavy price for organizational morale and culture. First, governors have increasingly meddled with the leadership of the Authority to ensure that loyalists occupy key roles, which has led to more rapid turnover in executive directors and chairmen. This challenges organizational continuity as each director and deputy attempts (to differing degrees) to both change and adapt to existing culture and staff struggle to adjust. Under such circumstances, longer term planning also becomes difficult. In our interviews with former Port Authority executive directors and staff, almost all commented on how culture had historically been an organizational strength and one that they had been tremendously proud of. While accounts of what the core culture entailed differed in their details, the broad themes were remarkably consistent in their invocation of the importance of regionalism and a commitment to world-leading excellence in project design and execution.

Heading into the 2010s, the Port Authority's finances were tight, it was subject to more political interference than ever before, and its internal culture had been weakened substantially (if not completely crushed). It was this combination of factors that created the context for the largest and most memorable scandal that the Authority has endured in its long history: Bridgegate.

"Time for Some Traffic Problems": Bridgegate and the Port Authority in the Cuomo/Christie Era

The George Washington Bridge is the most heavily used bridge in the world, carrying approximately 300,000 vehicles per day. Its fourteen lanes between Manhattan and Fort Lee in New Jersey connect with numerous highways, including the New Jersey Turnpike and the Cross-Bronx Expressway. On September 9, 2013, David Wildstein, the Port Authority's director of interstate capital projects and a loyalist of New Jersey's Republican governor Chris Christie, ordered the closure of two of the three lanes into the toll plaza from Fort Lee local streets. The three "local" tollbooths are dedicated to serve traffic feeding from Fort Lee as the result of a longstanding political agreement, while the remaining nine booths serve traffic from various highways. The closure of the two local tollbooths was described as part of a traffic study intended to determine whether to keep the local traffic arrangement in place in the future and the fact that Port Authority staff had been asked to collect data on the traffic patterns was used as proof of the study's legitimacy.

Under the best of circumstances, this would have greatly disrupted traffic patterns and increased congestion. However, the initial closures occurred during the morning rush hours and without any advanced warnings that would have permitted appropriate detours and signage to be installed for local traffic. In fact, Wildstein instructed Port Authority employees not to share information about the closures with police or public officials, and he kept the lanes closed for four straight days until the executive director, Pat Foye, ordered the lanes reopened.

The closures caused an estimated 2,800 vehicle hours of delays each day,[46] increasing some commutes that would normally take half an hour to over four hours. Fort Lee experienced days of clogged streets, hampering mobility and emergency responses. Wildstein (and his boss, Bill Baroni) asserted that the closure was part of the planned traffic study and that the lack of notice or alternative routing was to discover what would happen naturally under such circumstances. However, officials in both states were immediately suspicious of the timing; a study should be conducted when traffic volumes represent typical conditions, but that week included the first day of school and the anniversary of the September 11 terrorist attacks. Democratic legislators began to question whether there may have been political motivations. Furthermore, Port Authority engineers stated that they never close traffic lanes because computer-generated modeling is usually used to predict changes in traffic patterns. It was later revealed that neither Wildstein nor Baroni ever asked to review any of the data collected.[47]

These suspicions proved to be well-founded. The story that ultimately emerged was that three Christie loyalists (Wildstein, Baroni, and the governor's deputy chief of staff, Bridget Anne Kelly) devised the plan as political retribution against the Democratic mayor Mark Sokolich of Fort Lee who had failed to support Christie in his reelection campaign. A damning eight-word email from Kelly to Wildstein stating that it was "time for some traffic problems in Fort Lee" came to light in a New Jersey legislature probe of the incident. Wildstein later stated that Kelly confirmed to him in a phone conversation that she wanted "to create a traffic jam that would punish" the mayor and "send him a message."[48]

Mayor Sokolich repeatedly and unsuccessfully sought help from Baroni, texting, "Presently we have four very busy traffic lanes merging into only one toll booth . . . bigger problem is getting kids to school. Help please. It's maddening." Kelly mentioned this message in a text to Wildstein saying, "Is it wrong that I'm smiling?" After Kelly wrote that she felt bad for the kids, Wildstein replied, "They are the children of Buono voters," referring to Christie's Democratic challenger in the upcoming election.[49]

The public backlash was "swift and severe"[50] as Port Authority staff were ordered to testify before the New Jersey State Assembly and Christie became the butt of jokes on Saturday Night Live and every late-night TV comedy show. Shortly thereafter, Wildstein and Baroni resigned, and Governor Christie dismissed Kelly. A sixteen-month federal investigation ensued in which Kelly and Baroni were indicted on nine criminal counts, including conspiracy to commit fraud by "knowingly converting and intentionally misapplying property of an organization receiving federal benefits."[51] Both claimed they were not guilty. Wildstein pleaded guilty to conspiracy to commit fraud and conspiracy against civil rights.

Accounts of what actually happened, at who's behest, and who knew about the plan ahead of time remain muddled. Specifically, what role Christie played in the scandal has not been decisively established. Kelly maintained that she had always believed that the closures were part of a legitimate study that she and Christie had personally approved.[52] However, Christie denied all knowledge of the plan and evaded federal prosecution.

Whether or not Christie orchestrated the closures, or his associates independently acted on this behalf, the incident was only possible because of the steady erosion of political insulation described above. The fact remains that, political loyalists in the Authority felt empowered to use its resources in service of personal agendas in part because such behavior had become so common. Christie's massive wave of patronage appointments (including Wildstein, a high school friend) and his appropriation of Port Authority funds for New Jersey projects (to avoid raising taxes and reward loyalists) were all possible because of an organizational culture that would not challenge what was seen as gubernatorial privilege.[53] Pat Foye, the New York appointed executive director, claimed that he had no prior knowledge of the study, but he was reluctant to supersede the decisions of his New Jersey counterparts for fear of upsetting a delicate political balance. In a further illustration of this point, when Foye suggested to New York appointed commissioner Scott Rechler that the lane closures should be discussed in the executive session of the next board meeting, Rechler responded that "we should make raising Fort Lee a game-day decision, depending how New Jersey is behaving with respect to all of our pending issues."[54] In other words, a New York commissioner was willing to minimize the significance of the scandal in order to achieve New York's goals.

Episodes like this demonstrate decisively that the Port Authority's independence has been undercut to serve the governors' interests in direct opposition to the Authority's founding principles. After Bridgegate, calls to reform or even abolish the Port Authority sounded across the region, but gained only modest traction.

"Democracy on Hold": The Perils of Government without Politics

In the introduction to *Empire on the Hudson*, Jim Doig described his book as "the story of how Democracy was put 'on hold' in the New York metropolis—of how the passion for greater efficiency in transportation and for rapid economic growth, combined with some antipathy toward local political leaders, led state officials and civic leaders to drop their guard and yield responsibility for an important part of their destiny to an authority insulated from direct popular control."[55] By contrast, our account describes how democracy has been twisted in other ways as political power, wielded with varying degrees of impudence by self-interested governors, has been asserted on the Authority. This chapter describes how this occurred over the hundred years of its evolution and explores how these changes have diminished the Port

Authority's key coalition-building assets and changed the political calculus with respect to the two states that are its key stakeholders.

Before turning to the conclusion in the next chapter we want to weigh the competing priorities for organizational reforms. Given the history of the organization and the political age we inhabit, a reassertion of the Authority's original political independence seems both unlikely and unwise. It is easy to forget that the Port Authority was contested throughout its early years for being too independent of state and local interests and that Tobin's, and the Authority's, legacy is often compared to his contemporary Robert Moses and is cited as one reason for the backlash against Progressive-era independent authorities that ensued. It was no accident that Doig described the Port Authority as an "empire" on the Hudson. The political researcher Stephen Eide argues that while both Moses and Tobin were able to protect their agencies from external interference, "they also enjoyed a level of deference from the public and the media that is inconceivable today," noting that part of what made them such effective leaders was their ability to create an image of virtue in public service that meant that they enjoyed public support in most controversies that embroiled them.[56] For all of its effectiveness, it is, and has been, an organization that has kept secrets and done deals that may not stand up to public scrutiny. For decades, the board met behind closed doors and business dealings were not recorded for public oversight. Tobin's withholding of records in the congressional investigation described in chapter 3 showed the degree to which he believed, and behaved, as if the Port Authority's autonomy should not be subjected to the annoyances of democratic accountability. Yes he protected the Authority's interests and independence, but investigations revealed that its behaviors were also not always above reproach.

As governors became more activist in their stance toward the Authority and more willing to wield the veto to advance their agendas, the space for public oversight expanded. Except that gubernatorial supervision does not quite equate to democratic accountability. Doig presciently reflected that while the veto inserts a degree of political accountability, it requires that "supervising officials, in this case the two governors, demonstrate a kind of disciplined oversight—*resisting the natural tendency of elected leaders to use the authority for short term political gain*, while at the same time actively monitoring the Authority's proposals in relation to the governors' broad policy agenda."[57] Unfortunately, as documented in this chapter and elsewhere in this book, political leaders have been more than willing to use the Authority for political gain and to look the other way when their counterparts in the other state do likewise.

Following the Bridgegate scandal both governors called for an independent investigation of the Authority. The resulting *Keeping the Region Moving* report, issued by a bistate panel, recommended replacing the executive director and deputy executive director with a single chief executive officer selected by and accountable to the board, as well as replacing the board's chair and vice chair with either cochairs or rotating chairs from each state.[58] The report also recommended measures to promote transparency and ethical behavior such as issuing a new code of conduct and creating a chief ethics and compliance officer position. As the panel was completing its report in 2014, both state legislatures passed legislation with "almost unheard-of bipartisan support" to enhance accountability and transparency, such as a whistleblower program, open meetings, regular updates to the legislatures, and a chief executive officer overseen by the board of commissioners.[59] Both governors vetoed the bills, although they did indicate their support for many of the bistate panel's reform recommendations. State legislative leaders were convinced that the governors were not willing to sign legislation that ceded their control over the chair and executive director.[60]

Subsequent legislative attempts at reform have failed to gain gubernatorial support, including a bill that would have required rotating chairs.[61] However, the two governors did sign a bill in 2015 that subjects the Port Authority to the states' open records laws. Significantly, the Authority initiated a search for a chief executive officer in 2015 but did not fill the position. Instead the New York governor continued to select the executive director and the New Jersey governor still picked the chair. Similarly, the position of deputy executive director has not been formally eliminated. Regardless, some reforms have been implemented to increase transparency and public oversight of Port Authority affairs, reduce conflicts of interest, support whistle blowers, and promote more ethical behavior.[62]

As the Authority faces its next hundred years it must grapple with the consequences of this complicated political legacy. If we accept that some shackles on organizational freedom in the name of democratic accountability are appropriate, the challenge then is to also deliver the efficiency in regional transportation infrastructure development and governance that is its core mandate. As we discuss in the following chapter, only time will tell if it can rebuild its capability for bold regionalism or if it will remain a diminished, if still reasonably functional steward of regional mobility.

CHAPTER 10

Conclusion

Whether they like it or not, New York and New Jersey need each other and they both need the Port Authority. New York City maintains its role as a global center for business, media, and the arts thanks to the Port Authority, whose facilities help New York attract workers from a wide geographical area and connect it with the rest of the world. New Jersey is one of the country's wealthiest states because of the highways, buses, and trains that connect it to Manhattan. The number of people on both sides of the Hudson River who rely upon the Authority's facilities is mind-boggling. On a busy day, the PATH train carries more people than the entire population of Pittsburgh. The city of New Orleans has about 384,000 residents, approximately the same number of daily passengers that travel through the Authority's airports. The number of vehicles crossing the Authority's bridges and tunnels on a typical day is about the same as Detroit's population.[1]

This chapter first summarizes the lessons learned from the previous chapters about the Authority's ability to mobilize the region. The second part identifies lessons gleaned from the Port Authority's experience that are useful for other organizations and other regions. Third, we consider whether the Port Authority is positioned to address the region's needs and take advantage of opportunities that are needed to secure New York's position in the world.

Looking Back

By building supportive coalitions and overcoming numerous obstacles, the Port Authority's mission has evolved from improving rail freight to building and operating motor vehicle crossings, seaports, airports, heliports, bus stations, truck terminals, office towers, and industrial parks. The Authority's ability to build coalitions and complete projects in a timely manner has

Conclusion

eroded, however. For instance, in the 1920s the Authority needed about five years to plan, design, and build the Goethals Bridge. Chapter 7 describes how the Authority needed more than thirty years to perform those same steps for its replacement.

As explained throughout this book, the Port Authority's ability to seize opportunities, respond to its external environment, and implement its agenda has been shaped by its resources, autonomy, culture, and entrepreneurial leadership.

Resources

When the Port Authority was first established, its wherewithal to finance a wide range of infrastructure projects was not assured. A government agency with virtually no assets or tax revenue had to identify its own investment opportunities, convince investors to buy its bonds, and then generate sufficient revenue to pay back its bondholders. The Authority was given three key advantages over private firms: the states' power of eminent domain, the ability to borrow money at low interest rates, and monopoly power to prevent any potential competitor from constructing a motor vehicle crossing between the two states. After taking over the Holland Tunnel and completing the George Washington Bridge, the Authority watched its coffers swell as motor vehicle use soared.

Those income streams opened numerous opportunities for the Authority to expand its portfolio. For several decades after World War II, the Authority had to worry about where to spend its excess revenue before the governors tried to spend it or force the Authority to lower the tolls on its facilities. That is one of the reasons the Authority decided to move into the real estate business. It is worth stopping for a second to think about how remarkable it is that this organization (not a global corporation or a national government) built the world's tallest two buildings in the early 1970s. The Port Authority could borrow enough money to finance this bold initiative because its tolls and other user fees were a reliable and prodigious source of revenue.

The public and elected officials lauded the Authority's new bridges, tunnels, airports, and bus stations. Private firms appreciated the Authority's engineering capabilities and the enormous facilities it built to consolidate and distribute goods arriving by sea, truck, and rail. Few people outside the organization, however, understood how the Authority was shrewdly using its resources to bolster its own capabilities and power.

In its heyday, the Port Authority operated in a similar manner as one of America's elite private companies such as General Electric and IBM. The Authority offered higher salaries and more generous benefits than other public-sector organizations so that it could attract and retain the best and the brightest employees. For example, the executive director's salary in 1970 was $70,000 while the heads of New York State's largest agencies earned $37,275 and federal cabinet officers earned $60,000.[2] The Port Authority's work was exciting, and its staff had lavish work environments compared to most public agencies. Executives ate in a subsidized dining room with plush red carpeting and wood-paneled walls where waiters served food on white tablecloths.[3] The Authority was able to recruit graduates from prestigious law schools because it paid salaries on par with Wall Street firms. The Authority's lawyers had an extra perk, however, routinely taking helicopters from the roof of their Eighth Avenue headquarters when attending meetings at the airports and locations outside of Manhattan (fig. 10.1).[4]

The Authority even had its own research and development department that conducted numerous studies such as experimenting with automatic toll collection equipment as early as 1957. A fellowship program gave talented employees from any department the opportunity to conduct year-long research studies or pursue on-the-job training with an outside organization. For instance, in the 1960s, an engineer lived in Rome for a year so that he could learn more about designing and constructing concrete structures, while another engineer received his full salary to study crowd density. The Port Authority provided funds for these types of studies without even knowing whether they were going to use the research results.[5]

The Authority encouraged staff to engage with other transportation professionals in the nation and set up a highly regarded library staffed with trained reference librarians. As a leader in numerous fields, the Authority shared its technical knowledge at conferences and in journals, which is how it developed an international reputation for building and maintaining infrastructure. The Authority encouraged staff to further their education, and its management and executive training programs groomed future leaders.

The Port Authority muscled its way into new arenas because of its financial resources and its ability to hire talented and motivated staff. The Authority's departments developed expertise in a wide variety of fields—starting with rail and sea transportation, and then later in trucking, aviation, real estate, incinerators, and real estate. When Austin Tobin evaluated the potential of building a World Trade Center, he assigned twenty-eight staff members to

Conclusion

Fig. 10.1. A Port Authority helicopter landing on the roof of its Eighth Avenue headquarters in the early 1950s.
(Photograph reprinted by permission of the Museum of City of New York and the Port Authority of New York and New Jersey.)

work on it full-time, including experts in architecture, planning, finance, real estate, and law. The Port Authority was seen as an ideal government agency to build an international trade center because its staff worked with importers, exporters, and transportation and government officials across the globe. Likewise, the expertise that the Authority nurtured (and the reputation it earned) in dredging, maritime trade, and aviation gave it the credibility to take over Newark's airport and seaport.

Until the mid-1990s, the Authority had a prominent planning department that brought together experts to look at the regional economy, conduct research, and convene conferences about specific industries and important public issues. The planners' skills and their access to data made the Port Authority the de facto leader in addressing regional issues. The Authority leveraged its expertise with a communications department modeled after those found in private corporations. Its public relations department, with a budget envied by other government agencies, helped enhance the agency's reputation and expand its portfolio. The department produced films, brochures, magazines, and established a speakers bureau that spread the word about the Port Authority's accomplishments. As a result, the business community, civic groups, and the financial industry lauded the Authority, which helped the Authority gain support for new initiatives along with more ongoing sources of revenue.

The money train eventually dried up. The PATH system proved to be more expensive to operate, maintain, and upgrade than expected; former Port Authority chairman Tony Coscia referred to it as a "financial dog with fleas."[6] Likewise, the bus terminal became a financial albatross. The Port Authority could no longer build new bridges and tunnels, and its crossings began to reach their capacities. For decades, the Authority could count on more and more drivers paying tolls. For example, the number of vehicles using the Authority's crossings increased 60 percent in the 1950s and 49 percent in the 1960s. That growth was not sustainable for physical, political, social, and environmental reasons. In fact, since the 1990s, the number of vehicles has been relatively stagnant, which is why the Authority has had to rely upon frequent toll hikes.[7]

The Authority's staff can still manage complex projects, but it is no longer an entity that attracts the best and brightest young people. Employees now earn salaries more commensurate with other government workers, and the work of a stagnating public agency that outsources much of its creative work is less alluring to recent college graduates. Other budget cuts, such as those that slashed training programs, have inflicted persistent damage to the Authority's expertise, skills, and technological mastery.

Along with this reduction in resources has been the Authority's reputation. In the 1950s, the New York Yankees won the World Series six times, a remarkable feat. The Authority had its own stellar decade including opening the Lincoln Tunnel's third tube, the Midtown Bus Terminal, a Manhattan heliport, and the Newark truck terminal. In 1960, the writer Edward T. Chase wrote in *Harper's Magazine*, "With the possible exception of the Yankees, New York's most splendidly successful institution has been the Port of New York Authority." He reported that the Authority's integrity and accomplishments are undisputed.[8]

In the 1960s, neither the Yankees nor the Port Authority matched their successes of the previous decade. While the Yankees descended into mediocrity, the Authority was left bloodied and weakened by congressional hearings, a futile jetport battle, and cost overruns on the World Trade Center. In the 1990s, Mayor Rudy Giuliani's relentless attacks left it vulnerable to an executive director with a sharp budget knife. The damage to the Authority's reputation made it easier for governors to interfere with the Authority's independence.

The 2013 Bridgegate episode exposed the infiltration of politics into the Port Authority's once touted independence and rational decision-making processes. Although the Authority rebuilt the World Trade Center, the frequently delayed design and construction process, and the ridiculously expensive PATH station did not enhance its reputation. The Port Authority is frequently accused of hiring politically connected individuals, operating obsolete facilities, making decisions in secret, and having a bloated overpaid workforce. That reputation is difficult to change and has hurt its ability to mobilize the metropolis.

Autonomy and Culture

The Authority's loss of resources in recent years has gone hand in hand with a diminution of its autonomy. The Port Authority had been set up so that it could be run like a business with minimal political interference. The commissioners' terms are six years, longer than any of the elected officials in the region. Instead of having to rely upon legislative appropriations, the Authority ostensibly controls its own revenue sources. However, the governors have reined in the Port Authority's ability to spearhead new initiatives.

Chapter 8 documents the consequences of the changes in autonomy. In the 1960s, the Authority was given far-reaching powers regarding the World Trade Center's design, construction, and future tenants. After the terrorist attacks, even though the Port Authority owned the site, they were frequently told by the governors what to build and where to build it. The World Trade Center was only one example. By the late 1990s, executive directors and chairmen had to check in with the governors before making major decisions. Likewise, board members were told how to vote on matters deemed important to the governors.

At the same time, the states began siphoning away billions of dollars for their own priorities. For instance, the Port Authority took a leading role planning a new passenger rail tunnel between the two states.[9] After Governor Chris Christie canceled the project, he took $1.8 billion from the Port Authority's budget that was allocated to the project and shifted it to repair roads in New Jersey. He took a big piece of the Authority's pie—nearly two years' worth of toll revenues.[10]

The previous chapter referred to the "Noah's Ark of patronage"—a two-by-two for senior positions. Not only was there an executive director appointed by the New York governor and a deputy executive director appointed by the New Jersey governor, but that practice had extended to numerous other departments. The Authority had the equivalent of two chiefs of staff, two police directors, and two general counsels—one who answered to Trenton and the other to Albany. Having both states represented within the Port Authority's bureaucracy slowed down approvals for everything from changing bus terminal procedures to issuing press releases.[11]

As the Port Authority's resources and autonomy changed, so did its culture. Austin Tobin understood the importance of providing the Authority with a vision, a mission, and values. He poured significant resources into supporting morale, cross-training staff, and systematically appraising performance. The Authority's culture was shaped by its engineers, who applied scientific principles to building bridges, managing people, and solving problems. Many of them recognized the importance of forming coalitions.

For example, in the 1960s the Port Authority had traffic engineers with a national reputation for excellence. One of them, Leon Goodman, was asked to look at how to reduce the delays that buses in New Jersey were encountering as they entered the Lincoln Tunnel in the morning peak period. In an interview for this book, he remembered, "In those days, the Port Authority was open to new ideas." Goodman came up with a novel idea at the time—a contraflow lane for buses—where one highway lane that typically carried westbound traffic would be used exclusively for eastbound buses in the morning.[12] Looking back on his proposal, he talked about how he was encouraged at all levels of the Authority to pursue his idea, even though it was something that had never been done before and raised serious safety concerns. Moreover, the bus lane would not bring in any additional revenue and would require approvals from numerous police departments and jurisdictions. Today, he said, if I brought this idea to an executive director, "I would be laughed out of the office, if not fired."[13]

Over the course of several years, Goodman refined his bus lane concept. He and his team established liaisons with local, state, and federal highway departments to promote the concept. The Authority designed signs and

Conclusion

Fig. 10.2. Buses traveling west into New York City in the Exclusive Bus Lane while cars and trucks are traveling east.
(Photograph reprinted by permission of Port Authority of New York and New Jersey.)

pavement markers, along with posts that could be used to separate vehicles traveling in opposite directions. Goodman's active role in two professional engineering societies helped him gain external support. At the time, the Authority encouraged engineers to attend meetings of professional organizations where they would share ideas. "Now," he said, "they look at it like a junket."[14] To create the "exclusive bus lane," the Authority agreed to pay for construction costs on a roadway it did not own as well as ongoing costs including maintaining tow trucks and patrolling the bus lanes. Today, the lane is by far the nation's most heavily used and productive bus lane in the nation, typically saving commuters twenty to thirty minutes and carrying more than 1,800 buses and 60,000 passengers on a busy morning (fig. 10.2).[15]

In the 1990s, George Marlin and his top aides did not understand the importance of nurturing a culture that values people and encourages risk-taking. The chief engineer, Frank Lombardi, watched Marlin break the Authority's social contract and devalue institutional knowledge. Lombardi deplored the deterioration of his once-vaunted engineering department as engineers were discouraged from attending conferences and found it harder to stay up to date with new developments in their fields. As their benefits were cut and challenging work shifted to outside consultants, Lombardi found it increasingly difficult to attract and retain top staff.

This sentiment was echoed across many departments. Officials in the port department had been accustomed to being very active in professional associations and were sought out by organizations across the world to consult on projects. Lillian Borrone, a former port director, remembered that she felt that "your responsibility as an agency and as an employee is to be the best you could be and then to share that with the region and the world." She said, "the spirit of the Port Authority was built into us. We were educated that way. We were proud of what we were doing, and we believed in the role that we were playing."[16] During her tenure, staff in her department were involved in advising the Panama Canal Authority, working with the port of Shanghai on strategic development, and participating in United Nations committees. Like Leon Goodman, later port directors lamented that the budget to engage as broadly no longer existed and that opportunities to demonstrate global leadership had dwindled.

Despite all these challenges, some of those we interviewed were confident that the Port Authority has not fundamentally lost the culture that they felt was one of the agency's great assets. Rick Larrabee, a former port director, commented that even during the most sinister and politically charged moments of his tenure "there was a soul of the organization that persisted."[17] This perspective offers more than a glimmer of hope for the future evolution of an agency that has been savaged in the press and in political statements as lost, broken, and corrupt. It turns out that an organization with more than a century of accomplishments has some resiliency.

Entrepreneurial Leadership

Previous chapters described how entrepreneurial leaders built and deployed the Authority's internal assets to achieve their goals. Austin Tobin used a wide range of resources and took advantage of his autonomy to initiate new programs and move the Authority into new fields. He instilled a culture of innovation and the development of skills and expertise that helped him embark on new initiatives including taking over the region's three airports, tying the region's highways together, creating container terminals, and building the World Trade Center. He strategically gained support from the media, elected officials, business leaders, trade unions, and various civic groups.

Another entrepreneurial leader, Peter Goldmark, was only thirty-six years old when he was appointed executive director in 1977, at a time when the region was reeling from an economic recession and a fiscal crisis. In his previous position as New York State's budget director, he had helped both the city and state of New York avoid bankruptcy. In interviews for this book, the staff who worked for him uniformly described Goldmark as a visionary. David Gallagher remembered, "He made us all feel good about what we did."[18]

Goldmark wanted to avoid having the governors set priorities. He explained his strategy: "You have to be on the offense with the governors. We proposed five or six things. If half were declined, you still have the other half." He added, "you need to be debating your program not what they want."[19] Goldmark had much more autonomy than recent executive directors. He felt that his first loyalty was to the board of commissioners and the Authority itself. It is "hopeless to act on one governor's behalf," he said. Goldmark remembers turning down a request from the New Jersey governor, Brendan Byrne, to hire one of his daughters. And (as noted in chapter 6), when Governor Byrne told Goldmark to fire a Port Authority employee, Goldmark responded, "You can tell me you don't like my direction. If you want me to fire someone, you have to get my badge on my way out of the door."[20]

In 1978, Goldmark set up the Committee of the Future to identify the region's needs relating to transportation and economic development, and then recommend how the Authority should most effectively use its resources to address those needs. Approximately one hundred Authority employees participated in the committee's efforts over the course of eighteen months. The committee also had extensive outreach including a meeting attended by more than 400 representatives of government, labor, business, and academic and civic organizations. The committee focused on the region's inner ring (including Brooklyn, Bronx, Yonkers, Jersey City, Elizabeth, and Newark)—the areas that had been particularly hard hit by the region's loss of manufacturing jobs. While Manhattan was recovering and the suburban areas were thriving, the communities in between were shedding jobs and population. In these struggling urban areas, the Authority went on to build several industrial parks, a waste-to-energy incineration power station, a facility for the processing and sale of seafood, and a satellite communications center.[21]

These economic development initiatives were politically popular at the time. The private sector was not willing to take them on and the local governments did not have the resources to finance them. Goldmark said, "Industrial parks are manufacturing jobs; not something a governor can say no to."[22]

Although Goldmark reshaped the Authority's priorities, his successors were not enamored of Goldmark's legacy. They tried, with varied success, to shed the economic development facilities that he initiated, seeing them as efforts that took the Authority's energy, focus, and resources away from its core transportation responsibilities.

A third entrepreneurial leader, Lou Gambaccini, was a man with a passion for public service who found a home at a public agency that emphasized customer service and high standards, along with encouraging creativity even at the risk of failure. Gambaccini saw the Port Authority as a dynamic organization that combined the best of the public and private sectors. He mobilized the metropolis by creating TRANSCOM, TransitCenter, and initiating ferry services. Compared to building a bus terminal, adding a deck to the George Washington Bridge, or even building an incinerator, these initiatives needed relatively little money to launch. Gambaccini had to rely upon other resources, such as the Authority's and his own reputation, along with talented and motivated staff, to get them off the ground.

While we have profiled a few leaders here, entrepreneurial leadership was promoted throughout the organization. The culture of mentoring, professional development, and fostering advancement helped to develop these qualities across all branches and ranks. Contemporary practices appear to have harmed the potential to develop the same types of leaders and attract entrepreneurial senior staff.

Lessons for Regional Governance and Public Agencies

Our account of the Port Authority's past contains lessons that public agencies operating in other metropolitan areas and regions can learn from the ways in which the Port Authority has used its resources, autonomy, culture, and entrepreneurial leadership to mobilize the metropolis. The Port Authority, the nation's very first public authority, has long inspired elected officials, civic leaders, and government officials. In fact, it now has more than 35,000 copycats, providing a wide variety of public services.[23] Most of these public authorities and special districts have features similar to the Port Authority—independent revenue sources and appointed governing boards.[24] One can see the prevalence of public authorities simply by looking at which highway agencies accept E-ZPass, a list that includes the Illinois State Toll Highway Authority, Maryland Transportation Authority, Maine Turnpike Authority,

West Virginia Parkway Authority, North Carolina Turnpike Authority, and the Kentucky Public Transportation Infrastructure Authority. Using the Port Authority as a model, New Jersey entered into compacts with both Pennsylvania and Delaware to operate bridges and tunnels,[25] while New York has more than 1,000 public authorities employing more than 100,000 people.[26]

Public authorities have often been able to build projects faster than traditional government agencies because they are not subject to some of the same regulations and restrictions (such as civil service and legislative oversight). Authorities can also make decisions faster because they can focus on one issue, compared to state governors and legislatures that are responsible for a wide range of issues such as education, housing, and health. Authorities can also be the best vehicle for overcoming jurisdictional boundaries, and they can often better resist party politics and patronage. Public authorities have some fundamental flaws, though, such as encouraging people to use facilities in a manner that may be detrimental to the public's best interests. For example, the Port Authority benefits financially when more people drive over its bridges and park at its airports; however, the additional vehicles on state and local roads exacerbate the region's traffic jams, pollute the air, and contribute to climate change. Another criticism of public authorities is the way they have been used to circumvent provisions that restrict how much debt states can issue. In fact, the public authorities in New York have more outstanding debt than the state itself.

All public authorities are constrained to varying degrees by the competing interests of their stakeholders and by the political, economic, and social contexts within which they operate. This is true no matter how well-resourced, institutionally autonomous, culturally attuned to excellence, or well-led they are. The Port Authority's history demonstrates this again and again. These competing interests and external contexts have two important implications that offer value to those trying to understand and improve these types of organizations.

The Inevitability of Governance

Scholars and practitioners of infrastructure development have long grappled with the problem of political and institutional fragmentation. Problems, vexingly, do not seem to respect jurisdictional divisions or the boundaries of governments. As a result, infrastructure development, among other policy concerns, requires some degree of coordination at the regional level. This can take many forms, from regional tiers of government (notably the Portland and Minneapolis Metropolitan Councils in the United States) to voluntary and collaborative regional public sector organizations[27] (such as the many councils of governments) to looser and ad hoc coalitions.

The literature on regional planning and metropolitan governance has, in the past three decades, mostly moved away from advocating new or larger forms of regional government, recognizing that creating a metropolitan government and consolidating municipalities are often political nonstarters. Instead it has focused on either the creation of narrowly focused special purpose bodies (such as transportation authorities) or governance in the form of (quasi-) voluntary coordination arrangements between existing public entities and their partners. Governance, rather than *government*, is now required to plan regional futures because so many organizations clutter the policy landscape, for better or for worse. Governance relies on involving and persuading independent actors to adopt and execute a collectively developed plan. Decision-making bodies that bring together both public and private players feature collaboration, consensus-building, negotiation, and accommodation. In these collaborative organizations, governments participate but are sometimes only one of many actors. In their assessment of planning metropolitan futures, Mark Tewdwr-Jones and Daniel Galland argue that "governments today can be characterized as significant facilitators and mediators of services and implementation, and require significant collaboration and partnership across sectors to enact change."[28]

However, the problem, some critics say, is that nothing gets done when decisions are not binding and where organizations lack independent resources. Voluntary councils and other related bodies have fallen short of their architects' visions. David Hamilton asserts that voluntary collaboration has generally failed to develop strong political support from state and local governments. As a result, they remain advisory in nature without the means to implement their plans and unable to create a strong sense of a region for planning purposes.[29] While there is mounting evidence that these observations do not hold for all voluntary arrangements, Hamilton is not alone in critiquing this approach.

Our analysis of the Port Authority provides an important counterpoint to these views. The creature of a different age, the Authority had many of the characteristics that contemporary collaborative public entities lack: permanence, breadth of mandate, resources, autonomy, authority—*real power*. But it still could not function unilaterally. Instead, like many institutionally weaker organizations, the Authority had to rely on its ability to build coalitions to support its activities. For more than one hundred years, the Authority has done its fair share of leading, but since the beginning it also sometimes needed to accomplish its goals through mediation, facilitation, and collaboration. In this sense, the need for governance amidst institutional pluralism that Tewdwr-Jones and Galland observe is perhaps less a new feature of regional planning than something that has become more obvious and has intensified as policy landscapes have become more crowded and complex.

Despite being the central character in this book, it is important to emphasize that the Port Authority has almost always been one among many. For example, in the New York metropolitan area, no government institution is responsible for looking at the region's overall transportation problems and then evaluating and implementing projects to address the region's needs. The Port Authority, as extensive as it is, does not have jurisdiction over every road, crossing, railway, or bus network in the area. Consequently, it is significant that even the region with one of the most powerful public authorities in American history has suffered the challenges of institutional cacophony. Insufficient cooperation between transportation-related entities in the New York area is not a new phenomenon. In his book *1400 Governments*, Robert Coldwell Wood calls the region "one of the great unnatural wonders of the world"—an interrelationship of governments "perhaps more complicated than any other that mankind has yet contrived or allowed to happen."[30] During John Lindsay's 1965 mayoral campaign, he referred to "the ineffectiveness, the quarrels and the waste which characterize the hydra-headed and fragmented monstrosity of the city's transportation structure."[31] These problems persist to this day.

A core lesson that emerges from our study, and our contribution to debates on regionalism, is that governance is inevitable. Governance specifically involves voluntary collaboration and partnership between units of government, usually to solve difficult problems. Previous eras of regional planning relied on a top-down view of government, typically nationally or state led, and master plans (that were rarely ever fully implemented). Scholars who have studied regional planning issues have until relatively recently sought government solutions (e.g., institution creation or reform) to these problems rather than working across jurisdictional and functional boundaries. In this book, we demonstrate how the Port Authority had to rely on coalition-building to accomplish its goals. This was both because the political fragmentation described above meant that other actors frequently had an interest in Port Authority projects and because those ambitions were often at odds with the interests of one or both of the states that it served. Thinking regionally ruffles feathers, and robust coalitions were required to counter reluctance or outright opposition from the states and their agents.

The inevitability of governance and the importance of coalitions hold an important implication for public authorities. There is no neat institutional fix. This challenges those who argue that an organization lacking some type of institutional advantage prevents it from playing an effective regional role. We argue that the organizational attributes that matter are not always derived from institutional structures but that a combination of factors, which evolve over time, are what underpins the ability to build and sustain coalitions. Moreover, our research demonstrates that while formal structures tend not to change much, an organization's stock of these assets, and its ability to leverage them effectively, can vary significantly over time and from project to project. The same combination of attributes that serve an organization well might not be as effective decades later. Organizations like the Port Authority that have multiple and changing portfolios must be wary and manage expectations because assets can change into liabilities and vice versa.

This suggests that public authorities should look internally to understand how they can leverage their strengths and overcome their weaknesses to build coalitions. This involves taking stock of an organization's resources, autonomy and authority, culture and reputation, as well as its leadership and vision and then developing an understanding of how these can be used to position it as a leader or to persuade potential partners and allies. Organizations should assess how these core attributes function together to advance a set of goals. Where weaknesses are identified, these assets can, to a certain degree, be enhanced or defended.

The Port Authority's struggles are likely to be familiar to public authorities worldwide. These organizations exist to perform difficult tasks in fragmented and contentious political environments. While every organization will face its own unique constellation of challenges, they all must do so by leveraging their resources, autonomy, culture, and leadership to build supportive coalitions and carve out room to maneuver. These challenges and coalitions will be ever shifting, and they must negotiate and balance a series of trade-offs.

A Series of Trade-Offs

There is no single answer to who should build and operate transportation facilities, the optimal way to structure a public authority, and the best way divvy up powers between states, municipalities, and public authorities. Governments make trade-offs when they assign responsibilities and delegate powers to government agencies, especially trade-offs relating to the role of the private sector, autonomy, and resources.

When setting up public authorities, one of the basic questions is determining the appropriate roles of the private and public sectors. Although public authorities use private companies to perform many functions, an argument could be made for turning over more facilities to the private sector. For example, while Port Authority employees operate PATH trains, a private company built and operates the AirTrains that link terminals at Kennedy and Newark airports. Private firms can often provide services at lower costs than government organizations, but there are trade-offs and risks associated with ceding power to private companies that are focused on the bottom line and not necessarily on the best interests of the region's residents, the facility's customers, or the organization's employees. Although private firms are ostensibly more innovative, that is not always the case. The saga of Stewart Airport shows that a private firm was no better at attracting passengers and flights than two different public authorities and a state agency.

Setting up a public authority requires a delicate balance between ensuring that the organization is accountable to citizens and providing it with autonomy to perform its work efficiently and effectively. While there are an infinite number of ways to strike a balance between too little oversight and too much political interference, none of them are perfect.

Giving too much power to board members is unwise. The Port Authority kept information so secret in the 1960s that the U.S. House of Representatives cited the Authority's chair and executive director in contempt of Congress for refusing to turn over documents. Independent board members might be asked to prioritize the region's interests, but they will all have their own biases and interests. For instance, individuals with ties to logistic firms and homebuilding companies will weigh transportation improvements very differently than those affiliated with environmental organizations. Likewise, board members who frequently drive will weigh priorities differently than those who rely upon trains and buses.

Giving too little power to board members is also problematic because it would undercut one of the authority's most important and defining characteristics—an emphasis on long-term goals. If an authority is subject to political whims and shifts in power, its leaders will find it much harder to make long-term commitments and follow through on them. Independent board members are more likely to keep their facilities in a state of good repair because they are more willing than politicians to increase toll and fares when necessary. In fact, bond rating agencies prefer independent boards for that very reason. Rating agencies have lowered their ratings of the Port Authority's bonds when too much political interference is seen as diverting the Authority's resources and threatening its ability to pay off debt and fund needed capital projects.[32] Bond ratings are critically important to public authorities because they directly affect borrowing costs.

Obviously, governments cannot give public authorities carte blanche regarding their facilities and services. The question of who should make decisions and when appropriate oversight is needed is a matter of debate. Should the governors, the legislators, or even the voters themselves have a say? Should local governments have power? For example, the city of Elizabeth is heavily affected by the Port Authority's decisions because it is home to a marine terminal, the Goethals Bridge, and a portion of Newark Airport. One might argue that the city should have veto power regarding certain Authority decisions, but holding the region hostage to Elizabeth's parochial concerns might be detrimental to all the other region's residents. One thing is clear about the way that the Port Authority is set up, however. Its current situation is not ideal. If a governor's office is going to micromanage a public authority, there is little benefit to having a board at all, other than giving the governors someone else to blame whenever there is a traffic problem, airport delay, or a toll increase.

To achieve their goals, authorities need to have sufficient resources. Many of the Port Authority's leaders (notably Austin Tobin and Peter Goldmark) displayed an entrepreneurial and creative streak to ensure that future revenues could meet ongoing costs. The Port Authority's history shows how having control over its own revenues has gone hand in hand with autonomy. Authorities that are flush with cash and autonomous can provide higher-quality services. On the other hand, observers often see well-funded authorities as overly extravagant. That was certainly the case when the Port Authority was known for its art collection, helicopter fleet, executive dining room, and high salaries. An important lesson from the Port Authority's experience has been that resources are not just financial; public sector organizations need to cultivate other resources such as their expertise and reputation.

Organizations should have a clear sense of mission and cultivate an internal culture to pursue that mission. When we consider how the Port Authority's culture has evolved, two lessons stand out. First, the Authority was more productive when it could attract and retain a talented staff. It lured them with exciting work and salaries and benefits that surpassed other public sector organizations. Losing that advantage hurt the Port Authority, although it might have helped other government agencies in the region attract staff with better credentials. Second, public authorities with diverse responsibilities can develop a culture that emphasizes a broader mandate. For example, after taking over the PATH trains, the Port Authority began to promote a more efficient transportation system by focusing more on moving people rather than cars. That does not mean it always does so. For example, the George Washington Bridge has fourteen lanes of traffic, but none of them are reserved for trains, buses, shuttle vans, or other high-occupancy vehicles.

Vision and Perseverance

Another valuable lesson from the Port Authority's experience has been the way that far-sighted leaders brought stakeholders together to create long-term visions and then achieve them. They used the organization's technical know-how, analytic skills, and insights from outside experts to take advantage of opportunities and prepare for future needs. That is how Gambaccini improved travelers' access to information, coordinated construction projects, and helped agencies respond to incidents faster. Lillian Borrone helped save the port by gaining support for dredging, state-of-the-art port facilities, and international trade routes that benefited the East Coast. The Authority's insight and long-term outlook has helped the New York metropolitan area stay ahead of its competitors. For example, its planners have long understood the benefits of containerization. The Port Authority wrote the following about containerization's benefits: "saving in labor; preventing breakage and theft; through cost of equipment; through easy transfer of containers from car to float, terminal or truck chassis; by eliminating individual package handling, and by application of mechanical methods for handling containers." What is remarkable about this insight is the annual report in which it appeared—not in 1961 or 1951, but rather in 1921.[33]

It is important to acknowledge that the Port Authority's massive infrastructure and real estate portfolio would be hard to replicate today. Public authorities face enormous obstacles trying to build large-scale projects. They cannot easily do what the Port Authority once did: clear land in Midtown Manhattan to build a bus terminal, demolish Civil War-era buildings to create new port facilities, and fill in wetlands to expand airports. Completing an environmental impact statement in the United States often takes six years or longer.[34] Sustaining support for projects during such a lengthy review period is problematic since political and economic conditions are subject to change and political champions come and go. But the Port Authority shows that governments can still complete massive projects such as replacing the Goethals Bridge, rebuilding LaGuardia Airport, raising the Bayonne Bridge's deck, and rebuilding the World Trade Center. The Authority is entrusted to take on these projects because of its credibility and reputation, and it has learned how to be more transparent, patient, and responsive to local needs. It has also displayed perseverance in securing approvals and resources, whether it has been to build a ferry dock in Lower Manhattan or replace a bridge between Staten Island and Elizabeth.

Looking Ahead

New York did not magically become a global city. Generation after generation of New Yorkers created institutions and infrastructure that has allowed it to prosper. Port traffic in New York surpassed Baltimore, Boston, and Philadelphia because of New York's early nineteenth-century investments in canals. Thanks to trolley lines and railroads, the city later became a manufacturing center and magnet for immigrants. Bridges and tunnels improved the efficiency and reliability of moving goods, and the subways, highways, and airports helped New York become a global powerhouse. In recent decades, the pace of transportation improvements has dramatically slowed and that is an ominous sign for the city and the entire metropolitan area.

Increasingly, the battles between cities in the United States have become regional competitions because more Americans live in suburbs than cities. Although high-speed Internet access allows people to work from nearly anywhere, they are still flocking to urban areas. One-quarter of Americans live in just nine metropolitan areas, those centered around the cities of New York, Los Angeles, Chicago, Dallas, Houston, Washington, D.C., Philadelphia, Miami, and Atlanta.[35]

To maintain its prosperity, New York City needs New Jersey's factories and warehouses, as well as its workers. When large firms look around the country for new office locations, they recognize their future employees will scatter throughout a region, living in downtown apartments, suburban developments, and large exurban homes. The ideal office locations offer convenient and reliable access to jobs via both car and transit, along with nearby airports that offer frequent service with a wide range of destinations. Corporations based in the city see New Jersey as an important part of the region because so many of their workers and business partners live and work there. New Jersey is not some far distant land as some New Yorkers might perceive (or wish) it to be. For instance, the city of Hoboken is closer to the World Trade Center than many of Manhattan's other well-known landmarks such as Central Park, Times Square, and Grand Central Terminal.

Challenges

The Port Authority was forged from perceived threats to the region's economy. A century ago, the movement of goods along the Hudson River waterfront had become increasingly unreliable and expensive. This affected every segment of the region's economy from grocery expenses to the costs incurred by factories when they purchased raw materials and shipped out manufactured goods. Today, the regional network of facilities and services that enable travel and commerce experiences recurring congestion and delays. Drivers, air passengers, and bus and rail riders can all attest to these conditions. This is a regional economic problem because businesses and people will leave the New York metropolitan area if they are not satisfied with its quality of life and the costs of living and working there. If they do not see the government addressing current transportation issues and preparing for the future, they are less likely to stay and invest in New York.

New York's success is important not just for the region but for the nation as well. The value of all the goods and services produced in the New York metropolitan area is equivalent to the entire output of Canada, a country whose labor force is twice as big.[36] Losing the region's high paying jobs does not necessarily mean they will go to some other city in the United States. They may very well go to Singapore, Shanghai, or Seoul. These Asian cities have built transportation infrastructure on a scale and pace unimaginable to most Americans. Seoul, for instance, did not have any subway service until 1974, seventy years after New York opened its first line. Today, not only is Seoul's subway more extensive than New York's, it is also faster, more reliable, and far more pleasant to ride. By comparison, the Port Authority took over operations of the thirteen-station PATH system in 1962 and invested billions of dollars into improving stations, signals, and tracks. Although the Authority has considered numerous extension plans, PATH still has only thirteen stations.

The fundamental problem facing the Port Authority today is a lack of capacity at nearly all its major facilities. As discussed in chapter 3, even though the Port Authority and the region's airlines have improved every facet of the airports' amenities in recent years, this has done relatively little to increase the number of planes that can take off and land in a single day. Aviation industry experts predict that air travel will continue increasing thanks to globalization, higher disposable incomes, and lower air fares. Even if air travel only grows at a modest 2 percent annually, the number of passengers will double in thirty-five years. Unfortunately, New York Stewart International Airport is not attracting enough flights and passengers to help alleviate some of the chronic congestion and delays, which will only get worse, at the three major airports. The ports have their own capacity issue because they are constrained by space. For example, the Newark and Elizabeth marine terminals have some room to grow, but they are surrounded by water that cannot be filled in, and a turnpike and airport that cannot be readily moved.

Compared to the airports and the ports, the capacity problems associated with the region's roads, trains, and buses are more complex because they involve more people, jurisdictions, and government agencies. Not many New Yorkers are old enough to remember the last time the Port Authority built a bridge or tunnel, where one did not exist before. The festivities at that event, the 1937 opening of the Lincoln Tunnel, included a military parade, an artillery salute, and a speech by New York's governor, Herbert Lehman, lauding the Port Authority for "demonstrating that modern technical knowledge can be utilized for the common good with integrity and ability."[37] The Port Authority subsequently built two more Lincoln Tunnel tubes and the George Washington Bridge's lower level, but since the early 1960s the only new lanes added between the two states were those linked with replacing the Goethals Bridge. For environmental and political reasons, the Port Authority has no plans in place to expand any existing crossings, let alone build a new one.

In the twentieth century, the Port Authority was a world leader in squeezing more capacity out of existing bridges and tunnels. It held that distinction because of the region's constraints and the organization's willingness to innovate and experiment. For example, to rapidly detect and clear disabled vehicles in the 1960s, the Port Authority pioneered and integrated three technologies in the Lincoln Tunnel: closed-circuit TV cameras, automated devices embedded in the roadway, and radio-equipped gasoline-powered vehicles that could travel along the narrow catwalk (fig. 10.3).[38] Two Port Authority innovations later implemented to improve highway efficiency, managing

Conclusion

Fig. 10.3. Port Authority officer traveling in Lincoln Tunnel's catwalk car (1960). *(Photograph from the Lincoln Tunnel Collection, reprinted by permission of the Hoboken Historical Museum and the Port Authority of New York and New Jersey.)*

regional traffic through TRANSCOM and the Lincoln Tunnel exclusive bus lane, have both been replicated across the globe.

Even if the Port Authority could figure out how to add some more highway capacity, the region would still need to rely upon transit improvements because trains and buses are far more efficient than cars in moving large numbers of people. One highway lane can carry approximately 2,000 vehicles an hour while the Lincoln Tunnel's exclusive bus lane averages more than 17,000 riders per hour.[39] Although trains are even more efficient than buses, they have their own capacity constraints. The region's rail map looks remarkably like the one in place in the 1950s and will not significantly change in the foreseeable future. The metropolitan area's transportation agencies are having enough trouble maintaining their existing rail network, much of which dates back more than a century. Billions of dollars are needed every year to keep it in a state of good repair, let alone to bring it up to twenty-first-century standards.

Fig. 10.4. Bus ramps connecting the Port Authority's Lincoln Tunnel with its Midtown Manhattan bus terminal (c. 2006).
(Photograph reprinted by permission of Port Authority of New York and New Jersey.)

Given the political, financial, and environmental obstacles associated with adding new highway lanes or rail lines, expanding the bus system is a much more feasible option. That has been an area of Port Authority expertise for a long time. The opening of the Port Authority Bus Terminal in 1950 was a proud moment in the Authority's history. Located near Times Square in Midtown Manhattan, the $25 million bus terminal replaced individual terminals operated by bus companies that were scattered throughout Manhattan. The Authority demolished forty buildings, relocated about 600 families,[40] and connected the bus terminal with the Lincoln Tunnel via overhead ramps (fig. 10.4). Thousands of buses were taken off the city's streets every day and bus passengers saved as much as thirty minutes on each trip.[41]

Austin Tobin was eager to build the bus terminal and he was convinced it would turn a profit or at least be revenue neutral. The Authority would charge buses in the same way that airports earned fees from take-offs and landings. The terminal was also designed to generate considerable concession revenue from shops, display areas for advertisements, public phones, and nearly 1,000 lockers.[42] After the terminal opened, the bus terminal's shopping center (including a bowling alley and one of the city's biggest supermarkets) provided about 60 percent of the bus terminal's annual revenue.[43]

Today, the Port Authority's bus terminal is the busiest in the world, accommodating approximately 8,000 buses and 260,000 travelers on a typical day.[44] However, the cost to operate the terminal is more than twice the revenue it generates. Although the bus terminal has been upgraded and expanded since 1950, it is now a symbol of the Port Authority's inability to expand transit facilities. The *New York Times*, whose headquarters are located directly across the street, describes the terminal as dreary with leaky ceilings and dingy vestibules.[45] Referring to the Port Authority on late night TV, John Oliver said, "The only thing people think of when they hear its name is the Port Authority Bus Terminal, also known as the single worst place on planet Earth. It is a place where cockroaches run up to people screaming, 'please get me out of here; this place is disgusting.'"[46]

Port Authority officials have long referred to the bus terminal as obsolete in terms of passenger amenities as well as its inability to accommodate more buses and larger buses (such as double-deckers). Planning for a new terminal began in 2013, but the governors have repeatedly clashed over funding to replace it. Although the bus terminal is located in New York and is critically important to the city's economy, most of its users live and vote in New Jersey. That is why New York's governors have not been as keen as their counterparts to support a project that could cost $10 billion.[47]

Replacing the bus terminal building is extraordinarily expensive, but it is just one relatively small component of the interstate bus network that needs more capacity. The capacity issues are not easy to solve because they involve numerous government agencies and private bus operators. For example, a shortage of bus parking spaces at the terminal and on Manhattan's streets creates a problem that stretches across both states. Ideally, bus operators would have all their buses at or near the bus terminal before the afternoon rush hour begins. But since there are not enough bus parking spaces in Manhattan, the bus operators have to store their buses in New Jersey during the day. Then, right before rush hour, the drivers take their empty buses from New Jersey through the Lincoln Tunnel into Manhattan. Since the congestion levels at the Lincoln Tunnel and its approaches make it difficult to precisely time the buses, passengers waiting at the bus terminal often experience extensive delays when they try to go back home.[48] The resulting long lines, overcrowding, and unreliable services helps explain why *Buzzfeed* described the bus terminal as *"Dante's Inferno* of public transportation" in its article titled "17 Reasons Why Port Authority Is Literally Hell on Earth."[49]

Is the Port Authority Prepared to Lead?

The Port Authority is currently ill-equipped to address its own air, highway, bus, and rail capacity issues, let alone take on broader regional problems. In the past few decades, the Authority has focused on replacing and improving its existing assets, rather than broadening its mission. This is problematic because no public agency is championing the region as a whole, and building new infrastructure takes time to complete, and even longer before it fully benefits the region's residents and businesses.

As Port Authority executive directors, Austin Tobin and Peter Goldmark were motivated to find new investments for the Authority's resources before the governors identified their own projects or pressured the Authority to lower tolls. Today, Port Authority officials do not have to worry about having too much cash on hand because they need to generate more than $1.5 billion in income every year just to pay back their bondholders. Even though the bonds first issued to build bridges and tunnels were paid off decades ago, the Authority now has tens of billions of dollars in outstanding debt. This limits the Authority's ability to issue new bonds that would finance large new projects. As discussed in chapter 7, the Port Authority could not borrow enough money to replace the Goethals Bridge and instead had to enter into a private-public partnership where a private firm provided the financing.

The Authority also faces high costs associated with the age of its infrastructure. The Authority spends more than $4 billion per year on operating expenses and capital projects just to keep its facilities in a state of good repair and ensure efficient, safe, and secure operations.[50] Because facilities that are used at near-capacity levels can only be shut down for limited periods of time, maintaining them is complex and costly. Repairs frequently inconvenience thousands of travelers, which is one of the reasons why Staten Island elected officials supported replacing the Goethals Bridge rather than repairing it in the early 2000s.

The Port Authority's largest revenue sources are tolls, fares, aviation fees, parking, and the rents it collects from tenants. Increasing any of them can have a wide range of negative repercussions. The Authority could increase fees and rents at the airports, but those additional charges typically get passed on to airline passengers and can make the airports less competitive. Likewise, raising PATH fares is not in the region's best interest because it would discourage some people from using transit. Raising tolls is also problematic. Tolls are used in the New York metropolitan area to subsidize transit, but some drivers are paying a disproportionately high share of these tolls. For example, residents of Bay Ridge in Brooklyn who work in Elizabeth, now pay about $27 in tolls every day to cross the Goethals Bridge and Verrazzano-Narrows Bridge on their twenty-eight-mile roundtrip commute. Tolls are much higher than in the past even after accounting for inflation. For instance, a driver in a large truck in the early 1950s paid approximately $31 in today's dollars for a roundtrip on one of the Port Authority's crossings.[51] Now, the toll for large trucks ranges from $82 to $110 depending upon the time of day. These tolls add to the cost of goods and can hinder economic growth.

Along with limited resources, the Authority has less credibility and autonomy than it once had to complete projects efficiently. Although it rebuilt the World Trade Center, replaced the Goethals Bridge, completely renovated LaGuardia Airport, and raised the deck of the Bayonne Bridge, two of its most prominent assets are the Midtown Bus Terminal and the PATH station. To the detriment of the Port Authority's reputation, one is obsolete and unpleasant, while the other is seen as overly extravagant. The Authority's limited autonomy holds it back from spearheading new initiatives. Given its short leash from Trenton and Albany, the Port Authority is not in a strong position to muscle its way into new spheres that might be appropriate for a bistate agency.

The Port Authority and other New York government agencies are also hesitant to take on new initiatives because the city's high real estate and labor costs make it more expensive to build public works projects than in most other parts of the world. Likewise, obtaining necessary approvals and completing projects in a timely manner has become increasingly difficult because of extensive environmental regulations along with the public's sensitivity about disturbances and inconveniences associated with construction. In the late 1940s, the Port Authority knocked down an entire block of Midtown Manhattan buildings to clear land for its new bus terminal; those days are long gone.

The agency at the center of infrastructure development in the New York metropolitan region might be tarnished and worn, yet it still has pluck and relevance—if the organization is led by people who are allowed to prioritize regional needs. The region has no shortages of problems and threats that cross political boundaries. Most of the vexing and enduring problems that New York City and its suburbs face are regional in nature. For instance, rather than having each state work on its own, the Port Authority could coordinate a regional effort relating to climate change and its reliance on fossil fuels. The Authority already thinks holistically about the regional implications of flooding and warmer temperatures across a diverse portfolio of infrastructure assets; it could take on a leading role integrating climate change defenses and serve as a thought leader to unite government agencies. If the states want the Authority's responsibilities to stay within the transportation realm, the Authority would be ideally suited to take on three new tasks: improving bus services, coordinating new transportation technologies, and complementing air services.

As previously noted, improving bus services is an area that plays into the Authority's strength. Given the constraints on building new rail lines and roads—the region is eventually going to have to rely more on buses. That means the region will need to create more bus and/or high-occupancy vehicle lanes, prioritize buses at intersections, reduce transfer times, integrate fares, and enhance bus stops. These changes will require strong leadership involving a wide range of institutions, including the municipalities that control bus stops, the highway departments that maintain roadways, and bus operators in both the private and public sectors.[52] No public agency is better prepared to take on this role than the Port Authority.

A second role that matches the Port Authority's strengths is figuring out how to complement and supplement air services. Since the airports cannot accommodate unlimited growth, the region must figure out how to supplement flights with more robust intercity rail and bus options; otherwise, travel will be impeded to and from the region. No organization is in a better position than the Port Authority to lead this effort, since it has frequently studied and advanced projects that have overcome the limitations of the region's airports and bus and rail networks.

A third potential role for the Port Authority is serving as coordinator for the deployment of new technologies. The region would benefit from a consistent and coordinated approach to take advantage of autonomous vehicles (buses, cars, and trucks), delivery drones, smarter highways, and electric vehicles. A well-thought-out approach is far better than an ad hoc piecemeal effort. For example, the E-ZPass system has benefited travelers because it was set up as a regional system, while the region's transit users are stuck with a complex range of fare media and policies when they use trains, ferries, and buses.

Conclusion

The two states can address problems more effectively and efficiently when they cooperate. New York's governor Herbert Lehman understood that in 1937 when he proclaimed at the opening of the Lincoln Tunnel, "The people of New York and New Jersey have learned to approach their joint problems in a new way. They have grown beyond the stage of petty rivalries and narrow sectionalism. They have learned to look beyond immediate pressures and rather to seek long-term solutions to problems whose scope extends far beyond the limits of the state line."[53] To modern ears, Lehman's words seem idealistic, if not naïve and quaint.

New York and New Jersey are no different than two siblings. They might have conflicts and compete for resources, but their families are much better off when the siblings get along, address problems together, and work toward common goals. An important lesson from chapter 5's discussion about Lou Gambaccini is the value of examining problems and then working in a cooperative manner on an ongoing basis to solve them. The Port Authority can redefine its mission and it can evolve to take on new roles. The states have periodically revised the compact that created the Authority to meet the regional problems of the times, to keep abreast of new technologies, and take advantage of new laws.[54] In 1984, Peter Goldmark said, "It is central to the genius of the Port Authority that it is so constituted that each generation of leadership can rethink and reshape the Port Authority's mission." The question he applied to determine whether the Authority should take on a new initiative is still valid: would the private sector or another public agency be able to do it better?

Goldmark saw the Port Authority itself, not just its facilities, as a valuable resource to the region because it could provide quality and innovative services and act as a vehicle for regional cooperation. "The vast resources and potential of the Port Authority," he argued, "can be mobilized and applied more productively and effectively if we in this region can recognize that in the Port Authority we have a tested institution that is the envy of other parts of the country."[55]

The Authority can do more to mobilize the metropolis. Getting in the way are two states who are often unwilling to set aside their parochial concerns and give the Authority some independence to address the region's common problems. This should be disconcerting to policymakers and the public because if the region is seen as stagnating, New York and New Jersey will find it harder to retain and attract the people and businesses needed to keep the region moving, thriving, and prospering.

NOTES

Chapter 1

1. "Statement of Hon. Frank C. Ferguson, Chairman of the Port Authority," in U.S. Congress. Senate. Special Committee on Taxation of Governmental Security and Salaries. Hearings, Seventy-Sixth Congress, First Session, 1939.

2. Approximately 200 million tons of freight pass through NYC every year (per the NYC Department of Transportation, "Delivering New York: Smart Truck Management Plan for New York City," May 2021, 5) and more than 500 million tons of goods move through northern New Jersey (per the North Jersey Transportation Planning Authority, "Plan 2045: Connecting North Jersey," 2021, 5).

3. Public Authorities Information Clearinghouse of the Government Law Center (Albany Law School), "Welcome," www.publicauthority.org, available July 6, 2021.

4. Jean-Paul Rodrigue, "The Port Authority of New York and New Jersey," in *The Geography of Transport Systems*, https://transportgeography.org/?page_id=9527, available August 31, 2021.

5. New York State Canal Corporation, "Canal History," http://www.canals.ny.gov/history/history.html

6. William Ressman Andrews, "Important New York Port Improvements," *Popular Mechanics* 35, no. 6 (June 1921), 831.

7. Merchants' Association of New York, "Industrial Map of New York City," 1922.

8. Henry Collins Brown, *Valentine's City of New York: Guide Book* (New York: Chauncey Holt, 1920), 49.

9. Port Authority's 1940 Annual Report, 11.

10. Tamar Gutner and Alexander Thompson, "The Politics of IO Performance: A Framework," *Review of International Organizations* 5, no. 3 (2010): 227–48.

11. Jameson W. Doig, *Empire on the Hudson: Entrepreneurial Vision and Political Power at the Port of New York Authority* (New York: Columbia University Press, 2001), 13.

12. Doig, 274.

13. Edith Penrose, *The Theory of the Growth of the Firm* (New York: Oxford University Press, 2009).

14. Michael N. Barnett and Martha Finnemore, "The Politics, Power, and Pathologies of International Organizations," *International Organization* 53, no. 4 (1999): 699–732.

15. Paul A. Sabatier and Christopher M. Weible, "The Advocacy Coalition Framework:

Innovation and Clarifications" in *Theories of the Policy Process*, ed. Paul A. Sabatier (New York: Routledge, 2007), 203.

16. Tom Christensen and Per Laegreid, eds., *Autonomy and Regulation: Coping with Agencies in the Modern State* (Cheltenham: Edward Elgar, 2006).

17. Philip Mark Plotch, *Politics Across the Hudson: The Tappan Zee Megaproject* (New Brunswick: Rutgers University Press, 2018), 12.

18. Anthony R. Zito, "European Agencies as Agents of Governance and EU Learning," *Journal of European Public Policy* 16, no. 8 (2009): 1224–43.

19. Doig, 150.

20. Tamar Gutner and Alexander Thompson, "The Politics of IO Performance: A Framework," *Review of International Organizations* 5, no. 3 (2010): 227–48; Chad Hartnell, Amy Yi Ou, and Angela Kinicki, "Organizational Culture and Organizational Effectiveness: A Meta-Analytic Investigation of the Competing Values Framework's Theoretical Suppositions," *Journal of Applied Psychology* 96, no. 4 (2011): 677–94.

21. Barnett and Finnemore.

22. Doig, 121.

23. Gayl D. Ness and Steven R. Brechin, "Bridging the Gap: International Organizations as Organizations," *International Organization* 42, no. 2 (2009): 247.

24. Doig, 146.

25. Port Authority, "Proposed Budget," November 2021, 47.

Chapter 2

1. Jameson W. Doig, *Empire on the Hudson: Entrepreneurial Vision and Political Power at the Port of New York Authority* (New York: Columbia University Press, 2001), 8.

2. Doig, 5.

3. Doig, 5.

4. For a long time, rail passengers traveling to and from New York City faced the same challenge. In 1904, the Pennsylvania Railroad completed the first tube of its North River tunnels connecting its lines through New Jersey to Pennsylvania Station.

5. The New York Harbor Case, 47 I.C.C. 643, 739 (917).

6. Erwin Wilkie Bard, *Port of New York Authority* (New York: Columbia University Press, 1942), 27–28; Julius Henry Cohen, *They Builded Better Than They Knew* (New York: Julian Messner, 1946), 289–92.

7. Bard, 27; Cohen, 290.

8. In the 1920s, New York governors were elected to two-year terms, New Jersey governors to three-year terms. As to the salary issue, the effort to aid independence by installing several commissioners (thus insulating the top staff from political incursions) followed the model devised for the ICC (five members when created in 1887, later increased to twelve; members must be divided between the major political parties) and the Federal Trade Commission (created in 1914; five members, must be divided between the political parties).

9. Cohen, 289.

10. "Harbor Treaty Bill Again Under Fire," *New York Times*, April 10, 1920.

11. R. L. Duffus, "A Rising Tide of Traffic Rolls over NY," *New York Times*, February 9, 1930.

12. Chapter 7 provides more information about the Staten Island bridges. Also see Robert W. Jackson, *Highway Under the Hudson: A History of the Holland Tunnel* (New York: NYU Press, 2011), 212.

13. The Pennsylvania Railroad's North River tunnels into Penn Station were completed in 1901 (and are now used by Amtrak and New Jersey Transit). The Hudson & Manhattan Railroad's two tunnels (which make up today's PATH system) were completed in 1908 and 1909, respectively.

14. Angus Kress Gillespie, *Crossing Under the Hudson: The Story of the Holland and Lincoln Tunnels* (New Brunswick: Rutgers University Press, 2011), 19.

15. Doig, 166.

16. Six commissioners were added to the Port Authority, bringing the total to twelve, in order to accommodate the addition of several tunnel commissioners.

17. Doig, 168.

18. Donald Wolf, *Crossing the Hudson: Historic Bridges and Tunnels of the River* (New Brunswick: Rutgers University Press, 2010), 134.

19. Doig, 77.

20. Doig, 125.

21. Doig, 134 and fn 32.

22. Wolf, 133.

23. The institution of veto power is discussed in more detail in chapter 9.

24. Doig, 155.

25. Doig, 150.

26. Port of New York Authority, "Eighteenth Annual Report," December 31, 1938.

Chapter 3

1. Jameson W. Doig, *Empire on the Hudson: Entrepreneurial Vision and Political Power at the Port of New York Authority* (New York: Columbia University Press, 2001), 214–44. Page 239 refers to his appointment as executive director in June 1942.

2. Doig, *Empire on the Hudson*, 13.

3. Jameson W. Doig, "To Claim the Seas and the Skies: Austin Tobin and the Port of New York Authority," in *Leadership and Innovation: Entrepreneurs in Government*, edited by Jameson W. Doig and Erwin C. Hargrove (Baltimore: Johns Hopkins University Press, 1990), 104–12.

4. Doig, "To Claim the Seas and the Skies," 104–12.

5. Doig, "To Claim the Seas and the Skies," 104–12.

6. Port Authority's 1943 Annual Report (pages 14–15) and 1944 Annual Report (pages 21–22).

7. Port Authority's 1943 Annual Report, 15.

8. "New York as an Air Center," *New York Times*, December 2, 1945; Port Authority's 1945 Annual Report, 20–22.

9. Doig, "To Claim the Seas and the Skies," 104–12.

10. Port Authority's 1945 Annual Report, 8; Doig, "To Claim the Seas and the Skies," 104–12.

11. Doig, "To Claim the Seas and the Skies," 104–12.

12. "A Great Airport for Newark," editorial, *New York Times*, August 1, 1946.

13. "Port Authority Aid on Airfields Asked," *New York Times*, August 3, 1946.

14. Paul Crowell, "Airport Contract Signed by Mayor," *New York Times*, April 18, 1947.

15. Port Authority's 1959 Annual Report, page v.

16. Corporation for Economic and Industrial Research, "The Economic Relationship of Air Transportation to the Economy of the New Jersey-New York Metropolitan Area: A Study Prepared for the Port of New York Authority," August 1960, 84–85.

17. Air first exceeded ship in 1955 per "Air Travel Wins Top Rank in Port," *New York Times*, January 11, 1956.

18. Port Authority's 1949 Annual Report (page 41) and 1959 Annual Report (air terminals page).

19. Port of New York Authority, "A New Major Airport for the New Jersey-New York Metropolitan Area: A Report on Preliminary Studies," December 14, 1959, 9.

20. Corporation for Economic and Industrial Research, "The Economic Relationship of Air Transportation to the Economy of the New Jersey-New York Metropolitan Area," 93.

21. Leo L. Beranek, "The Noisy Dawn of the Jet Age," *Sound and Vibration* 41, no. 1 (2007): 94–100.

22. Port of New York Authority, "A New Major Airport for The New Jersey-New York Metropolitan Area," 9; David Gladfelter, "Jets for The Great Swamp," in *Cases in State and Local Government*, edited by Richard T. Frost (Englewood Cliffs, NJ: Prentice-Hall, 1961), 304.

23. Metropolitan Washington Airports Authority, "History," https://www.flydulles.com/iad/history, available October 18, 2020.

24. Port Authority's 1959 Annual Report, 2–5.

25. Port of New York Authority, "A New Major Airport," 17–25.

26. Bureau of the Census, "Population of Standard Metropolitan Statistical Areas: 1960 and 1950," April 10, 1961.

27. Port Authority's 1959 Annual Report, 2–5; Port of New York Authority, "A New Major Airport," 3.

28. Jameson W. Doig, "The Best as Enemy of the Good: The Port Authority's 4th Jetport, Lindenthal's Massive Span Over the Hudson, and the George Washington Bridge," *Journal of Urban History* 40, no. 6 (2014): 1123–37.

29. Cam Cavanaugh, *Saving the Great Swamp* (Frenchtown, NJ: Columbia Publishing, 1978), 23.

30. David Lyle, "Jersey Town Sees 'Ruin' in New Airport," *New York Herald Tribune*, December 6, 1959.

31. "2-Story Colonial Displayed on L.I.," *New York Times*, September 18, 1960; 1960 U.S. Department of Census, "Per Capita and Median Family Money Income in 1959, for States, Standard Metropolitan Statistical Areas, and Counties," July 30, 1965, tables 1–3.

32. Arie Y. Lewin, Melvin F. Shakun et al., "Case 3: The Fourth Jetport for Metropolitan New York: A Case Study," in *Policy Sciences: Methodologies and Cases*, edited by Arie Y. Lewin and Melvin F. Shakun (New York: Pergamon Press, 1976), 136; Gladfelter, "Jets for the Great Swamp," 306; Richard Witkin, "Is Jet Airport Needed?," *New York Times*, January 15, 1960.

33. Tom Barrett, "Plans for Jersey Jet Airport Revealed," *New York Herald Tribune*, December 15, 1959.

34. Port of New York Authority, "A New Major Airport," 2.
35. "New Airport That Is Needed," editorial, *New York Herald Tribune*, December 5, 1959.
36. "The Unwanted New Airport," *New York Times*, editorial, December 16, 1959.
37. "946–5 Against," *Daily Record* (Morristown), December 1959.
38. "Meyner Seeks More Jet Airfield Facts," *Daily Record*, December 8, 1959; "More Facts Necessary," *Daily Record*, December 16, 1959; "Meyner Trip Paid by PA," *Newark Evening News*, August 26, 1960; "Meyner: Trips on PA $$ Never Secret," *Daily Record*, August 27, 1960.
39. Great Swamp Watershed Association, "History of the Great Swamp," greatswamp.org/history-great-swamp, available October 18, 2020; Cavanaugh, *Saving the Great Swamp*, 30.
40. Port Authority's 1958 Annual Report, 56; Joseph C. Ingraham, "Relocation Is Almost Completed Near George Washington Bridge," *New York Times*, April 23, 1959.
41. Port Authority's 1957 Annual Report, 18.
42. Article about neighbors concerned about property values in Clarence Dean, "Plan for Airport Argued in Jersey," *New York Times*, January 14, 1960.
43. Andrew L. Pincus, "Estate Owners Vow Jetport Fight," *Newark Sunday News*, December 27, 1959.
44. Pincus, "Estate Owners Vow Jetport Fight."
45. Paul Amadio and John Moran, "Tell Plans for Fight on Jetport," *Daily Record*, December 19, 1959.
46. Amadio and Moran, "Tell Plans for Fight on Jetport."
47. David Miller, "Jetport Hoots at Meyner," *New York Herald Tribune*, July 13, 1961.
48. Cavanaugh, *Saving the Great Swamp*, 27.
49. Originally called the Jetport Action Association, the organization was later renamed the Jersey Jetport Site Association (JJSA).
50. "Group Fights to Shift Site of Jetport," *New York Herald Tribune*, December 30, 1959.
51. "Meeting of Steering Committee of Jetport Action Association held December 28, 1959 at New Fire House in Chatham," Box 1, The JJSA Collection, North Jersey History Center, Morristown and Morris Township Library; Joe Alex Morris, "Jetport Showdown in Jersey," *Saturday Evening Post*, December 17, 1960, 30, 84–86; Morristown and Morris Township Library, "Finding Aid to the Jersey Jetport Site Association Collection," http://mmtlibrary.org/HCFindingAids/jerseyjetport.xml, available October 18, 2020.
52. Edward R. N. Douglass and Albert S. Fulling, "Public Relations Proposals for Jetport Action Association," undated, 1–13, Folder 2, Box 1, JJSA Collection, North Jersey History Center, Morristown and Morris Township Library.
53. "Port Authority Speeches," Folder 4, Box 5, JJSA Collection.
54. Port of New York Authority's Aviation Department, "The Influence of a Major Airport on the Economy of Surrounding Areas," January 1960, Folder 10, Box 5, JJSA Collection.
55. JJSA, "J.J.S.A Newsletter," Issue 1, March 9, 1961, 1, Folder 13, Box 1, JJSA Collection.
56. Cavanaugh, *Saving the Great Swamp*, 53.
57. Cavanaugh, *Saving the Great Swamp*, 59; JJSA, "J.J.S.A Newsletter," Issue 1, March 9, 1961, 1, Folder 13, Box 1, JJSA Collection.

58. JJSA, "J.J.S.A Newsletter," Issue 1, March 9, 1961, 1, Folder 13, Box 1, JJSA Collection.

59. W. Stuart Landes (executive vice chair of JJSA), "Local Committees," February 5, 1960, Folder 5, Box 1, JJSA Collection.

60. "The JJSA Statement of Cash Receipts and Disbursements for the Period December 1, 1959, to December 31, 1960," Folder 8, Box 1, JJSA Collection.

61. Gladfelter, "Jets for The Great Swamp," 315.

62. "Frelinghuysen Says Jetport Dead," *Daily Record*, January 19, 1960.

63. George Cable Wright, "Jet Airport Plan Vetoed by Jersey," *New York Times*, January 19, 1960.

64. "Gov. Meyner: Cannot Make Jet Decision," *Daily Record*, January 26, 1960.

65. Gladfelter, "Jets for The Great Swamp," 317.

66. "Jetport Site Here Styled Only Fit One," *Daily Record*, December 21, 1959; "Port Authority," *CQ Almanac 1960*, 16th ed., Washington, DC: Congressional Quarterly, 1960, http://library.cqpress.com/cqalmanac/cqal60-880-28173-1331100; Peter Frelinghuysen, Jr., letter to Cong. Celler, December 23, 1959; Frelinghuysen, telegram to Morris County Daily Record, WMTR, and Associated Press, December 30, 1959 (both in Folder 8, Box 4, JJSA Collection).

67. "Port Authority," *CQ Almanac 1960*.

68. "Port Authority," *CQ Almanac 1960*; C. P. Trussell, "House Cites Three in Port Authority in Contempt Case," *New York Times*, August 24, 1960.

69. "Port Authority," *CQ Almanac 1960*; Cavanaugh, "Jets for The Great Swamp," 81–85; Peter Kihss, "House Study Told Insurance Agent Feted Port Aides," *New York Times*, December 1, 1960. Note that Tobin was supported by Governors Rockefeller and Meyner, who did not want federal officials meddling in their affairs.

70. George Cable Wright, "Jersey Senate Votes Full Inquiry on Port Agency Internal Affairs," *New York Times*, September 13, 1960.

71. Clarence Dean, "Jersey Senators Tour Facilities in Inquiry Into Port Authority," *New York Times*, December 16, 1960.

72. George Cable Wright, "Port Agency Bids on Hudson Tubes," *New York Times*, September 28, 1960; "Fears on Jetport Remain in Morris," *New York Times*, September 28, 1960.

73. Supplementary Listing Record for National Register of Historic Places Registration Form, Continuation Sheet for Hartley Farms, July 19, 1991, https://npgallery.nps.gov/GetAsset/1218db29-bfeb-436c-a678-fd557533f8ed, available October 18, 2020; William G. Wing, "Land Swap Thwarts Big N. J. Jetport," *New York Herald Tribune*, September 9, 1961.

74. "Living with Ike and Mamie," *Star-Ledger*, October 29, 2012.

75. Cavanaugh, "Jets for The Great Swamp," 94–111.

76. "U.S. Plans Refuge in Jersey's Swamp," *New York Times*, October 1, 1960.

77. Port of New York Authority, "A Report on Airport Requirements and Sites in the Metropolitan New Jersey-New York Region," 1961, 126.

78. Tom Barrett, "Jetport Called 'Impractical' At Site in Morris County," *New York Herald Tribune*, April 7, 1961.

79. Port of New York Authority, "A Report on Airport Requirements and Sites in the Metropolitan New Jersey-New York Region," 1961; Richard Witkin, "New Study Backs Jetport in Morris," *New York Times*, June 1, 1961.

Notes to Pages 62–67

80. Port of New York Authority, "A New Major Airport," 4.
81. Port of New York Authority, "A Report on Airport Requirements," 1.
82. "Meyner on Jetport—Have a Referendum," *New York Herald Tribune*, July 28, 1961.
83. "Meyner: Can't Bar Jets' Era," *New York Herald Tribune*, August 29, 1961.
84. Cavanaugh, "Jets for The Great Swamp," 148.
85. "His Political Foes Joyous Over Meyner Jetport," *New York Herald Tribune*, June 30, 1961.
86. Port Authority's 1963 Annual Report (page 18), 1964 Annual Report (page 29), 1965 Annual Report (page 36) and 1966 Annual Report (page 30).
87. "Group Fights to Shift Site of Jetport," *New York Herald Tribune*, December 30, 1959.
88. Robert J. Maso, *Contested Lands: Conflict and Compromise in New Jersey's Pine Barrens* (Philadelphia: Temple University Press, 1992), 76.
89. George Cable Wright, "Airport is Pushed for South Jersey," *New York Times*, August 9, 1960.
90. Austin J. Tobin, "When You Can't Get There From Here: Our Fourth Airport Crisis," speech to New York Chamber of Commerce, February 5, 1969, 9, Folder 10, Box 4, JJSA Collection.
91. Ronald Sullivan, "Port Unit Renews Bid for Jet Field in Great Swamp," *New York Times*, December 21, 1966.
92. Port of New York Authority, "Airport Requirements and Sites to Serve the New Jersey-New York Metropolitan Region," December 1966, 3. Similar wording was in the Port Authority's 1967 Annual Report (page 29), and in "Tobin for Forcing Air Rescheduling," *New York Times*, July 29, 1968.
93. Walter H. Waggoner, "Great Swamp: Island of Solitude Near Millions," *New York Times*, October 3, 1968.
94. U.S. Fish & Wildlife Service, "Release of Draft Comprehensive Conservation Plan," newsletter, May 2014, www.fws.gov/endangered/map/ESA_success_stories/NJ/NJ_story4/index.html
95. Edward, Hudson, "Port Authority Has 2d Choice for Jersey Jetport," *New York Times*, August 6, 1968.
96. Port Authority's 1968 Annual Report, 10.
97. Robert Lindsey "Airlines Support Solberg Airport," *New York Times*, March 19, 1969.
98. Port Authority, "A Report on Airport Requirements," 1961, 14.
99. Port Authority, "A Report on Airport Requirements," 1961, 15.
100. Port of New York Authority, "A Report on Airport Requirements," 1961, 15, 129.
101. "Jersey Nominees Clash on Jetport," *New York Times*, September 6, 1969 (Meyner was Cahill's opponent in the general election and he still supported building a new jetport).
102. Robert Lindsey, "Solberg Given Up as a Jetport Site," *New York Times*, November 15, 1969.
103. Tobin, "When You Can't Get There From Here," 12.
104. Port Authority's 1969 Annual Report, 25.
105. Port of New York Authority, "A New Major Airport," 16.
106. Port of New York Authority, "A New Major Airport," 11.
107. Port of New York Authority, "A Report on Airport Requirements," 1961, 37.

108. "Jetport Merry-Go-Round," editorial, *New York Times*, December 30, 1966.
109. "Tobin for Forcing Air Rescheduling," *New York Times*, July 29, 1968.
110. Edward Hudson, "Airlines Propose Alternate Plan to 4th Jetport," *New York Times*, October 27, 1965.
111. Edward Hudson, "Airline Proposal Picks Up Support," *New York Times*, November 6, 1965.
112. Regional Plan Association, "The Region's Airports," *Regional Plan News*, July 1969, page 2.
113. National Academy of Sciences and National Academy of Engineering, "Jamaica Bay and Kennedy Airport: A Multidisciplinary Environmental Study," Volume II, 1971, 24; Amedeo R. Odoni and Joseph F. Vittek (MIT Flight Transportation Laboratory), "Airport Quotas and Peak Hour Pricing: Theory And Practice," 1976, table 10; Martin Tolchin, "Airport Fees Rise for Private Craft," *New York Times*, August 1, 1968; Port Authority's 1968 Annual Report, 10.
114. Port Authority's 1969 Annual Report, 28; Port Authority's 1967 Annual Report, 29.
115. For example, Tobin did so in a May 7, 1969, letter to John P. Keith (RPA president) in Regional Plan Association, "The Region's Airports," *Regional Plan News*, July 1969, V. Appendix.
116. Doig, *Empire on the Hudson*, 298–312.
117. Jameson W. Doig, "Public Demands and Technological Response: Austin Tobin, Leo Beranek and the Advent of Jet Travel," *Journal of Aeronautical History*, Paper No. 2017/03, 2017, 30–40.
118. Pine Island was the name of the community in Orange County. Travel times per Port Authority, "A Report on Airport Requirements," 1961, 13–14.
119. Richard Witkin, "$1-Billion Is Asked for Stewart Airport," *New York Times*, April 25, 1973.
120. Richard Witkin, "Should Stewart Be Made Metropolitan Area's 4th Major Jetport?" *New York Times*, May 15, 1973; U.S. DOT and NYS DOT, "Design Report/Draft Environmental Impact Statement: Stewart Airport Access Improvement," Volume 1, March 1999, II-5.
121. Witkin, "Should Stewart Be Made Metropolitan Area's 4th Major Jetport?"
122. Edward Hudson, "Air-Cargo Line to Build Newburgh Hub," *New York Times*, May 27, 1978.
123. Lena Williams, "State Taking Two Airports From M.T.A.," *New York Times*, June 24, 1982; Douglas Cunningham, "American Exits with Stewart Set for Growth," *Times Herald-Record*, July 13, 2007; Lisa W. Foderaro, "A New Service Begins at Stewart Airport," *New York Times*, April 18, 1990; Tim Gilchrist, interview with Plotch, phone, September 17, 2020.
124. George Pataki, "Executive Order No. 8: Establishing the New York State Advisory Commission on Privatization and the New York State Research Council on Privatization," May 12, 1995.
125. Raymond Hernandez, "Plan to Lease Stewart Airport Is Approved," *New York Times*, November 27, 1997.
126. New York State DOT, press release, "Governor Pataki Hands Stewart Airport Keys to National Express (Orange County)," March 31, 2000.

Notes to Pages 70–73

127. "Air Traffic Congestion at LaGuardia Airport," Hearing Before the Subcommittee on Aviation of the Committee on Transportation and Infrastructure, House of Representatives, One Hundred Seventh Congress, World Trade Center, July 16, 2001, 43.
128. Chris Ward, interview with Plotch and Nelles, phone, October 28, 2020.
129. Port Authority's 2005 Annual Report, Schedule G.
130. A new runway could significantly increase capacity, but it would not be a panacea for the airport congestion problems because for safety reasons all the runways at the three airports could not be used simultaneously. Because planes can take off with headwinds and tailwinds, but not with winds that blow perpendicular, weather patterns dictate which runways could be used. Adding a parallel runway would have been helpful because one could be shut down for repairs while the other remained open, but airports cannot use parallel runways simultaneously unless they are situated nearly a mile apart. Moreover, air traffic controllers limit which runways can be used at any one time so that the planes near one of the three major airports do not collide with the planes departing and approaching from the other two. The constraints in the sky were equally problematic. The United States has designated air routes which are similar to highways for airplanes; along these routes planes must fly at a safe distance from each other. Air traffic controllers also limit the number of planes flying above the metropolitan area at any one time. With airlines operating more than 3,000 flights a day above the New York metropolitan area, its skies were one of the most congested and complex airspaces in the world. Together, the two problems—not enough runways and airspace constraints—created havoc for the airlines because if one of the airports did not have an available runway, an approaching plane was put into a holding pattern, which meant that other planes might be redirected from the region's airspace. Local weather conditions exacerbated the capacity constraints since the New York metropolitan area is subject to high winds, thunderstorms, heavy rains, and snow.
131. Patrick McGeehan, "New York Fliers May Get Choice a Bit Farther Out," *New York Times*, April 29, 2006.
132. McGeehan, "New York Fliers May Get Choice a Bit Farther Out."
133. Patrick McGeehan, "New Airport May Be Due, Officials Say," *New York Times*, July 1, 2005; Office of New York Senator Charles Schumer, "New Schumer Study Reveals for First Time LaGuardia, JFK and Newark Rank as Worst Three in Nation for Delayed Flights," news release, November 20, 2005; McGeehan, "New York Fliers May Get Choice a Bit Farther Out."
134. McGeehan, "New York Fliers May Get Choice a Bit Farther Out."
135. McGeehan, "New York Fliers May Get Choice a Bit Farther Out."
136. For example, Senator Charles E. Schumer helped obtain federal funds in 2006, per Schumer, "Schumer Announces $250,000 for Stewart International Airport," press release, August 2, 2006.
137. Lee Sander, interview with Plotch, phone, September 25, 2020.
138. Lee Sander, interview with Plotch, phone, September 25, 2020; Tim Gilchrist, interview with Plotch, September 17, 2020.
139. Tony Coscia, interview with Plotch and Nelles, phone, October 20, 2020; Judy Rife, "How the Deal Was Done," *Times Herald-Record*, November 1, 2007.
140. Port Authority, "Port Authority Executive Director Anthony E. Shorris Remarks

New York Building Congress Breakfast," press release, June 19, 2007; Tony Shorris, interview with Plotch and Nelles, phone, January 11 and 15, 2021.

141. Tony Shorris, interview with Plotch and Nelles, phone, January 11 and 15, 2021.

142. Tony Shorris, interview with Plotch and Nelles, phone, January 11 and 15, 2021.

143. Tony Coscia, interview with Plotch and Nelles, phone, October 20, 2020.

144. Patty Clark, interview with Plotch, phone, November 23 and 25, 2020.

145. Elliot Spitzer, "State of The State Address," Assembly Chamber, Albany, January 3, 2007.

146. Port Authority, "Acquisition of Stewart International Airport Lease and Assets from SWF Airport Acquisition, Inc. and National Express Corporation" in "Minutes of Special Board Meeting: Thursday, January 25, 2007," 5–7; Port Authority, "Agency Acts to Relieve Air Traffic Congestion at JFK, Newark, LaGuardia and Teterboro Airports, and Create Capacity for Future Passenger Traffic Growth," press release, January 25, 2007.

147. Port Authority's 2008 annual report, 16.

148. Port Authority, "Review of Stewart International Airport as an Opportunity to Expand Regional Airport Capacity," Board meeting minutes, November 16, 2006, 283.

149. Steven Rothman, interview with Plotch, phone, October 22, 2020; Rothman, email to Plotch, January 7, 2021; Tony Coscia, interview with Plotch and Nelles, October 20, 2020.

150. Committee Meeting of Assembly Transportation and Public Works Committee, Trenton, New Jersey, February 26, 2007, https://dspace.njstatelib.org/xmlui/bitstream/handle/10929/23896/t7642007a.pdf; Port Authority, "Acquisition of Stewart International Airport Lease and Assets from SWF Airport Acquisition, Inc. and National Express Corporation" in "Minutes of Special Board Meeting: Thursday, January 25, 2007," 5–7.

151. Tim Gilchrist, interview with Plotch, September 17, 2020; Port Authority, "Governor Spitzer, Port Authority, Hudson Valley Officials Mark First Day of PA Control of Stewart International Airport," press release, November 1, 2007.

152. Rife, "How the Deal Was Done."

153. Patty Clark, interview with Plotch, phone, November 23 and 25, 2020; Patty Clark, email to Plotch, December 31, 2020.

154. Port Authority, Committee on Capital Programs/Agency Planning Transcript, December 17, 2008; Port Authority, Committee on Operations Meeting Transcripts, February 9, 2012; Port Authority, Committee on Operations Meeting Transcripts, February 9, 2012.

155. Hilary Potkewitz, "Port Authority Will Struggle to Get Stewart Airport to Fly," *Crain's New York Business*, February 12, 2007; Judy Rife, "Port Authority Set to Buy Stewart Airport's Lease," *Times Herald-Record*, January 25, 2007.

156. Doreen Frasca, "Is Stewart Ready to be the Fourth New York Airport?" *New York Transportation Journal*, Fall 2006.

157. Port Authority, Committee on Operations Meeting Transcript, September 30, 2010.

158. Port Authority, Committee on Capital Programs/Agency Planning Transcript, December 17, 2008.

159. Port Authority, Committee on Capital Programs/Agency Planning Transcript, December 17, 2008

160. Stewart's baseline scenario was 393,100 "enplaned" passengers per FAA, Port

Authority, NYS DOT, and Delaware Valley Regional Planning Commission, "FAA Regional Air Service Demand Study of NY & NJ: Summary Report," May 2007, 17.

161. Stewart Airport passenger volumes were 141,098 (inbound), 140,656 (outbound), and 281,754 (total), per Port Authority, "Airport Traffic Report," 2015, table 2.5.1.

162. Edmond J. Harrison, interview with Plotch, phone, September 14, 2020.

163. Edmond J. Harrison, interview with Plotch, phone, September 14, 2020.

164. Ricky Radka, "New York (Stewart)—Bergen $225 Roundtrip," *Airfarewatchdog* (blog), December 27, 2018, https://www.airfarewatchdog.com/blog/50046050/new-york-stewart-bergen-225-roundtrip-nonstop-on-norwegian, available February 22, 2021.

165. "US Traffic Increases by 19% from 2008 to 2017; Stewart Was Fastest Expanding Airport Last Year," Airline Network News & Analysis (anna.aero), August 29, 2018; "Port Authority, Committee on Operations Transcript, September 26, 2019."

166. Lucie Young, "The Unknown US Airport That Could Change Transatlantic Travel Forever," *The Telegraph*, June 13, 2017.

167. Edmond J. Harrison, interview with Plotch, phone, September 14, 2020.

168. Judy Rife, "No Consensus on Stewart Rebranding," *Times Herald-Record*, May 19, 2015; Judy Rife, "PA Chief's Stewart Forecast," *Times Herald-Record*, March 21, 2007.

169. Edmond J. Harrison, interview with Plotch, phone, September 14, 2020.

170. "Harrison to Leave SWF Manager's Post," *Mid Hudson News*, February 6, 2020.

171. Patty Clark, interview with Plotch, phone, November 23 and 25, 2020; Patty Clark, email to Plotch, December 31, 2020.

172. RPA, "Upgrading to World Class: The Future of the New York Region's Airports," January 2011.

Chapter 4

1. International Chamber of Shipping, "Shipping and World Trade: Driving Prosperity," www.ics-shipping.org/shipping-fact/shipping-and-world-trade-driving-prosperity, and "Explaining Shipping," https://www.ics-shipping.org/explaining, available May 28, 2021.

2. Rose George, *Ninety Percent of Everything: Inside Shipping, the Invisible Industry That Puts Clothes on Your Back, Gas in Your Car, and Food on Your Plate* (New York: Henry Holt and Company, 2013), 2.

3. Howard S. Cullman (chair, The Port of New York Authority), "Our Port of Many Ports," *New York Times Magazine*, May 5, 1946.

4. This complex consists of six container terminals: APM Terminals, GCT Bayonne, GCT New York, Maher Terminals, Port Newark Container Terminal, and Red Hook Container Terminal.

5. Port Authority, "Capital of Commerce—The Port of New York and New Jersey: A Gateway for Global Trade," 2019, 4.

6. Port Authority, "Port of New York & New Jersey: 2019 Trade Statistics."

7. A forty-foot container holds approximately twice the contents of a twenty-foot container. The source for the contents of a twenty-foot container is icontainers, "What Fits in a 20-Foot Shipping Container?" https://www.icontainers.com/help/what-fits-20-foot-container, available May 28, 2021.

8. Anne Strauss-Wieder (North Jersey Transportation Planning Authority) in collab-

oration with the New York Shipping Association, "A 21st Century Supply Chain Critical to the Region and Nation: The 2020 Report on the Economic Value of the New York-New Jersey Port Industry," July 2020. Note that the region primarily includes New York and New Jersey but also extends into the Lehigh Valley in Pennsylvania, which houses many warehousing and distribution center activities.

9. See M. A. Mueller, B. Wiegmans, and J. H. R. van Duin, "The Geography of Container Port Choice: Modelling the Impact of Hinterland Changes on Port Choice," *Maritime Economics & Logistics* 22, no. 1 (2020): 26–52 for a discussion of hinterlands and port competitiveness. See also Richard Bergqvist and Gordon Wilmsmeier, *Dry Ports—A Global Perspective: Challenges and Developments in Serving Hinterlands* (Burlington, VT: Ashgate, 2016).

10. Increasingly, goods also travel by barge.

11. Robert G. Albion in collaboration with Jennie Barnes Pope, *The Rise of New York Port [1815–1860]* (New York: Charles Scribner's Sons, 1939); Steven Erie, *Globalizing LA: Trade, Infrastructure, and Regional Development* (Stanford: Stanford University Press, 2004).

12. These include current tenants; host communities; rail and terminal operators; federal, state, and local agencies; harbor pilots; shipping and labor management associations; labor associations; trucking and logistics companies; New York and New Jersey elected officials; transportation and planning authorities; commercial real estate and property management groups; technology leaders; academic institutions; and environmental justice groups. See Port Authority of New York and New Jersey (2019), 17.

13. A note on terminology: in maritime shipping, terminals refer to the places where freight is loaded/unloaded, stored before transport, and where logistics services are delivered. Carriers are the shipping companies that own, operate, or contract the vessels themselves. Some shipping lines own their own terminals.

14. Port Authority's 2019 Annual Report 2019, 90.

15. "New York-New Jersey Port Authority Compact of 1921," Article 6.

16. This point was driven home rather frequently as the Port Authority got underway. For example, New York governor Nathan Miller, speaking at a Brooklyn Chamber of Commerce event invoking the congestion of the ports, stated emphatically, "Let me say right here that *there is nothing whatever in the compact which interferes with the ownership and control and development by each of the municipalities within the district of their own waterfronts*. We want each municipality to own and control its dock and waterfront properties and development of them, the more the better" (emphasis added), per "Build Port or Pay Price, Says Miller," *New York Times*, October 30, 1921.

17. Erwin Wilke Bard, *The Port of New York Authority* (New York: Columbia University Press, 1942), 5.

18. "Crippling the Port," *New York Times*, March 23, 1920.

19. "Film Shows Need of Improving Port," *New York Times*, July 29, 1921.

20. A unified belt line is a rail line on which trains from multiple carriers can travel to reach collective infrastructure, such as unified rail yards or docks.

21. This is when carriers cooperate to share barges, when necessary, rather than running their own barges at less than full capacity and is a strategy to manage port and channel congestion.

22. An inland freight terminal is a site away from the waterfront where goods can be sorted and routed.

23. "City Versus Port," *New York Times*, January 3, 1922.

24. Some aspects were completed, for instance the inland freight terminal at 15th Street and 8th Avenue, but this made only a modest contribution to reducing port congestion. See Doig's *Empire on the Hudson* for a more detailed description of the Comprehensive Plan's downfall.

25. This involved suits "to protect the commerce of the port from attempts to increase rail or water rate handicaps or otherwise restrict its free flow" (Port Authority's 1934 Annual Report, 24).

26. See Port Authority's 1933 Annual Report, 20.

27. See Port Authority's 1942 Annual Report, 1–2. Also note that this time the focus was on trucking and transport costs and not necessarily the rail and lighter issue of previous decades. However, to the extent that trucking now figured more permanently in the port's value chain, this illustration was still used to make the case for the overall simplification of port operations and reduction of wasteful competition on cost competitiveness grounds.

28. Created in 1942 as the successor to the Department of Docks (1919–1942) and its predecessor the Department of Docks and Ferries (1898–1918).

29. Port Authority's 1945 annual report.

30. Harland Bartholomew and Associates report submitted by the Central Planning Board to the City of Newark Commission dated October 1945, cited in "Port of New York Authority: Hearings Before Subcommittee No. 5 of the Committee on the Judiciary, House of Representatives, Eighty-sixth Congress, Second Session: November 28, 29, 30, December 1 and 2, 1960," Serial No. 24, Part 2, printed by the U.S. Government Printing Office in 1961 for the use of the Committee on the Judiciary, 1765.

31. See chapter 3 for a more detailed discussion of this process.

32. See his request letter to the PA dated October 20, 1947—also cited in the Port Authority Annual Report 1947, 35.

33. Doig, *Empire on Hudson*, 266.

34. Port Authority's 1947 annual report, 6.

35. For a fascinating account of the shift in this industry, see Marc Levinson, *The Box: How the Shipping Container Made the World Smaller and the World Economy Bigger* (Princeton: Princeton University Press, 2008).

36. Brooklyn also had a vibrant shipping industry.

37. Port Authority's 1956 Annual Report.

38. Interview with Guy Tozzoli cited in Levinson (2008), 89. Official Port Authority statements on the acquisition of the Brooklyn piers tout the potential to restore the competitiveness of New York's ports by working together, but Tozzoli's statement suggests that it was a more political move to offset increased investment in New Jersey ports with some benefits for the New York side.

39. Jean-Paul Rodrigue, "The Port Authority of New York and New Jersey: Global Changes, Regional Gains and Local Challenges in Port Development," *Les Cahiers Scientifiques du Transport* 44 (2003): 55–75.

40. "10 Years of Container Shipping Bring Major Changes in Port," *New York Times*, August 29, 1972.

41. Levinson, 2008, 97.

42. Richard Levine, "New York Port Loses Top Spot to Los Angeles," *New York Times*, June 12, 1990.

43. Port Authority's 1983 annual report, 9.

44. Iver Peterson, "Imports by Rail Cut in Half Amount of Cargo Arriving at Region Docks," *New York Times*, January 13, 1992.

45. Peterson, 1992.

46. Lillian Borrone is highly respected among Port Authority professionals and, by all accounts, one of the most effective executives and leaders in every role she played during her long career in public service and at the agency. Her career and impact deserve more space than she gets in this short chapter. For more about her life and career see H. L. Schachter, "Lillian Borrone: Weaving a Web to Revitalize Port Commerce in New York and New Jersey," *Public Administration Review* 68, no. 1 (2008): 61–67.

47. Lillian Borrone, interview with Nelles, phone, June 6, 2020.

48. Erich E. Toll, "Bigger Relay Network Will Aid Neptune Orient Suez Canal Service to US," *Journal of Commerce*, November 3, 1991.

49. Port Authority's 1981 annual report, 23.

50. In 2019, 41.3 percent of total volume (imports/exports) through Port Authority ports originated or was destined for Southeast Asia per Port Authority, "2019 Trade Statistics."

51. John Holusha "Regional Market—New Jersey; Visions of Polluted Site Made Cargo Hub," *New York Times*, January 22, 2003; Port Authority 2019 annual report, 7.

52. C. G. Poore, "Program for a Great Port of New York," *New York Times*, April 13, 1930.

53. Tom Wakeman (PANYNJ's dredging program manager) in "Public Hearing before Senate Transportation Committee and Assembly Transportation and Communications Committee: Issues Related to Dredging in Port of New York and New Jersey," Trenton, June 22, 1995; Clifford J. Levy, "S.I. Terminal to Be Reopened by Sending Silt to Landfill in Utah," *New York Times*, June 22, 1995. In 2000, the "New York/New Jersey Harbor Navigation Study" recommended deepening the channel to at least fifty feet.

54. Port Authority's 1987 annual report, 15, and 1988 annual report, 19.

55. Governor's Dredged Material Management Team, "Dredging: What is the Best Approach for New Jersey? (Final Report of the Governor's Dredged Material Management Team)," 1994.

56. Wakeman, 1995; Levy, 1995. In 2000, the "New York/New Jersey Harbor Navigation Study" recommended deepening the channel to at least fifty feet.

57. Al Frank, "Tainted Mud From Harbor Dredging Will Get an $18 Million Ride To Utah," *Star-Ledger*, June 22, 1995; Levy, 1995.

58. Assemblyman Steve Corodemus in "Public Hearing before Senate Transportation Committee and Assembly Transportation and Communications Committee: Issues Related to Dredging in Port of New York and New Jersey," Trenton, June 22, 1995, 22–28.

59. Lewis Nagy (NJ DEP assistant commissioner), memo to Robert C. Shinn, Jr. (NJ DEP commissioner), November 28, 1995, in Folder: "Jane Kenny, Chief of Policy & Planning, Dredging: 4 of 4," Box 3: Subject Files, Appointments—Minority Issues, 1995, Series:

Governor Christine Todd Whitman, Office of Policy and Planning, Records of Jane Kenny, Chief, 1994–1995, New Jersey State Archives (Trenton, New Jersey).

60. Frank McDonough (director of maritime resources in NJ's Department of Commerce and Economic Development), memo to Christine Todd Whitman, Jane Kenny (chief of policy), and Judy Jengo (policy advisor), October 30, 1995, in Folder: "Jane Kenny, Chief of Policy & Planning, Dredging: 2 of 4," Box 3: Subject Files, Appointments—Minority Issues, 1995, Series: Governor Christine Todd Whitman, Office of Policy and Planning, Records of Jane Kenny, Chief, 1994–1995, New Jersey State Archives (Trenton, New Jersey).

61. Port Authority, Board materials, January 29, 1998, 9.

62. Brian Maher in Public Hearing, June 22, 1995, 51–57.

63. New York State Department of State Division of Coastal Resources and Waterfront Revitalization, "Dredging the Port: Maintaining Maritime Facilities in New York and New Jersey—Problems and Options," 1995.

64. Andrew C. Revkin, "2 Governors Plan Cleanup for Harbor," *New York Times*, October 6, 1996.

65. The Harbor Estuary Program helps to manage the biggest public resource in the nation's largest and most densely developed metropolitan area. Managing the estuary and its many services and uses is the shared responsibility of at least five core federal agencies; two states; eleven major sewerage agencies; hundreds of counties, cities, and towns; and millions of property owners. Critical stakeholders include maritime businesses and several hundred civic and community-based organizations. HEP brings these partners together to work collaboratively to develop and implement an Action Agenda that advances progress toward five long-term goals.

66. Scott Fallon, "Officials Mark Completion of N.Y. Harbor Channel Dredging," *The Record*, September 1, 2016.

67. Tom Wakeman, interview with Nelles, phone, December 11, 2020.

68. Northam, Jackie. "Cargo Overboard, Intense Rolling: The Risks of Fully-Loaded Mega-Container Ships," NPR, April 1, 2021.

69. Frank Caggiano, interview with Nelles, phone, December 10, 2020.

70. Port Authority's 1992 annual report.

71. Port Authority's 1995 annual report, 19, and 1996 annual report, 15.

72. Port Authority's 2006 annual report.

73. Bethann Rooney, personal communication with Nelles, September 6, 2021.

74. Rick Larrabee, interview with Nelles, phone, November 6, 2020.

75. Wakeman, December 11, 2020.

76. Wakeman, December 11, 2020.

77. Tedd Mann, "Computer Problems Leave Goods Stranded at New York Port," *Wall Street Journal*, August 4, 2013.

78. Bethann Rooney, interview with Nelles, phone, January 8, 2021.

79. Rooney, January 8, 2021.

80. Bethann Rooney, "A Focus on Port Performance in the Port of New York and New Jersey 'Taking a Fix,'" draft, December 2, 2013, 3.

81. Rooney, 2013, 4

82. Council on Port Performance, "Bylaws," August 1, 2014.

83. Council on Port Performance, "2018 Work Plan," 2018.
84. Jim Pellicio, interview with Nelles, phone, January 8, 2021.
85. Rooney, January 8, 2021.
86. Rooney, January 8, 2021. See also Mark Szakonyi, "JOC Uncharted: COVID-19 response shows NY-NJ Port Resilience," *Journal of Commerce*, June 12, 2020.
87. Costas Paris, "Shipping Companies Look at Sailing Away from Chocked Southern California Gateways," *Wall Street Journal*, February 8, 2021.
88. Wakeman, December 11, 2020.

Chapter 5

1. Lillian Borrone, interview with Plotch, phone, January 27, 2021.
2. Lou Gambaccini, "Leaving the City Better and More Beautiful," in *This I Believe: Philadelphia*, edited by Dan Gediman, Mary Jo Gediman, and Elisabeth Perez-Luna (Charleston, SC: The History Press, 2015), 127–28; Linda Spock, interview with Plotch, phone, June 2, 2020.
3. Lou Gambaccini, interview with Nicholas K. Tulach and Martin Robins, November 2012, Alan M. Voorhees Transportation Oral History Project and Archive, http://vtc.rutgers.edu/wp-content/uploads/2014/12/Interview_Lou_Gambaccini_2012.pdf
4. Gambaccini, November 2012.
5. Port Authority 1977 annual report, 33.
6. Lou Gambaccini, "Hearings Before the Subcommittee on Urban Affairs of the Joint Economic Committee Congress of the United States Ninety-Third Congress Second Session. April 8 and 29, May 6 and 13, and July 3, 1974," U.S. Government Printing Office, 1974, 60.
7. Spock, June 2, 2020.
8. "In Memoriam: Gambaccini: Half a Century of Service," *Passenger Transport*, August 20, 2018.
9. Robert Kelly, interview with Plotch, phone, May 4, 2020.
10. "Port Authority Plans Dial-a-Train Service," *New York Times*, March 12, 1978.
11. Lou Lumenick, "PA Approves Dial-A-Route Computer Plan," *The Record* (Bergen County, NJ), March 10, 1978.
12. Kelly, May 4, 2020.
13. Kelly, May 4, 2020.
14. Joseph F. Sullivan, "Byrne to Name Gambaccini Transport Commissioner," *New York Times*, April 6, 1978.
15. Martin Robins, interview with Plotch, phone, January 26 and 27, 2021.
16. Matt Edelman, interview with Plotch, phone, April 23 and 29, 2020.
17. Deborah Wathen Finn, interview with Plotch, phone, June 29, 2020.
18. Stanley Brezenoff, interview with Plotch and Nelles, phone, February 1, 2021; Vicky Kelly, interview with Plotch, phone, February 3, 2021.
19. Robins, January 26 and 27, 2021.
20. Suzanne Daley, "Traffic Up, Port Agency Plans Study," *New York Times*, January 14, 1984.
21. Spock, June 2, 2020.
22. Daley, January 14, 1984.

Notes to Pages 120–25

23. Spock, email to Plotch, July 27, 2020.
24. Daley, January 14, 1984; Anne Kornhauser, "Hoboken-N.Y. Ferry Wins Design Funds," *Jersey Journal*, June 14, 1985.
25. Joseph F. Sullivan, "Plans Predict Spurt on Hudson Crossings," *New York Times*, February 14, 1987.
26. Suzanne Daley, "Ferryboats Are Inspiring a New Wave of Enthusiasm," *New York Times*, August 25, 1985.
27. Ted Mann, "A PATH Link Going Offline for Weekends," *Wall Street Journal*, February 5, 2014.
28. Daley, August 25, 1985.
29. Stefan Fatsis, "Ferryboats Make a Comeback on the Waters of New York," *Los Angeles Times*, November 5, 1987.
30. Regional Plan Association (RPA), "Ferries in the Region: Challenges and Opportunities—Discussion Paper Prepared for the Working Forum on Ferries November 6, 2006," November 2006, 3.
31. Joseph F. Sullivan, "Amid the Gridlock, Travel by River Returns," *New York Times*, May 20, 1987.
32. George Cancro, interview with Plotch, phone, August 11, 2020.
33. Port Authority's 1985 annual report, 39 and 41.
34. Cancro, August 11, 2020.
35. Robins, January 26 and 27, 2021.
36. David Gallagher, interview with Plotch, phone, July 6, 2020.
37. Stephen Berger, interview with Plotch, November 9, 2020.
38. RPA, November 2006, 5; Amit Bhowmick, interview with Plotch, phone, April 27, 2020. The permanent facilities opened in Battery Park City in 2009 and Hoboken in 2011.
39. Cancro, August 11, 2020.
40. James Brooke, "Column One: Transport," *New York Times*, October 22, 1986.
41. Daniel Patrick Moynihan, 100th Cong., 2nd session, *Congressional Record—Senate*, October 21, 1988, 32461–32462.
42. Rosemary Scanlon, interview with Plotch, phone, January 18, 2021; Joseph F. Sullivan, "Rise of the Commuter Ferry," *New York Times*, September 29, 1987.
43. New York Metropolitan Transportation Council's 2018 Hub Bound Travel survey.
44. New York Metropolitan Transportation Council's 2018 Hub Bound Travel survey.
45. 53.7 million in 1985 (per Port Authority's 1985 annual report) and 81.7 million in 2018 (per Port Authority's 2018 annual report).
46. Marc Santora, "PATH to Resume Weekend Service to Lower Manhattan," *New York Times*, August 23, 2021.
47. David Andelman, "For Drivers in Manhattan the Situation Was Thick," *New York Times*, August 8, 1980; Robert D. McFadden, "Propane Gas Leak on Bridge to Jersey Causes Huge Tie-Up," *New York Times*, August 8, 1980; "With Washington Bridge Reopened traffic Shouldn't be Nightmare Again," *Jersey Journal*, August 8, 1980.
48. Valerie Briggs and Keith Jasper, "Organizing for Regional Transportation Operations: New York/New Jersey/Connecticut," Operational Dialogue Report No. FHWA-OP-01–138, 2001.
49. Kelly, May 4, 2020.

50. Sewell Chan, "Transit News is a Click Away, and About 5 Years Behind Schedule," *New York Times*, April 25, 2005.
51. Gambaccini, November 2012.
52. Robert Hanley, "Regional System Is Formed to Attack Traffic Tie-Ups," *New York Times*, November 21, 1986.
53. Marygrace Parker, interview with Plotch, phone, May 14, 2020.
54. Finn, June 29, 2020.
55. Finn, June 29, 2020.
56. Parker, May 14, 2020.
57. Parker, May 14, 2020.
58. Parker, May 14, 2020.
59. Gambaccini, November 2012.
60. Kelly, May 4, 2020.
61. Hanley, November 21, 1986.
62. Briggs and Jasper, August 2001.
63. David Judd, interview with Plotch, phone, July 2, 2020.
64. Tom Batz, interview with Plotch, November 22, 2016.
65. Ken Philmus, interview with Plotch, June 29, 2016.
66. Edelman, April 23 and 29, 2020.
67. Edelman, April 23 and 29, 2020.
68. John Baniak, "A Decade of Partnership, Evolution and Growth: The I-95 Corridor Coalition," https://rosap.ntl.bts.gov/view/dot/39364/dot_39364_DS1.pdf, accessed July 29, 2020.
69. Parker, May 14, 2020.
70. Filler, interview with Plotch, June 11, 2020, and June 18, 2020; "Solving New York City's Traffic Riddles: Ideas from Experts," *New York Times*, November 10, 1985.
71. Filler, June 11 and June 18, 2020.
72. Filler, June 11 and June 18, 2020.
73. Port Authority 1977 annual report, 13.
74. Richard Oram, interview with Plotch, phone, June 29, 2020.
75. Filler, June 11 and June 18, 2020.
76. Filler, June 11 and June 18, 2020.
77. Judd, July 2, 2020.
78. Filler, June 11 and June 18, 2020.
79. Filler, June 11 and June 18, 2020.
80. Judd, July 2, 2020.
81. Filler, June 11 and June 18, 2020.
82. Filler, June 11 and June 18, 2020.
83. Filler, June 11 and June 18, 2020.
84. Filler, June 11 and June 18, 2020.
85. Filler, June 11 and June 18, 2020.
86. Filler, June 11 and June 18, 2020; Oram, June 29, 2020.
87. Oram, June 29, 2020.
88. Filler, June 11 and June 18, 2020.

89. Sam Roberts, "Metro Matters; Tepid Incentive for Commuters: A $15 Subsidy," *New York Times*, October 8, 1987.
90. Port Authority's 1987 annual report, 16.
91. Milt Freudenheim, "Companies Offer New Benefits," *Berkshire Eagle* (Pittsfield, MA), November 20, 1988; "Commuters Called Hurt by Taxes," *New York Times*, July 3, 1988.
92. John Henry, "Check it Out," *Daily News*, November 29, 1987.
93. Oram, June 29, 2020.
94. Louis J. Gambaccini, "U.S. Economy, and Proposals to Provide Middle-income Tax Relief, Tax Equity and Fairness, Economic Stimulus and Growth," Hearings before the Committee on Ways and Means, House of Representatives, 102nd Congress, February 6, 1992, U.S. Government Printing Office, 1476–78.
95. Seth Faison, "Explaining the Check in 'TransitChek,'" *New York Times*, January 25, 1993.
96. "Case Study 10: TransitCenter (New York City)," in *Fare Policies, Structures And Technologies: Update, TCRP* (Transit Cooperative Research Program) Report 94, 2003, 154.
97. Judith C. Schwenk (U.S. Department of Transportation), "TransitChek in the New York City and Philadelphia Areas," Report #: FTA-MA-26-0006-96-1, October 1995, Table 2–8.
98. Filler, June 11 and June 18, 2020.
99. Oram, June 29, 2020.
100. Judd, July 2, 2020.
101. TransitCenter, "The Value of an Idea," January 31, 2014, https://transitcenter.org/the-value-of-an-idea
102. The E-ZPass system was the world's largest in the late 1990s and early 2000s.
103. Robert S. Foote (Port Authority), "Collection Problems and the Promise of Automatic Vehicle Identification," *Transportation Research Record* 494 (1974): 15–20.
104. James Brooke, "Machines to Sell L.I.R.R. Tickets by Credit Card," *New York Times*, July 8, 1986.
105. Glenn Rifkin, "Business Technology; Electronic Toll-Taking is Being Put to the Test," *New York Times*, September 9, 1992.
106. Rifkin, September 9, 1992.
107. Port Authority's 1989 annual report, 33.
108. Spock, email to Plotch, July 27, 2020.
109. Spock, June 2, 2020.
110. Susan Rosegrant, "E-ZPass: The Effort to Design and Implement A Regional Electronic Toll Collection System," Kennedy School of Government Case Program, C16-05-1818.0, October 31, 2005; Spock, July 27, 2020.
111. Spock, June 2, 2020.
112. Rosegrant, October 31, 2005.
113. Rosegrant, October 31, 2005.
114. Rosegrant, October 31, 2005.
115. Gallagher, July 6, 2020.

116. Gallagher, July 6, 2020.
117. Gallagher, July 6, 2020.
118. Port Authority's 1998 annual report, 13.
119. Rosegrant, October 31, 2005.
120. Port Authority's 1993 annual report, 16–17; Matt Edelman, email to Plotch, September 17, 2020.
121. Rosegrant, October 31, 2005; E-ZPass Group, home page, https://www.e-zpassiag.com, accessed March 24, 2022.
122. Filler, June 11 and June 18, 2020.
123. Oram, June 29, 2020.
124. Filler, June 11 and June 18, 2020.
125. Filler, June 11 and June 18, 2020.

Chapter 6

1. Former governors Byrne and Carey remembered that they relied on the independent-minded business leaders they had appointed to the board, per Ronald Smothers, "As Port Authority Stalls, Ex-Governors Urge Talks," *New York Times*, April 15, 2000.
2. James Dao, "Conservative Candidate: Angry Elbow to Giuliani's Right," *New York Times*, August 20, 1993.
3. Alison Mitchell, "The 1994 Campaign: The Mayor; Giuliani, Defying His Party, Backs Cuomo for 4th Term," *New York Times*, October 25, 1994.
4. Richard C. Leone, "Pataki's Politics; Everyone's Port Authority," *New York Times*, January 7, 1995.
5. "Mr. Pataki's Mediocre Choices," editorial, *New York Times*, January 12, 1995.
6. James Dao, "Governors Seek to Agree on Port Job," *New York Times*, January 14, 1995.
7. Dao, January 14, 1995.
8. Clifford J. Levy, "Pataki Nominee Is Elected to Run Port Authority," *New York Times*, February 10, 1995.
9. Iver Peterson, "A Pataki-Whitman Honeymoon Hits a Bump, on Port Authority," *New York Times*, January 13, 1995.
10. Clifford J. Levy, "Manager of Boston Subway Gets No. 2 Post at Port Authority," *New York Times*, April 27, 1995.
11. Levy, April 27, 1995; Port Authority, "Appointment of Executive Director," board materials, February 9, 1995, 105; Levy, February 10, 1995.
12. "Governors Should Bridge Port Authority Breach," *Star-Ledger*, April 23, 2000.
13. Jonathan P. Hicks, "Mayor Sharply Attacks Port Authority," *New York Times*, August 24, 1995; Andy Newman, "Port Authority May Increase Fees for Buses," *New York Times*, June 26, 1998.
14. Jonathan P. Hicks, "Mayor Sharply Attacks Port Authority," *New York Times*, August 24, 1995.
15. Christina Pretto, "N.Y.C. Mayor's Airport Buyout Plan Includes $2 Billion in Debt," *Bond Buyer*, June 3, 1996.
16. Vivian S. Toy, "Mayor's Office Attacks Port Authority Over Rent," *New York Times*, January 21, 1996.

17. Joseph B. Rose (NYC Department of City Planning), "A Critical Analysis of the Role of the Port Authority of New York and New Jersey," Summer 1995, 3.

18. Mark Green, "Follow the Money: How the Port Authority of NY and NJ has Favored New Jersey over New York," February 1996, 1–18.

19. Rose, Summer 1995, 1–10.

20. Rose, Summer 1995, 1–10.

21. Rothschild Inc., "The Port Authority of New York & New Jersey: A Preliminary Report to Mayor Rudolph Giuliani, Deputy Mayor John Dyson, Charles E. F. Millard (President, NYC Economic Development Corporation)," May 1996, available in NYC Municipal Library.

22. Mark Green, "Follow the Money: How the Port Authority of NY and NJ Has Favored New Jersey over New York," February 1996, 1–18.

23. Michael Tomasky, "Four Candidates and a Funeral," *New York Magazine*, May 12, 1997, 34–35.

24. "Don't Mess With Success," editorial, *New York Daily News*, October 26, 1997.

25. "Priorities at the Port Authority," editorial, *New York Times*, February 7, 1996.

26. David Kocieniewski, "Whitman Seeks to Restrict Spending on City's Airports," *New York Times*, January 16, 1999.

27. Charles V. Bagli, "2-State Dispute Over Shipping Lines' Lease Clouds Port Authority Future," *New York Times*, April 20, 1999.

28. George Marlin, interview with Plotch, Midtown Manhattan, November 17, 2019.

29. James C. McKinley, Jr., "Port Authority Is Proposing A Toll Freeze for a Year," *New York Times*, December 2, 1994.

30. George Marlin, interview with Plotch, Midtown Manhattan, November 17, 2019.

31. Clifford J. Levy, "Port Authority Uses Buyouts to Cut Its Costs," *New York Times*, September 3, 1995.

32. Richard Mroz, interview with Plotch, Haddonfield (NJ), July 8, 2019.

33. Al Frank, "300 P.A. Workers Take Early Retirement, 'Helping' Agency's Fiscal Picture," *Star-Ledger*, August 18, 1995.

34. Al Frank, "Plan To Streamline The P.A. Slashes Hundreds of Jobs," *Star-Ledger*, September 7, 1995.

35. PANYNJ, "Executive Director's Report," board materials, May 11, 1995, 167; "World Trade Center May Be Sold," *Star-Ledger*, May 14, 1995.

36. George Marlin, letter to editor, *New York Times*, September 13, 1995.

37. Levy, September 3, 1995.

38. Frank, August 18, 1995.

39. Paul Bea, interview with Plotch, phone, January 16, 2020.

40. PANYNJ, "Reduction in Force—Severance for Separated Employees," board materials, September 7, 1995, 328.

41. Al Frank, "Staff Cuts at P.A. Increase to 900," *Star-Ledger*, September 9, 1995; had been layoffs during the Depression, per Clifford J. Levy, "Era Ends at Port Authority as 160 Workers Are Laid Off," *New York Times*, September 16, 1995.

42. Al Frank, "Port Authority Streamlining Continues As High Projects Exec Steps Down," *Star-Ledger*, November 5, 1995.

43. Frank, September 7, 1995.

44. Neil MacFarquhar, "Port Authority Chief to Leave, After Cutbacks and Criticism," *New York Times*, January 18, 1997; plan to eliminate about 1,000 positions or 10 percent of the workforce per PANYNJ, 1994 annual report, 9.
45. Alice Herman, interview with Plotch, phone, August 13, 2019.
46. Richard Kelly, interview with Plotch, West Caldwell (NJ), August 12, 2019.
47. Kelly, August 12, 2019.
48. Former senior Port Authority official, phone interview with Plotch, February 10, 2020.
49. Lillian Borrone, interview with Plotch, phone, November 14, 2019.
50. Chris Dupin, "Borrone's Tenure Was Eventful, Productive," *Journal of Commerce*, December 17, 2000.
51. Borrone, November 14, 2019.
52. Dupin, December 17, 2000.
53. George Marlin, interview with Plotch, Midtown Manhattan, November 17, 2019.
54. Marlin, November 17, 2019.
55. John Haley, interview with Plotch, phone, October 7, 1999.
56. Richard Roper, interview with Plotch, phone, January 22, 2020.
57. Guy T. Baehr, "P.A. Faces Changes as Bigger Becomes Better," *Star-Ledger*, October 16, 1994.
58. Jacques Steinberg, "Port Authority Cuts Back on Free-Spending Ways," *New York Times*, February 4, 1992; Jane Fritsch, "Free Spending Survives Port Authority's Attempts at Restraint," *New York Times*, July 6, 1992.
59. Stanley Brezenoff, interview with Plotch and Nelles, February 1, 2021.
60. Rosemary Scanlon, interview with Plotch, phone, January 18, 2021.
61. Sandra Salmans, "Arts in New York Said to Generate $5 Billion a Year," *New York Times*, February 16, 1983; Scanlon, January 18, 2021.
62. Marlin, November 17, 2019.
63. Sheri Ernico, Bruce Boudreau, Dan Reimer, and Steve Van Beek, "Considering and Evaluating Airport Privatization," *ACRP Report* 66, 2012, 92.
64. Marlin, November 17, 2019; Clifford J. Levy, "Port Authority to Lay off 300 More Workers," *New York Times*, September 9, 1995; Bea, January 16, 2020; Levy, September 16, 1995.
65. Marlin, November 17, 2019.
66. Borrone, November 14, 2019; Wayne Barrett, "Pataki's Favorite Conservatives," *Village Voice*, October 27, 1998.
67. Marlin, November 17, 2019.
68. Former senior Port Authority official, February 10, 2020.
69. Clifford J. Levy, "Remarks on Airport Link by Port Authority Head Surprise Albany," *New York Times*, June 3, 1995; Neil MacFarquhar, "Port Authority Chief to Leave, After Cutbacks and Criticism," *New York Times*, January 18, 1997.
70. Robert Boyle, interview with Plotch, phone, July 19, 2019.
71. Al Frank, "The Odd Trio: A Trader, an Ambassador and a Builder," *Star-Ledger*, May 9, 1999.
72. Peter Goldmark, interview with Plotch and Tindall, Upper East Side, October 16, 2019.

73. Boyle, July 19, 2019.
74. Philip Lentz, "Angry Governor Eyes Breakup of Port Authority," *Crain's New York Business*, March 24, 1997.
75. Bagli, April 20, 1999.
76. Boyle, July 19, 2019.
77. Charles V. Bagli, "Pataki Rejects Whitman's $120 Million Deal to Keep Shipping Lines," *New York Times*, April 13, 1999.
78. Ron Shiftan, interview with Plotch, Rumson (NJ), June 11, 2019.
79. Haley, October 7, 1999.
80. "Governors Should Bridge Port Authority Breach," April 23, 2000.
81. Smothers, April 15, 2000.
82. Smothers, April 15, 2000.
83. "Region Depends on States' Cooperation—The Kean-Byrne Dialogue," *Star-Ledger*, April 30, 2000.
84. Al Frank, "Border War Still Stalls Maersk, Port Authority," *Star-Ledger*, December 12, 1999.
85. Christine Todd Whitman, interview with Plotch, phone, March 6, 2020.
86. Whitman, March 6, 2020.
87. Joan Verplanck, interview with Plotch, phone, June 5, 2020.
88. New Jersey Petroleum Council, in "Public Hearing before Senate Transportation Committee and Assembly Transportation and Communications Committee: Issues Related to Dredging in Port of New York and New Jersey," Trenton, June 22, 1995, 174X–175X.
89. International Longshoremen's Association, New Jersey Petroleum Council, in "Public Hearing before Senate Transportation Committee and Assembly Transportation and Communications Committee: Issues Related to Dredging in Port of New York and New Jersey," Trenton, June 22, 1995, 181X.
90. Brian Maher, in public hearing, June 22, 1995, 51–57.
91. New York Shipping Association, in Public Hearing, June 22, 1995, 176x–178x.
92. Charles V. Bagli, "Port Authority Struggles to Keep 2 Shippers," *New York Times*, February 14, 1999; "Lillian C. Borrone Talks About the Port Authority's Plan to Keep Shipping Lines From Moving Out," *Business News New Jersey*, February 22, 1999.
93. Charles V. Bagli, "As Governors Spar, Shippers Weigh Leaving," *New York Times*, April 7, 1999.
94. Bagli, February 14, 1999.
95. Bagli, February 14, 1999.
96. Al Frank, "Port Makes Finalist Cut—Shipping Lines Mulling Two Others for East Coast Hub," *Star-Ledger*, December 11, 1998.
97. Bagli, February 14, 1999.
98. Frank, December 11, 1998; Boyle, July 19, 2019.
99. Chris Ward, interview with Plotch and Nelles, phone, October 28, 2020.
100. Bagli, February 14, 1999.
101. Frank, December 11, 1998.
102. Bagli, February 14, 1999.
103. Frank, December 11, 1998; Al Frank "Port Tenants Float a Move—Two Biggest Shippers Court Other Cities' Ports," *Star-Ledger*, May 13, 1998.

104. "Regina Maersk," *Vinalogs Container Transportation*, accessed January 11, 2020, https://www.container-transportation.com/regina-maersk.html

105. Frank, December 11, 1998.

106. Al Frank, "Jerseyan Gets No. 2 P.A. Post," *Star-Ledger*, September 9, 1998.

107. Shiftan, June 11, 2019.

108. Frank, December 11, 1998.

109. Bagli, April 7, 1999.

110. Bagli, February 14, 1999; Boyle, July 19, 2019.

111. New Jersey's Director of Maritime Resources, draft version of "Port Dredging: The Plan for 1996," 1995 in Folder: "Jane Kenny, Chief of Policy & Planning, Dredging: 2 of 4," Box 3: Subject Files, Appointments—Minority Issues, 1995, Series: Governor Christine Todd Whitman, Office of Policy and Planning, Records of Jane Kenny, Chief, 1994–1995, New Jersey State Archives (Trenton, New Jersey), 1–5.

112. Jim Devine (Sea-Land General Manager), interview with Plotch, phone, June 8, 2020.

113. Al Frank, "The Ship of Respect Sank Feb. 23," *Star-Ledger*, May 9, 1999.

114. Bagli, April 20, 1999.

115. Frank, May 9, 1999.

116. Frank, May 9, 1999; Bagli, April 20, 1999.

117. Ronald Smothers, "Port Authority Rift Revealed States' Competitive Instincts," *New York Times*, June 6, 2000; Boyle, July 19, 2019.

118. Frank, May 9, 1999.

119. Smothers, June 6, 2000; Frank, May 9, 1999.

120. Bagli, April 20, 1999.

121. Boyle, July 19, 2019; Senior Port Authority official, interview with Plotch, phone, January 13, 2020, and January 27, 2020; Bagli, April 20, 1999.

122. Ronald Smothers, "Port Authority and 2 States Discuss Lease for Terminal," *New York Times*, December 23, 1999.

123. "Tolls Steady, Tunnels to go High-Tech Under P.A.," *Star-Ledger*, May 28, 1999.

124. Bagli, April 7, 1999.

125. Bagli, April 13, 1999.

126. Bagli, April 20, 1999; Charles V. Bagli, "Rally to Promote Port Leases Widens Gap Between States," *New York Times*, April 10, 1999.

127. Bagli, April 10, 1999.

128. Charles V. Bagli, "2 Shippers Agree to Stay in Harbor," *New York Times*, May 8, 1999.

129. Al Frank, "Governors Get Time to Work Out Differences," *Star-Ledger*, April 8, 1999.

130. Bagli, April 13, 1999.

131. Bagli, February 14, 1999.

132. Bagli, February 14, 1999; Verplanck, June 5, 2020.

133. Frank, April 8, 1999.

134. Smothers, April 15, 2000.

135. Bagli, April 7, 1999.

136. Bagli, April 10, 1999.

137. Bagli, April 13, 1999.
138. Frank, May 9, 1999.
139. Frank, May 9, 1999.
140. Greg Storey, interview with Plotch, phone, July 15, 2019.
141. Frank, May 9, 1999.
142. Borrone, November 14, 2019.
143. Bagli, February 14, 1999.
144. Bagli, April 13, 1999.
145. Jim Devine (Sea-Land general manager) discussed the "withdrawal liability exposure" in his interview with Plotch, phone, June 8, 2020; Alan F. Schoedel, "A Matter of Definition," *Journal of Commerce*, March 8, 1987.
146. Bagli, May 8, 1999.
147. Frank, December 12, 1999; Smothers, June 6, 2000; Al Frank, "Airline Execs Press 2 Governors to Make Peace," *Star-Ledger*, April 30, 1999.
148. Al Frank, "P.A. Agenda Stalls Over Impasse on SeaLand-Maersk—Pataki is Reluctant to Sign off on Cargo Hub," *Star-Ledger*, October 1, 1999.
149. Al Frank, "P.A. to Hold Line on Fares and Tolls," *Star-Ledger*, December 8, 1999; Frank, October 1, 1999.
150. Al Frank, "Governors Are at it Again," *Star-Ledger*, October 31, 1999.
151. Frank, October 31, 1999.
152. Frank, October 31, 1999; Frank, December 12, 1999.
153. Smothers, December 23, 1999.
154. Goldmark, October 16, 2019; PANYNJ, 1982 and 1983 annual reports.
155. Neil MacFarquhar, "New York Boycotts Port Authority's Meeting," *New York Times*, December 17, 1999.
156. "Governors Should Bridge Port Authority Breach," April 23, 2000.
157. Smothers, April 15, 2000; "Governors Should Bridge Port Authority Breach," April 23, 2000.
158. "Governors Should Bridge Port Authority Breach," April 23, 2000.
159. Smothers, April 15, 2000.
160. Mroz, July 8, 2019.
161. Mroz, July 8, 2019.
162. Former senior Port Authority official, January 13, 2020.
163. Goldmark, October 16, 2019.
164. Charles H. Heying, "Civic Elites and Corporate Delocalization: An Alternative Explanation for Declining Civic Engagement," *American Behavioral Scientist* 40, no. 5 (1997): 657–68.
165. Bea, January 16, 2020.
166. Dupin, December 17, 2000.
167. Ronald Smothers, "Feud Over How Port Authority Spends Money Creates an Impasse," *New York Times*, February 24, 2000.
168. Smothers, February 24, 2000.
169. "Region Depends on States' Cooperation—The Kean-Byrne Dialogue," April 30, 2000.

170. Lautenberg and Moynihan, letter to Pataki and Whitman, April 20, 2000, in Folder: "Washington Office, Records of Lance Giles, Port of New York & New Jersey," Series: Governor Christine Todd Whitman, Office of Policy and Planning, Records of Jane Kenny, Chief, 1994–1995, New Jersey State Archives (Trenton, New Jersey); Al Frank, "Budget Vote Could End P.A. Logjam," *Star-Ledger*, April 27, 2000.

171. Ronald Smothers, "Hopes Are Raised, Then Dashed, Over Stalemate at Port Authority," *New York Times*, April 28, 2000.

172. Frank, April 27, 2000.

173. Smothers, April 28, 2000; Al Frank, "P.A. Fails to Break Lengthy Impasse," *Star-Ledger*, April 28, 2000.

174. Smothers, April 28, 2000; Frank, April 28, 2000.

175. Frank, April 28, 2000.

176. Smothers, April 28, 2000.

177. Mroz, July 8, 2019.

178. Pat R. Gilbert, "Port Authority Feud Tying Up Billions," *Bergen Record*, May 25, 2000. Article found in folder "Washington Office, Records of Lance Giles, Port of New York & New Jersey," Series: Governor Christine Todd Whitman, Office of Policy and Planning, Records of Jane Kenny, Chief, 1994–1995, New Jersey State Archives (Trenton, New Jersey).

179. Smothers, June 6, 2000.

180. Ronald Smothers, "Governors End Port Authority Rift That Blocked Billions in Projects," *New York Times*, June 2, 2000.

181. Smothers, June 2, 2000; Ronald Smothers, "Trade Center Leasing Project Goes Forward," *New York Times*, June 28, 2000.

182. Smothers, June 2, 2000; Mroz, July 8, 2019.

183. Smothers, June 2, 2000; PANYNJ, annual report 2000; PANYNJ, "Minutes of Special Board Meeting," June 2, 2000.

184. Andrew Tangel, "Port Authority Executive Balked at Penn Station Lease," *Wall Street Journal*, January 12, 2016.

185. Andrew Tangel, "Port Authority Chairman Trashes Old Lease," *Wall Street Journal*, February 18, 2016.

186. Smothers, June 2, 2000; Port Authority's 2000 annual report; Port Authority, "Minutes of Special Board Meeting," June 2, 2000.

187. Mroz, July 8, 2019.

188. Port Authority, "2011 Trade Statistics: The Port of New York and New Jersey," July 2012.

189. Eric Lipton, "New York Port Hums Again, with Asian Trade," *New York Times*, November 22, 2004.

190. Devine, June 8, 2020; Gregory Richards, "Massive $450 Million Port Terminal Opens in Portsmouth," *Virginian-Pilot*, September 7, 2007; "APM Opens Va. Deep-Water Container Terminal," *Transport Topics*, September 10, 2007.

191. Frank Lombardi, interview with Plotch and Nelles, phone, November 4, 2020.

192. Lombardi, November 4, 2020.

193. Paul Bea, "Do Something. But Not Just Anything," *MTS Matters* (Martin Transpor-

tation System blog), May 2, 2014, https://mtsmatters.com/2014/05/02/do-something-but-not-just-anything

Chapter 7

1. Doig, *Empire on the Hudson*, 89.
2. FHWA, "State Motor Vehicle Registrations, By Years, 1900–1995," https://www.fhwa.dot.gov/ohim/summary95/mv200.pdf
3. Population of New York City was 5,620,048 and Staten Island was 116,531 in 1920.
4. "The Arthur Kill Bridges," *New York Herald Tribune*, August 1, 1925.
5. "Mainland Links to Staten Island," *New York Times*, August 29, 1926; "The Staten Island Bridges," editorial, *New York Times*, September 15, 1926.
6. "Bridge or Tunnel Across Arthur Kill," *New York Times*, August 12, 1923.
7. "Bridge or Tunnel Across Arthur Kill," August 12, 1923; the New York and New Jersey Vehicular Tunnel Commission was responsible for building the tunnel.
8. "Tunnel Board Takes up New Tunnel Project," *Jersey Journal*, August 9, 1923.
9. "Tunnel Advocates Tell Silzer His Bridge Plans Won't Do," *Jersey Journal*, December 27, 1923; "Silzer Urges Plan of Port Authority," *New York Times*, January 23, 1924.
10. "Argue on Four Bridge Bills," *Jersey Journal*, February 17, 1925.
11. "Smith Proposes Port Authority and Tunnel Commission Merge," *Engineering News Record*, March 8, 1923, 464; Robert W. Jackson, *Highway Under the Hudson: A History of the Holland Tunnel* (New York: NYU Press, 2011), 159–60.
12. *Laws of the State of New York Passed at the One Hundred and Forty-Seventh Session of the Legislature* (Albany: J. B. Lyon Company, 1924), 406; Doig, *Empire on the Hudson*, 99–100; Port Authority, 1926 annual report.
13. Port Authority's 1924 annual report, 5.
14. Port Authority's 1925 annual report, 13.
15. Port Authority's 1923 annual report, 21.
16. "Hudson Men Urge Bridge Bill in Trenton," *Jersey Journal*, January 27, 1925; "Booming Northern New Jersey," editorial, *Jersey Journal*, February 10, 1925; "Bayonne Bridge Hearing to See Case Answered," *Jersey Journal*, February 14, 1925; "Legislature Agrees on 4 Interstate Bridge Bills," *Jersey Journal*, February 17, 1925.
17. "Work Is Pushed on Harbor Bridges," *New York Times*, November 21, 1926.
18. "The Staten Island Bridges," *New York Times*, September 15, 1926.
19. "Seeks Competition to Finance Bridge," *New York Times*, January 4, 1926.
20. "Bridges to End Staten Island's Isolation," *New York Times*, September 12, 1926.
21. Port Authority's 1925 annual report, 20 and appendix.
22. "Bridges to End Staten Island's Isolation," September 12, 1926.
23. "Arthur Kill Spans Shown in Models," *New York Times*, July 29, 1925; Port Authority's 1925 annual report, 19.
24. "Kill Van Kull Span is Urged at Hearing," *New York Times*, December 1, 1927.
25. "Smith Warns Roads at Bridge Exercises," *New York Times*, June 21, 1928.
26. "Smith Warns Roads at Bridge Exercises," June 21, 1928.
27. Mabel Abbott, "Staten Island at Last Linked with Mainland," *New York Times*, June 10, 1928.

28. "Tomorrow's Bridge Celebration," editorial, *Jersey Journal*, June 19, 1928.
29. "Two States Open Bayonne Bridge, Forming Fifth Link," *New York Times*, November 15, 1931.
30. Gail Radford, *The Rise of the Public Authority: Statebuilding and Economic Development in Twentieth-Century America* (Chicago: University of Chicago Press, 2013), 125.
31. New York Temporary State Commission on Coordination of State Activities, "Report of the Temporary State Commission on Coordination of State Activities Report of Activities for The Year 1953–1954 and First Interim Staff Report on Public Authorities Under New York State," 1954, 24.
32. Port Authority's 1950 annual report, 27.
33. Port Authority's 1952 annual report, 11.
34. Joseph C. Ingraham, "Tunnel-Traffic Link," *New York Times*, October 5, 1952.
35. Jameson W. Doig, "Regional Conflict in the New York Metropolis: The Legend of Robert Moses and the Power of the Port Authority," *Urban Studies* 27, no. 2 (1990): 201–32.
36. Doig, 1990, 201–32.
37. Doig, 1990, 201–32.
38. Doig, *Empire on the Hudson*, 121; Julius Henry Cohen, *They Builded Better Than They Knew* (New York: Ayer Publishing, 1946), 330; advocates for the Bayonne Bridge had expected that drivers would be able to take the Holland Tunnel to Jersey City, drive over the Bayonne Bridge to Staten Island and then cross the Goethals Bridge or Outerbridge to central and south Jersey. However (per Julius Henry Cohen, 313), after the Pulaski Skyway was built, revenues of the two Staten Island bridges went down while revenue from the Holland Tunnel went up.
39. "Plans New Bridge Over Kill Van Kull," *New York Times*, February 8, 1927; Port Authority's 1950 annual report, 27.
40. The Clearview Expressway, Cross Bronx Expressway Extension (I-295), and the Alexander Hamilton Bridge were part of this plan.
41. Doig, 1990, 201–32.
42. Doig, 1990, 201–32.
43. Joseph C. Ingraham, "Vast Traffic Study Planned by Port and Bridge Bodies," *New York Times*, February 15, 1954.
44. Port Authority's 1954 annual report, 7–16.
45. "Excerpts from Governor Harriman's Message on the 1955–56 State Budget," *New York Times*, January 31, 1955.
46. Port Authority's 1954 annual report, 14–15.
47. Port Authority's 1954 annual report, 14–15.
48. Port Authority's 1954 annual report, 14–15.
49. Port Authority's 1956 annual report, 28.
50. Port Authority's 1959 annual report, 32.
51. Joseph C. Ingraham, "News Analysis; Now, More Roads," *New York Times*, November 23, 1964.
52. Port Authority's 1960 Annual Report (page 26) and 1969 Annual Report (page 18).
53. Port Authority's 1984 annual report, 16, "Port Authority Laments Growing Hudson Logjam," *Sunday Register* (Red Bank, NJ), April 1, 1984, A3.

Notes to Pages 187–90   337

54. Amit Bhowmick (retired Port Authority senior transportation planner), interview with Plotch, phone, April 27, 2020.

55. New York City Planning Commission, "Shaping the City's Future: New York City Planning and Zoning Report," Spring 1993.

56. Port Authority's 1980 annual report, schedule F; Port Authority's 1985 annual report, 48.

57. Along a thirty-five-mile stretch, the interstate ran over the Goethals Bridge and then along the Staten Island Expressway, Verrazzano-Narrows Bridge, Gowanus Expressway, Brooklyn–Queens Expressway, Kosciuszko Bridge, Grand Central Parkway, Triborough Bridge, and Bruckner Expressway; confirmed by Uchenna Madu (New York State Department of Transportation) in email to Plotch on June 1, 2020.

58. Lou Venech (retired Port Authority general manager of regional transportation policy), interview with Plotch, phone, April 20, 2020.

59. Port Authority's 1985 annual report, 20.

60. Richard Eisen, "New Staten Island Bridge Hinges on P.A. Vote," *Staten Island Advance*, June 9, 1993; U.S. Coast Guard, "Staten Island Bridges Program, Modernization and Capacity Enhancement Project, Final Environmental Impact Statement/Section 4(f)," October 1997, volume 1, 2–2.

61. "P.A. Seeks Info On Its Customers," *Staten Island Advance*, November 21, 1991.

62. Amit Bhowmick, interview with Plotch, phone, April 27, 2020; Lou Venech, interview with Plotch, phone, April 20, 2020.

63. Eisen, June 9, 1993.

64. Port Authority's 1990 annual report, 27.

65. The estimated cost was $300 million compared to $400 million for replacing the existing bridge with a wider one, per Sharon Hoey, "Authority Still Eyeing New Span Bridge Decision by April," *Staten Island Advance*, June 14, 1992.

66. Maryann Spoto, "Port Authority Unveils Goethals Bridge Plans," *Star-Ledger*, October 19, 1990.

67. Port Authority's 1923 annual report, 21–23.

68. Eileen A. J. Connelly, "Brezenoff: Keep Open Mind on Goethals Twin," *Staten Island Advance*, December 26, 1993.

69. Jeff O'Heir, "Crime Tops List of Concerns on South Shore," *Staten Island Advance*, August 14, 1994.

70. The Port Authority's 1960 annual report (page 26) had counts that included both east- and westbound traffic. In August 1970, the Port Authority doubled its toll for eastbound drivers and eliminated the toll for westbound drivers. After that, the Authority stopped counting the number of vehicles crossing in the westbound direction. In 1990 (per Authority's 1990 annual report, 82), 27.622 million vehicles crossed the bridge in the eastbound direction.

71. Sharon Hoey, "Surprise! Island Residents Spend Most Time Commuting," *Staten Island Advance*, May 17, 1992.

72. Hoey, June 14, 1992.

73. Richard Eisen, "P.A. Will Begin Review of Plan for New Bridge," *Staten Island Advance*, June 11, 1993; Connelly, December 26, 1993.

74. Staten Islanders with cars registered on the island could purchase prepackaged tokens at a discount.

75. Craig Schneider, "Lesson Missed in 1990 Bridge," *Staten Island Advance*, October 16, 1991.

76. U.S. Coast Guard, October 1997, S-3; Eisen, June 11, 1993; Tracey Porpora, "P.A. to Air Its Plan for a Goethals Twin," *Staten Island Advance*, October 5, 1993.

77. U.S. Coast Guard, October 1997, S-8.

78. U.S. Coast Guard, October 1997, S-15–S-18.

79. Eileen A. J. Connelly, "Transit Study to Look at Hudson River Crossing," *Staten Island Advance*, October 4, 1994.

80. Judy L. Randall, "P.A. Memo: Islanders Deserve Better Shake," *Staten Island Advance*, February 19, 1995.

81. Eileen A. J. Connelly, "Goethals Plan Now Includes Railway," *Staten Island Advance*, December 13, 1994.

82. Sharon Reier, *The Bridges of New York* (New York: Dover Publications, 1977), 116. Note that the Authority reduced construction cost by omitting the provision for rapid transit on the Outerbridge Crossing, per the Port Authority's 1928 annual report, 38.

83. Tri-State Transportation Campaign, "Citizens Action Plan," 1993, 29.

84. Tri-State Transportation Campaign, "Molinari Says Port Authority Goethals Plan Would Dump Traffic on S.I.," *Mobilizing the Region*, March 10, 1995; Plotch, *Politics Across the Hudson* (New Brunswick: Rutgers University Press, 2018), 48–61; Eileen A. J. Connelly, "BP Objects to Goethals Twin," *Staten Island Advance*, June 9, 1995.

85. Eileen A. J. Connelly, "Would Goethals 'Twin' Ease Congestion Woes?" *Staten Island Advance*, October 31, 1993.

86. Tri-State Transportation Campaign, "Goethals Project Still 'Evil Twin' for S.I.," *Mobilizing the Region*, October 22, 1999.

87. Tri-State Transportation Campaign, "Port Authority Pounds Pavement to Sell Bridge Twin," *Mobilizing the Region*, August 3, 1995,

88. Tri-State Transportation Campaign, "Congestion Pricing: A Primer," November 1999, www.tstc.org/reports/pricingprimer.pdf

89. Eileen A. J. Connelly, "Bridge Plan Looks Like Evil Twin," *Staten Island Advance*, June 14, 1995.

90. John Marchi, "Remarks by Senator John J. Marchi, Public Hearing—June 13, 1995," in U.S. Coast Guard, "Staten Island Bridges Program, Modernization and Capacity Enhancement Project, Final Environmental Impact Statement/Section 4(f)," October 1997, volume 3, S.14.

91. Susan Molinari, "Testimony: Staten Island Bridges Program, Modernization and Capacity Enhancement Project," in U.S. Coast Guard, October 1997, volume 3, F.13.

92. "Bridging the Gap," editorial, *Staten Island Advance*, June 11, 1995.

93. Howard Golden (Brooklyn Borough president), letter to Rear Admiral J. L. Linnon (U.S. Coast Guard) August 18, 1995; Kenneth Fisher (NYC Council) and Ed Towns (congressman), letter to Gary Kassof (U.S. Coast Guard), July 24, 1995. Letters are both in U.S. Coast Guard, October 1997, volume 3, C8 and F11.

94. New York State Board of Elections, "Vote Cast for Governor and Lieutenant Gov-

Notes to Pages 193–98 339

ernor by Party of Candidates: New York State by County—November 8, 1994," https://www.elections.ny.gov/NYSBOE/elections/1994/gov94.pdf, George Marlin, interview with Plotch, phone, May 30, 2020.

95. Chris Ward (director of Port Authority's Port Commerce Department), letter to editor, *Staten Island Advance*, October 16, 1997.

96. Andy Newman, "Port Authority Is to Consider Bridge Parallel to the Goethals," *New York Times*, January 27, 1998; Rich Cirillo, "Port Authority to OK Funds For Goethals Twin," *Staten Island Advance*, January 27, 1998.

97. "BP Opposed Funding for Bridge," *Staten Island Advance*, January 31, 1998.

98. "BP Opposed Funding for Bridge," January 31, 1998.

99. Peter Rinaldi, interview with Plotch, phone, April 30, 2020; Connelly, "Months of Headaches on Outerbridge?" *Staten Island Advance*, March 12, 1995.

100. Rinaldi, April 30, 2020.

101. Rinaldi, April 30, 2020.

102. Michael Wagner, "Even though the P.A. Has Made it a Top Priority, the Question Remains: To Twin or not to Twin the Goethals Bridge?" *Staten Island Advance*, April 1, 2001.

103. Ken Philmus, "The Port Authority of New York and New Jersey Agency Impacts from 9/11," May 7, 2002, in author's possession.

104. Ken Philmus, interview with Plotch, phone, April 16, 2020.

105. Philmus, May 7, 2002.

106. Seth Solomonow, "Officials Warming to the Idea of Replacing Goethals," *Staten Island Advance*, October 3, 2004.

107. "Bridge Work—The Issue," editorial, *Staten Island Advance*, June 26, 2003.

108. Lou Venech, email to plotch, July 1, 2020.

109. Karen O'Shea, "NASCAR Track Seen as Huge Boon to Island's Economy," *Staten Island Advance*, June 4, 2004.

110. "A Bridge Too Old," editorial, *Staten Island Advance*, October 8, 2004.

111. Hoey, May 17, 1992; Richard Eisen, "1995 Start is Target for Electronic Tolls," *Staten Island Advance*, June 30, 1993.

112. Seth Solomonow, "New Span for Goethals Gaining Steam," *Staten Island Advance*, October 6, 2004.

113. Port Authority's 1985 annual report, 48, and 2003 annual report, 83.

114. "Bridge Work—The Issue," editorial, *Staten Island Advance*, June 26, 2003.

115. Clifford J. Levy, "New York Looks to S. I. Site to Revive Port," *New York Times*, September 27, 1994.

116. Lou Venech, interview with Plotch, phone, April 4, 2020.

117. Rich Cirillo, "Bridges: Bumpy Days Ahead," *Staten Island Advance*, February 26, 1999; John Reel, "CB 3 Panel Discusses Plans for Bridge Repair," *Staten Island Advance*, March 12, 1996.

118. Michael Wagner, "P. A. Funds Study to Decide Fate of Goethals Bridge," *Staten Island Advance*, September 11, 2003.

119. Venech, April 4, 2020.

120. Venech, April 4, 2020.

121. U.S. Coast Guard, "Draft Environmental Impact Statement Pursuant to 42 U.S.C. §4321 et seq. of the National Environmental Policy Act (NEPA) of 1969, as amended: Goethals Bridge Replacement Project," May 2009, Executive Summary, ES-3.

122. New Jersey Department of Transportation, "Route 278, Goethals Bridge Replacement," in "FY 2014–2023 Statewide Transportation Improvement Program," https://www.nj.gov/transportation/capital/stip1423/sec3/routes/rt278.pdf

123. Ronald Smothers, "Port Authority Extends Lease of a Renamed Newark Airport," *New York Times*, August 30, 2002; Jeffrey E. Stoll, "Tax Relief Sought," *New York Times*, October 24, 1976; Colette Santasieri, "Port of Call or Port of Conflict: The Evolution of The Port of New York and New Jersey, Port-City Relationships, and the Potential for Land Use Conflicts on the Newark Bay Waterfront," New Jersey Institute of Technology dissertation, 2012, 253; Christian Bollwage, interview with Plotch, April 17, 2020.

124. Bollwage, April 17, 2020.

125. Joann Papageorgis, interview with Plotch, phone, June 4, 2020.

126. Bill Baroni, interview with Plotch, phone, June 17, 2020.

127. Bollwage, April 17, 2020; Jonathan Jaffe, "Elizabeth Ends Slowdown Aimed to Block Port Deal," *Star-Ledger*, October 15, 1999.

128. Federal Highway Administration, "Project Identification Number (PIN): X77047; Goethals Bridge Replacement: Staten Island, New York And Elizabeth, New Jersey," 6–8, https://old.panynj.gov/bridges-tunnels/pdf/goethals-rod.pdf, available June 21, 2020.

129. Joseph C. Ingraham, "Traffic Jams Due as Jersey Lags," *New York Times*, February 17, 1964.

130. Steve Strunsky, "Port Authority Approves Goethals Bridge 'Link' with Routes 1&9," *Star-Ledger*, July 25, 2013; Port Authority, "Committee on Capital Planning, Execution and Asset Management Meeting Transcripts July 24, 2013," https://corpinfo.panynj.gov/files/uploads/documents/board-meeting-information/board-committee-meeting-presentations/7-24-13_Committee_on_Capital_Planning%2C_Execution_and_Asset_Management_Transcript.pdf

131. Port Authority, "Port Authority Approves 10-Year Capital Plan Outlining Critical Regional Transportation Needs," press release, December 14, 2006; Port Authority, "Port Authority 2007–2016 Capital Plan: Project List," December 14, 2006, 11.

132. Gerald Stoughton (retired Port Authority's director of the Office of Financial Analysis and general manager of Corporate Capital Planning, Management and Budget Department), interviewed by Plotch, April 9, 2020.

133. Steve Strunsky, "Port Authority Asks Private Investors to Finance New Goethals Bridge," *Star-Ledger*, May 12, 2010.

134. Craig Schneider, "Bridge Repair Tab: $750,000," *Staten Island Advance*, December 11, 1991; Stephanie Slepian, "Ship Scrapes Bayonne Bridge," *Staten Island Advance*, October 25, 2003; Craig Schneider, "Ship's Pilot Blamed for Bridge Crash," *Staten Island Advance*, May 12, 1992.

135. Philmus, April 16, 2020.

136. Chris Dupin, "Max Headroom," *JoC Week*, August 26–September 1, 2002, 50; "Bayonne Bridge Too Low for Today's Massive Ships," *Staten Island Advance*, October 19, 2009; Port Authority, U.S. Coast Guard, "Bayonne Bridge Navigational Clearance Program: Final Environmental Assessment," May 2013, 1-5 to 1-6.

Notes to Pages 202–7

137. Stoughton, April 9, 2020.
138. George Marlin, interview with Plotch, phone, May 31, 2020.
139. Tony Shorris, interview with Plotch, phone, January 15, 2021.
140. Brian Davis, Rob Holmes, and Brett Milligan, "Isthmus," *Places*, December 2015, https://placesjournal.org/article/isthmus-panama-canal-expansion
141. U.S. Army Corps of Engineers, "Bayonne Bridge Air Draft Analysis: Prepared for the Port Commerce Department," September 2009, https://www.scribd.com/document/20 3425176/Bayonne-Bridge-Air-Draft-Analysis; Port Authority, "Next Steps to Address Bayonne Bridge Navigational Clearance," c. 2009, https://www.panynj.gov/content/dam/port-authority/about/studies-and-reports-pdfs/Bayonne-bridge-Air-Draft-Analysis-paper.pdf
142. Maura Yates, "Bayonne Bridge Fix Could Cost $2B," *Staten Island Advance*, October 27, 2008; "A Bridge Too Low," editorial, *Staten Island Advance*, June 29, 2008.
143. Papageorgis, June 4, 2020; Baroni, June 17, 2020; Chris Ward, interview with Plotch and Nelles, phone, October 28, 2020.
144. Ward, October 28, 2020.
145. Peter Tirschwell, "Bayonne Bridge Replacement Gains Favor," *Journal of Commerce*, April 23, 2009.
146. The following three web pages from the NationsPort.org's website as of April 24, 2010, are available at Archive.org: "Representative" (www.nationsport.org/reps.html), "Initiatives" (www.nationsport.org/init.html), and "Home" (www.nationsport.org).
147. Timothy Carroll, "Gov Brings His Hammer to the Bayonne Bridge," *Observer*, September 21, 2010.
148. Rob Anthes, "Bridgegate Saga Showed Bill Baroni as We Didn't Know Him," *Community News* (NJ), March 29, 2019, https://communitynews.org/2019/03/29/bridgegate-saga-showed-bill-baroni-as-we-didnt-know-him
149. Baroni, June 17, 2020.
150. Governor Chris Christie, "Governor Chris Christie Appoints Senator Baroni to Port Authority," press release, February 19, 2020.
151. Baroni, June 17, 2020.
152. Baroni, June 17, 2020.
153. Baroni, June 17, 2020.
154. Baroni, June 17, 2020.
155. Papageorgis, June 4, 2020.
156. Baroni, June 17, 2020.
157. Papageorgis, June 4, 2020.
158. NYC DOT, "New York City Bridge Traffic Volumes 2010," May 2012, 11 (2010 round-trip bridge traffic numbers); Frank Lombardi, interview with Plotch and Nelles, phone, November 4, 2020.
159. Papageorgis, June 4, 2020.
160. Papageorgis, June 4, 2020.
161. Papageorgis, June 4, 2020.
162. Baroni, June 17, 2020; Papageorgis, June 4, 2020.
163. Papageorgis, June 4, 2020.
164. Papageorgis, June 4, 2020.
165. Ward, October 28, 2020.

166. Steve Strunsky, "Miraculous Engineering to Heighten the Bayonne," *Staten Island Advance*, January 30, 2011; Neil Genzlinger, "A Bridge Too Low and a Lesson for Visionaries," *New York Times*, July 8, 2011.

167. Russ Buettner, "Port Authority Land Purchase Is Boon to Bayonne, and Christie," *New York Times*, June 8, 2014; Ward, November 13, 2020.

168. John Ambrosio, "2 Bayonne Parks Will Be Moved Due to Bayonne Bridge Raising," *Jersey Journal*, August 12, 2013.

169. Baroni, June 17, 2020; Papageorgis, June 4, 2020.

170. Port Authority, U.S. Coast Guard, "Bayonne Bridge Navigational Clearance Program: Final Environmental Assessment," May 2013, 20–28.

171. Gerald Stoughton and other Port Authority officials looked at bringing in private partners on the Bayonne Bridge. Although private construction firms would build the bridge (as they did all of the Authority's infrastructure), a long-term maintenance contract for the Bayonne was less appealing than the Goethals Bridge. Construction firms would rather enter into long-term contracts on a new bridge that they design and build themselves, rather than a bridge that was originally built in the 1920s. Per Gerald Stoughton (retired Port Authority's director of the Office of Financial Analysis and general manager of Corporate Capital Planning, Management and Budget Department), interviewed by Plotch, phone, April 9, 2020.

172. Strunsky, January 30, 2011.

173. Erik Bascome, "Reaching New Heights," *Staten Island Advance*, July 16, 2018.

174. Susan Lunny Keag, "It Was Thrilling," *Staten Island Advance*, February 21, 2017.

175. Sam Roberts, "High Above the Water, but Awash in Red Tape," *New York Times*, January 2, 2014.

176. The White House, Office of the Press Secretary, "We Can't Wait: Obama Administration Announces 5 Major Port Projects to Be Expedited," July 19, 2012.

177. Baroni, June 17, 2020.

178. "Skanska Breaks Ground on Bayonne Bridge Project," *Real Estate Weekly*, July 3, 2013, https://rew-online.com/skanska-breaks-ground-on-bayonne-bridge-project

179. Steve Strunsky, "Miraculous Engineering To Heighten The Bayonne," *Staten Island Advance*, January 30, 2011 (Baroni said it would cost a little more than $1 billion).

180. Ward, October 28, 2020.

181. CMA CGM Group, "The CMA CGM Theodore Roosevelt to Inaugurate New Bayonne Bridge," August 28, 2017, https://www.cma-cgm.com/local/germany/news/90/the-cma-cgm-theodore-roosevelt-to-inaugurate-new-bayonne-bridge-largest-ship-ever-to-call-at-port-of-new-york-and-new-jersey

182. Steve Strunsky, "Colossal Container Ship to Pass Under Raised Bayonne Bridge," *Star-Ledger*, September 2, 2017.

183. Kathleen Dalton, *Theodore Roosevelt: A Strenuous Life* (New York: Alfred A. Knopf, 2002), 16.

184. Baroni, June 17, 2020.

Chapter 8

1. New York World's Fair, "Your World of Tomorrow," 1939, 3–11.

2. "Dewey Picks Board for Trade Center," *New York Times*, July 7, 1946; James Glanz

and Eric Lipton, *City in the Sky: The Rise and Fall of the World Trade Center* (New York: Macmillan, 2003), 29–30.

3. "Permanent Fair Bill is Signed by Dewey," *New York Times*, April 22, 1946; "Dewey Picks Board for Trade Center," July 7, 1946.

4. Angus K. Gillespie, *Twin Towers: The Life of New York City's World Trade Center* (New York: New American Library, 2001), 32; Glanz and Lipton, 2003, 31.

5. Edward T. Chase, "Lindsay Challenges the PA," *The Reporter*, June 30, 1966, 24, http://www.unz.com/print/Reporter-1966jun30-00023

6. "The Pier Plans Analyzed," *New York Times*, May 3, 1948; Paul Crowell, "City to Consider $270,000,000 Plan for Waterfront," *New York Times*, May 16, 1947; "Program of Promise," *New York Herald Tribune*, May 18, 1947; the corporation initially lost out to the NYC Department of Marine and Aviation per Goodhue Livingston, letter to the editor, "How to Build Trade Center," *New York Herald Tribune*, September 23, 1961; "Trade Group Asks Wind-Up," *New York Times*, January 7, 1949.

7. Aldrich had been chair of Chase National Bank, the predecessor to Chase Manhattan Bank.

8. Abraham Stein describes David Rockefeller's interests and motivations in his PhD dissertation on pages 82 through 88.

9. Port Authority's 1957 annual report, 73, and 1958 annual report, 68.

10. Jameson W. Doig, *Empire on the Hudson: Entrepreneurial Vision and Political Power at the Port of New York Authority* (New York: Columbia University Press, 2001), epilogue; Abraham Stein, 52–53.

11. Stein, 52, 66, 98–99.

12. Port Authority's 1958 annual report, 39–40.

13. Austin Tobin, letter to Governor Nelson Rockefeller, Governor Robert Meyner, Governor Abraham Ribicoff (Connecticut), Mayor Robert F. Wagner, February 10, 1959, 9, folder: "Rail Transit 1959 (including Moses & AJT letter)," Box 24, Empire on the Hudson research files, New Jersey State Archives.

14. Port Authority's 1954 annual report, 13.

15. Stein, 117.

16. "Another Argument for World Trade Center," *New York Herald Tribune*, May 24, 1961.

17. Port Authority's 1960 annual report, 5.

18. Gillespie, 2001, 5.

19. Port Authority's 1958 annual report, 4–6.

20. Port Authority's 1959 annual report, 37–39.

21. Gillespie, 2001, 183; Downtown Lower Manhattan Association, "World Trade Center: A Proposal for the Port of New York," January 27, 1960, downloaded from Anthony W. Robins's website: https://anthonywrobins.com/resources/world-trade-center-2/

22. Tobin's weekly report to the commissioners, February 2, 1960, in Plotch's possession.

23. Austin J. Tobin, memo to Roger Gilman (director of Port Development), "World Trade Center," September 2, 1959, in Folder "WTC 1959, 1960, Empire on the Hudson research files," New Jersey State Archives.

24. Glanz and Lipton, 2003, 33–34.

25. NYC Department of Parks & Recreation, "The Battery," accessed May 24, 2019, https://www.nycgovparks.org/parks/battery-park

26. Downtown Lower Manhattan Association, "World Trade Center: A Proposal for the Port of New York," January 27, 1960, Robins's website.

27. Gillespie, 2001, 183; "355 Million World Trade Center Backed by Port Authority Study," *New York Times*, March 12, 1961.

28. "City as Trade Capital," *New York Times*, May 5, 1960.

29. Glanz and Lipton, 2003, 40.

30. Port of New York Authority, "World Trade Center," press release, January 20, 1964, located in New Jersey State Library.

31. Glanz and Lipton, 2003, 55.

32. "World Trade Center Presentation," internal Port Authority document, October 1973, Plotch's personal possessions (received from Jameson Doig); Gillespie, 2001, 34.

33. Port of New York Authority, "A World Trade Center in the Port of New York: A Report by The Port of New York Authority on the Need for and Feasibility of a World Trade Center in the New York-New Jersey Port District," March 1961, Robins's website.

34. John Molleson, "Moses Backs World Trade Center Plan," *New York Herald Tribune*, January 28, 1960; Tobin's weekly report to the commissioners, February 2, 1960, 7–12, in Plotch's possession.

35. "Wagner Backs World Trade Center Project," *New York Herald Tribune*, March 16, 1961.

36. "The World Trade Center We Must Have," editorial, *New York Herald Tribune*, March 14, 1961; "A World Trade Center," *New York Times*, March 14, 1961.

37. New York-New Jersey Port Authority Compact of 1921, Article XI.

38. Sloan Colt, "The Port of New York and the Challenge of World Trade," speech at World Trade Luncheon, New York, May 18, 1959, 2–3, Box 6, Empire on the Hudson research files, New Jersey State Archives.

39. "H. & M. Fight to Win Riders," *New York Times*, September 29, 1960; Abraham Stein, "The Port Authority of New York and New Jersey and the 1962 PATH-World Trade Center Project," PhD diss. (New York University, Graduate School of Business Administration, 1980); Port Authority, annual report 1964, 22–24.

40. George Cable Wright, "Port Agency Bids on Hudson Tubes," *New York Times*, September 28, 1960; George Cable Wright, "Jersey Senate Votes Full Inquiry on Port Agency Internal Affairs," *New York Times*, September 13, 1960.

41. Wright, September 13, 1960.

42. Sam Pope Brewer, "Port Agency Bars U.S. Investment of Inner Affairs," *New York Times*, June 13, 1960.

43. Port of New York Authority's Port Development Department, Planning Division, "Trans-Hudson Study," July 1959, folder: Rail Transit: 1958–59, Box 10, Empire on the Hudson research files, New Jersey State Archive, 2, 69–70.

44. Walter Hamshar, "Marine, Aviation and Railroads," *New York Herald Tribune*, May 5, 1960.

45. H&M Railroad was bankrupt since 1954 per Port Authority's 1960 annual report.

46. Port Authority indicated it was willing to take over the H&M, per Wright, September 28, 1960.

Notes to Pages 220–23

47. Gillespie, 2001, 38
48. Gillespie, 2001, 38; "Merchants Oppose Plan that State Buy H&M," *Jersey Journal*, August 29, 1961; "Port Agency Bill Fought in Jersey," *New York Times*, March 24, 1961.
49. Glanz and Lipton, 2003, 57; Stein, 77–78.
50. Sandra Van De Walle (Port Authority counsel), interview with Plotch, New York City, May 22, 2019.
51. Glanz and Lipton, 2003, 58.
52. "New Tube Link: Bigger Bite from P.A Demanded by Hughes," *Jersey Journal*, December 26, 1961; "P.A. Eyes Journal Sq. Updating," *Jersey Journal*, December 23, 1961; Richard Hunt, "Port Unit Offers Compromise Plan on Trade Center," *New York Times*, December 23, 1961; Joseph O. Haff, "Jersey City Gets Terminal Plans," *New York Times*, June 26, 1962; Port of New York Authority, 1961 annual report, 1961, 32; Stein, 80, 135.
53. "Hughes Starts," editorial, *Jersey Journal*, December 26, 1961.
54. Gillespie, 2001, 40.
55. Port of New York Authority, "The Hudson and Manhattan World Trade Center Project," 1962, available in New Jersey State Library.
56. Stein, 72–81, 137–40.
57. Russell Porter, "2 Governors Back H.&M. Compromise; Bills on Hudson Tubes and World Trade Center to Go to Legislatures," *New York Times*, February 11, 1962; Layhmond Robinson, "Assembly Votes H.&M. Revamping," *New York Times*, March 7, 1962; for text of law, see New Jersey's Laws of 1962, chapter 8 available at https://babel.hathitrust.org/cgi/pt?id=ucl.b3683797;view=1up;seq=63
58. List of supporters identified in letter from Guy Tozzoli (director of World Trade Department) to William A. Schmidt (General Services Administration), March 15, 1965, and in letter from Austin Tobin to Thomas J. Cuite (City Council), August 10, 1964, Robins's website.
59. RPA referred to its 1961, 1962, and 1966 support in Regional Plan Association, "Regional Plan Calls Trade Center Step Toward Better District," news release, March 30, 1967, Box 9, Empire on the Hudson research files, New Jersey State Archives; "Hearing is Held on Trade Center," *New York Times*, May 3, 1966.
60. Thomas Schiavoni, "The Port of New York Authority's World Trade Center," senior thesis, Princeton University, 1972, 80.
61. John F. Kennedy, "Q & A Following Address at the Economic Club of New York," December 14, 1962, Waldorf Astoria Hotel, New York, American Rhetoric Online Speech Bank, https://www.americanrhetoric.com/speeches/jfkeconomicclubq&a.html
62. Glanz and Lipton, 2003, 89 and 101.
63. Gillespie, 2001, 47.
64. There were thirteen blocks on site, per Chase, June 30, 1966.
65. Glanz and Lipton, 2003, 59.
66. Gillespie, 2001, 46; Anthony W. Robins, *The World Trade Center* (Sarasota, FL: Pineapple Press and Omnigraphics, 1987), 40–41.
67. Bernard Stengren, "Biggest Buildings in World to Rise at Trade Center," *New York Times*, January 19, 1964.
68. Downtown Lower Manhattan Association, January 27, 1960.
69. Chase, June 30, 1966.

70. Port of New York Authority, *Annual Report 1964*, 11.
71. Gillespie, 2001, 76–77.
72. 1964 annual report, 12–13.
73. Port of New York Authority, "World Trade Center in the Port of New York," 1964, Robins's website; "World Trade Center," via Port of New York, January 1964, Robins's website.
74. New York, Department of City Planning (City Planning Commission), "The World Trade Center: An Evaluation," March 1966, New York City Municipal Library.
75. The city council considered a resolution that would have opposed the trade center, per letter from Austin Tobin to Thomas J. Cuite (City Council) on August 10, 1964, Robins's website.
76. Glanz and Lipton, 2003, 62–87; Edith Evans Asbury, "Downtown Merchants Parade to Protest World Trade Center," *New York Times*, July 14, 1962.
77. Gillespie, 2001, 44.
78. Van De Walle, May 22, 2019.
79. "Port's Acquisition of Railroad Voided," *New York Times*, February 20, 1963; Appellate Division of the Supreme Court of New York, First Department Courtesy Sand. Shop v. Port of N.Y. Authority, 17 A.D.2d 590 (N.Y. App. Div. 1963).
80. Paul Crowell, "World Trade Center Here Upheld by Appeals Court," *New York Times*, April 5, 1963; Port of New York Authority's 1962 annual report, 34, and 1963 annual report, 32, 44.
81. Gillespie, 2001, 48; "Hearing is Held on Trade Center," *New York Times*, May 3, 1966; "Port Body Scores Trade Center Foe," *New York Times*, April 27, 1966; Clayton Knowles, "New Fight Begun on Trade Center," *New York Times*, February 14, 1964.
82. Clayton Knowles, "New Fight Begun on Trade Center," *New York Times*, February 14, 1964.
83. Richard Roth (Emory Roth & Sons), Western Union telefax to John B. Oakes (*New York Times* editor), February 14, 1964, Robins's website; Lee Jaffe (Port of New York Authority's director of public relations), press release, February 14, 1964, Robins's website.
84. Robert VanDeventer (executive editor at Port of New York Authority), email to Philip Plotch, April 14 and April 17, 2019.
85. Austin J. Tobin to File April 18, 1966, "Meeting with Deputy Mayor Price and Deputy Commissioner Halberg, re: World Trade Center," folder: PNYA—Materials from John Bunner, Box 9, Empire on the Hudson research files, New Jersey State Archives; "Weekly Report to the Commissioners from the Executive Director," November 28, 1966, folder: "The Port of NY Authority, Weekly Report to the Commissioners, January 1966–November 1966," Box 14, Angus K. Gillespie Papers (R-MC 086), Special Collections and University Archives, Rutgers University Libraries.
86. Austin Tobin, remarks to New York Building Congress, Astor Hotel (New York), September 29, 1965, Warren T. Lindquist papers (FA102), Series 1, 1970, Accession, Box 27, Rockefeller Archive Center, Sleepy Hollow, NY.
87. Committee for Reasonable World Trade Center, "Coming Soon: The New York Ghosts," advertisement, *Daily News*, March 28, 1968, 25.
88. Two documents written by Michael W. Moynihan (Port Authority director of public

affairs) in the file titled "World Trade Center," Box 9, Empire on the Hudson research files, New Jersey State Archives: "Ottinger-Scheuer Meeting with Civic Organizations on World Trade Center," June 5, 1967, and memo to Austin J. Tobin, June 8, 1967, "Congressman Bingham's Views on WTC-TV interference."

89. Charles G. Bennett, "Delay is Sought on Trade Center," *New York Times*, February 9, 1966.

90. Robert Alden, "Business Leaders Press Tax Battle in City Hall Talk," *New York Times*, April 8, 1966; Robert Price (deputy mayor and chair of City of New York Negotiating Committee for the World Trade Center), memo to Tobin May 27, 1966, Box 9, Empire on the Hudson research files, New Jersey State Archives.

91. New York City Department of City Planning (City Planning Commission), "The World Trade Center: An Evaluation," March 1966, available at New York City Municipal Library.

92. "Delay is Sought on Trade Center," *New York Times*, February 9, 1966.

93. Joseph C. Ingraham, "Fee Rise Offered at Trade Center," *New York Times*, April 23, 1966; Gillespie, 2001, 42; Glanz and Lipton, 2003, 59.

94. Glanz and Lipton, 2003, 148; Price, May 27, 1966.

95. New York City Department of City Planning, March 1966, 27, available at New York City Municipal Library on 31 Chambers Street in Manhattan.

96. New York City Department of City Planning, March 1966.

97. Price, May 27, 1966.

98. "Mayor Rebuffed on Trade Center," *New York Times*, July 13, 1966.

99. The following materials are in a folder titled "PNYA—Materials from John Bunner, WTC: PNYA-NYC Detailed Negotiations" in Box 9 of the Empire on the Hudson research files at the New Jersey State Archives: Tobin to File, April 27, 1966, "World Trade Center Vault Permit, Etc."; Tobin to File, "Conversations of June 9 with Mayor Lindsay and Deputy Mayor Price," June 10, 1966; Governor Nelson Rockefeller to John Lindsay, June 21, 1966; S. Sloan Colt to John V Lindsay, June 27, 1966; Austin J. Tobin, Sidney Goldstein, Rosaleen C. Skehan, Richard C. Sullivan, Memorandum to File, "Meeting with Mayor Lindsay and the Mayor's Negotiating Committee on the World Trade Center—June 28, 1966, and Related Discussions—June 29, 1966," July 5, 1966; "Trade Center Pact Backed by Hughes," *New York Times*, August 5, 1966; "Hughes Warns City on Veto of Center," *New York Times*, July 26, 1966.

100. "Trade Center Pact Backed by Hughes," August 5, 1966; "Hughes Warns City on Veto of Center," July 26, 1966.

101. "Hughes Okays PA-N.Y. Pact," *Newark News*, August 9, 1966.

102. "Weekly Report to the Commissioners from the Executive Director," August 8, 1966, folder: "The Port of NY Authority, Weekly Report to the Commissioners, January 1966–November 1966," Box 14, Angus K. Gillespie Papers (R-MC 086), Special Collections and University Archives, Rutgers University Libraries.

103. "Maintaining Port's Supremacy," editorial, *New York Times*, August 4, 1966. Payments in lieu of taxes estimated to be $6,175,000 for the first year of completed occupancy, per 1966 annual report, 9.

104. Gillespie, 2001, 52–53; Glanz and Lipton, 2003, 169–70; George Horne, "City is

Unexcited by Pier Proposal," *New York Times*, July 21, 1966; George Horne, "Port Authority Proposes Modernized Piers for Superliners," *New York Times*, July 20, 1966; Austin Tobin, "Weekly report to the commissioners from the executive director for the week ending August 8, 1966"; Office of the Mayor (John V. Lindsay), press release 309–66, August 3, 1966, Warren T. Lindquist papers.

105. Maurice Carroll, "Port Authority is Urged to Build World Trade Center in Harlem," *New York Times*, May 27, 1966; Will Lissner, "Harlem Studied for State Office," *New York Times*, July 25, 1966; Mccandlish Phillips, "Rockefeller Hails Harlem Building," *New York Times*, October 14, 1966; Paul Hofmann, "State Office Site Picked in Harlem," *New York Times*, December 7, 1966.

106. "TV Mast Offered on Trade Center," *New York Times*, February 24, 1966; "Accord Reached on Trade Center," *New York Times*, February 24, 1966; Lawrence Van Gelderoct, "North Trade Center Tower to Get TV Transmitters," *New York Times*, October 17, 1974; Port Authority 1967 annual report, 13.

107. Chase, June 30, 1966.

108. Glanz and Lipton, 2003, 33–34.

109. Gillespie, 2001, 45–46; "State Will Rent at Trade Center," *New York Times*, January 14, 1964; Terence Smith, "Agreement Near on Trade Center," *New York Times*, August 3, 1966; William J. Ronan, unpublished memoir, World Trade Center chapter, 6–7, William J. Ronan papers, Series 1, Personal Papers, 1945–1988, Box 15, Rockefeller Archive Center, Sleepy Hollow, NY.

110. Damon Stetson, "Building Unions Back Rockefeller as Labor's Friend," *New York Times*, September 21, 1966.

111. Chase, June 30, 1966.

112. Gillespie, 2001, 199; Glanz and Lipton, 2003, 207, 223.

113. Austin Tobin, letter to Roger Starr (executive director of Citizens Housing and Planning Council of New York), March 29, 1965, Robins's website.

114. Port of New York Authority, "Notes for Meeting with Real Estate Committee of the Downtown-Lower Manhattan Association," 17, Box 10, Empire on the Hudson research files, New Jersey State Archives.

115. Steven V. Roberts, "Approval Voted for Trade Center," *New York Times*, June 23, 1967.

116. "The World Trade Center," editorial, *New York Times*, January 20, 1964.

117. "Reviewing the Trade Center," editorial, *New York Times*, April 12, 1967.

118. Gillespie, 2001, 69; ". . . Trade Center Escalation," *New York Times*, December 30, 1966.

119. Total cost was about $1.1 billion, per Port Authority, "Fact Sheet: The World Trade Center in the Port of New York-New Jersey," June 1984, Robins's website.

120. Port Authority 1973 annual report, 39.

121. Tobin was pushed out per Van De Walle, May 22, 2019.

122. Paul Goldberger, *The City Observed: New York: A Guide to the Architecture of Manhattan* (New York: Random House, 1979).

123. Reference to acrophobia in Minoru Yamasaki, letter to Ada Louise Huxtable (*New York Times*), April 10, 1973, page 3, folder: "The Port Authority of New York and New

Jersey, Report to the Commissioners, January-December 1973," Box 14, Angus K. Gillespie Papers (R-MC 086), Special Collections and University Archives, Rutgers University Libraries; John Gallagher, *Yamasaki in Detroit: A Search for Serenity* (Detroit: Wayne State University Press, 2015), 92.

124. Brian Thompson (McKinsey) letter to John Brunner (Port Authority World Trade Department), July 23, 1971, Box 9, file: PNYA—Materials from John Brunner, Box 9, Empire on the Hudson research files, New Jersey State Archives.

125. Gillespie, 2001, 186.

126. Port Authority, "A World Trade Center Management Contract?" internal document, September 20, 1973, Plotch's personal possessions (received from Jameson Doig).

127. Port Authority, "World Trade Center Presentation," internal document. October 1973, Plotch's personal possessions (received from Jameson Doig).

128. Port Authority annual reports.

129. Henry Klingman, letter to Jameson Doig, September 8, 1992, Plotch's personal possessions (received from Jameson Doig).

130. Henry Klingman, letter to Jameson Doig, September 8, 1992, Plotch's personal possessions (received from Jameson Doig).

131. Port Authority, September 20, 1973.

132. Glanz and Lipton, 2003, 223.

133. Glanz and Lipton, 2003, 225, 233.

134. Port Authority's 1978 annual report, 35, and 1983 annual report, 34.

135. Charles V. Bagli, "Trade Center, Once Sneered At, Lures Rich Suitor and $3.2 Billion," *New York Times*, February 23, 2001.

136. Lynne B. Sagalyn, *Power at Ground Zero: Politics, Money, and the Remaking of Lower Manhattan* (New York: Oxford University Press, 2016).

137. Ron Shiftan, interview with Plotch, Rumson, NJ, June 11, 2019.

138. Andy Newman, "Plan to Lease Trade Center Is Near a Vote," *New York Times*, September 24, 1998.

139. Former Port Authority attorney, interview with Plotch, January 13, 2020.

140. Lynne Sagalyn, interview with author, Upper West Side, March 29, 2019; Bagli, February 23, 2001.

141. Charles V. Bagli, "Deal Is Signed to Take Over Trade Center," *New York Times*, April 27, 2001.

142. Port Authority, "Governor Pataki, Acting Governor Difrancesco Laud Historic Port Authority Agreement to Privatize World Trade Center," press release, July 24, 2001.

143. Cherrie Nanninga, interview with Plotch, West 23rd Street, October 21, 2019.

144. Paul Goldberger, *Up From Zero: Politics, Architecture, and the Rebuilding of New York* (New York: Random House, 2005), 86.

145. Port Authority, "PATH Rail History," accessed May 24, 2019, https://www.panynj .gov/about/history-path.html (PATH won top American Public Transportation Association prize for heavy rail system in 1998).

146. Port Authority's 1961 annual report, 31, referred to the annual expected subsidy. Port Authority 2000 annual report, 53, refers to the Authority's cumulative investment into the PATH system. The 1960 annual report, 46, referred to the $83.5 million investment.

147. Port Authority's 1963 annual report, 37, and 2000 annual report, 10.

148. New York, Department of City Planning (City Planning Commission), "The World Trade Center: An Evaluation," March 1966, 48–50, available at New York City Municipal Library.

149. Eric Benson, "Planes, The," *New York Magazine*, August 26, 2011.

150. Ron Shiftan, speech at University of Virginia, October 19, 2002, text in Plotch's personal possession.

151. Senior Port Authority official, interview with Plotch, January 13, 2020.

152. Rachel O'Donoghue, "The Missing Bodies: Why Half of September 11 Victims in Twin Towers Were Never Found," *The Star* (UK), September 11, 2017.

153. "Fighting to Live as the Towers Died," *New York Times*, May 26, 2002.

154. Quentin Brathwaite (Port Authority's Assistant Director for World Trade Center Construction), interview with Plotch, World Trade Center, May 22, 2019.

155. Shiftan, June 11, 2019.

156. Ryan McKaig "News in Brief: Sinagra Named NY-NJ Port Authority Chair," *Bond Buyer*, December 3, 2001; Martin Z. Braun, "New Boss Tapped for N.J. Sports Agency as Port Authority's Eisenberg Stays Put," *Bond Buyer*, October 3, 2001.

157. Neil MacFarquhar, "Port Authority Chief to Leave, After Cutbacks and Criticism," *New York Times*, January 18, 1997: Tim Gilchrist, phone interview with Plotch, May 24, 2019; Doig, 2001, epilogue.

158. Port Authority of New York and New Jersey, "Executive Director's Transition Book: Comprehensive Department Overview," Chief of Staff section, December 2001, Box 90 (Transition Reports—Port Authority of New York and New Jersey), Series: Governor James Edward McGreevey, Office of Policy and Planning Subject Files, 2002–2005, New Jersey State Archives.

159. Sagalyn, 90–91.

160. Note that New York State legislature and New York City council held their own public hearings.

161. Charles Gargano, *From the Ground Up: Rebuilding Ground Zero to Re-engineering America* (New York: Post Hill Press, 2019), 11–12.

162. Rupal Parekh, "Silverstein, Insurers Settle WTC," *Business Insurance*, May 27, 2007, https://www.businessinsurance.com/article/20070527/ISSUE01/100022003/silverstein-insurers-settle-WorldTradeCenter-claims; Sagalyn 107, 580–81, 647, 653.

163. Katia Hetter "Terrorist Attacks/Silverstein Promises to Rebuild Towers," *Newsday*, September 18, 2001.

164. Goldberger, 2005, 64.

165. "Principles and Preliminary Blueprint for the Future of Lower Manhattan" (revised one is on my PC).

166. LMDC press release, April 9, 2002.

167. New York City Department of City Planning, "The World Trade Center: An Evaluation," March 1966, 16; Robins, 1987, 40–41.

168. David W. Dunlap, "Girding Against Return of the Windy City in Manhattan," *New York Times*, March 25, 2004.

169. Robins, 1987.

Notes to Pages 240–47

170. Goldberger, 2005, 95–97.
171. Sagalyn, 89, 194.
172. Port Authority's 2000 annual report.
173. Tom McGeveran, "Port Authority Reasserts Grip on Towers Site," *Observer*, May 6, 2002, https://observer.com/2002/05/port-authority-reasserts-grip-on-towers-site/
174. Edward Wyatt, "Pataki's Surprising Limit on Ground Zero Design," *New York Times*, July 2, 2002.
175. LMDC, "Port Authority and Lower Manhattan Development Corporation Unveil Six Concept Plans for World Trade Center Site, Adjacent Areas and Related Transportation," press release, July 16, 2002.
176. "Port Authority: Flawed By Design," *New York Daily News*, July 20, 2002.
177. Bobby Cuza "Speaking Their Minds," *Newsday*, July 21, 2002.
178. Goldberger, 2005, 104–7.
179. David W. Dunlap, "Officials Favor Larger Site for Trade Center Complex," *New York Times*, July 15, 2003; Sagalyn, 186, 188, 247.
180. Goldberger, 2005, 112.
181. LMDC and Port Authority, "The Public Dialogue: Innovative Design Study," February 27, 2003, 1, accessed January 16, 2020, http://www.renewnyc.com/content/pdfs/public_dialogue_innovative_design.pdf
182. Julie V. Iovine, "Turning a Competition into a Public Campaign; Finalists for Ground Zero Design Pull Out the Stops," *New York Times*, February 26, 2003; Goldberger, 2005, 160.
183. LMDC, "Guiding the Process: The Public Dialogue and Lower Manhattan Revitalization Initiatives," April 2005.
184. Goldberger, 2005, 166–67.
185. LMDC, "The Lower Manhattan Development Corporation and Port Authority of New York & New Jersey Announce Selection of Studio Daniel Libeskind," press release, February 27, 2003; LMDC "Selected Design for the World Trade Center Site as of February 2003," http://www.renewnyc.com/plan_des_dev/wtc_site/new_design_plans/selected_design.asp. Note that the original South Tower was 1,362 feet tall, and the North Tower was 1,368.
186. Alex Frangos, "Property Report: Uncertainties Soar at Ground Zero," *Wall Street Journal*, October 20, 2004.
187. Scott Raab, "The Truth About the World Trade Center," *Esquire*, September 2012.
188. Edward Wyatt, "Pataki Offers a Timetable for Downtown," *New York Times*, April 25, 2003.
189. National September 11 Memorial & Museum, "Chairman Michael R. Bloomberg," accessed May 24, 2019, https://www.911memorial.org/chairman-michael-r-bloomberg
190. "Westfield America, Inc. Closes on Deal for Retail Component of World Trade Center," PR Newswire, July 24, 2001.
191. Goldberger, 2005, 86.
192. The World Trade Center does have some parking for building tenants.
193. Judith Dupre, *One World Trade Center: Biography of the Building* (New York: Little Brown, 2016), 109.

194. Deborah Sontag, "The Hole in the City's Heart," *New York Times*, September 11, 2006.
195. Alex Frangos, "The Property Report: Costs, Tensions Rise at World Trade Center," *Wall Street Journal*, May 11, 2005.
196. Sagalyn, 169–73.
197. Rupal Parekh, "Silverstein, Insurers Settle WTC," *Business Insurance*, May 27, 2007, https://www.businessinsurance.com/article/20070527/ISSUE01/100022003/silverstein-insurers-settle-WorldTradeCenter-claims
198. Sagalyn, 408–15, 441–52.
199. "Wanted: Leadership at Ground Zero," editorial, *New York Daily News*, March 31, 2006.
200. Charles V. Bagli, "Political Chiefs Iron Out Plans for 9/11 Site," *New York Times*, April 6, 2006.
201. Sagalyn, 405–73; Charles V. Bagli "Unified Financial Plan Is Presented for Ground Zero," *New York Times*, April 20, 2006; LMDC, "Governor Pataki, Governor Corzine and Mayor Bloomberg Announce World Trade Center Site Global Realignment Agreements and New Milestones," press release, September 21, 2006.
202. Shannon Harrington, "Green light Expected for Transit Hub," *The Record* (NJ), July 28, 2005.
203. Port Authority, minutes of Board meeting, July 28, 2005, 308; Tony Shorris, memo to Eliot Spitzer, Paul Francis, Tim Gilchrist, and Avi Schick, March 7, 2008, in Plotch's possession.
204. David W. Dunlap, "How Cost of Train Station at World Trade Center Swelled to $4 Billion," *New York Times*, December 2, 2014.
205. Port Authority, October 2, 2008; LMDC, "Scenario 1—FTA/LMDC Cost Contributions—$750M FTA and $130M LMDC," internal memo, January 14, 2005, Plotch's personal possession; Port Authority official, interview with Philip Plotch, New York, 2019.
206. New York State Board of Elections, "2002 Election Results," accessed May 24, 2019, https://www.elections.ny.gov/2002ElectionResults.html
207. Dunlap, December 2, 2014.
208. Alan Riding, "His Signature Is Bold: Architect, Artist, Engineer," *New York Times*, December 31, 2000.
209. Andrew Rice, "The Folly of Santiago Calatrava's WTC Station," *New York Magazine*, March 12, 2015; Sontag, September 11, 2006; Herbert Muschamp, "Filling a Creative Void at Ground Zero," *New York Times*, August 1, 2003.
210. Sontag, September 11, 2006.
211. Cathleen McGuican, "Calatrava Takes Flight," *Newsweek*, February 23, 2004.
212. Nicolai Ouroussoff, "Architecture Review; A Hub of Hope and Memory," *Los Angeles Times*, January 24, 2004.
213. Sontag, September 11, 2006.
214. Sagalyn, 50; David W. Dunlap, "Approval Expected Today for Trade Center Rail Hub," *New York Times*, July 28, 2005.
215. Rice, March 12, 2015; Dunlap, December 2, 2014.
216. Frank Lombardi, interview with Plotch and Nelles, phone, November 4, 2020.
217. Tony Shorris, interview with Plotch and Nelles, phone, January 11, 2021.

Notes to Pages 252–56

218. Tony Shorris, interview with Plotch and Nelles, phone, January 11 and 15, 2021.
219. Tony Shorris, memo to Eliot Spitzer, Paul Francis, Tim Gilchrist, and Avi Schick, March 7, 2008, in Plotch's possession.
220. Shorris, March 7, 2008.
221. Shiftan, interview with Plotch, Rumson, NJ, June 11, 2019.
222. Tim Gilchrist, phone interview with Plotch, May 24, 2019.
223. Shorris, January 11 and 15, 2021.
224. Shorris, March 7, 2008.
225. Gilchrist, May 24, 2019.
226. Gilchrist, May 24, 2019.
227. Chris Ward, interview with Plotch and Nelles, phone, November 13, 2020.
228. Eliot Brown, "Paterson Officially Launches Review of Trade Center Timetable," *Observer*, June 11, 2008.
229. Chris Ward, interview with Plotch, phone, January 26, 2021.
230. Chris Ward, letter to Governor David Paterson, June 30, 2008; Port Authority, "World Trade Center Report: A Roadmap Forward," October 2, 2008.
231. Sagalyn, 549.
232. Federal Transit Administration (FTA) Lower Manhattan Recovery Office, "Permanent World Trade Center, Port Authority Trans-Hudson Terminal Project, LMRO Monthly Report: March 2007."
233. Ward, November 13, 2020.
234. Sagalyn, 544.
235. Rice, March 12, 2015.
236. Larry Higgs, Bob Jordan, Dustin Racioppi, and Michael Symons, "Press Investigation: Inside the Port Authority's Money Machine," *Asbury Park Press*, April 7, 2014.
237. Materials in response to a Freedom of Information Law request sent by Daniel Duffy (Port Authority) to Charles Bagli (*New York Times*), https://corpinfo.panynj.gov/files/upl oads/documents/freedom-of-information/foi-fulfilled-requests/14507-O.pdf, available on April 15, 2019; Rice, March 12, 2015.
238. Lombardi, November 4, 2020.
239. Anonymous, phone interview with Plotch; Sagalyn, 556–57.
240. Ward, November 13, 2020.
241. "Port Authority Workers Move Into Four World Trade Center," *NBC New York*, October 27, 2014, https://www.nbcnewyork.com/news/local/Four-World-Trade-Center-Opens-Port-Authority-Lower-Manhattan-280526692.html
242. Quentin Brathwaite, interview with Plotch, World Trade Center, May 22, 2019; Shiftan, June 11, 2019.
243. The Council on Tall Buildings and Urban Habitat declared in 2013 that the spire on top of One World Trade Center should be considered when measuring the height of the building.
244. Jonathan O'Connell, "The Lower Manhattan Revival, Now Featuring One World Trade Center," *Washington Post*, October 31, 2014.
245. Office of the State Comptroller, "The Transformation of Lower Manhattan's Economy," Report 4–2017, September 2016, 1–2, https://www.osc.state.ny.us/osdc/rpt4-2017 .pdf

246. Roof broadcasting per NAB Pilot, "Broadcasting Returns to Lower Manhattan," accessed May 19, 2019, nabpilot.org/broadcasting-returns-to-lower-manhattan

247. Ivan Pereira, "Oculus, World Trade Center PATH Hub, to Make Long-Awaited Debut," *AM New York*, March 1, 2016; note that the Port Authority did hold an event in the Oculus in May to celebrate the people who worked on the site, including the first responders, per Christopher Maag, "Port Authority Leaders Hold Ceremony to Dedicate World Trade Center Oculus," *The Record* (Hackensack, NJ), May 26, 2016.

248. "They Cleaned Our Clock," editorial, *Daily News*, March 4, 2016; Dana Rubinstein, "Port Authority Declines to Celebrate Calatrava-Designed Transportation Hub," *Politico*, February 22, 2016, www.politico.com/states/new-york/albany/story/2016/02/port-authority-declines-to-celebrate-calatrava-designed-transportation-hub-031488; Sean Carlson, "Port Authority Chief Declines WTC Hub Ribbon Cutting, Citing Project's Costs," *WNYC*, February 22, 2016, www.wnyc.org/story/port-authority-chief-declines-wtc-hub-ribbon-cutting-citing-projects-costs

249. Michael Kimmelman, "A Soaring Symbol of a Boondoggle," *New York Times*, March 3, 2016.

250. Tony Coscia, interview with Plotch and Nelles, phone, October 20, 2020.

251. Ward, October 28, 2020.

252. Alison Bowen, "WTC Head Chris Ward Admits Success and Failure, Too," *Metro*, August 31, 2011.

Chapter 9

1. Roosevelt's address at the dedication of the George Washington Bridge, per "Science: Biggest Bridge," *Time*, November 2, 1931.

2. James B. Stewart, "From (Crumbling) Airport to (Broken) Escalators," *New York Times*, February 8, 2018; "Port Authority Is So Bad, It's a National Joke," editorial, *Star Ledger*, June 11, 2018.

3. Regional Plan Association, "Restructure the Port Authority to Function as a Regional Infrastructure Bank," November 2017.

4. Seth Barron, "Why the Port Authority Is an Unmanageable Mess," *New York Post*, January 24, 2016.

5. Jameson W. Doig, *Empire on the Hudson: Entrepreneurial Vision and Political Power at the Port of New York Authority* (New York: Columbia University Press, 2001), 66.

6. "An Accountable Port Authority," *New York Times*, November 5, 2006.

7. Stephen J. Smith, "It's Time to Kill the Port Authority of New York and New Jersey," *Next City*, January 15, 2014; Rick Cotton and Kevin O'Toole, "The Port Authority Needs a Rescue," op-ed, *New York Daily News*, June 11, 2020.

8. Mike Vilensky and Andrew Tangel, "Cuomo Wants More Control over Port Authority, State Agencies," *Wall Street Journal*, December 22, 2016.

9. Philip Rocco and Chloe Thurston, "From Metaphors to Measures: Observable Indicators of Gradual Institutional Change," *Journal of Public Policy* 34, no. 1 (April 2014): 35–62.

10. Doig, 2001, 49.

11. Doig, 2001, 58

12. "Joint Resolution Granting Consent of Congress to an Agreement or Compact Entered into Between the State of New York and the State of New Jersey for the Creation of the Port of New York District and the Establishment of the Port of New York Authority for the Comprehensive Development of the Port of New York," 67th Congress," Sixty-Seventh Congress (1921), Sess. I. Ch. 77, https://tile.loc.gov/storage-services/service/ll/llsl//llsl-c67/llsl-c67.pdf, 174, available September 10, 2021.

13. Doig, 2001, 49.

14. U.S. Constitution, Article I, Section 10, Clause 3.

15. Interestingly, the clause itself is phrased as a limitation on state autonomy to enter into interstate agreements but it also enables approval by Congress. Doig (2001, 50) notes that Cohen very creatively perceived the potential positive uses of the clause to create an enduring interstate agency. See for more detail on the clause and its use in interstate compacts: "Congress and the Port of New York Authority: Federal Supervision of Interstate Compacts," *Yale Law Journal* 70, no. 5 (1961): 812–20; Emanuel Celler, "Congress, Compacts, and Interstate Authorities," *Law and Contemporary Problems* 26, no. 4 (1961): 682–702.

16. Other contemporary uses of the Compact Clause revolved around the regional use of water resources. The Colorado River Compact (1922) was the first of many interstate agreements to manage river basins and watersheds using this model.

17. Frederick L. Zimmermann and Mitchell Wendell, *The Interstate Compact Since 1925* (Chicago: The Council of State Governments, 1951).

18. Doig, 2001, 50–51.

19. "Joint Resolution Granting Consent of Congress," 1921.

20. See Doig, 2001, 52 and 424 fn13.

21. Louis Gambaccini, "The Port Authority of New York and New Jersey," in *Public Enterprise: Studies in Organisational Structure, edited by V. V. Ramanadham, 131–63* (New York: Routledge, 1986).

22. Julius Henry Cohen, letter to editor, *New York Times*, March 9, 1947.

23. Doig, 2001, 150.

24. "New Jersey Defies Protest on Bridge," *New York Times*, March 27, 1927.

25. Doig, 2001, 149.

26. Doig, 2001, 472, fn14.

27. Doig, 2001, 186–87.

28. Doig, 2001, 337.

29. Tony Shorris, interview with Plotch and Nelles, phone, January 11, 2021.

30. "Restore Integrity at the Port Authority," op-ed, *New York Times*, February 20, 2012.

31. While there have been predictable money generators (bridges, tunnels, airports) and losers (PATH), some assets have flipped from one to the other column of the ledger. The Port Authority Bus Terminal was previously profitable and became a loser in the 1980s. The World Trade Center was originally unprofitable only to become successful later on. The ports have generally operated at a slight loss or slight surplus, never tipping the balance too drastically in any one direction.

32. Navigant, "Report to the Special Committee of the Board of Commissioners of the Port Authority of New York and New Jersey," September 2021.

33. See Steve Strunsky, "How Much Did Gov. Chris Christie Know About the Port Authority's Proposed Toll Hikes?," *Star Ledger*, August 9, 2011, for allegations that Governor Christie was aware of toll increases and had planned to put pressure on the agency to roll it back to appear tough and effective (a reduced fare was approved shortly thereafter) and to initiate an audit into the agency's finances to prove that it was inefficiently run.

34. Dana Rubinstein, "Port Authority Officials Answer Questions on a Christie-Cuomo Audit, But Say Little," *Politico*, February 9, 2012.

35. Port Authority's 1945 annual report, letter from commissioners to governor in preface.

36. Doig, 2001, 260.

37. Jameson W. Doig, "Fixing the Port Authority," *Newsday*, February 2, 2014.

38. Richard Roper and Linda Bentz, "Politics Running Roughshod over the Port Authority of NY/NJ," *Star Ledger*, March 15, 2012.

39. Former senior Port Authority official, interview with Plotch, phone, January 13, 2020.

40. Charles H. Heying, "Civic Elites and Corporate Delocalization: An Alternative Explanation for Declining Civic Engagement," *American Behavioral Scientist* 40, no. 5 (1997): 657–68.

41. Paul Berger, "N.J. to Honor Outgoing Port Authority Commissioner Who Clashed with Cuomo," *Wall Street Journal*, June 20, 2017.

42. Lipper was not the only target of Cuomo's ire. New Jersey appointed chairman John Degnan had also frequently been in his crosshairs and subject of a public spat over the Port Authority Bus Terminal (among other topics). See Dana Rubinstein, "With Christie Mia, Cuomo Goes into Attack Mode at the Port Authority," *Politico*, November 29, 2016.

43. Ryan Hutchins, "Cuomo Pushes Again for New Powers at Port Authority," *Politico*, January 23, 2017.

44. Jameson W. Doig and Mary Durfee, "Cross-Border Hostilities and Regional Planning in the United States and Canada," *Journal of Planning History* 18, no. 4 (November 2019): 239–57.

45. Melissa Klein, "Gov. Andrew Cuomo Slow to Name New Members of NY State Boards," *New York Post*, May 8, 2021.

46. Kate Zernike, "The Bridge Scandal, Explained," *New York Times*, May 1, 2015.

47. *Kelly v. United States*, 140 S. Ct. 1565, 206 L. Ed. 2d 882 (2020).

48. *Kelly v. United States*, 140 S. Ct. 1565, 206 L. Ed. 2d 882 (2020).

49. Shawn Boburg, Abbott Koloff, and Stephanie Akin, "New GWB Files, Same Callous Jokes," *The Record*, February 27, 2014.

50. *Kelly v. United States*, 140 S. Ct. 1565, 206 L. Ed. 2d 882 (2020).

51. Kate Zernike and Marc Santora, "2 Indicted in George Washington Bridge Case," *New York Times*, May 1, 2015.

52. Katherine Landergan, "Former Christie Aide Bridget Anne Kelly, Known for Role in Bridgegate, Running for Office," *Politico*, January 25, 2021.

53. Doig and Durfee, November 2019, 252.

54. Kate Zernike and Noah Remnick, "Port Authority Chief Testifies Christie Ally Pressured Him to Reclose Lanes to Bridge," *New York Times*, September 21, 2016.

Notes to Pages 277–85   357

55. Doig, 2001, 2–3.
56. Stephen Eide, "Let's Break Up the Port Authority," *City Journal*, Summer 2016.
57. Doig, 2001, 23 (emphasis added).
58. The Special Panel on the Future of the Port Authority, "Keeping the Region Moving," December 26, 2014.
59. Jesse McKinley, "Cuomo and Christie, Defying Legislatures, Reject Bill to Overhaul Port Authority," *New York Times*, December 27, 2014; A3417/S2181 in New Jersey and A3944C/ S7721 in New York, https://www.njleg.state.nj.us/bills/BillView.asp
60. "Christie, Cuomo Reject Far-Reaching Port Authority Reform Bill, Support Smaller Changes," *Star-Ledger*, December 28, 2014; Loretta Weinberg (New Jersey senator), interview with Plotch, Teaneck (NJ), December 12, 2019; Bob Gordon, interview with Plotch, Fair Lawn (NJ), November 25, 2019.
61. "Senate, No. 708; State of New Jersey, 217th Legislature," 2016, https://www.njleg.state.nj.us/2016/Bills/S1000/708_I1.htm; Salvador Rizzo, "Christie Vetoes Bills Including Port Authority Reforms," *The Record*, May 23, 2016.
62. These involve reforms to make more board meetings public and publicize agendas, facilitate public comment processes, revamp the ethics code, and revise the agency freedom of information policy. See Port Authority, "Port Authority Board Continues Reform Initiatives to Enhance Transparency and Governance Practices," press release, October 22, 2014.

Chapter 10

1. Populations per 2020 census (Pittsburgh: 302,971, New Orleans: 383,997, Detroit: 639,111). The number of PATH passengers on July 24, 2019, was 311,317, the number of airport passengers in 2019 was 140.5 million, and the number of eastbound vehicles on its six crossings was 122.2 million, per Port Authority, "Port Authority Airports and Road and Rail Network Report Record Passenger and Cargo Volumes for 2019," press release, February 3, 2020. The number of westbound vehicles on the crossings is assumed to be the same as the number of eastbound vehicles.
2. Charles R. Holcomb, "State Salaries Are Not Small," *Ithaca Journal*, February 4, 1970.
3. John Fruin, interview with Plotch, phone, March 27, 2020.
4. Sandra Van De Walle, interview with Plotch, Manhattan, May 22, 2019; Jacques Steinberg, "Port Authority Cuts Back on Free-Spending Ways," *New York Times*, February 4, 1992.
5. Port Authority's 1959 annual report, 21, 1969 annual report, 41, 1968 annual report, 41; Fruin, March 27, 2020.
6. Tony Coscia, interview with Plotch and Nelles, phone, October 20, 2020.
7. Traffic volumes (in thousands) per Port Authority annual reports: 1950 (59,525), 1959 (94,974), 1960 (96,207), 1969 (143,617), 1999 (123,611 eastbound), 2019 (122,228 eastbound).
8. Edward T. Chase, "How to Rescue New York from Its Port Authority," *Harper's Magazine*, June 1, 1960.
9. The project to refurbish rail tunnels between New York and New Jersey, known as

the Access to the Region's Core (or ARC) tunnel, was canceled by New Jersey governor Chris Christie in October 2010. The project was revived partly due to the Port Authority's advocacy and leadership in convening regional stakeholders and has been reimagined as the Gateway Program spearheaded by Amtrak.

10. Revenues from both tolls and fares was $1.07 billion in 2010 and $1.15 billion in 2011 per Port Authority's 2011 annual report, schedule D-1.

11. Mark Muriello (former deputy director of the Port Authority's Tunnel Bridges & Terminals Department), interview with Plotch, January 14 and 18, 2020.

12. Leon Goodman, interview with Plotch, phone, August 7, 2019.

13. Goodman, August 7, 2019.

14. Goodman, August 7, 2019.

15. Port Authority, "Exclusive Bus Lane," https://www.panynj.gov/bridges-tunnels/en/lincoln-tunnel/xbl.html, available May 21, 2021; Port Authority, "Lincoln Tunnel Exclusive Bus Lane Enhancement Study," newsletter, March 2005; Mark Muriello, "The Lincoln Tunnel Exclusive Bus Lane: The Nation's Most Productive Managed Lane," in FHWA, "12th International HOV Systems Conference: Improving Mobility and Accessibility with Managed Lanes, Pricing, and BRT Conference Proceedings," February 2, 2017, https://ops.fhwa.dot.gov/publications/12hovsysconf/breakout7.htm

16. Lillian Borrone, interview, Nelles, phone, November 30, 2020.

17. Rick Larabee, interview, Jen Nelles, phone, November 6, 2020.

18. Interviews with Plotch (on phone unless noted): Anne Strauss-Wieder (May 13, 2020), David Gallagher (July 6, 2020), Alice Herman (August 6, 2019), Deborah Wathen Finn (June 29, 2020), Gerald Stoughton (April 9, 2020), Jeff Green (January 13, 2020), Ken Philmus (April 16, 2020), Richard Kelly (West Caldwell, NJ, August 12, 2019), Martin Robins (March 17, 2020), Larry Lennon (New York, October 16, 2019).

19. Peter Goldmark, interview with Plotch and Tristan Tindall, New York, October 16, 2019.

20. Goldmark, October 16, 2019.

21. Port Authority's 1978 annual report, 4; Port Authority, "Regional Recovery: The Business of the Eighties," 1982; U.S. Department of Transportation, "Transportation and Urban Economic Development," June 1982, 98–113.

22. Goldmark, October 16, 2019.

23. Public Authorities Information Clearinghouse of the Government Law Center (Albany Law School), "Welcome," www.publicauthority.org, available July 6, 2021.

24. James M. Smith, "Special-Purpose Authorities," in *The Wiley Blackwell Encyclopedia of Urban and Regional Studies* (2019), 1–4.

25. United States Government Accountability Office (GAO), "Interstate Compacts: Transparency and Oversight of Bi-State Tolling Authorities Could Be Enhanced," GAO-13-687, August 2013.

26. Thomas P. DiNapoli (NYS comptroller), "Public Authorities by the Numbers," January 2017.

27. David Miller et al., *Discovering American Regionalism: An Introduction to Regional Intergovernmental Organizations* (New York: Routledge, 2018); David Miller and Jen Nelles, "Order Out of Chaos: The Case for a New Conceptualization of the Cross-Boundary Instruments of American Regionalism," *Urban Affairs Review* 56, no. 1 (2020): 325–59; Jay

Rickabaugh, "Regional Public Sector Organizations: A Broader Taxonomic Classification to Cross-Pollinate Empirical Research," *Public Administration* (August 6, 2021).

28. Mark Tewdwr-Jones and Daniel Galland, "Planning Metropolitan Futures, the Future of Metropolitan Planning: In What Sense Planning Agile?," in *Metropolitan Regions, Planning and Governance*, edited by K. Zimmermann, D. Galland, and J. Harrison, 225–34 (Cham, Switzerland: Springer International, 2020), 231.

29. David K. Hamilton, *Governing Metropolitan Areas: Growth and Change in a Networked Age*, 2nd ed. (New York: Routledge, 2014), 249.

30. Robert C. Wood, *1400 Governments: The Political Economy of the New York Metropolitan Region* (Cambridge, MA: Harvard University Press, 1961), 1.

31. John V. Lindsay, "A Modern Transportation System for New York City," campaign white paper, 1965, 1–2.

32. U.S. GAO, August 2013; Fitch Ratings, "Fitch Downgrades Port Authority of NY & NJ's Bonds to 'A+'; Removed from Negative Watch," January 19. 2021, https://www.fitchratings.com/research/infrastructure-project-finance/fitch-downgrades-port-authority-of-ny-nj-bonds-to-a-removed-from-negative-watch-19-01-2021

33. Port Authority's 1921 annual report, 20.

34. Council On Environmental Quality (Executive Office of The President), Environmental Impact Statement Timelines (2010–2018), June 12, 2020, https://ceq.doe.gov/docs/nepa-practice/CEQ_EIS_Timeline_Report_2020-6-12.pdf

35. Per the 2020 U.S. Census, 24.95 percent of Americans live in these metropolitan areas.

36. Mark Perry (American Enterprise Institute), "Understanding America's Enormous $20.6T Economy by Comparing US Metro Area GDPs to Entire Countries," December 18, 2019.

37. "Texts of Addresses of Officials at the Formal Opening of the Lincoln Tunnel" and "Lincoln Tunnel Is Opened with Festive Ceremonies," *New York Times*, December 22, 1937.

38. Port Authority's 1965 annual report, 51, and 1960 annual report, 27.

39. Lanes consisting entirely of passenger vehicles with good weather and ideal roadway geometry have higher than 2,000 per hour capacity levels, per Federal Highway Administration, "Traffic Data Computation Method Pocket Guide," August 2018, 15. The exclusive bus lane operates approximately four hours on weekdays and averages more than 18.5 million passengers a year, per Port Authority of New York, "Exclusive Bus Lane," https://www.panynj.gov/bridges-tunnels/en/lincoln-tunnel/xbl.html, available August 17, 2021.

40. "City Begins Moving Bus Site Families," *New York Times*, November 20, 1948.

41. Port Authority's 1952 annual report, 36.

42. Port Authority's 1950 annual report, 102.

43. Port Authority's 1952 annual report, 34.

44. Port Authority, "Port Authority Unveils New Plan for Bus Terminal Replacement," press release, January 21, 2021.

45. Patrick McGeehan and Winnie Hu, "Notorious Port Authority Bus Terminal May Get a $10 Billion Overhaul," *New York Times*, January 21, 2021

46. John Oliver, "New York's Port Authority: Last Week Tonight with John Oliver (HBO)," https://www.youtube.com/watch?v=44fCfJQV7yQ, August 4, 2014.

47. Patrick McGeehan, "Governors Compromise on Port Authority Plan," *New York Times*, December 8, 2016.

48. WSP/Parsons Brinckerhoff, "Trans-Hudson Commuting Capacity Study: Summary Report," prepared for the Port Authority, September 2016, 4; WSP/Parsons Brinckerhoff, "Trans-Hudson Commuting Capacity Study, Appendix A (Interstate Bus Network—Operational and Service Strategies—Lincoln Tunnel Corridor/PABT Facility Strategies)," September 2016, 21; Muriello, January 14 and 18, 2020.

49. Rawan Eewshah, "17 Reasons Why Port Authority Is Literally Hell on Earth," *BuzzFeed*, November 10, 2015.

50. $8.8 billion was allocated to renew and maintain assets over ten years, per Port Authority, "Capital Plan: 2017–2026," February 16, 2017. The Authority's 2021· operating budget allocated $3.3 billion for operating expenses and $1.6 billion for debt service, per Port Authority, "Port Authority Releases Proposed 2021 Operating and Capital Budgets for Public Review and Comment," press release, November 19, 2020.

51. Joseph C. Ingraham, "Port Authority Car Tolls Cut 20% for Buyers of 25 Rides," *New York Times*, June 15, 1951.

52. Muriello, January 14 and 18, 2020.

53. "Texts of Addresses of Officials at the Formal Opening of the Lincoln Tunnel" and "Lincoln Tunnel Is Opened with Festive Ceremonies," *New York Times*, December 22, 1937.

54. Port Authority's 1949 annual report, 4.

55. Port Authority's 1984 annual report, 5.

INDEX

Note: Page numbers in *italics* indicate maps and figures. Numbers followed by n refer to endnotes.

Access to the Region's Core (ARC) tunnel, 285–86, 357–58n9
Air France, 216
air traffic control, 66–68
airports, 10–11, 24, *25*, 217; capacity problems, 49–54, 66–73, 77–80, 280, 300; fees and rents, 68, 146, 304–5; flight delays, 68, 70–71, *71*; green-field, 72; improvements, 50–51, 148, 297; national alliance, 68; opposition to, 58–63; Orange County opportunity, 69–77; passenger estimates, 53, 66; privatization, 70–75, 153; proposed sites, 54–65, *62*, 71–75; revenues, 50–51; runways, 66. *See also specific facilities by name*
AirTrains, 147, 295
Albion, Robert, 83
Aldrich, Winthrop, 214
Alitalia, 216
American Airlines, 161, 164, 216
American Public Transportation Association, 115, 134
American Society of Civil Engineers, 209
Ammann, Othmar, 48; Bayonne Bridge work, 180, 208; George Washington Bridge work, 10, 16, 19–20, 43–44, 266

Amtrak, 118, 357–58n9
Arthur Kill, 174, *175*
Asian trade, 97–98, *99*, 99–100
Astor, John Jacob III, 57
Atlantic City Expressway, 138
automobiles. *See* motor vehicles
autonomous vehicles, 306
autonomy: of board members and executives, 50, 141, 167, 211–12, 252–53, 288–89; erosion of, 29, 46, 142, 161–62, 172, 193, 211–12, 252, 261–62, 266–71, 285–88; financial, 7, 51, 264, 269–71; institutionalization of, 262–65; organizational, 16–18, 42–43, 46–48, 294–96, 305; political, 7, 46, 263

Baltimore, Maryland port, 160–61, 164
Banana Docks, 92
Bankers Trust Company, 57
barges, 153
Barnett, Michael, 18
Baroni, Bill, 200, 204–8, 212, 275–76
Bathgate (Bronx, New York), 25
Battery Park City, New York, 122–23, *221*, 229, 232, 235
Batz, Tom, 128–29

361

Bayonne, New Jersey, 81–82, 207
Bayonne Bridge, 24, *25*, *211*; clearance and elevation, 23, 173, 180, 201–12, *209*, *210*, 298; construction, 180, 342n171; construction timeline, *38*, 42, 114; design, 191–92, 208; location, 173, *175*, *184*; opposition to, 180; planning, 177; replacement costs, 205; ridership, 183, 191–92, 205; toll revenues, 202
Bea, Paul, 123, 128, 149, 157, 167, 172
Bell Labs, 58
Berger, Stephen, 122, 132–33
Betts, Roland, 242
Biden, Joe, 208
Bingham, John, 227
Bloomberg, Michael, 239, 243, 247–48, 257
Boeing, 66, 77
Bollwage, Chris, 199–200
bonds, 178, 200–201, 263–64, 304; covenants, 216; ratings, 296; tax-exempt, 49, 68, 247
Borrone, Lillian: interstate conflict, 157–59; leadership, 76, 102–4, 111, 150–51, 167, 273, 288, 297, 322n46; port operations, 76, 99–105, 111, 150–51, 157–59, 164, 297; vision and perseverance, 297
Boyle, Robert, 154–55, 158–62, 168–70, 193
brain drain, 151, 171–72, 238
Brazil: trade offices, 53
Brezenoff, Stanley, 148, 151–52, 191
Bridgegate, 2–3, 23–24, 212, 275–77, 285
bridges, 24, *25*; interstate compacts, 291; privatization, 201; Staten Island, 173–98, *175*, 201–12; tolls, 178, 191; traffic volumes, 270–71; upgrading, 187. *See also specific bridges by name*
Brooklyn, New York, *32*, 82, 88, 95, 170, 235
Brooklyn–Queens Expressway, 337n57
Bruckner Expressway, 337n57
Burnham, Daniel, 216
bus lanes, 286–87, *287*, 301, *302*, 359n39
bus services, 197, 271, 300, 306
bus stations, 24, 53, 155, 216–17. *See also* George Washington Bridge Bus Station; Midtown Manhattan Bus Terminal
Bush, George W., 242, 256–57
business community, 29–30, 42; transit service tax benefits, 130–33, *134*, 134–35; World Trade Center tenants, 230–34, 255–56
Business Week, 268
Buzzfeed, 304
Byrne, Brendan, 118, 154–56, 165–68, 289

Caggiano, Frank, 105
Cahill, William, 64–65
Calatrava, Santiago, 250–58, *258*
Canada, 105, 299
capacity problems, 7–13; at airports, 49–54, 66–73, 77–80, 280, 300; innovations for squeezing more capacity out of bridges and tunnels, 300–301, *301*; planning for additional capacity, 196–97; ways to expand capacity, 120–21, 187
capital improvements, 107–8; dredging, 100–104; ExpressRail, 104–7
Carey, Hugh, 69–70, 165–66, 272
carpooling, 197
Celler, Emanuel, 60
Chase, Edward T., 284
Chase Manhattan Bank, 214–15, 233
Chelsea Piers sports complex, 95
Chicago, Illinois: trade offices, 53, 217
Christie, Chris: ARC tunnel work, 285–86; Bayonne Bridge elevation, 204–9, *209*, 212; Bridgegate, 2–3, 23–24, 212, 275–77; Port Authority appointments, 274–77
Ciano, Peter, 189
Citizens Housing and Planning Council, 221–22
Citizens Union, 221–22
Civic Alliance to Rebuild Downtown New York, 239, 242
civil engineering, 209
Clark, Patty, 75, 79
Clearview Expressway, *184*
Cleveland, Ohio: trade offices, 53, 217

Index

climate change, 306
coalitions and coalition-building, 7–20, 280–81, 286, 292–94
Cohen, Julius Henry, 7, 29, 31–37, 42, 48, 262–65
Colorado River Compact, 355n16
Colt, S. Sloan, 219
Commerce and Industry Association of New York City, 218
communication networks, 107–11, 113
competition: architectural, 242–43; between cities, 298; global, 81–84, 96–107; interstate conflict, 146–48, 154–71, 234, 252, 262–63, 280, 307; between Lower and Midtown Manhattan, 215; between ports, 81–84, 96–107, 159–65, 170–71, 208, 216; between private automobiles and public transportation, 190, 215–16; for real estate, 224–27; regional, 159–65, 170–71, 208, 263, 298; World Trade Center redevelopment battle, 239–43
Comprehensive Plan, 19, 43–44, 87–88
computer problems, 109–11
congestion pricing, 192–97
congestion problems, 140–42; early management efforts, 86–88, *87*; at the ports, 86–88, *87*, 109; Staten Island bridges, 185, 187, 196–97, *197*; Staten Island Expressway, 190; at the tunnels, 119
Conrail, 105
conservation, 63
container shipping, 91–96, *94*, *106*, *107*, 203, *211*; benefits of, 297; channels for, 100–104, 159, 202; competition between ports, 81–84, 96–107, 159–60, 170–71; routes, 209–10
Continental Airlines, 161, 164
Coopers & Lybrand, 233
Coroedmus, Steve, 102
Corzine, Jon, 247–48
Coscia, Anthony (Tony), 71–74, 247–49, 259, 284
Council on Port Performance, 110–11, 113

COVID-19 pandemic, 77, 107, 110–11, 113
Cracchiolo, Anthony, 250
creativity, 14–15
credibility, 196
Cross-Bronx Expressway, 187, 275
Cullman, Howard S., 82
culture: of innovation, 216, 288; of mentoring and professional development, 290; organizational, 18–19, 42, 115–17, 140–43, 150, 161–62, 172, 211, 216, 233, 238, 272–77, 285–91, 296–97; of patronage, 260, 276–77; and World Trade Center, 233
Cuomo, Andrew, 274
Cuomo, Mario, 144, 156, 163–65, 356n42
customer service, 116–20

Daily News, 147, 242, 247
DeCota, Bill, 70–73, 75
Degnan, John, 356n42
Delaware: New Jersey compact, 291
delivery drones, 306
DelliBovi, Alfred, 133
Deloitte & Touche, 149
Denver International Airport, 71–72
Depression years, 267–68
Devine, James, 159
Dewey, Thomas E., 11, 214
Dodge, Geraldine Rockefeller, 61
Dodge, Marcellus Hartley, 61
Doig, Jameson, 9, 28–29, 39, 261–63, 266–69, 272, 277–78
Donovan, Kathy, 153
Douglas DC-6, 66
Downtown Alliance, 239
Downtown-Lower Manhattan Association, 214–18
dredging, 100–104, 157, 170–71; disposal sites, 101–3, 157; funding, 158; ongoing efforts, 202
Dufree, Mary, 274
Dulles Airport, 54
Dyer, George R., 41

E-ZPass, 135–41, 290–91, 306, 327n102; development of, 22; Interagency Group, 138–40; logo color, 139; public support for, 196
economic analysis, 76, 151–53, 157
economic development initiatives, 289–90
Edelman, Matt, 118, 128, 140–41
Eide, Stephen, 278
Eisenberg, Lewis (Lew), 148, 160–62, 238
Eisenhower, Dwight D., 54, 61, 182
elected officials. *See* politics
electric vehicles, 306
electronic tolls, 115; E-ZPass system, 22, 135–41, 290–91, 306, 327n102; privacy concerns, 139
Elizabeth, New Jersey, *175*, 176, 296; container shipping, *106*, *107*; docks, 81–82; industrial parks, 25; Marine Terminal, 25, *106*, 157, 170–71, 199–200, 217, 235, 300; Port Elizabeth, 12, 94–95, 199; support for Goethals Bridge replacement, 199–200
Empire State Building, 217
England: trade offices, 53, 217
entrepreneurial leadership, 20, 50, 288–90
Environmental Defense Fund, 102
environmental impact statements, 190–93, 198–99, 208, 297–98
environmental issues, 57, 61–63, 185–86; climate change, 306; Great Swamp National Wildlife Refuge, 64, *65*; Great Swamp Wilderness Act, 64; green-field airports, 72
Erie, Steven, 83
Essex County, New Jersey, 69
ethical behavior, 279
executive dining, 132, 150–52, 282
expertise, 254–55; brain drain, 151, 171–72, 238; deference to, 29; demonstration of, 42; development of, 50, 171–72, 190, 282–83; technical, 15–16, 181
ExpressRail, 105–7

fare cards, 141
fares, 304–5; PATH system, 121, 147–48, 162, 165–71, 234, 270–71, 284, 305

Farley Post Office, 161, 170
Federal Aviation Administration, 64, 153
federal funding, 128, 133, 184, 254
fellowships, 282
Ferguson, Frank, 267–68
ferry services: commuter ferries, 121; early services, 86–87, *87*, 140–41; between Manhattan and Staten Island, 191; revival, 120–23; ridership, 121; support for, 135–36, 215, 290
Filler, Larry, 130–32, 135, 141
Finn, Deborah Wathen, 125
Finnemore, Martha, 18
Florio, Jim, 156
forecasting, 76, 153
Fort Lee, New Jersey, 275–76
Foye, Pat, 257–58, 275, 277
Freedom Tower (One World Trade Center), 243, 248, *248*
freight operations: dockside cargo handling, 104–7; Manhattan piers, 91–96, *92*. *See also* container shipping
freight rates, 31
Frelinghuysen, Peter, Jr., 58, 60–61, 63
Frelinghuysen, Rodney, 208
Frigand, Sidney, 151
funding: accusations of misuse, 146–48, 154–56; for dredging, 158; federal, 128, 133, 184, 254; financial autonomy, 7, 51, 264, 269–71; financial resources, 15–17, 181, 254, 269–71; for roadways, 184
future directions, 298–307

Gallagher, David, 289
Galland, Daniel, 292
Galvin, John, 267
Gambaccini, Lou, 22; as architect of adaptation, 115–17; commitment to improving transportation, 141; ferry services, 120–23, 135–36; focus on coordination, 117–20; gospel according to, 120; leadership, 290, 297, 307; legacy, 115–16, 123, 136–38, 140–41; TRANSCOM work, 123–30, 136; Trans-Hudson Task Force

Index

work, 120, 130, 186–88; TransitCenter work, 132–36; vision, 125–26, 129–30; Washington, DC contacts, 133
Garden State Parkway, 124
Gargano, Charles, 155–56, 160–62, 165–66, 170, 238
Gateway Program, 357–58n9
geography, 30–34
George, Rose, 81
George Washington Bridge, 24, *25*, 180, *186*, 187; Bridgegate, 2–3, 23–24, 212; construction, 2, 9–10, 43–46, *45*, 264; construction costs, 180; construction timeline, *38*, 39, 42, 114; design, 16, 19, 43–44, 183, 191–92; emergency closures, 124; expansion, 114, 211, 216–17; lanes of traffic, 114, 297; legacy, 45–46; location, 173; lower level, 57, 183–85, *184*, *186*, 211, 300; opening, 30, 45; revenues, 264, 281; ridership, 181–85, 191–92; support for, 15, 20; traffic management, 129, 275–76; upper level, *184*, 185, *186*
George Washington Bridge Bus Station, 24, 135
Gilchrist, Tim, 72, 74
Gillespie, Angus Kress, 39–41
Gilman, Roger, 182–85
Giuliani, Rudy, 144–48, 154–55, 196, 285
Glendening, Parris, 160
global shipping, 81–84, 96–107
Goethals, George, 41, 176, 210
Goethals Bridge, 24, *25*, *181*, *201*; construction, 177, *179*, 281; construction timeline, *38*, 42, 114, 180; expansion efforts, 188–94; life expectancy, 202; location, 173, *175*, *184*; name, 176; planning, 176; public opinion about, 189–98; rehabilitation, 194–95; replacement, 23, 72, 173, 194–201, *201*, 203, 211–12, 298, 300, 304; safety issues, 196–97, *197*, 199; tolls, 137, 190, 201–2, 305; traffic volume, 201, 205
Goldberger, Paul, 231–32
Goldmark, Peter, 154, 165–68, 233–34, 289–90, 296, 304, 307

good neighbor policy, 207
Goodman, Leon, 286–88
Google: Eighth Avenue headquarters (New York City, NY), 1, 2
Gore, Al, 103
governance: gubernatorial veto power, 10, 44–46, 62, 153–54, 166, 218–19, 229, 239, 265–73, 278–79; lessons for, 290–98. *See also* leadership; politics
Gowanus Expressway, 337n57
Gowanus Grain Terminal, 88–91
Grand Central Parkway, 337n57
Grand Central Terminal, *221*
Great Depression, 27, 47
Great Swamp (New Jersey): airport initiative, 54–65, 219
Great Swamp National Wildlife Refuge, 64, *65*
Great Swamp Wilderness Act, 64
Green, Mark, 147
gubernatorial privilege, 277
gubernatorial veto power, 10, 44–46, 153–54, 166, 265–73, 278–79; and Great Swamp airport, 62; and World Trade Center, 218–19, 229, 239

Hague, Frank, 267
Haley, John, 145, 149–51, 156, 273
Halifax, Canada port, 102, 160
Hamilton, David, 292
Harbor Estuary Program (HEP), 103, 323n65
Harlem state office building (New York City, NY), 229–30, 235
Harrison, Edmond, 76–77
Hedden, Walter, 49–51
helicopters, 152, 282, *283*
heliports, 53, 284
Hell Gate Bridge, 43
Henderson, Henry, 145
Herald-News, 185
Herald Tribune, 185, 218
Herman, Alice, 149
High Line, 82

high-occupancy-vehicle (HOV) lanes, 197, 306
highways: elevated, 226; innovations, 300–301; interstate, 182–84, 216; regional, 182, 184; smarter, 306
Hoboken, New Jersey: ferry service, 86–87, 87, 122–23; location, *221*, 299; population, 55; revitalization, 235
Holland, Clifford, 41
Holland Tunnel, 24, 180; construction, 27, 30, 37–43, 176, 264; construction timeline, *38*; design, 41; location, *25*, *184*; opening, *40*; revenues, 42, 264, 281, 336n38; traffic management, 47, 119, 140–41; traffic volume, 181–82
HOV (high-occupancy-vehicle) lanes, 197
Howland Hook, 25, 197
Hudson & Manhattan Railroad (H&M Railroad): acquisition of, 61, 116–17, 155–56, 219–20, *223*, 235, 272; railroad line, *221*; tunnels into Penn Station, 311n13
Hudson River, *25*, 30, *221*; crossings, 181–82, 264; Little Island, 95, *96*; piers, *34*; traffic along, 5, 6
Hudson River Park, 95
Hudson Tubes. *See* Hudson & Manhattan Railroad (H&M Railroad)
Hughes, Charles E., 178
Hughes, Richard, 63–64, 220–21, 228–29
Hurricane Sandy, 108, 111, 113, 123
Hylan, John, 36

I-80 (Bergen-Passaic Expressway), 183, *184*
I-95 Corridor Coalition, 129
I-278, 188
Ideal X, 94, *94*
Idlewild Airport, 50–52. *See also* John F. Kennedy Airport
Illinois State Toll Highway Authority, 290
Imperatore, Arthur, 123
industrial parks, 25, 148, 289–90
information management: coordination of, 16, 117–20; "The Manhattan Traveler" map, 135, *136*; TRANSCOM (Transportation Operations Coordinating Committee), 126–30, *127*, 135–41, 186–87, 290, 301
information sharing, 282, 287
innovation, 29, 50, 209, 216, 288, 300–301, *301*
intermodal transportation, 104–7
Internal Revenue Service (IRS), 130
Interstate Commerce Commission (ICC), 31
interstate cooperation, 157–59, 165–71, 262–64, 280, 307; conflict over World Trade Center redevelopment, 234, 252
interstate highways, 182–84, 216
intraregional competition, 159–65, 170–71, 208, 263, 298
investigation, 279

Jaffe, Lee, 51, 222–23
Jersey City, New Jersey, *221*, 235; Journal Square, 220–21; railroad yards, 31, *32*, 35
Jersey Jetport Site Association (JJSA), 58–63
John F. Kennedy Airport, 6, 10–11, 24, 50; acreage, 55; AirTrains, 295; flight delays, 70–71, *71*; improvement efforts, 11, 78, 161, 164; International Arrivals Building, 153; location, *25*, *62*, 69; noise impacts, 166; parking garage, 73; privatization, 153
Johnson, Lyndon, 64
Journal Square, *25*

Kean, Thomas, 126, 146, 156, 165–66
Keeping the Region Moving report, 279
Kelly, Bridget Anne, 275–76
Kelly, Richard, 149–50, 191
Kelly, Robert, 118, 126–27, 137, 141
Kennedy, John F., 222
Kentucky Public Transportation Infrastructure Authority, 291
Kiley, Bob, 132–33
Kill Van Kull, 174, *175*, 202
Kimmelman, Michael, 257–58
Klingman, Henry, 233

Index

KLM-Royal Dutch Airlines, 216
Koch, Ed, 133
Kosciuszko Bridge, 337n57

labor unions, 153
LaGuardia Airport, 10–11, 24, 50–52, *52*; acreage, 55; improvement efforts, 78, 298; location, *25*, *62*, *69*
landfill, 55
Larrabee, Rick, 108, 202, 288
Larson, Morgan, 267
Lautenberg, Frank, 128, 168
law enforcement, 103, 123–30
leadership, 24, 42, 271–74; early, 29; entrepreneurial, 20, 42, 48–50, 288–90; global, 288; lessons learned, 297–98; political appointments, 143–45, 151, 160, 167, 171, 267–69, 273–77, 282, 286; training and preparation for, 282, 304–7; vision and perseverance of, 297–98. *See also specific leaders by name*
Lehman, Herbert, 300, 307
Lehman Brothers, 167
Leone, Richard, 144–45, 169
Levin, Neil, 236
Levinson, Mark, 91
Levy, Gus, 167
Libeskind, Daniel, 243
library, 153, 282
light rail, 207
Lincoln Tunnel, 24; construction, 27–30, 46–48, 57, 268; construction timeline, *38*, 114; electronic toll collection, 136–37; Exclusive Bus Lane, 286–87, *287*, *301*, *302*, 359n39; expansion, 284; improvements, 300, *301*; location, *25*, *184*; opening, *47*, 300; traffic management, 47, 140–41; traffic volume, 181–82
Lindenthal, Gustav, 43
Lindsay, John, 227–29, 293
Lipper, Kenneth, 273–74
Little Island, 95, *96*
lobbying, 123, 128, 133, 157–58, 167, 204

Lombardi, Frank, 171–72, 205, 251, 255, 287–88
London, England: trade offices, 217
Long Island, 31, 215
Long Island Daily Press, 185
Long Island Rail Road (LIRR), 118
longshoremen, 111, 163–64
Longshoremen's Association, 163
Los Angeles, California: port operations, 97
Los Angeles Times, 250
Lower Manhattan, 187; competition with Midtown Manhattan, 215; Downtown-Lower Manhattan Association, 214–18; going around, 181–86, *184*; piers, *32*; population, 256; redevelopment after September 11, 2001 attacks, 238–39; subway stations, 238–39
Lower Manhattan Development Corporation (LMDC), 238–41
loyalists, 151, 154, 159–66, 193, 238–39
Lufthansa, 216

Maersk, 105, 158–64, 168, 171
Maher, Brian, 102, 164
Maher Terminals, 105, 109–11
Maine Turnpike Authority, 290
maintenance costs, 270–71
Manhattan, *33*; Banana Docks, *91*; dock operations, 88, *91*, 91–96, *92*; ferry services, 191; as geographic obstacle, 31; going around Lower and Midtown Manhattan, 181–86, *184*; Lower Manhattan, *32*, 187, 215, 238–39, 256; Midtown, 187, 215; piers and terminals, *34*, 95, 235; population, 256; recreational venues, 95, *96*; subway stations, 238–39; Upper East Side, 215
"The Manhattan Traveler" map, 135, *136*
Marchi, John, 193
marine terminals, 25, *25*, 53, 164, 320n13. *See also* ports; *specific facilities by name*
marketing alliances, 100

Marlin, George: appointment to Port Authority, 145, 160, 169, 273, 287–88; campaign for mayor of New York City, 144; Goethals Bridge work, 202; personality, 154; staff reductions, 148–54, 171–72, 287–88; TRANSCOM work, 129
Maryland Transportation Authority, 290
mass transit. *See* transit services
Maxwell School of Citizenship and Public Affairs (Syracuse University), 116
McGraw, Donald C., Jr., 57
McKinsey & Company, 217
McLean Trucking, 93–94, 112
media relations, 42, 181, 184–85; interstate conflict, 146–48, 154–56; news leaks, 56–57; for World Trade Center project, 226. *See also* public relations
megaprojects, 216
Menendez, Robert, 208
mentoring, 290
Metropolitan Transportation Authority (MTA), 130–32, 141, 191; airports, 69, 74; World Trade Center redevelopment, 247, 250. *See also* New York City Subway
Meyner, Robert, 55, 57, 62–63, 219
Midtown Manhattan, 187, 215; going around, 181–86, *184*
Midtown Manhattan Bus Terminal, 24, 53, 284, 302–4; air rights, 155, 164, 170; bus ramps, 302, *302*; bus services, 6, 271; construction, 297; expansion, 216–17; location, *25*; profitability, 355n31
Miller, Nathan, 320n16
Milton, John, 267
Minneapolis Metropolitan Council, 292
Mirones, Matthew, 196
Molinari, Guy V., 192, 194
Molinari, Susan, 193
Molinaro, James, 195
Moore, A. Harry, 266–67
Moore, William H. II, 57
Morris County, New Jersey: opposition to airports in, 58–63, 78; population growth, 55; proposed Great Swamp airport, 54–65
Moses, Robert, 11, 51, 63, 183, 226, 278
MOTHER (Manhattan Operating Trans-Hudson Electric Railway). *See* PATH
motor vehicle facilities, 174; bridges, 24, 25, 37–38, *38*, 173–89, *175*, 207; capacity constraints, 121; crossings, 24, *25*, 37–38, *38*, 87–88, 114, 119–21, 180–82, 264; early projects, 37–38, *38*; going around Lower and Midtown Manhattan, 181–86, *184*; parking facilities, 246; revenues, 39. *See also* roadways; *specific facilities by name*
motor vehicles, 190, 215–16; congestion problems, 86–88, *87*, 140–42, 185, 187, 190, 196–97, *197*; vs public transportation, 190, 215–16; volume of, 37, 174, 284
Moynihan, Daniel Patrick, 168
Mroz, Richard, 166, 169
mud dump, 101

The Narrows, 174, *175*, 183
NASCAR, 196
National Express Group, 70, 72
National September 11 Memorial & Museum, 247; construction, 243, *249*; dedication, 256–57, *257*; location, *245*
NationsPort, 204
Neptune Orient Lines, 99–100
networks: political, 153–54; professional, 131–33, 138, 282; social, 107–13; transportation, 155–56
New Deal, 47
New Jersey: compacts, 291; confidence in the Port Authority, 19; conflict with New York, 146–48, 154–65, 167–71, 234, 252, 262–63, 280, 307; container facilities, 83–84, 160; Department of Transportation, 118; drinking age, 199; elected officials, 144; Garden State Parkway, 124; gubernatorial veto power, 239, 265–67; Morris County, 55; port congestion problems, 86–87, *87*; proposed Great Swamp airport site, 54–65, *62*; proposed

Index

Pine Barrens airport site, 62, 63; Staten Island bridges, 173, *175*, 176–90, 202, 210–12; Whitman administration, 170
New Jersey Chamber of Commerce, 157, 163, 204
New Jersey Harbor, 82
New Jersey Interstate Bridge and Tunnel Commission, 37–38, *38*, *40*
New Jersey Transit, 118, 131, 140–41, 191
New Jersey Turnpike, 124, 126, 138, 275
New York Chamber of Commerce, 31, 42
New York City, New York, 188; 111 Eighth Avenue, 1, 2, *283*; airports, 51–53; Department of Marine and Aviation, 88–89; elected officials, 144; employment levels, 119; ferry services, 191; as gateway for world commerce, 49–50; Harlem state office building, 229–30, 235; marine terminals, 91–96; motor vehicles, 37; population, 4, 55, 119; rise of, 4–7; World Fair, 213–14. *See also* Manhattan
New York City Subway, 223–24; extension, 183; fares, 147, 171; improvements, 135; Lower Manhattan stations, 238–39; No. 1 line, 250
New York City Transit Authority, 118. *See also* Metropolitan Transportation Authority (MTA); New York City Subway
New York Harbor, *32*; dredging, 101, 157–58; economic benefits, 82; Harbor Estuary Program, 103
New York Herald Tribune, 56, 175
New York magazine, 147
New York Post, 260
New York Shipping Association (NYSA), 82, 108–9, 158
New York State: conflict with New Jersey, 146–48, 154–65, 167–71, 234, 252, 262–63, 280, 307; Department of Transportation, 69–70; drinking age, 199; elected officials, 144; interstate highways, 188; Orange County, 69; Pataki administration, 170; public authorities, 180–81, 291
New York State Bridge and Tunnel Commission, 37–38, *38*
New York State Thruway, 138
New York State Thruway Authority, 17, 139
New York Stock Exchange, 162
New York Times, 52, 56, 71, 95, 137, 147, 218, 226, 231, 250, 257–58, 261, 264; description of the Port Authority Bus Terminal, 303
New York Waterways, 123
New York Yankees, 284–85
Newark, New Jersey: Central Planning Board, 89; Marine Terminal, 53, 81–82, 157, 170–71, 199, 217, 235, 300; population, 55; truck terminal, 284
Newark Bay, 103
Newark Evening News, 56
Newark Legal & Communications Center, 25, 153–54
Newark Liberty International Airport, 10–12, 24, 50–53; AirTrain, 147, 295; improvement efforts, 78, 89, 161, 164; location, 25, 62, 69; runways, 66; terminals, 147
Newark News, 267
Newark Sunday News, 57
news leaks, 56–57
NIMBY (Not in My Back Yard), 56, 58
noise buffers, 63, 68–69
noise impacts, 65, 74, 166
North American Wildlife Foundation, 61
North Carolina Turnpike Authority, 291
North Jersey Transportation Planning Authority, 82
North River, 311n13
North River Bridge Company, 43
Northeast Corridor Commuter Rail Agencies Committee, 118
Norwegian Airlines, 76–77
NYNJ Link, 201

Obama, Barack, 208, 256–57
ocean dumping, 101–3, 157

O'Dwyer, William, 52–53, 89
Oliver, John, 303
One World Trade Center (Freedom Tower), 243, 248, *248*, 255–56, *256*
O'Neill, Hugh, 163
Oram, Richard, 133–34
Orange County, New York: airport opportunity, 69–77
Ouroussoff, Nicolai, 250
Outerbridge, Eugenius, 176
Outerbridge Crossing, 24, *25*; construction, 177, *178*; construction timeline, *38*, 42, 114, 180; location, 173, *175*, *184*; name, 176; planning, 176; revenues, 336n38; ridership, 205
Outstanding Civil Engineering Achievement Award (ASCE), 209

pagers, 127
Pan American World Airways, 54
Panama Canal, 203, 208, 288
Papageorgis, Joann, 205–7
Parker, Marygrace, 125–26, 129
parking benefits, 134–35
parking facilities, 246
parking fees, 304–5
parking subsidies, 130
parks, 95
Pataki, George: bid for Port Authority break up, 154–56; bid to revamp resource allocation, 159–71; Port Authority appointments, 144–45; privatization of Stewart Airport, 70, 72; Staten Island projects, 101, 193; subsidies for cargo barges, 153–54; World Trade Center work, 234, 238–43, 247–51
Paterson, David, 253–54
Paterson News, 185
PATH (Port Authority Trans-Hudson) system, 118–19; capacity problems, 120–21; control center, 125; creation, 116–17, 155–56, 223, 311n13; fares, 121, 147–48, 162, 165–71, 234, 305; financing, 191; improvements, 299; magnetic fare cards, 141; name, 222; operating expenses, 121, 146–47, 235, 284; passenger volume, 120, 235, 271, 280, 357n1; signal system, 121; stations, 25, *25*, 236, 299; subsidies, 146–47, 155, 234–35, 270; train lengths, 121; train line, *25*; TransitCheks, 141; Transportation Hub, 3, 249–52, 255, 285, 305
patronage, 172, 260, 267–69, 274–77, 286
Penn Station, 161, 170, *221*, 311n13
Pennsylvania: New Jersey compact, 291
Pennsylvania Turnpike, 138
Penrose, Edith, 14
perseverance, 297–98
personal protective equipment (PPE), 111
Perth Amboy, New Jersey, *175*, 176
Philmus, Ken, 129, 194–98, 202
Pine Barrens (New Jersey): proposed airport site, *62*, 63
Pine Island, 316n118
Pittsburgh, Pennsylvania: trade offices, 53, 217
policy analysis, 151–53, 157
political accountability, 278–79
politics, 28–29, 142; appointments, 143–44, 151, 160, 167, 171, 267–69, 273–77, 282, 286; of balancing state benefits, 271–74; Bridgegate, 2–3, 23–24, 212, 275–77, 285; early incursions, 265–69; elected officials, 144; election campaigns, 144–45; former governors, 165–69, 267; independence from, 29, 42, 260–79; interstate conflict, 146–48, 154–71, 234; loyalists, 275–77; opposition to World Trade Center, 226–27; patronage, 172, 267–69, 274–77, 286; political networks, 153–54
pollution, 103
Port Authority bus terminal. *See* Midtown Manhattan Bus Terminal
Port Authority of New York and New Jersey (Port Authority, also known as Port of New York Authority): administration, 153; airport operations, 49–80, *71*, 153; assets, 1; Aviation Department, 54–55,

Index

71–72; balancing state benefits, 271–74; Board of Commissioners, 24, 26, 36, 146, 149, 161–69, 211, 254–55, 263–74, 295; bonds, 178, 200–201, 216, 263, 296, 304; budget cuts, 284; budget deficits, 148; bus operations, 24, 53; capacity, 7–20; capital budget, 169, 200, 360n50; capital expenditures, 146–47, 304; centennial, 2, 141; challenges, 2–3, 36; civil engineering awards, 209; coalitions, 7–20; Committee of the Future, 289–90; communications department, 284; Comprehensive Plan, 19, 43–44, 87–88, 262; copycats, 3; development bank, 165, 169, 171; E-Z-Pass, 22, 135–41, 290–91, 306, 327n102; early political incursions, 265–69; early successes, 27–28, 37–48, 38; economic analyses, 152–53; economic development initiatives, 289–90; Eighth Avenue headquarters (New York City, NY), 1, 2, 283; engineering department, 171–72, 287–88; environmental impact statements, 190–93; establishment, 27–28; evolution, 87–88, 165–69, 172; executive dining room, 152, 282; executive director, 271–74, 282, 289; executives, 143–45, 160, 172, 254, 271–74; expertise, skills, and technological mastery, 15–16, 42, 50–51, 282–83; fellowship program, 282; ferry services, 120–23, 140–41; financial resources, 15–17, 181, 254, 269–71; first port acquisition, 88–91; founding, 34–37; free lunches, 132; future directions, 298–307; good neighbor policy, 207; government affairs office, 151; headquarters, 232–33; helicopters, 152, 283; heliport operations, 53; income streams, 281; as infrastructure agency, 84–96; initiatives, 6–7; internal resources, 14; investigation of, 279; leadership, 20, 24, 42, 48–50, 69, 115–17, 145, 167, 171, 267–68, 271–74, 304–7; legacy, 278; library, 153, 282; lobbying, 123, 167; major facilities, 24–25, 25; maritime mandate, 85–86; marketing alliances, 100; media relations, 184–85; mission, 87–88, 161–62, 280–81; as model public authority, 180; Office of Economic and Policy Analysis, 151–53, 157; office spaces, 232–33; operating budget, 168–69, 360n50; operating expenses, 149, 215, 304; organization structure, 26, 26; organizational autonomy (*see* autonomy); organizational culture (*see* culture); original mission, 37; original proposed plans, 37; origins, 4–7; planning department, 283–84; police force, 146; port department, 288; port operations, 53, 81–96, 158–59; preparation for the future, 304–7; priorities, 174; profitability, 270–71; project approvals, 72; public relations, 51, 56–59, 156, 169, 181, 184–85, 189–98, 224–26, 284; public support for, 180; ratification, 261–63; real estate taxes, 227; reform attempts, 279; regional partnerships, 114–42; regional significance, 2; reputation, 284; research department, 152–53, 156, 282; resources, 14–16, 29, 42, 181, 238, 281–85; revenues, 171, 200–201, 215, 281, 304–5, 358n10; road operations, 116, 188; salaries, 282, 284; speakers bureau, 284; staff and employees, 26; staff appointments, 143–44, 151, 160, 167, 171, 267–69, 273–77, 282, 286; staff reductions, 148–54, 267–68; Staten Island bridges, 173, 175, 176–90, 202, 210–12; tenants, 232–33; trade promotion offices, 53, 152, 217; training programs, 284; TRANSCOM operations center, 127, 127; transformation, 144; TransitCenter offices, 132–35; truck terminals, 53; veto power, 7, 263; work environment, 282; workforce, 236–38, 284, 287–88, 296–97. *See also specific facilities, projects, and officials*
Port Compact, 7, 35–36, 263, 265
Port Elizabeth, New Jersey, 12, 94–95, 199
Port Newark, New Jersey, 12, 25, 25, 89–93, 94, 159

Port of Baltimore (Maryland), 160–61, 164
Port of Halifax (Canada), 102, 160
Port of London Authority, 35
Port of New York, 4–7, 6, 36, 53
Port of New York and New Jersey: capital improvements, 100–108; competitiveness, 81–84, 96–107; Council on Port Performance, 110–11, 113; economic benefits, 82–83; information portal, 110; networks, 107–11; resilience, 107–11; shipping channels, 100–104; traffic, 298
Port of Shanghai (China), 288
Portland Metropolitan Council, 292
ports, 11–13, 112–13; advocacy for, 204; competition between, 81–84, 96–107, 159–65, 170–71, 208, 216; congestion problems, 86–88, 87, 109; construction, 297; dockside cargo handling, 104–7; early management efforts, 86–88, 87; leases and fees, 159–64, 170, 199; Manhattan operations, 91, 91–96, 92; Port Authority operations, 53, 84–96, 158–59, 355n31; regional economic impact, 157. *See also specific facilities by name*
Portsmouth, Virginia, 171
potato travels, Mrs. Jones', 86–88, 87
Premo, Jerry, 117
prestige, 196
Price, Robert, 227–28
prioritization, 174, 289, 295, 305–6
private automobiles. *See* motor vehicles
private sector. *See* business community
privatization, 161, 164, 170–72; of airports, 70–75, 153, 295; of bridges, 201; lessons for, 295; resistance to, 233; of transit services, 155–56; of World Trade Center, 161, 164, 170, 233–34
professional development, 150, 171–72, 282–83, 290
professional networks, 131–33, 138, 282, 287–88
profitability, 155–56
Progressive Era, 7, 18, 28–30
propaganda, 58–59, 226

public authorities, 180–81; lessons for, 290–97. *See also specific authorities by name*
public opinion, 146–48, 189–98
public-private partnerships, 201
public relations, 51, 184–85, 284; for Goethals Bridge replacement work, 198; for Great Swamp airport efforts, 56–59; interstate conflict, 146–48, 156; news leaks, 56–57; for World Trade Center, 224–27
public service, 172, 264
public transportation. *See* transit services
Public Works Administration, 47
Puerto Rico: trade offices, 53, 217
Pulaski Skyway, 336n38

quality-of-life issues, 196
Queens County, New York, 69, 215

radio frequency identification (RFID) tags, 22, 110, 136–40
Radio Row, 224–26, 225
rail services, 174, 219–20; capacity constraints, 121, 300–301; for commuters, 215–16; crossings, 121; future directions, 306; infrastructure, 264; lines on motor vehicle facilities, 207; maintenance demands, 301; Northeast Corridor Commuter Rail Agencies Committee, 118; original plans, 37; rail-to-ship services, 105; ship-to-rail services, 105; unified belt lines, 320n20. *See also specific lines, systems*
rational planning, 29
real estate, 25, 224–26, 281
Rechler, Scott, 277
recreational venues, 95
Regina Maersk, 159
regional balance, 272
regional competition, 159–65, 170–71, 208, 263, 298
regional governance, 290–97
regional highways, 182, 184
regional partnerships, 114–15, 140–42, 306;

Index

coordination of services, 117–20; E-Z-Pass, 22, 135–41, 290–91, 306, 327n102; ferry services, 120–23, 140–41; with police agencies, 123–30; TRANSCOM (Transportation Operations Coordinating Committee), 126–30, *127*, 135–41, 186–87, 290, 301; transit benefits, 130–32; TransitCenter, 132–35, 140–41
Regional Plan Association (RPA), 11, 79, 163, 221–22, 260
regionalism, 264, 271–72
research and development, 152–53, 282
resilience, 107–11
resources, 14–16, 29, 281–85; demonstration of, 42; financial, 15–17, 181, 254, 269–71; importance to public authorities, 296; internal, 14; Port Authority as regional resource, 307; regional, 263, 307
Rinaldi, Peter, 194–95
roadways: bus lanes, 286–87, *287*, 301, *302*; capacity problems, 300–301; electronic toll lanes, 139; elevated highways, 226; federal funding, 184; high-occupancy-vehicle (HOV) lanes, 197, 306; interstate highways, 182–84; maintenance issues, 116; Port Authority operations, 116, 188; regional highways, 182, 184; smarter, 306. *See also* bridges; tunnels; *specific projects*
Robins, Martin, 130–31, 141, 240
Rockefeller, David, 214–17, 219, 230, 233, 240
Rockefeller, John D., Jr., 214, 240
Rockefeller, Nelson, 69, 214, 219–20, 228–30, 240
Rockefeller Center, 215, 217, 240
Roebling Company, 266
Ronan, William, 230
Rooney, Bethann, 108–11
Roosevelt, Franklin D., 1, 42, 48–49, 180, 260
Roosevelt, Theodore, 210
Rothman, Steve, 74
Rothschild Inc., 147
Route 1/9, 200

Saint Lawrence Seaway, 216
San Juan, Puerto Rico: trade offices, 217
Sander, Lee, 72
Sartor, Anthony, 254–55
satellite communications, 289
scandals, 253, 260
Scanlon, Rosemary, 152
seafood processing, 289
Sea-Land, 105, 158–64
Seaport World Trade Center (Boston, MA), 217
seaports. *See* ports
secrecy, 295
security issues, 195–96, 246
Seoul, South Korea, 299
September 11, 2001 attacks, 23, 73, 123, 195–96; National September 11 Memorial & Museum, 243, *245*, 247, *249*, 255–57, *257*
Seymour, Joseph (Joe), 239, 241–42, 250
Shanghai, China port, 164
Shapiro, George, 229
Shiftan, Ron, 160, 166, 236–38
shipping, 81–84, 96–107; Banana Docks, *91*; carriers, 320n13; competition between ports, 81–84, 96–107, 159–64, 170–71; container, 82–84, 91–96, *94*, 97–98, 100–104, *106*, *107*, 159–60, 170–71, 203, *211*, 297; Manhattan port operations, *91*, 91–96, *92*; Port Authority port operations, 53, 84–96; rail-to-ship services, 105; ship-to-rail services, 105; terminology, 320n13
shipping channels: deepening, 100–104, 202–3; improvement projects, 101
shipping routes, *99*, 99–100, 209–10
Shorris, Tony, 73, 77, 203, 251–53, 268
Shostal, H. Claude, 163
signage, 125, 129
Silverstein, Larry, 234, 239, 247–48, 257
Silzer, George, 41, 43, 48, 176–78, 180, 266
Sinagra, Jack, 241–42
Singapore, 100
Sires, Albio, 208

smart highways, 306
Smith, Al, 41, 48, 176, 266
social networks, 107–13
Sokolich, Mark, 276
Solberg Airport, 64
Soviet Union, 219
speakers bureau, 284
Spitzer, Eliot, 72–74, 250–53
Spock, Linda, 117, 137–38, 141
staff: brain drain, 151, 171–72, 238; development of expertise, 150, 171–72, 282–83, 290; early retirement program, 149; expert, 15–16, 42, 50; Port Authority workforce, 236–38, 284, 287–88, 296–97; reductions, 148–55, 171–72, 287–88; salaries and benefits, 115, 282, 284
Staten Island, 173–76, 175, 183; bridges, 173–98, 175, 201–12; cargo facilities, 82; ferry services, 191; population growth, 174, 189–90, 211; port facilities, 95, 170, 197–98; rail connection, 197–98; support for Goethals Bridge replacement, 189–98; transit services, 191, 194
Staten Island Advance, 193, 195–96
Staten Island Expressway, *184*, 188–90, 197, 337n57
Staten Island Teleport, 25, 153–54
Stewart Air Force Base, 62, 69
Stewart International Airport, 24, 62, 69–78, 295, 300
Storey, Greg, 163–64
suburban developments, 55, 182, 215
Suez Canal, 99, *99*, 99–100
Suez Canal Authority, 100
supply chain disruptions, 109–10
Switzerland: trade offices, 53, 152
Syracuse University, 116

Tappan Zee Bridge, 17
Taro, Nick, 158
taxes, 7, 130–31, 144–45, 227–28, 277
technical expertise. *See* expertise
television, 227, 300
terrorism: 1993 truck bomb, 246; September 11, 2001 attack, 23, 73, 123, 195–96, 235–37
Teterboro Airport, 24, *25*, 53, 62, 67–68, 74
Tewdwr-Jones, Mark, 292
Theodore Roosevelt, 210
Throgs Neck Bridge, 183–84, *184*
Times Herald-Record, 77
Tobin, Austin: airport initiatives, 49–57, 60–65, 68–69, 78, 219; departure from the Port Authority, 348n121; highway initiatives, 182; leadership, 20, 49, 115, 150, 269, 286, 288, 296, 304; legacy, 278; political independence, 168, 268; Port Authority Bus Terminal work, 302–3; port initiatives, 89–91; railroad initiatives, 219–20; World Trade Center work, 214–31, 233, 282–83
Austin J. Tobin Plaza, 240, *241*
tolls, 120, 205, 215, 264, 281, 304; congestion pricing, 192–97; E-ZPass collection system, 22, 135–41, 290–91, 306, 327n102; electronic collection systems, 115, 136–39; increases, 148, 169, 270–71, 284, 305; Staten Island bridges, 178
tourism, 152
Tozzoli, Guy, 222
trade: Asian, 97–98, *99*, 99–100; Port Authority offices, 53, 152; responding to shifts in, 97–100; shipping routes, *99*, 99–100, 209–10. *See also* World Trade Center
traffic conditions, 205; assessment of, 188; congestion pricing, 192–97; congestion problems, 86–88, *87*, 140–42, 185, 187, 190, 196–97, *197*; safety issues, 196–97, *197*; Staten Island, 190; trucks for the ferry in Hoboken, 86–87, *87*
traffic engineers, 286
traffic incidents, 123–24, 129; accidents, 188, 201
traffic management, 182–85, *184*, 286, 300; Bridgegate, 2–3, 23–24, 212, 275–77, 285; integrated, 125–26, 129, 140–41

Index

traffic patterns, 182, 275
traffic studies, 275–76
traffic volumes, 270–71
train services. *See* rail services
TRANSCOM (Transportation Operations Coordinating Committee), 126–30, *127*, 135–41, 186–87, 290, 301
Trans-Hudson Task Force, 120, 130, 186–88
Trans-Manhattan Expressway, *184*
transit services, 205, 216; benefits of, 117; calls for improvements, 191; competition with private automobiles, 190, 215–16; expansion of, 120–23; intermodal, 104–7; privatization, 155–56; promotion of, 115; for Staten Island commuters, 191; tax benefits, 130–33, *134*, 134–35, 141. *See also individual agencies*
TransitCenter, 132–36, 140–41, 290
TransitCheks, 133, *134*, 135, 141
transparency, 279
travel patterns, 182, 186–87
Tremaine, Morris, 180
Tribeca, 235
Triborough Bridge, 337n57
Triborough Bridge and Tunnel Authority, 137, 139, 181, 188
Tri-State Transportation Campaign, 192, 194, 196
truck terminals, 1–2, 49, 53, 84
trucks and trucking, 37, 86–87, *87*, 93–94, 110, 173–74
Trump, Donald, 234
trust, 196
tugboats, 180
tunnels, 175–76, 187, 270–71, 280, 291. *See also specific tunnels by name*

unified belt lines, 320n20
United Nations (UN), 288
United States Army Corps of Engineers, 101, 103
United States Coast Guard, 199, 208

United States Constitution: Compact Clause, 34–35, 263, 265, 355n16
United States Court of Appeals, 60
United States Department of the Interior, 61
United States Department of Transportation, 254
United States House Judiciary Committee, 60
United States Supreme Court, 225
urbanization, 185–86, 298
user fees, 281

VanDeventer, Robert, 226
Verplanck, Joan, 157, 163
Verrazzano-Narrows Bridge, 182–85, 188–89, 209–10, 337n57; location, *184*; tolls, 137, 305
veto power: gubernatorial, 10, 44–46, 62, 153–54, 166, 218–19, 229, 239, 265–73, 278–79; limitations, 7, 263
Virginia, 171
vision, 20, 125–26, 297–98
visioning, 152–53

Wagner, Robert F., 12, 167, 218, 227
Wakeman, Tom, 104, 108–9
Wall Street Journal, 247
Ward, Chris, 159, 193, 203, 206–9, 253–55, 259
Washington, D.C.: airport location studies, 54; metropolitan population, 55; trade offices, 53, 217
waste-to-energy incineration power station, 289
water treatment facilities, 103
Waterman Steamship Company, 93
Wendell, Mitchell, 263
West Shore Expressway, 193
West Virginia Parkway Authority, 291
Westchester, New York, 215
Westfield, 246–47
wetlands, 55
White House, 208

Whitman, Christine Todd, 102, 144; dredging work, 157–58, 170; and Giuliani's rhetoric, 148; Goethals Bridge replacement, 200; and Pataki, 168–71; Port Authority appointments, 145, 156, 159–67, 171–72, 273; Port Authority staff reductions, 148, 153; World Trade Center work, 234

Wien, Lawrence, 225–27

Wildstein, David, 275–77

Wiley, John, 64

Wilson, Edwin, 55

Windows on the World, 236

Wolf, Donald, 39

Wood, Robert Coldwell, 293

World Trade Center (New York, NY), 1–2, 25, *25*, *232*; annual revenues, 234, 241; collapse, 236, *237*; construction, 2, 6–7, 61–63, *225*, 231, 285; design, 222–24, 230–33, *244*, 250; hotel, 148; location, 218, 220–21, *221*, 299; management, 233–34; name, 217; office spaces, 231–32; One World Trade Center (Freedom Tower), 243, 248, *248*, 255–56, *256*; opposition to, 224–31; parking facilities, 246; PATH station, 236, 240, 249, 251, 257–58, *258*; privatization, 161, 164, 170, 233–34; profitability, 230–37, 355n31; proposal, 213–22, *221*, 223; reconstruction, 72, 200–203, 206, 237–43, *245*, 246–48, *248*, 248–55, 271, 285, 298; rents, 234; reopening, 255–58; safety analysis, 226; security issues, 246; September 11, 2001 terrorist attack, 23, 73, 195, 235–37; site evaluation, 148; support for, 231; television antennas, 229–30; tenants, 230–34, 255–56; Austin J. Tobin Plaza, 240, *241*; Transportation Hub, 3, 249–52, 255, 285, 305; truck bomb (1993), 246; Windows on the World, 236

World Trade Center Houston, 217

World Trade Center New Orleans, 217

World Trade Center San Francisco, 217

World Trade Corporation, 214, 230

World War II, 27

World's Fair (1939), 213–14

Yamasaki, Minoru, 222, 231–32, 250–51

Yankees, 162

Yermack, Larry, 137, 140

Zimmerman, Frederick, 263

Zipf, Peter, 205, 208

Zurich, Switzerland: trade offices, 217